JERRY WHITE

Zeppelin Nights

London in the First World War

VINTAGE BOOKS
London

Published by Vintage 2015

2 4 6 8 10 9 7 5 3 1

Copyright © Jerry White 2014

Jerry White has asserted his right under the Copyright, Designs and
Patents Act 1988 to be identified as the author of this work

This book is sold subject to the condition that it shall not, by way of
trade or otherwise, be lent, resold, hired out, or otherwise circulated
without the publisher's prior consent in any form of binding or cover
other than that in which it is published and without a similar condition, including this condition, being imposed on the subsequent
purchaser.

First published in Great Britain in 2014 by The Bodley Head

Vintage
20 Vauxhall Bridge Road,
London SW1V 2SA

www.vintage-books.co.uk
global.penguinrandomhouse.com

A CIP catalogue record for this book is
available from the British Library

ISBN 9780099556046

The Random House Group Limited supports the Forest Stewardship
Council (FSC®), the leading international forest-certification
organisation. Our books carrying the FSC label are printed on FSC®-
certified paper. FSC is the only forest-certification scheme
supported by the leading environmental organisations, including
Greenpeace. Our paper procurement policy can be found at www.
randomhouse.co.uk/environment

Typeset in Sabon by Palimpsest Book Production Ltd, Falkirk, Stirlingshire
Printed and bound by CPI Group (UK) Ltd, Croydon, CR0 4YY

**London Borough
of Southwark**

B

SK 2486584 2	
Askews & Holts	10-Feb-2015
942.1083 HIST	£10.99 ✓

For Rosie

CONTENTS

Preface: London and the First World War   ix

1	An Immense Sense of Waiting	1
2	An Altogether New London: 1914	27
3	A War for Purity	47
4	The All-Invading Alien	69
5	Work, Work, Work	93
6	Zeppelin Nights: 1915	115
7	Come Home, Come Home, You Million Ghosts	137
8	In Imminent Fear of an Earthquake: 1916	157
9	Harlot-Haunted London	177
10	Everyone Is So War-Weary! 1917	199
11	The Curse Is Being Removed	225
12	The News Is NOT Good! 1918	247
13	The Most Wonderful Day in All Our Lives	267

Acknowledgements   277
Illustrations   279
Notes   281
Bibliography   325
Index   341

PREFACE: LONDON AND
THE FIRST WORLD WAR

FOR most of us the very thought of 'London at war' means just one thing – the Blitz. That extraordinary drama so dominates the idea of wartime London that it is hard to imagine the city and its people affected in any special way by the war of 1914 to 1918. Of course, the Londoners must have shared in the misery and sacrifice of that greatest of all British wars. Many will know there was some bombing of a kindergarten nature and that the tremendous bombardments on the Western Front were at times audible in the capital. But these would seem to rank as sideshows, a puppeteer's dress rehearsal for 1939 to 1945, especially the cataclysm of 1940–41.

The truth is much more interesting. From the moment war was declared at 11 p.m. on Tuesday 4 August 1914, London became the hub of an ever-enlarging leviathan of total war. Londoners almost without exception were caught up body and soul in its maw. The war utterly dominated the city's life. It changed everything – not just for those four and a quarter years of the most destructive war that human history had ever witnessed but for generations after. Even in the twenty-first century Londoners still live with many of the consequences of the First World War.

The war had this impact because London occupied a far more dominating place in both nation and empire in 1914 than it did even twenty-five years later. The national and imperial war effort was directed from London in almost every theatre of operations. A large part of the nation's munitions were manufactured there. Almost every British soldier on his way to active service moved through it and most spent some time there. Soldiers in their hundreds of thousands from Australia and New

Zealand, Canada and the USA saw something of the sights of London, from St Paul's to the Alhambra Theatre, from the Houses of Parliament to the brothels of the Waterloo Road. It was to London that the wounded were brought bleeding from France and Belgium, even from Gallipoli and Mesopotamia, and to London that refugees from the war-torn territories came seeking respite and perhaps to start a new life. And it was London that epitomised the wholehearted commitment – and from time to time the fearful stresses and disturbances – of a nation under nerve-breaking strain, daily affected by the shifting fortunes of total war. Small wonder that this strategic centre of the British and imperial war effort was considered a legitimate target for military aggression; and small wonder too that the very notion of 'civilian' should be blurred when so many adult Londoners were effectively mechanics in this great machine of war.

I have tried to tell the story of this astonishing time, a protean moment in the history of London in the twentieth century, by focusing on the daily life of the Londoners. Leading politicians, senior officials, high-ranking army officers, society celebrities have some place in this story and the royal family from time to time makes an important appearance. All these, of course, were Londoners too. But I have tried to capture most of all the daily experience of the mass of Londoners: the diarists, men and women, who recognised from the moment of war's declaration or a few days before that they were living in momentous times; the memoirists of all classes who recorded their experiences after the event; the individuals running some of London's public and private institutions as the fortunes of war impacted on their working lives – something, in short, of the lives of patriots and pacifists, wounded soldiers and nurses, businessmen and 'munitionettes', clergymen and thieves, bluestockings and prostitutes. In doing so, and despite so much misery coming the way of so many, I have tried to bear in mind the food writer Hallie Eustace Miles's hope when she came to publish her wartime diary a dozen years after the Armistice that it might 'help to remind people of what a *wonderful* place London was in War-time'.[1]

AN IMMENSE SENSE OF WAITING

MAY Day, London, 1914. Thousands of workers took a holiday on this warm sunny Friday and marched from all corners of the city, as for some years past, to a great demonstration in Hyde Park. The day was notable this year for the large numbers of foreign workers present. They were given their own 'international platform, where several languages were spoken', French and German prominent among them. The London building workers, embroiled in an ill-tempered lockout, had two platforms to themselves, and The Times's good-natured report noted specially the 'Juvenile Socialists' around the stage of the London Socialist Sunday School Union, whose meeting opened with a hymn. 'The demonstration passed off very quietly,' the paper thought.[1]

But not quite. Earlier in the day, some 600 marchers from west London, including a section from the National League of the Blind, were crossing the Edgware Road at Church Street, Marylebone, close to the slum district of Lisson Grove. At the front of a queue of traffic waiting in her car for the procession to cross was Mrs Hilda Beatrice Hewlett, a famous flyer, the first British woman to hold a pilot's licence. According to the police, Mrs Hewlett waited about three minutes and then drove on, 'scattering the processionists in all directions'. 'She stopped after being called to three times, and when her name and address had been taken, she remarked, "Now move them (i.e., the crowd) out of the way or I will drive over them."' The crowd 'was incensed, and but for the intervention of the police would have over-turned the car'. In her defence at the magistrates' court in early June, Mrs Hewlett claimed she had driven off only when the marchers had passed and left a space, when she 'at once sounded her hooter and crossed the road'. But she too confirmed the mood of the crowd as ugly. 'Immediately a large crowd of very rough people collected round and mounted the car, yelling "Suffragette! We will teach you how to behave to the working classes." As a matter of fact, she herself belonged to the working class' – Mrs Hewlett stretched a point here: she was a Church of England vicar's daughter – 'and was not a suffragette. Had she not had her big dog with her in the car she believed that they would have attacked her.' The magistrate accepted that her words to the police were not a threat but merely concern for the crowd's safety and fined her 40s for dangerous driving with 2s costs.[2]

This was an incident small but telling. For London in that early summer of 1914 was a divided city where the divisions were not held in check by politeness or reserve. The widest fracture had opened along the fault line of class and Mrs Hewlett and the May Day workers' march had exposed an open wound of mutual mistrust and loathing in which violent language, even violent actions, were never far from the surface. The outbreak of war, less than two months away though utterly unthought of when Mrs Hewlett received comeuppance of a sort, would heal some divisions. But the festering class divide in London would prove the most difficult of all to paper over.

If London in the last few months before the outbreak of war in 1914 was in many ways at war with itself, it remained a city of unparalleled greatness, like nothing else the modern world had ever seen. With a population of 7.25 million, Greater London was nearly twice the size of Greater Berlin and larger than the municipalities of Paris, Vienna and St Petersburg combined. If it overshadowed its European competitors, London dwarfed the major provincial centres of Great Britain. It was home to more people than all that Edinburgh, Dublin, Belfast, Cardiff, Manchester, Salford, Liverpool, Birmingham, Glasgow, Bristol, Portsmouth, Southampton, Nottingham, Bradford, Leeds and Sheffield could together muster.[3] The growth of London that had staggered the nation and the world throughout the nineteenth century was now slowing in the first decade or so of the twentieth, but even so Greater London had added a net 67,000 people (more than the population of Blackpool, for instance) every single year between 1901 and 1911. And to accommodate them, some 140,000 houses and flats had been built in the decade after 1901, though these numbers too were slowing before 1914. Almost all these new houses were in the London suburbs, and most were designed for middle-class occupation.[4]

A significant part of London's population growth was made up by immigration. London's draw on young people of working age had never abated in the countries of Britain and the provinces of England. But for thirty years and more, London had attracted increasing numbers from continental Europe too. The largest of these minorities was made up of Russians and Russian Poles, mainly Jews, who clustered most of all in the East End of London. In 1911 they totalled some 68,000, not counting those born in Britain since their great emigration had begun thirty years before. The next largest migrant group by far was the German-born, over 30,000 in the County of London and 5,000 or more in the outer suburbs, two-thirds of them men; another 10,000 or so Austro-Hungarians, mostly Austrians with a significant number of Jews living with their co-religionists in the East End, might be added to the German-speaking minority in London. They all far outnumbered the French, London's oldest-established European minority, 14,000 of them in the County of London in 1911, and the Italians, around 12,000. All of these foreign-born communities had increased in number since 1901 and in all likelihood continued to do so in the few years immediately before 1914.[5]

That year London was a more cosmopolitan city than it had been for centuries past. The Germans, who will concern us most, were long-established in both the East End (especially Whitechapel) and the West End (especially Soho and St Pancras north of Oxford Street), with suburban communities at all points of the London compass. Charlotte Street, west of Tottenham Court Road, was the main West End artery, known as 'Charlottenstrasse' and famous for its German restaurants and clubs. In the rest of London there were a dozen German churches, a Salvation Army German Corps, a German Hospital at Dalston, two German-language newspapers, a great German Gymnasium at King's Cross, and associations for every interest group, from amateur theatricals to chess players, cyclists to military men. German merchants, traders, stockbrokers and bankers had carved out an important niche in the City; the German governess had become a necessity in many upper-class homes; and the German waiter among proletarian migrants, and bakers and barbers among tradesmen, had become what seemed like irreplaceable fixtures in London's economic life. With their high rates of inter-marriage with English women and their readiness to stay in London rather than return 'home', no foreign community was more integrated than the Germans. August 1914 would change all that. The painful fracture between the London Germans and their hosts would be a new and dramatic feature of the years to come.[6]

The greatest division in London life of course – enduring and unbridgeable – was between rich and poor. This was the fundament of class difference and of class loathing. The gap was probably widening in material terms – there was little improvement in the living standards of the London poor in the years after the death of Queen Victoria and the London rich got richer, certainly if measured by the growing numbers of metropolitan millionaires.[7] It seems too that the gap widened culturally. Much commentary comes to us in the aftermath of the war, when a nation's sacrifice cast a glare both lurid and jaundiced on the excesses of the insouciant London rich before 1914, but perhaps only hindsight could do the times proper justice. Stephen McKenna, the civil servant nephew of a Liberal Cabinet minister and wealthy banker, saw it by 1921 in apocalyptic terms:

> Those who remained in London and those who periodically returned thither in the five years before the war alike discovered that they were in a new imperial Rome in a new silver age. All who had waited for the passing of Victorianism were rewarded for their patience by finding a vacuum which they were free to fill in what way soever they chose; and to the task they brought unbounded energy, almost unbounded wealth, a vigorous dislike of restraint and an ingenuous ignorance of tradition. Never, in the recorded history of England, has the social power of money been greater; never has the pursuit of pleasure been more wide-spread and successful; never has the daily round . . . been brought nearer to the feverishness, the superficiality and the recklessness . . . of the French in the years immediately before the first revolution.[8]

McKenna is borne out by the sycophantic attention paid by the London press to the trivial daily preoccupations of aristocrats and plutocrats in Mayfair and Belgravia and Kensington during the London Season from May 1914. The comings of Lord and Lady St Levan to Belgrave Square or Lady Beaumont's entourage to Eaton Square or Admiral Sir Francis Bridgeman to Claridge's Hotel; the goings of Lord and Lady Wellesley from London to the Hôtel Lotti, Paris, or Lady Alice Shaw-Stewart, leaving for Scotland; and the doings of the Hon. Mrs Devereux at the Ritz, where she gave a dinner-dance for her daughter Blanche, or of the Brunners, who hosted a dance at 43 Harrington Square, where the various rooms boasted yellow and white irises, pink carnations and crimson ramblers and where Corelli

Windeatt's band played for the dancers, all filled scores of column inches of tiny print and endless lists of names and titles.[9] It was said of these last pre-war Seasons that 'the entertainments grew in number and magnificence. One band in a house was no longer enough, there must be two, three even.'[10]

On these nights of the Season the London poor would stare and wonder from the pavement, kept back from the carriages, cars and red carpets by obliging police constables. The poor could be an unwelcome sight. A regular 'lady' diner in these years at the Café Royal in Regent Street 'always ordered a wing of chicken in browned butter sauce' for her Pekinese, for which 'an expensive cushion and chair were kept specially'. When it was suggested to her that the remainder of the chicken might 'be given to some of the poor people who used to come to the back door', she 'turned round, and with a look as cold as marble said: "I hate poor people, they depress me."'[11]

Well they might. There were, for one thing, so many of them. And they were, for another, so very poor. The social investigator and shipping magnate Charles Booth had reckoned in the early 1890s that of some 4.2 million people living in the County of London, about 3.5 million (82 per cent) were working class (working with their hands in some way) and of these 1.3 million could be classed as living below the poverty line. That was 30.7 per cent of all Londoners in the inner area, split between the 400,000 or so '"very poor"' – 'at all times more or less "in want"', 'ill-nourished and poorly clad' – and 'the "poor"', not in want but whose lives nonetheless were comfortless and 'an unending struggle', readily cast into the ranks of the very poor by accidents of sickness, bereavement or industrial dislocation.[12]

That things were little different twenty years on was revealed by the Fabian Women's Group's study of North Lambeth published in 1913. Their business was not with 'the poorest people of the district. Far from it!', but with those where the breadwinner was in fairly regular work and receiving a wage of 18s to 26s a week, average earnings for the labouring poor. The never-ending struggle of these families to maintain decent levels of nourishment, cleanliness and respectability in home and person, their vulnerability to sudden impoverishment, the constant nagging worry over the health and well-being of children, and the interminable vexations of worn-out housing and overcrowded homes, were unsentimentally laid before London's reading public, though to little apparent effect on the conscience of the rich.[13]

The fundamental causes of family poverty in London were twofold: low wages and irregularity of employment. Most working-class families suffered during the course of their lives from both, especially when the breadwinner did not possess a special skill of high value in the labour market. For the 'unskilled', competition from the huge agglomeration of workers in London kept wages low and hours irregular, long hours alternating with slack times. These pressures affected in particular 'general labourers' among men – the poor condition of the casual dock workers in the Port of London had long been notorious – and seamstresses and cleaners among women.

It was among the tailoring workers, women and men, that 'sweating', the extreme subdivision of labour, the production of a garment broken down to its smallest components and given to low-skilled workers at the very cheapest wage rates, had become a byword for exploitation in the years before the war.[14] Not all manufacturing industries treated their workers this badly, but poor working conditions in elderly workshops, often filthily kept, were pretty general among the 800,000 and more employed in manufacturing in the County of London in 1911, men and women both. Something similar was true for the nearly quarter of a million men employed in transport and goods handling and many of the 130,000 in building, both industries especially subject to work stoppages due to the vagaries of the weather. And while regularity of employment characterised the working lives of most of the 200,000 live-in female domestic servants in the County, their careers were dogged by poor wages, long hours and petty restrictions, especially for the majority employed as skivvies or all-purpose maids in one-servant households.[15]

The privations of London's workers in 1914 did not end at poverty and economic exploitation. The London housing problem was perhaps the city's most grievous nuisance, on a scale not seen elsewhere. Low wages, long hours, poverty, these were evils besetting the whole of the British working class at the time – indeed, wages were generally higher in London than outside (though the price of provisions was higher too). But the exorbitant cost of London housing, and the cramped space and battered accommodation it bought, combined in a problem of monumental scale and intransigence. Working-class suburbs, especially in outer east London, had done something to ease overcrowding in London by 1911. Even so, three-quarters of a million people lived at a density of two persons per room or more.[16]

There were, though, consolations. Charles Booth had recorded of the London poor twenty years before that 'Their lives are an unending struggle, and lack comfort, but I do not know that they lack happiness.'[17] Many London pleasures cost nothing – the parks, the heaths and commons were within walking distance, the excitements of the streets and markets were available during both day and night. And most could afford the occasional treat. Money could be scrimped together or garnered from a windfall or, very often, borrowed from the pawnbroker, that ubiquitous banker to the poor.

There was also more to spend it on. The quality and quantity of entertainments open to the London working class improved greatly in the years after Victoria. There were some fifty-three theatres in inner London, some in working-class districts like Kennington, Whitechapel, Hoxton, Bethnal Green and Poplar, and a further fifty-one music halls and variety theatres catering largely to a popular trade. Entrance to the halls cost 2d to 2s and was even free some nights to soldiers and Territorials in uniform (or it was in south London in 1911).[18] Here the jokes and songs that were the currency of collective life gained a universal circulation. At Christmas 1913, for instance, Chris Massie, a wayfaring casual labourer lodging in Hoxton with 'an old lady' and her two sons, one a boxer and the other a pickpocket, played unendingly 'It's a Long Way to Tipperary' on the family gramophone: 'That Christmas we danced and sang and drank beer to the melody', already made famous in the halls.[19] And another London entertainment, the cinema, though a relative newcomer was quickly becoming popular. Some forty-nine 'cinematograph theatres' were licensed in 1911 but in 1913 there were 363, with many other places also licensed to show films.[20]

All these entertainments provoked the disgust, and even anger, of those who took it upon themselves to police the morals of the London worker. Chief among them were the churches, especially the established church. Church membership and attendance in London were generally a middle-class habit, and a minority one at that.[21] Frustration at the churches' lack of progress in involving working people in organised religion had long been a source of class tension, if not enmity. It was the churches' lay members who made up the great bulk of voluntary 'social workers' and 'missionaries'. Among many, priggishness, censoriousness and superiority knew no bounds. For those who claimed to have the interests of the poor at heart the dominant tone was of pity tempered by contempt. In this worldview fun was never innocent but involved some infraction of a standard that few would have presumed to set for themselves. Here is Alexander Paterson, a south London social worker and by no means the sternest censor, contemplating working lads and their enjoyments in 1911:

> Attendance at a music-hall as a weekly practice is commonly held to denote a careless and irreligious life; and though there may be in all districts some good men and steady lads who are not ashamed to frequent these places, it is still a safe rule that the worst boys are the *habitués*, and the best boys do not go at all. At the best it is a poor entertainment, at the worst it is the gate to every temptation, and no man who is trying to help a boy can view with anything but apprehension his return to the gallery door.[22]

By far the most obnoxious pleasure of the London working class was drink. That was the view, anyhow, of all those whose work or hobby it was to amend the workers' behaviour. In 1913 there were 6,566 licensed premises in which 'liquor' – the word itself shivered many tender spines – might be consumed, and only 400 of those were hotels and restaurants. The pubs and beer houses of the metropolis seemed to many the very domain of the devil. They undermined not only goodness but usefulness to employer and to society at large. That drink was, unsurprisingly given the living conditions of so many, a mainstay in making the best of things, the numbers of arrests for drunkenness on the streets of London might stand as testament. In 1911 the Metropolitan and City Police arrested and prosecuted some 62,700 persons for being drunk, two-thirds of them for aggravated offences.[23] At its worst, drunkenness exacerbated the miseries of poverty and fuelled domestic terror and violence, especially against women and children. It was these ill effects of drink in London before 1914 that made many working people firm advocates of one of the several branches of the temperance movement.

For many reasons, then, the London working class – outnumbering the rest by four to one in inner London – proved suspect, distasteful, even loathsome to those with power in the metropolis. And the politics and practice of class struggle in these years made everything more tense, even warlike. Working-class resentment at the condition of the many found expression in two main ways. The more powerful was industrial organisation. There were growing numbers of union members with well-stocked 'war-chests' and a truculent determination to improve the unionists' lot despite the resistance of employers. The second was a widening allegiance to socialism as a political movement. London socialism was fractured and fissiparous, but there were common messages that workers could readily agree with: shared ownership of land and industry, a society organised to better the lot of the many not the few, loyalty among workers that transcended national boundaries so that it seemed a worker in Berlin had more in common with the ordinary Londoner than a Mayfair aristocrat or industrialist. These ideas had powerful resonance. A 'new spirit of dissatisfaction with economic conditions' was plainly apparent to David Lloyd George, a radical Liberal politician whose roots and sympathies lay close to the respectable God-fearing working man and who was Chancellor of the Exchequer in the Liberal government of 1908 to 1915.

> Workers were agitating for a higher standard of life and a more dignified status than they had enjoyed in the past. From 1911 onwards there was a steady development of strike action, and in the summer of 1914 there was every sign that the autumn would witness a series of industrial disturbances without precedent.[24]

That was especially true of the mining and heavy industrial districts of the country, but there was turbulence in London too. Throughout 1914 the London building workers had been in dispute with the master builders over union recognition. Walkouts on building sites because unionists refused to work with non-union men had provoked a backlash among the employers at a time when house construction and other building had been unusually flat. After many such 'lightning strikes' a walkout at the Pearl Assurance offices site in Holborn at the end of 1913 had proved the final straw and from 24 January 1914 a general lockout by the masters laid off some 30,000–40,000 men and shut every big site in the capital, including County Hall, the London County Council's new home on the South Bank.[25]

The masters presented the men with 'The Document', a personal agreement requiring them to sign a pledge to work with any employee, unionist or not, before they would be taken on again. Surprisingly, in an industry where collective solidarity had long been undermined by traditions of casual labour and self-employment, the men held firm, indeed firmer than their leaders. The dispute gripped the trade union world – hence two of the ten platforms that May Day in Hyde Park

were devoted to the building workers and their cause. Later that month
it seemed that the dispute might spread to the provinces, with the masters
talking of a national lockout to bring the London men to heel.[26] By
June, after nearly six months out of work, only the stonemasons had
voted to accept a compromise offered by the employers and their members
returned to work in early July. But the other building unions rejected a
similar agreement after numerous ballots, despite their leaders urging a
settlement. As late as Wednesday 29 July there was an 'ultimatum' from
the master builders threatening once more a lockout nationwide.[27]

That spring and summer in London were marked by industrial strife
in every direction. In May the militant London and Provincial Union
of Vehicle Workers threatened a 'general strike' on the buses over hours,
wages and paid holidays, and there was trouble on the trams over the
employment of boys in men's jobs in late July.[28] A strike in May at
Pink's jam factory in Southwark saw attacks on carmen driving wagons
from the yard, the warehousemen demanding higher wages and an end
to boy labour; the works closed pending negotiations.[29] A public
campaign by shop assistants for shorter working hours tried to win
over London churches and metropolitan borough councils in May.[30]
And on Friday 3 July a strike at the Royal Arsenal, Woolwich, the
nation's premier armaments factory, brought out 1,500 men, members
of the Amalgamated Society of Engineers. One of their number had
refused to erect a machine on a concrete bed laid by non-union labour
and had been sacked, bringing the Royal Gun Carriage Department to
a halt. A day later and some 8,000 were out seeking 100 per cent trade
union membership – 97 per cent were thought already to be members
– and almost all the Arsenal's 10,000 workers were on strike by Monday.
Mass-picketing round the Arsenal gates led to some violent scenes,
though these were quickly quelled by the strike committee, anxious to
get public opinion on the workers' side. Even Prime Minister Herbert
Asquith was involved in settling the dispute. After four days the sacked
worker was reinstated pending a Court of Inquiry into the dispute, and
the Arsenal returned to normal working on 9 July.[31]

This truculent mood spread to unlikely terrain. Also in July the West
Ham Board of Guardians refused to administer poor relief in protest
at interference by the District Auditor – *The Times* promptly labelled
the row 'The Guardians' Strike'; and a dispute on the Great Western
Railway (GWR) at Paddington briefly brought the dining-car service
to a halt on West Country trains.[32]

Most worrying of all was the threat of a Triple Alliance – the phrase borrowed from European diplomacy, the partnership of Austria, Germany and Italy from 1882 – involving the miners', railwaymen's and transport workers' unions. Negotiations began in late May to establish that a strike by one union would mean a strike by all, London railwaymen prominent among the militants. The threat of a coalfields dispute in remote Durham or Ebbw Vale bringing the national rail network to a halt and closing the Port of London took on nightmarish possibilities for government and business. The unions debated and endorsed the Alliance through June, with sympathy strikes becoming the biggest guns in the workers' industrial armoury, ready-primed for that autumn's negotiations over pay and conditions. The prospect provoked both fear and wrath. In July the Reverend William Inge, Dean of St Paul's, denounced trade unions as 'criminal combinations whose leaders deserved to be executed as rebels against society'.[33]

London workers, then, had played their part in the 'new spirit of dissatisfaction' that was such a feature of the time, and so ominous for the times ahead. But it was a different sort of struggle that truly enlivened the streets and public life of the metropolis that spring and summer. The suffragette campaign of votes for women had entered a uniquely violent phase. By the very nature of political power – as the seat of government and home to both Parliament and (for much of the time) the royal family – London was the militant suffragettes' main battlefield. When those marchers in the Edgware Road on May Day saw Mrs Hewlett drive into the crowd they thought they were seeing yet another violent suffragette stunt, and who could blame them for leaping to conclusions? For the suffragettes, with astonishing energy, organisation, physical courage and reckless unconcern for the consequences, were bringing their cause into London's streets and public buildings and were the subject of conversation at every breakfast table of the well-to-do and every proletarian taproom in the metropolis.

Throughout May, June and July there were suffragette attacks on London art galleries, with pictures slashed at the Royal Academy, the National Gallery and the Tate; a mummy case was smashed at the British Museum; there were violent demonstrations, with assaults on police lines outside Buckingham Palace, at Bow Street magistrates' court and in Victoria Park; there was organised window-breaking in West End shopping and residential streets; home-made bombs exploded at the Metropolitan Tabernacle, Elephant and Castle, and at Westminster

Abbey; bombs were discovered at St George's, Hanover Square, and St John's, Smith Square, and bomb-making equipment was found at Lauderdale Mansions, Maida Vale; church services were disturbed by suffragette demonstrations at Brompton Oratory, Westminster Cathedral, the Abbey and St Paul's. In June a possible plot to disrupt London's drinking-water supply required police protection of the Metropolitan Water Board's reservoirs. In the background was continuous news of hunger strikes and the operation of the 'Cat and Mouse Act' – women released from prison when too weak to be detained further were rearrested when their health recovered – and of women chaining themselves to railings and inside public buildings. Everywhere 'Votes for Women' resounded in the parks and stared out from posters.[34]

The suffragettes were by no means all middle-class women – an active, vociferous and persuasive East London Federation of the Suffragettes had many working-class supporters and local leaders supporting Sylvia Pankhurst from their headquarters at Old Ford Road, Bow. But the overwhelming tone of the suffragettes' national leaders, including their most audacious militants, had much arrogant class hauteur about it. During these same spring and summer months, an increasingly violent backlash developed among Londoners against the suffragettes' more extreme antics, and while much of this was plainly gender-based – middle-class medical students frequently threw themselves into the anti-suffragist fray – some just as plainly originated in that class feeling we glimpsed against Mrs Hewlett in the Edgware Road. So, for instance, women speakers were assaulted by crowds in Hyde Park and Clapham Common, and suffragettes were more than once rescued by police from a potential ducking on Hampstead Heath;[35] and at the Lyons Corner House in Coventry Street, Piccadilly Circus, haunt of the West End shop assistant, two suffragettes distributing leaflets 'were pelted with cutlery, sugar, bread and cake' – the trouble continued when they took refuge in the lift, which then stuck between floors, 'missiles being thrown at them through the cage'.[36]

We might leave the last word to poor Miss Marguerite Fedden, writing to The Times from the Halcyon Club, Cork Street, Mayfair, on 25 June:

On Sunday last I was walking through Hyde Park on my way to an 'At home' in Kensington, and I stood for a few minutes by a suffragette platform to listen to one of the speakers. I was standing perfectly quietly when some man recognised me as having been one of the speakers at the previous Thursday's Religious League's demonstration. At a hint from him a huge horde of hooligans gathered round me and began to hurl opprobrious epithets at me, and because I stood silent and did not reply they grew unruly and obscene. (It was impossible for me to get away.)

Suddenly there was a stampede with me in the middle to the Serpentine, my hat and veil were torn to ribbons, my haircombs stolen, my umbrella smashed, my dress bespattered with eggs and torn, and my foot badly crushed. I should have been trampled to death if it had not been for the bravery of a police inspector, who, with the help of a few men and at the risk of his life, rescued me and took me for safety to the police-station.

What is our country coming to when such scenes can be enacted in the pleasure-parks of our great Metropolis? . . . As a member of the public who helps to pay for Hyde Park, I claim protection from assault when I choose to walk in it on any future Sunday.[37]

There were, fortunately, other preoccupations in London that summer besides strike threats, picket lines and the excitements provided by the militant suffragette campaign. Most of all, the weather was generally lovely from the end of May to early September, far drier and warmer than average and especially sunny in June. The Londoners made the best of it, despite the closure of many art galleries for fear of further suffragette 'outrages'. Whit Monday, 1 June, saw the start of the Anglo-American Exhibition at the White City, Shepherd's Bush, where 100,000 turned up to see a cowboy ranch and 'Real Wild West' with 'reproductions' of New York and its skyscrapers and the recently opened Panama Canal. The Anglo-Spanish Exhibition opened at Earls Court Exhibition, there was the usual Whitsun flying display at Hendon Aerodrome, and thousands of picnickers flocked to the Crystal Palace and stayed for the fireworks after dark. The Zoo was packed with some 50,000 visitors, there in part to see the fake mountains of the Mappin Terraces, opened for the first time that very day. Outside, in Regent's Park, the annual carthorse parade had a 'stream of gaily-decked animals and newly-painted carts, stretching as far as the eye could see'. Day-tripping to the seaside or country filled the railway stations, with 110,000 travelling to Brighton alone over the holiday weekend and a record number of passengers leaving Paddington for the West Country. And back in London heaths, commons and parks were turned over to music and dancing as dusk settled – this year the waltz held sway, few attempting

the '"new-fangled" creations like the Tango and the Maxixe'. There
had, in short, never been such a Whitsun and many looked forward to
something like a return bout at the August Bank Holiday, just two
months away.[38]

In the meantime, July saw the climax of the year's London Season.
The Henley Regatta opened on the 1st and a fortnight's summer sales
on the 6th; Gentlemen and Players met at cricket at both the Oval and
Lord's, sharing the honours over the two matches; the air race from
London to Paris and back aroused great interest at Hendon once more
and a fortnight's shooting took place at Bisley. There were extraordinary
scenes at the Eton v. Harrow two-day cricket match at Lord's when
Eton triumphed in a nail-biting finish to a 'tremendous' ovation and
pitch invasion by thousands of spectators in top hats and tails, 'a black
sea, over which light and dark blue handkerchiefs waved tempestuously
from walking sticks'. Celebrations continued that night at Olympia
with Edward Prince of Wales and a first team of aristocrats joining in
the fun.[39] It was at Olympia too, a few days later, that the most eagerly
anticipated heavyweight boxing contest of the century so far took place
on Thursday 16 July. 'One thing only mattered in London at the end
of July, 1914,' recalled the Fleet Street journalist Ferdinand Tuohy, and
that was 'whether Carpentier could beat Gunboat Smith.'[40] He did,
controversially in six rounds out of a scheduled twenty, amid unprecedented scenes. Some 60,000 without tickets clustered around Olympia,
the streets impassable, the 'French colony' emptied to cheer on their
champion while Americans waved 'miniature Stars and Stripes' for the
Gunboat. The New York papers were agog with the '"Boxing madness
of London"'.[41]

Followers of the shooting matches at Bisley from 13 July would have
noted that unusually the first week's competitions had been given over
to the Territorials and 'shot for under conditions in accordance with
War Office requirements'.[42] For talk of war, and the central part the
army might play in it, was very much in the air this summer. But that
talk was of civil war in Ireland. After interminable vexatious debate and
negotiation, Asquith's Liberal government had at last fixed on proposals
for Irish Home Rule, provoking fury in much of the 'loyal' Protestant
province of Ulster. A potentially mutinous army, or officer elements
within it, had raised the prospect of a war that could have not just
Irishman against Irishman but British soldier fighting British soldier. A
political crisis not seen in Britain for centuries threatened the country

with a loaded rifle and absorbed almost the whole attention of government and Parliament. Compared to the metropolitan anxieties of industrial strife or the violent public tactics of the suffragettes, this third and
greatest crisis of Liberal Britain had little resonance on the streets of
London or among the Londoners. There were a few indoor political
meetings and one great outdoor Unionist rally on Saturday 4 July at
the London County Athletic Grounds, Herne Hill; there, in perfect
weather, some 10,000 turned out to hear Sir Edward Carson pledge to
'fight it out to the finish' and offer 'no surrender'.[43] Despite this low
public profile in London, Irish Home Rule and the prospect of civil war
were what the papers meant when they wrote of 'The Crisis' for the
whole of spring and the early summer of 1914 and most of July.

Things changed with remarkable suddenness from Friday 24 July.
At first it was apparent only to a very few. That afternoon the Cabinet
met in Downing Street to discuss the partition of Ireland, now a
political inevitability but one where the details of a settlement remained
not just elusive but explosive. The 'margin in dispute,' recalled Winston
Churchill, First Lord of the Admiralty, 'was inconceivably petty. The
discussion turned principally upon the boundaries of Fermanagh and
Tyrone. To this pass had the Irish factions in their insensate warfare
been able to drive their respective British champions.' In a justly famous
passage written a few years later, Churchill described what happened
next, somewhere around 5 o'clock on Friday 24 July 1914.

> The discussion had reached its inconclusive end, and the Cabinet was
> about to separate, when the quiet grave tones of Sir Edward Grey's voice
> were heard reading a document which had just been received from the
> Foreign Office. It was the Austrian note to Serbia. He had been reading
> or speaking for several minutes before I could disengage my mind from
> the tedious and bewildering debate which had just closed. We were all
> very tired, but gradually as the phrases and sentences followed one
> another, impressions of a wholly different character began to form in my
> mind. This note was clearly an ultimatum; but it was an ultimatum such
> as had never been penned in modern times. As the reading proceeded it
> seemed absolutely impossible that any State in the world could accept
> it, or that any acceptance, however abject, would satisfy the aggressor.
> The parishes of Fermanagh and Tyrone faded back into the mists and
> squalls of Ireland, and a strange light began immediately, but by percep-
> tible gradations, to fall and grow upon the map of Europe.

I always take the greatest interest in reading accounts of how the war came upon different people; where they were, and what they were doing; when the first impression broke on their mind, and they first began to feel this overwhelming event laying its fingers on their lives. I never tire of the smallest detail, and I believe that so long as they are true and unstudied they will have a definite value and an enduring interest for posterity; so I shall briefly record exactly what happened to me.

I went back to the Admiralty at about 6 o'clock. I said to my friends who have helped me so many years in my work that there was real danger and there might be war.[44]

These were the first inklings of a possible pan-European war to reach London. Some, such as Grey and Asquith and their closest advisers, may have had feasible forebodings before, but even for Churchill, very much in the inner circle, the Irish question had obliterated all else from the political horizon.

This first intimation of Friday 24 July was still the possession of a small political and social elite and it did not spread much wider over the weekend. An anonymous lady diarist living in Kensington noted that there was 'very little interest on the part of the English public' in the Balkans that weekend; on Sunday (the 26th) a friend was unconcerned about a holiday to Belgium in the following week; and on Monday another continued to plan her trip to St Petersburg and Finland during August. Only on Tuesday 28 July, with Austria's declaration of war on Serbia, did another friend abandon her next week's holiday in the Austrian Tyrol, though hopeful 'the "fracas might settle down there in a few days . . ."' She was just one of a small minority bothering to alter their continental tours at this time. It was only on Wednesday 29 July that the Kensington diarist observed 'People in the streets beginning to show an interest in the situation, nearly every man buying an evening-paper'.[45] Thus it was that people later spoke of this astonishing, bewildering and utterly unexpected war, striking like lightning from a clear sky that sunny late July and early August of 1914.[46]

When the prospect, even likelihood, of a European war struck home, on or around Wednesday 29 July, the general belief still was that Britain should and would keep out of it. Most of the press, apart from *The Times*, set itself against British intervention. A majority in the Cabinet throughout the remainder of July was against joining the conflict, even should France be invaded and overwhelmed by Germany.[47] Unsurprisingly,

Londoners continued to go about their normal business, prudently protecting their own interests where they had the means to do so.

On their minds most of all were their holidays. Despite the general talk of war from 29 July, the confident hope that Britain would not be involved meant that almost every London public institution adjourned for the summer as they had always done – the London County Council on that very day, for instance. And ordinary Londoners got away too. Edward Ezard, from Nine Elms, Battersea, about fifteen years old, the son of a bank clerk's respectable widow, was holidaying with family friends in Eastbourne, where 'war was in the air. Groups assembled on the top promenade by the pier awaiting the latest edition of the paper.' Thomas Hancock Nunn, a prominent Hampstead philanthropist and social worker in his fifties, was with his wife in their little retreat at Shoreham, Kent, 'a small wooden hut built on to an old railway milk-van' on a ridge of shingle near the beach. Georgina Lee, from South Kensington, forty-five though with a two-year-old son, her husband a prominent London solicitor, began her holiday in Somerset on Friday 31 July. At Paddington she found the trains disrupted by a strike of GWR shunters, with everyone facing a long wait at the station: 'A sense of impending calamity hanging over everyone, overcame the ordinary reserves [sic] of English people. Tongues were loosened, people spoke of their experiences.' Indeed, every London railway station was 'besieged' by thousands that last Friday of July, 'bound for all parts of England and for every kind of holiday'. The coming weekend was August Bank Holiday and the plans for railway excursions and special trains, or for steamboat trips from London to Southend or Margate, remained unaffected by prospects of a European War.[48]

But not all Londoners looked on stoically, if they looked at all. The threat of war even without Britain involved had begun to stoke a financial crisis from 27 July. Within forty-eight hours, war preparations in Russia, Germany, France and Belgium meant that the world financial system had largely ceased to function. London, in Lloyd George's words, was 'the financial centre of the world' and this was the greatest crisis the City had ever known. Virtually all foreign trading was brought to a halt. On Friday, 31 July, the London Stock Exchange closed indefinitely, Lloyd's suspended business except the insurance of war risks and the bank rate doubled from 4 to 8 per cent, the highest since 1873. 'People,' a banker noted, 'are getting really alarmed and are flocking to the Bank of England to change notes for gold', with long queues forming outside the Bank doors. The City, with so much money and so much trade staked on foreign goodwill, was in utter 'panic'.[49]

The financial crisis that came to a head that Friday impacted mostly on a small elite, but repercussions went far wider. After all, over 350,000 worked in the City. Most were men, most lived in London or commuted from nearby and many were heads of households. The ripples of anxiety spreading out from Threadneedle Street and Cornhill made themselves felt in 'hoarding', the widespread buying up of extra supplies – not yet 'panic-buying' – that had begun to take effect by that same Friday when so many Londoners left for their holidays. The anonymous lady diarist from Kensington noted on 30 July: 'People laying in coal, groceries etc: some for two months. Price of flour, grain, etc. raised.' And next day John James Sainsbury, seventy years old but still very much hands-on chief of his great London grocery chain, warned his managers that people would buy in much larger quantities than normal and that they should stop 'the small shopkeeper and restaurateur' trying 'to avail themselves of our present prices'. By the end of Friday some shops had almost run out of flour, one lady in 'a leading store' carrying off a sackful 'in triumph in a waiting motor-car'.[50]

Anxiety increased over the weekend. On Saturday 1 August, stores like Harrods and many London clubs were refusing to give gold for cheques or in change. Statisticians noted the first general rise in food prices that day – they would go on rising rapidly in the week ahead. Hoarding continued to create shortages in the shops and the bank rate rose again to 10 per cent. Yet the contradictory motion of London life continued with much going on as normal. This being August Bank Holiday, 'normal' meant day trips and summer holidays. Again the railway stations were packed, though there was feverish interest in the news: France had mobilised the day before in the light of German threats against Russia, France's ally. It was from around now that a passion for diary-keeping 'in this "time of trouble"' became a national preoccupation.[51]

Among the many getting away, if only for the day, Frederick Willis, a young Bermondsey hatter, took advantage of the traditional day off granted by his firm on Bank Holiday Saturday, took a tram to Purley in Surrey and walked out in his best clothes with his girl. At the Swan and Sugar Loaf in Croydon they came upon a crowd of cyclists, two of whom he knew: 'We fell to talking about the International situation.

My two acquaintances, who had just been reading the paper, told me of the latest developments, and we came to the conclusion that war was inevitable. None of us had the faintest idea of what it meant to us personally.'[52]

For some others that day, though, what it might mean for them became just a little clearer. The London Rifle Brigade, a 'crack Territorial Regiment', were to begin their annual training exercises at Beachy Head, near Eastbourne. They arrived at their camp at 4.30 in the afternoon only to be told they had to return to London immediately to await orders.[53]

Indeed, the threat of war was beginning to penetrate everywhere. On Saturday night Ferdinand Tuohy was sent out by the editor of his Sunday paper to write up 'War scenes in the West End'. At first he found business as usual.

Piccadilly Circus that Saturday night hard on fifteen years ago. The theatres just emptying on the surging, twinkling scene; on the pavement a London crowd of that day – young men, mostly what we liked to call 'bounders'; 'gay' women [prostitutes] in longish dresses and picture hats . . . a few frothy, giggling flappers running the domestic gauntlet for an hour or two; old treading roués, eyes alone alert; 'Varsity Youth 'just down' and bent on a wonderful night; opera-hatted 'Johnnies' sauntering with magnificently-knobbed sticks, white gloves, and an air of benign tranquillity; intermingling with it all, the babel and jostle of Soho. Ghost crowd!

Presently a newspaper van drew up with a skid outside the Tube.

'Germany Declares War on Russia. Speshul!'

The news flashed from lip to lip. People paid a penny to see it blurred in the stop-press. Passers-by formed in knots. Yes, this was 'it'. Within a few minutes the whole of Coventry Street was agog.[54]

Next morning, Sunday 2 August, the continental news of the day before began to sink in. It was added to most worryingly during the day. Germany demanded a right of way through Belgium and made incursions across the French border, while Russia invaded East Prussia. A general continental war was no longer inevitable, it was under way. In London the financial crisis deepened as a royal proclamation extended the due date for payment of bills of exchange (a promise to pay on goods traded) by one month – this was a 'moratorium', a word so unusual it had to be explained in the newspapers. It gave some relief to all those whose trading debts became due in the next four weeks. What would happen after that no one knew. The anxiety now brought crowds to Whitehall and Downing Street, hoping for news by being closest to events, as though a politician's face glimpsed in the street might tell the future. Church congregations in London, as elsewhere, were unusually large. The Archbishop of Canterbury took the afternoon service at Westminster Abbey and spoke of the duty of the nation and the citizen: 'Steadiness and self-control' for both were 'sacredly imperative'.[55]

Even so, suffragette demonstrations interrupted services at both the Abbey and St Paul's and in general there was, as late as Sunday 2 August, almost universal doubt – perhaps hope against hope – that the conflagration spreading from the Balkans need involve the nation in war. Yet a great fear was in the air. This was the time when, five days or so after the seriousness of the situation began to dawn on Londoners, the disparate components of an anti-war movement showed their mettle. Hectic organisation had begun around 30 July, when the newly formed Neutrality League under the leadership of Norman Angell opened an office in Whitehall. With other 'peace bodies', the League organised a leafleting campaign that 'flooded' London. Anti-war rallies were organised in north London on the Saturday night and, most famously, in Trafalgar Square on Sunday afternoon. Thousands attended, marches converging – just like May Day – from every direction, from St George's Circus in Southwark, the East India Docks in Poplar, from Kentish Town in the north and Victoria in the west. The speakers included Keir Hardie, H. M. Hyndman, Ben Tillett and other leaders of the London labour movement. There was a torrential thunderstorm, but the only trouble came from 'hilarious, excited young men' who 'pushed their way through the crowd, waving their hats and sticks, and singing *Rule Britannia*', much in the spirit of the Eton and Harrow match at Lord's three short weeks before.[56]

Many Germans and Frenchmen were in the anti-war crowd at Trafalgar Square that afternoon and were quiet enough, considering their nations were effectively at war. But during the day many took a late opportunity to leave by rail and ship for the Continent from Victoria, 'their exceedingly grave countenances testifying to their anxiety'. Elsewhere London's minorities adopted a more bullish tone; some 6,000 people, it was said, 'led by the enthusiastic French residents of Soho', marched through the Mall cheering the continental mobilisations, and boastful celebrations had gone on in German and French restaurants through the Saturday night of 1–2 August.[57]

Yet still, on the following Sunday night the mood of Londoners remained ambivalent, though tilting to an acceptance that war involving Britain was more likely than not. That evening, after the Trafalgar Square demonstration, R. M. Fox, a socialist mechanical engineer from north London, spoke at a peace rally in Hyde Park.

> People were realizing the gravity of the situation now, and they listened in intent silence while I pledged myself to do everything possible to oppose war . . . Suddenly the high-pitched voice of a woman cut across the meeting: 'Are we to wait till the Germans murder us in our beds?' A quiver passed through the crowd as if a field of corn were shaken by the wind. It was the beginning of war panic.[58]

And just half a mile away a crowd gathered outside Buckingham Palace to cheer the King and his family.[59]

Next day, 3 August, Bank Holiday Monday, everything became clearer. Germany declared war on France and the implications of its demand for a passage through Belgium began to sink in. The neutrality of Belgium had been guaranteed since 1839 by most European powers, including Prussia and Britain. A German invasion of Belgium, plainly not an aggressor in any continental struggle, seemed an affront to international decency. From this moment, for the vast majority of the British people, the nation's involvement in a war looked likely to be necessary, even essential, if its honour meant anything. The change of mood infected almost all the British Cabinet too. This was the turning point, experienced nearly everywhere. That day a young London Territorial noted, 'The one topic is – "Are we coming in?" It will be a black shame if we do not stand by our friends.' The socialists Beatrice and Sidney Webb were convinced that 'if Belgian neutrality was defied we had to go to war'. 'Even staunch Liberals', Beatrice wrote on Monday, 'agree that we had to stand by Belgium', the position that Grey put the same afternoon to a tense and crowded House of Commons; almost all in the chamber wholeheartedly agreed.[60]

The emerging consensus for intervention now found louder expression in the streets of London. Thousands turned out in the fine weather to mill about Whitehall and Downing Street and outside the Houses of Parliament. But if there was one dominant emotion on 3 August it was bewilderment. There 'is no enthusiasm about the war', thought Beatrice Webb; 'at present it is, on the part of England, a passionless war, a terrible nightmare sweeping over all classes, no one able to realize how the disaster came about'. John Middleton Murry, a man of letters living in Chelsea with the writer Katherine Mansfield, both usually far remote from the passage of events, found themselves seized by 'a fever of unrest'. 'We drifted about London, bought newspapers, read them in the tea-shops: in the evening we swirled with the crowds from one embassy to another, here caught in strange momentary eddies of mass-emotion, and flung aside, bewildered. We were neither for war nor against it . . .' The journalist Philip Gibbs saw 'no blood-lust' in the London streets: 'None of the old Jingo spirit which had inflamed great crowds before the Boer War was visible now or found expression.' Beatrice Brown, a thirteen-year old schoolgirl from Swiss Cottage, later recalled 'the tension, the groups of people standing about, waiting. I remember the feeling of them waiting. My uncle, walking with me, said, "I expect you will never forget this day."' The novelist Mary Hamilton detected 'a vague unformulated dread' weighing on people in the streets: 'A great silence, an immense sense of waiting, held them all.' Even the dense crowds outside Parliament were 'opposed to demonstration', with little singing or cheering. There were, though, patriotic scenes outside Buckingham Palace that evening, with cheers for the King and royal family, clearest symbol for many, even in this divided city, of national pride. And although leafleting by pacifists and neutrals continued in London – 'ENGLISHMEN, DO YOUR DUTY and keep your country out of A WICKED AND STUPID WAR' – the distributors got short shrift from the crowds.[61]

This day also saw the quickening of a movement back to London. Some cut short their holidays, like the pacifist Frederick Pethick-Lawrence and his wife, trying to do something to help avert the catas-trophe but finding 'we were mere straws upon the stream'. Thomas Hancock Nunn felt it his duty to be on hand should people in Hampstead need him. Others, like Frederick Robinson, a successful South Africa shipper with offices in Old Broad Street who lived in rural Surrey, just wanted to be close to events and motored to London to get the latest news. Perhaps most felt as he did: 'The thousands who had scattered four days earlier to every part of England poured back,' Stephen McKenna thought, 'on a common impulse, to London. There, all felt, they would gain readier news, when the silence and isolation of the country had become unbearable.' This rush back to London, according to Ford Madox Ford, 'was the great rout of the 3-8-14'.[62]

That evening made more visible the presence of troops in London. They had been gathering, as we have seen, but their appearance almost everywhere became a poignant warning for the first time of just what might be at stake. In Tooting, the south London newspaperman Alfred Hurley recalled the call-up of the retired reservists and 'the pitiful scenes that night at the Broadway, when wives and children bade farewell to . . . the Old Contemptibles', and there were similar leave-takings at Charing Cross and Victoria stations. John Middleton Murry and Katherine Mansfield 'stood, clasping hands, by the railings of the Green Park, late at night, while a Highland regiment – someone said the Black Watch – marched to the station, and our hearts were big within us, hot with the sadness and the beauty of their ordered going'.[63] That same night – or probably that night, the Foreign Secretary couldn't be sure in retrospect – Sir Edward Grey received a friend in his office:

> We were standing at a window of my room in the Foreign Office. It was getting dusk, and the lamps were being lit in the space below on which we were looking. My friend recalls that I remarked on this with the words: 'The lamps are going out all over Europe; we shall not see them lit again in our life-time.'[64]

Next day, Tuesday 4 August 1914, events moved quickly to what had now with breathtaking suddenness become a foregone conclusion. In light of the German demand for passage through Belgium, inevitably rejected, Britain sought in the early hours of Tuesday morning an assurance that Germany would respect Belgian neutrality. A few hours later German troops invaded Belgium. The British government responded with an ultimatum requiring a 'satisfactory answer' on Belgian neutrality 'before midnight' Berlin time, 11 p.m. in London.

News of these events became rapidly known to the crowds that continued to throng the capital. The Bank Holiday had been extended to 6 August to deter any run on gold while millions of the very first issue of £1 and 10s notes were being printed. Many were still on holiday and some continued to leave for the country or seaside as normal. Beatrice Brown left London that day, for instance, encountering 'great crowds on Paddington Station – other families going, like us, for their holiday, but I felt a menace'. Many others were swept into the streets, which remained packed throughout the day around Whitehall, Parliament Square and Buckingham Palace. The weather was once again perfect: 'Young men in straw hats were in the majority. Girls in light calico dresses were numerous.'[65]

And now something like 'war fever' did grip many Londoners, with patriotic songs sung and cries of 'Down with Germany!' At the heart of things, the anti-war minority continued to make its presence felt around the plinth of Nelson's Column, but the general mood was overwhelmingly in favour of British intervention. It affected even a convinced pacifist like Pethick-Lawrence, who mingled with the London crowd late in the evening: 'I too, in spite of my loathing of war, felt that, granted the circumstances as they were at the twelfth hour, a refusal to come to the help of France and Belgium would have been a breach of faith.' For almost everyone everywhere, this was a righteous war.[66]

As the day wore on and the news of the British ultimatum became known, the tension grew and the main thoroughfares became more and more crowded, and by nightfall Whitehall and Parliament-street, Trafalgar-square, and the Mall were packed with cheering masses. Scores of motor-cars carrying men and women in evening dress wound slowly around them. Union Jack and tricolour favours of the Royal Standard were to be seen everywhere. Flags were waved from cabs, omnibuses, and private cars. The plinth of the Nelson Column, the pedestals of the statues in Whitehall, the windows of Government offices served as grandstands for the demonstrators. From time to time field-guns and ammunition wagons lumbered by. The glimpse of a khaki tunic was the signal for fresh outbursts of enthusiasm.

The excitement reached its height outside Buckingham Palace, where a vast crowd had gathered early in the evening, growing denser as time wore on. The Victoria Memorial was black with people. Numbers of motor-cars were drawn up near the Palace gates. For more than four hours the singing and cheering of the crowd was maintained without a break.

At 7 o'clock the King responded to the demonstration. With the Queen and the Prince of Wales and Princess Mary he appeared on the accustomed balcony and was greeted with tumultuous cheering, the singing of the National Anthem, and 'He's a jolly good fellow.'[67]

The crowd had assembled most expectantly about the doors of the Foreign Office in Downing Street. That was where any German reply before the deadline would first be received. Formal communications had broken down under the strain of intense diplomatic traffic, but news 'from a reliable quarter' revealed that the British demand 'had been summarily rejected'. At 11 p.m. Britain declared war on Germany.[68]

Within minutes word had reached the street and in an instant was in everyone's mouths, from Whitehall to Buckingham Palace. It was received with loud and prolonged cheering. There were similar scenes throughout London. The writer C. H. Rolph's father was a City of London police inspector and travelled home late each night to Fulham. Getting out of the tube at Hammersmith Broadway, he found the trams weren't running, 'immobilized by the crowds'. As he began the long walk home he heard from the thousands outside Hammersmith Town Hall a sudden great cheer 'of excitement and belligerence' as the news of war was telephoned through to the town clerk.[69]

In the Café Royal that night J. B. Booth, a Fleet Street journalist well known in the more louche corners of the West End, drank in the scene:

A dazed excitement was the prevailing note . . . The Chelsea set, with the usual female appendages, was inclined to boisterousness, but the men from Fleet Street and the theatre world talked in undertones; no one could foresee an hour into the future, and it was by intelligent anticipation of the future that both crafts had their livelihood. The smoke-laden air was full of rumour of papers closing down, of theatres shutting . . .

I think there was not a man there who did not realise that we were at the death-bed of the old pleasant order of things; that life, as we had known it, lived it, and loved it, was at an end for ever.[70]

He was right. The world would never be the same again. And nor would London.

2

AN ALTOGETHER NEW LONDON:
1914

IN the small hours of Wednesday morning, 5 August, Ernest Thurtle, a City clerk, was woken in his Brixton flat by 'a newsboy calling out "Special! Special! England declares war on Germany. Heavy fighting in the Channel!"'[1] By breakfast all London knew that war had come. The weight of this enormous change pressed heavily on almost everyone's mind, difficult to take in, shocking to contemplate. 'The sense of the momentous import of the outbreak of war in 1914,' recalled the Hampstead peace campaigner and social psychologist Caroline Playne some seventeen years later, 'still lingers in the minds of those who were consciously overwhelmed by it at the time.'[2]

Reactions were no doubt infinitely varied but one common strand was personal fear for one's own and one's family's welfare. For the poor it was fear of unemployment and of a breadwinner snatched away, and so even deeper poverty. For most there seemed the likelihood of some industrial dislocation, financial chaos, food shortages. Only some of these things could be bolstered against. Where money could run to it, anxiety expressed itself in a redoubling of the food panic among the better off. 'The well-to-do people in London have, in quantities lost their heads,' wrote the lady diarist in Kensington that day. 'They are buying enormous stores of food, as if for siege provisions . . . Taxis today are laden with provisions people are taking home.'[3] 'Things have begun to crumble about us', the *Times* journalist Michael MacDonagh noted in his diary that same Wednesday. Walking from his home in Clapham to the Army and Navy Stores in Victoria Street, he saw every provision shop 'thronged with buyers . . . principally of the middle class, looking well dressed and comfortably off'. At the Stores, armed with 'my own little list', he joined 'a long line of customers waiting to be served' but had to give up after a two-hour wait.[4] The Kensington diarist noted the case of a woman who had telephoned Barker's, the local provision store, at 4 a.m. to order food and coal from the night watchman to the value of £65, a whole year's income for one of the North Lambeth families studied by Maud Pember Reeves in 1913.[5]

This 'rush for food' was greatly resented among those with no money to spare. MacDonagh reported a few days later that the 'angry outcry against the hoarding of food' had led to 'women loaded with parcels' being stopped by other women in the streets 'and roughly deprived of their parcels', and delivery vans were rifled. Some instances reached the local papers. There was reportedly a 'food riot' at a Bermondsey grocer's where women refused to accept a hike in prices on 5 August – goods were swept from the counter and 'flung about', with threats to wreck the place, until the police arrived; the shop prudently closed for the day. And fears of resentment could be even worse than the thing itself, grounded in that class mistrust and hostility that underpinned so much of contemporary London life: 'they say burglars, & people who may starve later, are marking the houses where [hoarding] is done, in order to raid them later on.'[6]

The food panic abated quickly enough, prices peaking on Saturday 8 August and then falling towards – though never again reaching – their late July levels.[7] Within a few days, hoarding and talk of a food panic had largely evaporated. There was another step taken towards normality in the financial situation as banks reopened after their enforced holiday on Friday 7 August and the bank rate was lowered to 6 per cent. Perhaps with the food panic in mind there was no rush to withdraw deposits. Unsurprisingly, however, the banks having last opened on the previous Saturday, there were queues at every branch to get money. Gold, though, was only given in small amounts, with the rest in silver and notes, including the new £1 Treasury notes – 'poor specimens of engraving', Frederick Robinson, the City merchant, thought them.[8] A few days later the Bank of England restored much confidence in the City by announcing that it would discount, or lend money on, any unpaid bills after the end of the one-month's moratorium, the government guaranteeing the Bank's losses. A breathing space on other debts over £5, excluding wages, was also granted by a further moratorium until 4 September, which was subsequently extended. It did not, however, cover weekly rents, the main debt of working-class Londoners. At the same time the less well off found some sources of credit drying up – Sainsbury's, like most popular grocers, refused to give credit from 6 August.[9] So after the initial shock, even panic, arising from the declaration of war there were welcome signs of something approaching 'business as usual', the great propaganda catchphrase of this opening period of war on the home front.[10]

There were signs too that some of the open wounds of pre-war Britain might after all be closing. Immediately after the declaration, Sylvia Pankhurst later wrote, 'frantic private efforts were being made to secure the release of the Suffragette militants' from prison, and within a week the Home Secretary, Reginald McKenna, agreed a general amnesty, releasing all the women without requiring any undertaking from them. There were some mishaps and the last unruly behaviour seems to have taken place as late as 27 August. But by then Mrs Emmeline Pankhurst and her daughter Christabel had thrown their considerable energy and organising power into the war effort. The last issue of the *Suffragette* newspaper was published on 7 August (it later became *Britannia*) and around the 15th the Pankhursts announced that the militant campaign was at an end. 'Votes for Women' as an objective had not been abandoned but that particular war would now be pursued by other means. The suffragettes' abandonment of militant campaigning trickled out in press notices from the middle of the month as staff, premises and whole organisations went over to 'war work' of one form or another – the Church League for Women's Suffrage, the Conservative and Unionist Women's Franchise Association, the National Union of Women's Suffrage Societies, the Women's Social and Political Union and others all shifted tack in this way.[11] Of less concern to Londoners, the divisions in Ireland were quelled for a year and more with an outbreak of unity among nationalists and unionists over the necessity for war and its vigorous prosecution.

This new understanding of the national interest was also widely shared within the labour movement. It took many on either side of the class divide by surprise. Almost overnight, many labour leaders abandoned the internationalism in which they had long been steeped, rejected transnational worker solidarity to prevent war as a utopian dream and fell readily into martial step. The 'bulk of the Labour Movement became vociferously patriotic' and that was true for both industrial and political arms. The Triple Alliance was effectively suspended for the duration; strikes quickly ended on 5 August or soon after, and even the adamantine builders' dispute was eventually settled on 14 August when the last of the building unions, the plasterers, agreed to the terms offered in June. Most of London's leading labour figures, such as Will Crooks in Woolwich, Will Thorne in West Ham, Robert Blatchford of the *Clarion*, the veteran former Marxist H. M. Hyndman, Ben Tillett of the transport workers and Jimmy Thomas of the railwaymen among others, became active on the recruitment platforms.[12]

It proved easier for labour men to go along with the war than for pacifists. The outbreak of war was a terrible blow to the peace groups in London. Their morale was shattered, their ranks thinned, their message was everywhere unpalatable, but they never gave up altogether. Of the working-class groups, most active were the Herald Leagues, networks of socialists selling the *Daily Herald*, the paper most associated with George Lansbury, the staunchly pacifist and suffragist former MP for Bow and Bromley. The Leagues had been in existence since 1912, but in the week before the war new groups had formed to spread an internationalist message of peace. These generally wilted and died away with the shock of 4 August. The most resilient was the North London Herald League, which continued to campaign against the war at open-air meetings in Finsbury Park or nearby, 'Sunday after Sunday', the only organisation to do so in London through 1914. But even the *Herald* suffered. Its circulation fell so sharply that about a month after war was declared it moved to weekly circulation.[13]

The militant socialist Independent Labour Party (ILP) tried hardest to keep internationalism alive and generally opposed the war, contrary to the position of the large majority of Labour MPs and activists. The ILP's opposition to the war was led by Keir Hardie and Ramsay MacDonald, both well known in London though not at this time metropolitan MPs. The party's grass-roots membership seems to have organised little collective anti-war activity in London for the remainder of 1914. Individual socialists were, however, brave enough to oppose the war in public – two Shoreditch borough councillors were arrested and charged with insulting words and behaviour at a street meeting in Hoxton and bound over in October 1914, for instance.[14] Among middle-class pacifist organisations, the Neutrality League continued to leaflet for a time after 5 August but then quickly collapsed. Some former members helped establish the generally anti-war Union of Democratic Control in late 1914, though it too had little impact on the streets of London in these first four months of war.[15]

The great majority sharing in this bellicose national unity included the churches – almost all denominations and sects and almost all clergymen. In the days before war many had played a part in the London peace movement, but they seem to have apostatised with an easy conscience. Even the Quakers wavered before reaffirming their historic pacifist allegiance; when they did they suffered many defections as a consequence. Elsewhere, from virtually every pulpit congregations were told of their Christian duty to wage war and 'pray for the victory of our arms' with a 'clear conscience'. 'War is allowed by God in the working out of His plan,' the rector of St Peter's, Walworth, confidently affirmed on Sunday 9 August, and many other comforting formulations were marshalled to convince Christians that killing was not murder. Some went further. The rector of St Matthew's, Brixton, had the church's prayer books re-covered in khaki and used the crypt as a rifle range.[16]

Exceptions among the clergy appear to have been very few. Perhaps because of this they suffered all the pains of anathema. The case of the Reverend Kaye Dunn, pastor of the Manor Chapel, Southwark Park Road, Bermondsey, became a local sensation in early September 1914. At that time the papers everywhere were filled with news of German atrocities, real and imagined, in Belgium. It was not a good time to publish his monthly newsletter reflecting on his return from holidaying in Germany just before war was declared: 'What a delightful people the Germans are. How kind to the stranger. How human, how cousinly, how Christian', with rather too much of the same. His musings were greeted in working-class Bermondsey with what the *South London Press* coyly called 'considerable indignation'. Tempers boiled over when Dunn tried to speak against the war at an open-air prayer meeting near his chapel on the night of Friday 11 September. A large and angry crowd threatened to overturn the rostrum when Dr Alfred Salter, a local general practitioner and ILP activist who also opposed the war, tried to bring peace to this tiny corner of south-east London. Salter was well known and widely respected locally. '"Dear friends," he began. "You ain't got no friends here," shouted a man in the crowd.' Salter stepped aside and the rostrum was overturned, Dunn's harmonium thrown down and Dunn himself 'severely mauled', though women supporters did their best to protect him. Eventually he was forced by 'a perfect hurricane of missiles' to flee home to the chapel. His windows were broken and 'other damage done of a serious nature'. Dunn had to leave the district. When he subsequently took his place at a meeting of Bermondsey

Borough Council he was cold-shouldered by his fellow councillors. Though there were rumours that he would return to Bermondsey, he appears to have given up living and preaching there for good.[17]

Class feeling was no doubt mixed up with patriotism here – the clergy were rarely popular in working-class London – and of all the pre-war wounds class was the hardest to heal. The cut was too deep, too visceral, the gap in understanding too wide to permit of anything much more than dislike on either side. Many middle-class people thought, for instance, that there would be 'bread-riots' among the poor in London should war be declared, but those who behaved most badly, as we've seen, were people like themselves. When Georgina Lee saw her uncle off at Paddington Station on 5 August she was 'surprised to see the platforms filled with poorly-dressed men whom we took for unemployed come to make a disturbance'; in fact they were army reservists rejoining their regiments. The East End clergy were apparently told 'in confidence' that they couldn't join the services because east London might be shelled from the river 'and panic and rioting ensue'. Beatrice Webb noted in her diary how John Burns, the former workers' leader from south London who resigned from the Cabinet over the declaration of war, told her, '"We shall see the unemployed marching down Whitehall to destroy the House of Commons."' The war would bring the classes together in some ways, making it easier, for instance, to hold conversation in streets, buses and the ubiquitous queue; some even thought in 1914 that 'out of the war there has been born in London a new democracy'. But fear and mistrust never broke down entirely in the capital; indeed, they revived as the war went on.[18]

Nor were class differences reconciled by experience in the trenches and elsewhere in the armed forces. There was a 'gaping distinction between officers and men', officers ordered never to board a bus in London or carry a parcel in the streets, whether in uniform or in mufti. Even when middle-class men joined the ranks, as many unwilling to wait for a commission did as volunteers on the outbreak of war, differences in language, education, habit and outlook were immense. When Hamilton Gibbs reported as a trooper to the cavalry depot at Woolwich on 3 September he encountered 'Bad smells, bad beer, bad women, bad language'; he found the smell from his fellow troopers' naked bodies hardest to live with.[19]

Having decided 'it was my war too', Gibbs 'took a taxi and went round London' to see what was happening to the long queues of 'city men, tramps, bricklayers, men of all types and ages' he had seen lining up to volunteer. 'Every recruiting office looked like a four-hour wait. I was in a hurry. So I went by train to Bedford' and joined up there. Indeed, men in khaki and men queuing to shoulder arms had been a dominant impression of those first days of London's war. Crowds gathered round the many Territorial and regimental headquarters to witness mobilisation on 4 and 5 August – there were cheering crowds at the several south London depots in Kennington, Southwark and Camberwell, for instance, now guarded by sentries with bayonets fixed. Reservists and Territorials marching to the railway stations for their journeys to camp were watched by crowds on their way to work, 'staring at us curiously. Many cheered and waved their hats.' But still the mood was more of anxiety than jingoism. Rudolf Rocker, a German-born anti-war anarchist, in London for many years, watched with others in Trafalgar Square as a contingent of troops marched to Waterloo Station. When men in two cars draped in Union Jacks arrived and tried to rouse people in a chorus of 'Rule Britannia', 'there was no response from the silent crowds' and the cars moved on.[20]

Official efforts to get men into khaki, however, were all around. Recruitment posters were pasted on walls from 6 August – 'Your King and Country need YOU' in blue letters on a white background with deep red border; and similar placards were attached to most London taxis before the end of the month. Recruitment offices opened everywhere in London. The best-remembered were the central recruitment office at Old Scotland Yard, Whitehall, a tented village at Horse Guards behind Downing Street and the Treasury, and at St Martin-in-the-Fields, Trafalgar Square – a true marriage of church and state that. But every London borough opened one or more recruitment offices in municipal buildings. In Croydon, for instance, 'the walls of the town were plastered' with signs 'To the Recruiting Office', 'huge arrows all pointing the way', as early as 5 August. Often these municipal offices recruited to local regiments – the 10th Battalion of the County of London Regiment ('Hackney's Own') at Mare Street, the 22nd Battalion was 'Bermondsey's Own', the 23rd Battalion was Battersea's, Wimbledon recruited for the East Surreys, and so on.[21]

Among middle-class volunteers a similar clustering was apparent, but the attachments here were less local and more of background and education. A day or so after 4 August, H. C. Meysey-Thompson, educated at Marlborough, applied to the Inns of Court Officer Training

Corps at Lincoln's Inn, 'confined to University and Public School men':
'A great many of my friends joined at the same time as I did, and I
kept on discovering old School and University friends whom I had not
seen for years.'[22]

Volunteering in these early months of the war frequently proved
disappointing. The physical condition of the London working class was
so poor in 1914 that many failed to meet the exacting standards then
enforced – requirements would later be reduced, and reduced again and
again as the struggle dragged on. So in September 1914, at a Stepney
recruiting meeting, 150 men volunteered but only fifteen passed the
preliminary medical inspection; the rest were sent home. The lower
middle classes could be similarly affected. Richard Church, a 21-year-
old civil servant living in south London, volunteered for the Army
Cyclists' Corps on 5 or 6 August but failed because of short sight and
a weak chest; and Ernest Thurtle, the City clerk from Brixton, was
rejected by a Guards regiment as too scrawny, though later in 1914 he
was allowed into the London Regiment. When men were accepted in
these early months they generally found employers patriotically keen
to let them go, with many – from Bermondsey Borough Council at one
extreme to the Reform Club in Pall Mall at the other – agreeing to pay
half-wages or a supplement to their army pay to ensure they suffered
no financial detriment for their sacrifice.[23]

Who were these early volunteers? Most were working men, if only
because the large majority of young men in London were of the working
class. But for many reasons the lower middle classes and above were
over-represented among volunteers, especially in London. The volunteering rate among industrial workers of eligible age nationally has
been estimated at 28 per cent, while 40 per cent of men employed in
financial services, commerce, the professions, hotels, restaurants, theatres
and so on – all jobs largely represented in London – joined up. This
difference seems to have had little if anything to do with class disaffection or any enduring resentment against a nation and society which
had done so little for the poor in times of peace, but other reasons are
not hard to find. Working-class men in London were in general less
well fed and less fit than middle-class Londoners, and some (like engineers, skilled dock workers and others) were less dispensable to the war
effort. It is likely that the over-representation of middle-class employment in London was one factor in generating a relatively high recruitment rate there among men of eligible age – 14.3 per cent (107,000

recruits) by 12 November 1914 compared to 10.2 per cent in England, Wales and Scotland overall.[24]

Yet despite the queues outside the recruitment offices, the marching columns of volunteers in civilian clothes, the presence everywhere of men in khaki, the levels of recruitment remained a source of anxiety in London throughout 1914. The fall of the Belgian fortress at Namur and the retreat of the Allied armies from Mons at the beginning of the last week of August led to vociferous public debate over how to get more men to enlist. A pessimistic assessment of the British Army's chances without more men and equipment, sent from Amiens by *The Times*'s war correspondent, was published prominently in the Sunday edition of the paper on 30 August. 'On Sunday London was in a panic,' Sir William Mansfield, the Lord Chancellor and soon to become Viscount Sandhurst, noted in his diary; it was 'criminal to publish it', he thought.[25]

The 'panic' acted like a shot of adrenalin to recruitment, 4,000 men enlisting next day compared to some 1,600 a day for the preceding week. But once awakened, anxiety was not allayed. The number of men volunteering was never enough. Recruitment propaganda redoubled through September, the month Alfred Leete's unforgettable Kitchener poster made its first appearance on London's walls, and in the music halls songs and skits urged men to go. Favourite was 'Your King and Country Want You' by Paul Rubens, with its famous line 'Oh, we don't want to lose you but we think you ought to go' – Hallie Miles had it sung at lunchtimes in her husband's fashionable restaurant in Chandos Street, Trafalgar Square, 'by way of getting more "loafers" to enlist'. Banners were flung across the City's Mansion House warning, 'Citizens of London, we must have more men'; the Lord Mayor's Show on 9 November became a 'military display in khaki'; and the funeral of Lord Roberts, hero of wars in Afghanistan and South Africa, at St Paul's nine days later was quickly turned to account with posters in London asking, 'He did his Duty. Will you do Yours?'[26]

These public manifestations of anxiety quickly became more personal. The novelist Arnold Bennett, then forty-seven, confided to his journal on 4 November, 'If one thinks about recruiting one soon gets obsessed by [the] number of young men about the streets.' It was around this time that the 'White Feather' nuisance began. On 10 November Frederick Robinson noted 'a sort of persecution going on': 'Girls go about offering <u>white</u> feathers and write letters to friends, urging them to enlist, and wanting reasons why not.' Perhaps his civil servant son had received one or other, possibly both, of these offensive messages, though he doesn't say so. It was a fine way for women to behave, he thought, given the nuisance they'd made of themselves before the war.[27]

The position of women had already provoked anxiety and for different reasons. The spectre of women and children cast suddenly into poverty by their men leaving for war, unable to fend for themselves as work dried up at home through economic uncertainty, and with all the promise of discontent that would bring about, was a nightmare that occurred to others besides John Burns. Widespread, even catastrophic, distress had been anticipated from the very outset. On 4 August, before war was declared, the Prime Minister established a government committee to coordinate the relief of distress caused by the coming war and on the 6th a National Relief Fund was launched by the Prince of Wales to solicit charitable donations for what was fully expected to be an overwhelming problem, especially and most dangerously in London. Regional committees to oversee relief were established, John Burns chairing the one for London, its members including the Fabian socialist Beatrice Webb; below that a network of subcommittees, chaired by local mayors, determined relief arrangements in London's localities. These were energetic efforts, widely supported. Money poured in to the National Relief Fund from middle-class givers, perhaps with those 'bread-riots' in mind – £2 million by 3 September, £3 million by 5 October.[28]

At first there was no shortage of need. Local branches of the Soldiers' and Sailors' Families Association (SSFA), who administered relief funds to servicemen's dependants, quickly registered thousands of cases, 180 in South Hackney alone on a single day, 12 August, for instance. Sylvia Pankhurst's East London Federation of Suffragettes, its efforts now put full-time into campaigning for infant welfare, unemployment relief and social work, saw babies 'ill from starving', whole streets affected by unemployment, poverty not helped by delays and confusion in the War Office in paying separation allowances to the wives and children of men who volunteered or had been called up. The seventy-two branches of the SSFA in London had handled 90,000 cases by late November, mainly advancing money owed by the War Office in this way and helping dependants such as elderly parents not covered by the official scheme. There were no doubt desperate cases: Stephen Hicks, a Stepney boy about eight years old, lived with his widowed mother; when his two wage-earning older brothers joined the army his mother couldn't provide for him and he was taken into a children's home in Mile End. Ultimately, though, widespread distress proved short-lived, one of many unfulfilled anxieties felt on the outbreak of war.[29]

However, in other ways the effects of the war on London were immediate, transformative and lasted as long as the war itself. People returning to London who had left in peacetime and came back after 4 August found it changed in every direction. Hallie Miles, returning from a seaside break soon after the declaration, thought it 'like an altogether new London'. The streets full of marching men by night and by day the children banging old tin pails and adults whistling patriotic melodies struck her most.[30] For the writer H. G. Wells, in town from his Essex home, it was the appearance of the streets:

> Everywhere there were the flags of the Allies; in shop windows, over doors, on the bonnets of automobiles, on people's breasts, and there was a great quantity of recruiting posters on the hoardings and in windows ... There were also placards calling for men on nearly all the taxicabs. The big windows of the Norddeutscher Lloyd in Cockspur Street were boarded up, and plastered thickly with recruiting appeals.

Wells noticed in these very early war days in London 'an impression of great unrest' in the streets, with 'a quite unusual number of drifting pedestrians. The current on the pavements was irritatingly sluggish. There were more people standing about, and fewer going upon their business.'[31] Winifred Tower, returning to South Kensington on 15 October after three months and more on the Isle of Wight, noted more purpose about things but an altered London:

> As we drove from the station we passed an enormous detachment of recruits marching over Waterloo Bridge, line after line of them, in their ordinary civilian clothes, mostly pale-faced city clerks: it was a most impressive sight. We soon got used to that sort of thing though, there were soldiers everywhere in every stage of their training and equipment. Some had complete uniforms and civilian headgear, some had only a uniform cap, others had a bandolier or a pair of puttees . . .[32]

The traffic too was different. Wells noted 'fewer omnibuses and less road traffic' and the reasons were not hard to find. A number of London General Omnibus Company (LGOC) motor buses had been 'commandeered' for troop movements in the first two days of war and 2,500 of its men were called up as reservists and Territorials or had volunteered by the end of the 1914; in September fifty buses were sent to Belgium with more to follow, and in October 300 more were sent to move troops during the First Battle of Ypres. In all, some 1,300 of the LGOC's 3,000 buses had been requisitioned for war duty by the end of the year. Taxis also fell away sharply as some motor cabs were converted to ambulances and as horses were taken for the army: there were over a thousand fewer motor cabs in London and 544 fewer hansoms and horse-drawn cabs by the end of 1914. Demand had fallen as well: an urge for economy was said to be driving middle-class people from taxis onto buses and trams even before the end of August. There were other traffic changes too. When Arnold Bennett came up to London from his house in Essex on 4 November he noted in his journal, 'Girls driving motor-cars'.[33]

If streets and traffic were quickly transformed by war, then so were London's parks and open spaces. In Hyde Park 'motor-buses, furniture vans, & carts are collected for transport purposes'; long lines of horses were picketed in Green Park; troops were camped at Bishop's Park, Fulham – C. H. Rolph, just thirteen, could hear 'bugles calling Reveille, Cookhouse, Last Post, etc.' from his bedroom window; H. C. Meysey-Thompson practised infantry attacks in Richmond Park in the south-west and there were military exercises on Wanstead Flats in the far east – indeed, every green space in London seemed at the army's beck and call.[34] London was to all practical effect a city under military occupation. Not since the aftermath of the Gordon Riots in the summer of 1780 had London seen anything like this: 'We used to watch them drilling in the Park, signalling, doing physical drill or riding in Rotten Row. You had to be careful in walking across the open space by the Marble Arch, or you suddenly found yourself up against a solid wall of Kitchener's Army.'[35]

But there was one other change overtaking London that no one failed to mention. That was in the appearance of the city at night. From the very outset, Londoners saw themselves close to the front line of war. There were immediate fears, as we have heard, that London would be shelled by a German task force from the river, and in the autumn a pontoon bridge was built by the Port of London Authority from Gravesend to Tilbury with a 600-foot removable section for navigation. Such was the urgency that the work was done in three and a half hours.[36]

Most, however, thought the real risk to London came from the air. The capacity of the Germans' Zeppelin airships to drop bombs on London had been recognised by ordinary Londoners from the beginning. Official precautions were immediate and plainly apparent. An anti-aircraft gun was spotted on the roof of the Foreign Office by a resident of Queen Anne's Gate as early as 10 August, and that same month the lake in St James's Park was drained to stop its moonlight glitter providing an aiming mark for nearby Buckingham Palace. Paris suffered its first air raids in August and Londoners too put themselves 'on the look-out' for Zeppelins: 'people walk about looking skywards. And the example is infectious . . .' The Admiralty took over air raid precautions from the overstretched War Office in early September, and even on the first of that month it was thought by Winston Churchill, First Lord, that Zeppelin raids were imminent. By early September searchlights were 'sweeping the sky in great circles – & on the top of Gresham College', in the City, noted the young Mary Coules, living in Acton; 'at the back of Daddy's office, there is an aeroplane gun. One night it was uncovered – but nothing came of it.'[37]

Many Londoners now began to make their own preparations for the raids that were generally expected and publicly discussed. London businesses considered whether to insure their properties against air attack – the Eustace Restaurant in Chandos Street did in October and the Reform Club thought about it but let the matter stand over.[38] Householders took action according to their means. Winifred Tower lived in prosperous Prince's Gate by the Royal Albert Hall:

> People began to make preparations for Zeppelin raids: one big wine dealer was reported to have let several of his cellars, and people we knew had furnished theirs and slept with big coats and hand-bag for valuables by the bedside. Most people had water or buckets of sand or fire extinguishers on every landing. We rather laughed at this at first but by degrees everyone came round to taking certain precautions.[39]

The night did indeed appear the most worrying time, and not just because of the fear of Zeppelins. The long evenings of August gave way to earlier lighting-up times in September. From Thursday 10 September, in accordance with a 'request' from the Metropolitan Police Commissioner, shops obscured their outside lights and 'sky-signs' were turned off; the number of lamps lit in the streets was reduced and tramcar lights were not turned on. This was an experiment to allow a naval airship to observe the city from the air over the next few nights. The experiment proved inconclusive and was extended. Then, at the request of the Admiralty, as a precaution against Zeppelin attack, the Home Secretary issued an order in early October that made the arrangements permanent. It applied to street lamps (extinguishing many except in thick fog and painting black the tops of those still lit); to sky-signs and other illuminated advertisements (all extinguished); internal lighting in shops (reduced); windows in tall buildings and skylights (covered); even naphtha flares in street markets (banned).[40]

Those who experienced London's second blackout twenty-five years later remembered the darkness from 1914 as 'no more than a dim-out'. It was true enough that in the main streets it remained fairly easy to see one's way. Arnold Bennett walked in early November from the National Liberal Club in Whitehall Place to the Reform in Pall Mall: 'London not so dark as I expected, owing to lamps in the centre of roads throwing down a volume of light in the shape of a lamp-shade (they are blackened at top).' And a month before, the writer H. Rider Haggard thought London 'a curious place just now. The lighting is about as bright only as that which I remember as a boy, when the gas lamps were few and burned dully and electric lamps were unknown.' Some found the novelty appealing – 'I shall never forget the first time I ever saw the stars above Piccadilly,' young Mary Coules enthused in her journal – and others with a writer's or painterly eye delighted in it: Wells thought the darkness gave London 'a Rembrandtesque quality' with 'mysterious arrangements of brown shadows and cones and bars of light'; and John Galsworthy found the Strand 'all jewelled and enamelled' – '"what beauty!"', he makes a character say.[41]

But for most Londoners this wartime darkness was a big change, and not for the better. Familiarity with it bred despondency, even depression. Rider Haggard thought that with the reduced lighting 'the town looks melancholy, and so are its inhabitants. Outwardly things are much the same, but there is a gloom in the air. Business is shocking', with restaurants and clubs half empty and the usual 'lines of magnificent motors' in Pall Mall and Waterloo Place now all gone. Similar feelings, differently expressed, were apparent in Hackney, with its great mixture of classes, middle class and even well-to-do in the north, working class and even poor in the south:

London is going to bed earlier . . . It is not the fear of Zeppelin bombs that is keeping folks at home, but the growing sense of depression that settles upon one as he peregrinates the streets. London when the lights are low is a dull, almost eery place, and the average individual has no difficulty in deciding that

Go East, Go West, home's best.[42]

One more reason to stay at home was the increased danger of the London streets. Many London MPs pressed in the House of Commons for a relaxation of the street-lighting regulations because of rising numbers of traffic accidents. In the capital, in September and October 1913, 101 people were killed in street accidents; in the same two months in 1914 the figure was 163. Not all these accidents happened at night, however, and police and government were reluctant to admit to any significant impact of the restrictions.[43]

By the time the darkened streets had begun to take their toll on the spirit of the Londoners it had become apparent just how much else there was to worry about. London had long been the hub of the nation's health services. It was home to the country's greatest medical schools and one of the world's richest markets for private healthcare provided by top specialists. Its venerable teaching hospitals had unrivalled traditions of professionalism and care for very diverse populations. And London sent doctors and nurses all over the Empire and beyond. It was clear that much of the burden of caring for British casualties from the front would fall on London. But just how quickly this would happen, and just what extraordinary demands it would make on London's hospitals, had not been foreseen.

From soon after the declaration of war there was a rush to provide more hospital beds in London to meet the casualties expected from the fighting in France and Belgium, including many private hospitals that were quickly adapted from residential premises. The Kensington division of the Red Cross began a hunt for hospital premises as early as 14 August. And two weeks later the journalist R. D. Blumenfeld, American-born but London-based and founder of the Anti-Socialist Union, lamented the absence of 'country-house parties' at weekends because houses were all being turned into hospitals. The large majority of these very numerous private hospitals in and about London would be for officers only.[44]

But the main burden of these early weeks fell on the London general hospitals, though not all were equally affected. Guy's, on the South Bank and well placed for Waterloo Station, offered help to the War Office but was told ample beds were available elsewhere; they would not receive their first casualties until November. The London Hospital in Whitechapel offered 500 beds at the outbreak of war and were told on 28 August that no casualties would come for five or six weeks. But the British Expeditionary Force was retreating from Mons with considerable losses and two days later, on Sunday 30 August, the first British wounded reached London. The London Hospital was told this when the men were on the train from Southampton to Waterloo and was asked to take 100 and to collect them from the station. The hospital had no transport of its own. A telephone call was made to a hospital governor, chairman of Lyons the bakers and caterers, who arranged for fourteen horse-drawn bread vans to be on hand to collect them. The soldiers arrived at the hospital at 9 o'clock at night to the cheers of an East End crowd clustered round the yard. An hour or two later the hospital was asked to take a further 150 men; somehow 172 beds were got ready and 200 arrived. The wounded officers received at Waterloo that night had a different welcome. They were taken in motor ambulances to the military hospital at Millbank, Westminster.[45]

Some chaos was unavoidable at first – the circumstances were so exceptional, the city's resources so unprepared to meet them. But even as large flows of wounded men into London continued over the next few months the transport arrangements remained makeshift, with insufficient motor ambulances available to carry the numbers involved and the London County Council not yet equipped with any adequate ambulance service of its own. This was a breach that began to be filled by the Red Cross's London Ambulance Column, formed this year and soon expanded with help from wealthy donors and businesses to provide some 140 ambulances by the New Year. Even so, at the end of October arrangements still seemed amateurish: the military casualty landing station at Southampton would telegraph the number of men arriving to Horse Guards, headquarters of the London District of the army; from there a clerk would telephone the civilian transport coordinator, who then dispatched 'the forty-five or forty-six motor cars loaned to him' by wealthy donors.[46]

From the end of August onwards it was the railway stations that became the closest point of contact between London and the war. That applied to all London's stations, for men on leave countrywide often left from them and returned to them when their time at home was over. But it was true most of all for the stations serving the south coast, especially Charing Cross, London Bridge, Victoria and Waterloo. For the American writer F. Scott Fitzgerald, who fought in France in 1918, Waterloo was forever the epitome of wartime London, 'still sad with the war', as he put it in 1934.[47] Hospital trains would be met by silent crowds and when large numbers of casualties were expected many gathered at hospital gates to see them safely in. The cheers that greeted the first casualties from Mons would not last long. By the end of September at Charing Cross Hospital, conveniently close to the station, a 'big white flag with the Red Cross on it is flying' from the roof 'and right across the street is a long white banner fixed, with the legend "QUIET – FOR THE WOUNDED". A policeman stands at the top of the street and lets no traffic down it. The Strand traffic slows down as it comes to this sacred spot . . .'[48]

This outward sign of the direct effect on London of the carnage in France, just 200 or so miles away, was inevitably followed by others. British casualties were very heavy from the end of August. Private grief at first seems to have kept itself to itself and public signs of bereavement took some time to show. R. D. Blumenfeld thought that, even a month after Mons and despite knowing 'a dozen families at least where death has come to bring sorrow', 'one sees no sign of mourning in the streets'. It would soon arrive. Michael MacDonagh, a reliable witness, noticed on 28 September how 'the wearing of black by women . . . is becoming more and more noticeable in the streets'.[49] And the diarist W. N. P. Barbellion, only in his twenties, sick and lonely but a keen observer of London and its ways, was struck in mid-October when

In the Tube, a young widow came in and sat in front of me – pale-faced, grief-stricken, demure – a sort of 'Thy Will be Done' look. The adaptability of human beings has something in it that seems horrible. It is dreadful to think how we have all accommodated ourselves to this War.[50]

By October too many of London's local newspapers were carrying paragraphs reporting the deaths at the front of local worthies and printing a 'Roll of Honour' of local dead, missing and wounded, week by week.[51]

In this autumn of suffering, the very streets dressed as it were in mourning after dusk, London struggled to offer its normal consolations.

Things were not so bad in daylight. By mid-December the traffic in the streets had restored itself (though buses and taxis never recovered their numbers during the war), pavements seemed unusually thronged and the shops as lively as ever. The restaurants were full at lunchtimes and the tea rooms packed to bursting in the afternoons.[52] But at night the stresses of war were more apparent. Everyone felt it because everywhere was affected. Even the London clubs, a gentleman's refuge from daily anxieties for generations, noticed the strain. The Reform Club in Pall Mall had among its members in 1914 the Prime Minister (Herbert Asquith), the Home Secretary (Reginald McKenna), the President of the Board of Trade (Sir Walter Runciman) and the Parliamentary Secretary to the Board of Education (Christopher Addison); the writers J. M. Barrie, Hilaire Belloc, Arnold Bennett, Erskine Childers, Robert Ross and H. G. Wells; the industrialists Lord Devonport, Sir Alfred Mond and Alexander Siemens; the philanthropists Andrew Carnegie and Charles Booth of London social-survey fame; the publishers Cecil Harmsworth, Thomas Fisher Unwin and John Lane of the Bodley Head. It was one of Liberal England's great institutions. Yet it began to creak and groan from the foundations upwards almost as soon as war was declared. There was no end to the London Season in 1914, no retreat to the country house, so the club's usual summer closure for cleaning and repairs was suspended to allow members to continue to meet there. The 7 p.m. Saturday set dinner was stopped to avoid food waste and replaced with a limited à la carte menu; familiar staff left in platoons – no fewer than fifty had gone and had to be replaced by 17 December; complaints about insolent new pageboys, bad manners and inattentive service, and the inability to cash cheques for gold all plagued the secretary.[53] As we shall see, things would only get worse.

Of far greater importance to the ordinary Londoner were the theatres and music halls of the West End and elsewhere. The dark streets hit theatreland hard. All advertising signs were switched off and foyer lights dimmed. Some theatres opened in the afternoons and closed in the evenings a few days a week; most brought forward their opening hours to accommodate the new darkness. Theatre business was uneven, responding (as Arnold Bennett, a successful London playwright at this time, thought) to news from the front, falling away with a setback, perking up when the Germans were in difficulties. By December, 'London has ceased to be a city of pleasure. The theatres close as early as they can; there are no more supper-parties at the great hotels; the night clubs

are shut.' In this first winter of the war, 'The theatre, paying half salaries and charging a little more than half prices, just manages to keep
its doors open – and that chiefly thanks to our soldiers.'[54]

Christmas gave the West End a chance to shine, metaphorically at
least. Pantomime had always been a staple of theatres in the London
suburbs and remained so, but now the West End too caught the idea
of drawing out an audience by entertaining the children; somehow it
was more acceptable this winter than adults being seen to seek pleasure
on their own account. So pantomime and other children's entertainments
were the main feature of the West End theatres at Christmas, with some
suburban productions moving into the centre (Cinderella taking her
coach from Crystal Palace to the Aldwych, for instance). J. M. Barrie's
Peter Pan had its eleventh successive year at the Duke of York's, St
Martin's Lane; Raffles was again played by Gerald du Maurier at the
Apollo, Shaftesbury Avenue; and there was a new two-part adaptation
by Sir Herbert Beerbohm Tree of David Copperfield at His Majesty's,
Haymarket (Tree played both Wilkins Micawber and Dan'l Peggotty).
Dickens seemed to comfort many this first – most hoped the only –
Christmas of the war.[55]

The war, of course, intruded even on the stage. 'Tipperary' had now
'become the British National Anthem No. 2', incongruously worked into
the overture to Sleeping Beauty at Drury Lane, having smoothly made
the transition from music hall to regular theatre; in the same production
George Graves sang his topical new hit 'Sister Susie's Sewing Shirts for
Soldiers', and refugees, toy soldiers and a noisy howitzer all made an
appearance. Henry V at the Shaftesbury Theatre seemed fresh-minted
for the times, even though celebrating victory over the wrong enemy.[56]

The weather that Christmas was foul. On Boxing Day, a Saturday,
'wind and rain and sleet in the morning and fog in the evening' kept
many at home: 'Rarely have the streets been so deserted on a Bank
Holiday', The Times reported. For those who did venture out the fog
made the return home 'unpleasant and tardy'.[57] The grim weather seemed
to fit many people's mood. Even so, the shops had been unusually full
that Christmas. When Christopher Addison visited Gammage's toy store
in Holborn early in December to buy bicycles for his children he was
'surprised at the crush of people shopping. One would never have
thought there was a war on.' Michael MacDonagh too thought the
shops as 'thronged as I have ever seen them'; in particular, money
'seemed to be plentiful'.[58]

But having money to spend, even spending it, did not always lift the spirits this Christmas. Many thought any celebration inappropriate when so much misery was abroad. The London Hospital, for instance, cancelled its usual Christmas entertainments on the wards, though it went ahead with Christmas dinner; perhaps the miniature rifle range it set up that same month in a corridor of the outpatients' department offered some diversion. And in the homes of the comfortable middle classes sympathy seemed to lie more with the unreformed Scrooge than the ghost of Christmas Present. 'It is horrid cold weather,' Georgina Lee wrote in her diary. 'We are doing practically nothing in the way of Christmas presents, only for the children . . . No family presents.'[59] Frederick Robinson felt the same, with most people sending fewer cards or none at all, and none of the usual festivities in the hotels, the whole season being marked by restraint and depression.[60]

In working people's homes perhaps the availability of ready money – so exceptional for so many – was cause enough for celebration in itself: it was reported that there were twice the numbers of charges of drunkenness in the North London Magistrates' Court this year than there had been at Christmas 1913.[61]

Drink was indeed a problem at Christmas 1914, though for a different reason: it was harder to get than at any time in living memory. For as if the fact of war were not bad enough by itself, there seemed to be a conscious strategy to eliminate pleasure from public life – and from private life too. Beatrice Webb, living in Grosvenor Road, Pimlico, made the point well in her diary as winter approached in 1914 and the dreary night-time began to take effect:

The darkening of London, now the days are short, adds to the national sobriety but also to the national gloom. It is reported that Berlin and its suburbs are blazing with light so as to produce optimism. Our government seems to think that what our people want is increased anxiety and seriousness: they certainly have helped to create a consciousness of personal peril by absence of light and absence of liquor . . .[62]

Something more was going on here than fear of Zeppelins. But what?

3

A WAR FOR PURITY

Had there not crept a softness over the nation, a passion for amusement, a love of luxury among the rich, and of mere physical comfort among the middle class? Not such was the nation which made the Empire, and which curbed the Armada.[1]

THE Bishop of London's call to arms at St Paul's Cathedral on the first Sunday of the war ranged widely over the duties of the Londoners in the calamitous conflict that had just begun. But his theme of war as a cure for the ills of the nation and its capital city resonated with many. One week later *The Times*, in a sermon of its own, took up the theme of war's benefits, stressing the value 'of its discipline' as a 'painful, but salutary, remedy for softness, slackness, sensuality . . .'[2]

The Bishop and *The Times* mined a deep seam of puritanism that had battled long but unsuccessfully with the evils of metropolitan existence. A peacetime survey of the work of the London churches published in 1914 intoned a frustrated lengthy litany of enduring immorality and sin, with much getting worse not better: congregations shrinking in the central districts as the middle classes leave for the suburbs; insufficient churches in outer London; 'indifference' to religion both among the poor and in 'respectable villadom'; 'two out of three' young people 'practically heathen' and 'thoroughly out of control when thirteen or fourteen years of age', '"idling about"' . . . and "growing up thoughtless, selfish and undisciplined"'. Virtue and religion were undermined by the amusements of the Londoners, especially the poor: there was much 'impurity in the streets'; 'gambling is widespread and difficult to eradicate'; there were too many public houses and an 'increase of drinking among women'; in the cinema, the pictures 'usually shown in the poorer districts [are] sensational and on the whole demoralising'; and there was 'Sunday desecration', with men at home 'in shirt sleeves with pipes in their mouths when they should be in a place of worship'. 'In two directions only,' the report concluded, 'is religious interest manifested, and here superstition might be the better word to use.' These were 'Watch-Night', New Year's Eve, when 'every church in a London slum will be crowded to the doors', and at the '"churching" of women' after childbirth. 'But apart from this religion is of use very largely for what can be got out of it.'[3]

Many of these complaints had been familiar among churchmen and lay Christians in London for generations. Yet efforts among a broad puritan and evangelical alliance to reform society and its manners had remained undaunted, continually adapting to changing circumstances, frequently finding new targets for amendment and imaginative ways to present their case afresh. And new allies were readily gathered, even from apparently unlikely sources, for puritans were to be found everywhere. In 1911 a manifesto of the National Council on Public Morals had sought to unite morality and the new pseudo-science of eugenics in a campaign for the sanctity of marriage, an increase in the legitimate birth rate, isolation of the 'feeble-minded', censorship of pernicious literature and the moral education of the young, all in the interests of 'race-regeneration'. The manifesto won broad support among medical men; it had an appeal too among radicals – its signatories included Ramsay MacDonald and Beatrice Webb.[4]

When the Council helped provoke a national moral panic over 'White Slavery', the alleged abduction and trafficking of women for prostitution at home and abroad, it found allies in the militant feminist wing of the suffragettes. Christabel Pankhurst's slogan from 1912 became 'Votes for Women and Chastity for Men'. She warned women against the dangers of marriage, claiming that men were almost universally infected with one venereal disease or another. The purity agenda of the Pankhursts' militant Women's Social and Political Union attracted many clergymen and social workers to the cause of women's suffrage during 1913 and 1914.[5] Prominent among them was Arthur Foley Winnington-Ingram, the Bishop of London. And within the churches young men were urged to vows of chastity until marriage in organisations like the nonconformists' Alliance of Honour and the Church of England's White Cross League; both claimed large allegiance within the lower middle classes in particular, many London clerks and shopmen among them.

A puritan alliance had also formed to combat the evils of drink. The temperance movement was of long standing and had spread widely beyond the walls of the churches. Through nonconformism it had penetrated into the ranks of the Liberal and Labour parties, where it had an explicitly political edge, the brewers and distillers providing a large element of Conservative Party funding. David Lloyd George, born in Manchester but brought up by a devout Christian and teetotal uncle in North Wales, was the most famous temperance politician of his day. Though not himself an abstainer and though he later lost his Christian faith, Lloyd George continued to preach temperance in and out of Parliament. His maiden speech in the House of Commons in 1890 had been against drink and he was an able propagandist for local prohibition rather than a national ban, making the sale of 'liquor' subject to a local veto.[6] Other politicians sought ineffectually over the years statutory enforcement of drink restriction, even prohibition and compulsory teetotalism: within Labour's ranks Philip Snowden, from a strict nonconformist background in Yorkshire and one of the Party's most fervent anti-war propagandists from 1915, led the charge against drink, advocating state control of brewing and distilling. And outside Parliament the Band of Hope and similar organisations drew working people and others into the teetotal ranks nationwide; they had numerous followers in London, where a 'temperance syllabus', pointing up the health evils of drink, was followed in many elementary schools by 1914.[7]

The temperance movement also had support in the army, where other components of masculine purity had long had considerable influence. The public school ideals of muscularity, bodily and moral cleanliness, fair play and faith in God designedly equipped many young men for life in the armed services. Beyond the upper classes, the Boy Scout movement, the Church of England's Boys' Brigade and an extensive network of university settlements, almost all blending manliness with Christianity in one form or another, sought to extend these virtues to working-class boys. But it was among the officer class that the 'soldier-saint' was a most powerful icon and had been since the 1850s at least. By 1914 a surprising number of senior officers in the British Army, including some drawn out of retirement by the emergency, were deeply steeped in a cult of puritan manliness formed on temperance, celibacy for single men and monogamy for the married, and an unquestioning faith in God and the Church of England.[8]

Lord Kitchener of Khartoum, who had walked in the steps of one of the greatest of all soldier-saints, General Charles George Gordon, was made Secretary of State for War on 5 August. He was unmarried and a temperance advocate. Kitchener famously urged celibacy on his troops and refused to equip the British Expeditionary Force (BEF) of 1914 with condoms as prophylactics against venereal disease, alone among the rival armies of Europe, preferring to rely on exhortation: 'In this new experience you may find temptations both in wine and women. You must entirely resist both temptations, and, while treating all women with perfect courtesy, you should avoid any intimacy.'[9] Field Marshal Lord Roberts, recalled to active service in August 1914 although he was eighty-two years old, was thought 'an almost perfect type of the Christian hero', a keen temperance man, his life untroubled by the temptation of women.[10] Generals Sir Ian Hamilton and Sir Francis 'Frankie' Lloyd, the latter General Officer Commanding the London District and responsible for military organisation and discipline in the capital, were both well-known temperance speakers. General Sir Douglas Haig, 'convinced that he had been led to the Western Front by God's hand', noted with disgust in his diary how much 'liquor' his guests took at dinner.[11] And General Sir Horace Smith-Dorrien, commander of the BEF's 2nd Army in 1914, would go into battle for the extreme wing of the puritans when he returned to London later in the war.

For all these very varied groups within the British ruling class the declaration of war in August 1914 came as a golden chance to correct the years of sensuality and licence since the death of Victoria, 'years which, of all in recent times, the ingrained puritanism of the English would most gladly forget. Under the shock of war,' wrote Stephen McKenna a few years later, 'it became fashionable to look upon this wanton life as an offence to God, which the scourge of God was being used to end . . .' War, then, was an *opportunity* – a keyword of the first twelve months of hostilities – to redeem a nation made soft by luxury, vicious by lust, spineless through liquor, undisciplined through democracy. This was a holy war, not just against the evils of Prussianism abroad but the evils of sin at home. It was a restorative, rebuilding, remaking, re-Christianising a corrupt society.[12]

The mechanisms of moral reform would become more complex and ubiquitous as the war grew older, but the foundations were laid early, on 8 August, by the passing into law of the Defence of the Realm Act – universally, and with ironic humour, known as DORA. Under succeeding Acts (at least nine) and the regulations made under them, almost every aspect of civil society became shaped and constricted by the state. Both at the time and after people wondered how the liberty-loving British succumbed to DORA's ensnaring wiles. The main reason was that most saw the nation fighting for its life in a just struggle where compromise and half-measures had no place. But another was because DORA indulged influential puritan prejudices that saw war correcting the wrongs of the past.

The most important target of puritans throughout the war was drink, and drink lay behind the first of many moral panics that gripped the middle-class imagination and led to a reaction by DORA. In the early days this was one of several gendered anxieties provoked by the war – women being the dangerous, weaker, more easily tempted sex. It concerned a question already vexing purity reformers long before August 1914: the tendency, real or imagined or just more visible to the public gaze, of women to resort to the pub and beerhouse more frequently than they had done before. A sustained call for a 'Teetotal War' had followed Kitchener's order for abstinence in the BEF in August. Publicity then was aimed at soldiers and recruits, and especially urged that men in khaki should not be treated to beer or spirits by well-meaning citizens. But early in October 1914 there built a crescendo of anxiety about working-class women and drink. Soldiers' wives were said to be misspending their separation allowances in the public house. Margaret Taylor of Cowley Street, near Westminster Abbey, and a worker for the Soldiers' and Sailors' Families Association, complained that 'day after day women come to us assuring us they and their children are starving, they have no soles to their boots, and pleading for larger grants from the society. And all the time puffing into our faces fumes of whisky, gin, and the like . . . Cannot the same power that is making our soldiers teetotal make their wives teetotal too?'[13]

Everywhere that October the problem of 'Tippling Among Women' became a metropolitan sensation. An unpublished 'inquiry' in 'every London borough' was said to provide 'one continuous list of complaints of increased drinking and drunkenness' among women often too befuddled to look after their children. Temperance reformers stood outside pubs in working-class districts to count the women going in – 750 in one Hoxton public house in a four-hour period, it was said, and 411 in another. London magistrates greedy for press attention called for women to be excluded from pubs altogether. They were backed by prohibition organisations like the South London Catholic Five Hundred and the Hackney and East Middlesex Band of Hope, and no doubt others. Bermondsey Borough Council resolved to consider withdrawing payments made to the wives of staff who had joined up if any woman was reported to the council for drinking too much. The letters columns of the daily and local London press were filled with the female tippling menace, not least to the fighting morale of men at the front, who might return to 'find their women-folk degraded and besotted by excessive indulgence in alcohol'. And puritanically minded patriots like H. Rider Haggard confided to their diaries observations of women drinking in pubs: 'If I had my way I would shut every one of them down at sun-down . . .'[14]

Was there anything in this? Some women were almost certainly drinking more. It would be surprising if they were not, many working-class women – as the rector of St George the Martyr, Southwark, put it – being 'better off now than they have ever been in their lives'.[15] Perhaps more important was the unprecedented strain they laboured under, their men in France or at sea, with an almost total news blackout in which rumour ran riot. But many experienced observers were sceptical about the panic, blaming it on increased attention from the middle classes towards elements of working-class culture that had been there long before the war but had gone unnoticed. Rider Haggard, for instance, noted a scene while walking in proletarian Harrow Road around 3 o'clock one afternoon – 'a group of women, all young and all with children, outside a public-house. There they stood, drinking very strong-looking beer, while their poor babies shivered in the bitter cold.' But this increased visibility of women drinking was almost certainly a product of the Children Act 1908, which banned young children from pubs. Some commentators, like the socialist and pacifist Charlotte Despard (the doting sister of Sir John French, Commander-in-Chief of the BEF), denied there was any drunkenness in the poor London-Irish community she lived among at Nine Elms, Battersea. Even the Charity Organisation Society, its instincts generally punitive, recognised that many women turned to the pub to 'hear the news' rather than drink heavily. In all, it's difficult to disagree with Helen Fraser, a suffragette and worker among the poor, who thought that a 'great deal of this talk' came from middle-class women who before the war 'had never done social work, and who knew nothing of real conditions' now going about 'among the people and [who] were shocked and overwhelmed by what were unfortunately normal wrong conditions, and lost all sense of perspective'.[16]

This particular scandal over women and drink died down as quickly as it had flared up. Nevertheless it was not without its effects. As early as 7 September 1914, to deter drinking among soldiers and recruits on leave, pub closing hours in London were shortened at both ends of the day. Before the war pubs could open from 5 a.m. till 12.30 a.m.; now they could only open from 8 a.m. (with exceptions for certain areas) and had to close at 11 p.m. In the midst of the tippling-women panic, from 19 October the closing time in London was again brought forward from 11 p.m. to 10 p.m., and in the munitions-making districts of Greenwich and Woolwich to 9 p.m. Then, from 9 November, London's pub-owners agreed with the Metropolitan Police that licence conditions should be varied to stop women being served with drink before 11.30 a.m. Though grumbles about working women and drink never entirely stopped during the war, the worst of the panic had evaporated by the end of November 1914.[17]

Or rather, the panic moved on. Working-class women continued to be the main source of puritan anxiety but in another guise – the sexual misconduct of women, whether stimulated by liquor or not. Many social workers were scandalised by unmarried women claiming separation allowances intended for 'wives'. The widespread tradition of cohabitation among working men and women in London was a shock to charity workers coming fresh to the lives of the metropolitan poor. From late 1914 through early 1915 there was an unsuccessful agitation within the churches, among London Boards of Guardians (the poor-law authorities) and within relief organisations to stop or at least reduce the separation allowances to common-law wives. The SSFA, who administered relief to the dependants of servicemen, was for a time torn apart by the issue, with many local committee members resigning rather than be responsible for the endowment of sin.[18]

The morals of working women, married or not, continued to vex the authorities throughout the war. In October 1914 the Army Council asked the Metropolitan Police Commissioner to keep soldiers' wives under surveillance so that allowances might be stopped to 'the Unworthy'. 'Of course there was a public outcry' against the suggestion, Sylvia Pankhurst recalled. But even so the Home Office later in the year continued to assert that the police should 'convey a timely warning of the results of misconduct' to women receiving allowances. How much contact there was between the police in London and the army over these matters is unclear – Pankhurst thought cooperation was 'a dead letter'. But certainly soldiers' complaints of their wives' infidelity were passed throughout the war by the War Office to the women police – a wholly new puritan arm of the state that we shall meet later – to investigate, leading to the withdrawal of allowances in some cases at least.[19]

The anxieties attaching especially to soldiers' wives, their morals and excessive drinking, expanded readily to girls and unmarried women generally. 'Khaki fever', a compulsive passion to be around soldiers, was said to have infected young women in London and the garrison towns soon after war was declared. The Young Women's Christian Association and other organisations appealed for financial aid to fight temptation with 'social and educative recreation'. And from the spring of 1915 a new panic erupted, this time about unmarried mothers and illegitimate births under the cry of 'War Babies'. This term, when originally coined around September 1914, had been innocuously applied to the offspring of men serving with the colours. It now came to represent the fruits of reckless immorality among young women whose willpower had been unbuttoned by drink and khaki. By April 1915 the War Babies' and Mothers' League, with offices in South Molton Street, Mayfair, was said to have 'dealt with over 4,000 cases' of mothers aged from sixteen to forty. That month the Women's Imperial Health Association invited some '60 ladies' from many organisations to a conference at Hanover Square to discuss the problem; excitement was such that many others not invited 'arrived by motor and otherwise' and held their own impromptu meeting on the doorstep. Mrs Pankhurst's Women's Social and Political Union devised a scheme for adopting girl war babies, boys apparently adequately catered for elsewhere. But by June a committee of churchmen had concluded that the war-babies scare had been a figment of a frenzied imagination fuelled by the daily press and that there had been no great rise in illegitimacy. The Bishop of London 'repudiated with righteous indignation the idea that the men in training were behaving badly as a body'; he thought that 'As a whole the women had behaved well' too.[20]

The truth, as often, was mixed but in general the Bishop seems to have been right. There was a marginal increase in the numbers of registered illegitimate births in London during the war, hardly out of step with estimates of the rise in population as a whole (17,329 in 1911–14, 17,538 in 1915–18). Only in Woolwich, a great troop-quartering and munitions-making district, was there a marked rise and even there the four years 1915–18 accounted for just 512 illegitimate births (compared to 299 in 1911–14). On the other hand, because the number of births in London fell drastically by over 20 per cent in these years compared to the four years before the war, the proportion of illegitimate births to all births rose from 3.9 per cent to 5 per cent. And infanticide became an even more marked feature of working-class London life than it had been, as we shall see in later chapters.[21]

It was around the time of the war-babies panic that the drink question moved to a definitive resolution. It is unsurprising that the opening bombardment was fired by David Lloyd George, then still Chancellor of the Exchequer. Disquiet about the inadequate supply of munitions, especially guns and shells, provoked the formation of a Cabinet committee to investigate the causes of the problem on 21 February 1915. No problem was more complex. It involved the organisation and control of industry, labour shortages and restrictive practices intensified by the reappearance of industrial discontent in Scotland and elsewhere, inadequate supplies of chemicals, metals and other materials, and a lack of technical and managerial expertise in government, especially in the War Office, whose responsibility, to add to all its other worries, munitions were. Many of these things had been recognised by government and measures begun to remedy them. But on 28 February Lloyd George, in a speech at Bangor, with brazen intellectual sleight of hand, laid one main cause for the nation's failures before the public:

> you must remember, a small minority of workmen can throw a whole works out of gear. What is the reason? Sometimes it is one thing, some-times it is another, but let us be perfectly candid. It is mostly the lure of the drink. They refuse to work full time, and when they return their strength and efficiency are impaired by the way in which they have spent their leisure. Drink is doing more damage in the War than all the German submarines put together . . . .[22]

It says much about the benighted condition of the official mind and the state of class relations in the country that Lloyd George's analysis was swallowed neat, with only a few angry voices, generally representing organised labour, raised in opposition. His speech was immediately seized upon by churchmen, both clerics and lay, as 'A Great Opportunity'. Within days, in early March, it had become 'The Great Opportunity' for 'a great national act of amendment and contrition', as the Bishop of Croydon put it.[23] The response to Lloyd George's speech quickly took the arguments beyond the sphere of munitions and other industrial production and made the drink issue what it had always been, a movement towards the moral reformation of the nation, especially its working people. All elements in the pre-war puritan alliance shouldered arms as at one command.

Teetotal fundamentalists continued to beat the drum of complete prohibition, sometimes gaining new allies. A letter-writing campaign, directed at Lloyd George, was said to have produced 50,000 letters and postcards in support of total suppression of drink manufacture and sale; the campaign advertisement cited Lloyd George's ringing phrase to a delegation of shipbuilders – 'We are fighting Germany, Austria, and Drink, and as far as I can see the greatest of these deadly foes is DRINK.'[24] The anti-drink movement was fortified by the King. Lloyd George had suggested to him that a personal lead from the palace could have a salutary effect in the nation and on 30 March George V wrote to the Cabinet to say he was prepared to relinquish alcohol in his family and household for the duration. The Cabinet accepted his offer and his letter was published on 6 April. But of the Cabinet only Lord Kitchener at the War Office followed suit. Lloyd George, whose drink intake was modest, stayed quiet. When Lord Rosebery, a prominent Liberal peer, was asked his view on the drink question he replied that 'he relied on the unerring judgment of the Prime Minister', Herbert Asquith, a heavy and unrepentant drinker. And when teetotal MPs moved prohibition in the nation, or even a ban on liquor in the House of Commons, they were roundly defeated. These mixed messages did not go unnoticed among ordinary people, and the agitations of abstinence and prohibition movements fell on stony ground among Londoners. Indeed, the spectre of prohibition induced another sort of panic among the wine-and-spirit-drinking metropolitan middle classes: R. D. Blumenfeld noted in his diary on 17 April 'the rush of people to replenish their cellars in anticipation of temperance legislation by Mr. Lloyd George'.[25]

There is no doubt, though, that the anti-drink commotion unleashed by Lloyd George was received with enthusiasm among puritanical and class-conscious elements of the London middle classes. We might cite the unpublished diary of Edith Marjorie Bunbury, a charity worker living in Lyndhurst Road, Peckham, who noted with approval Lloyd George's Bangor speech and deplored the drink-sodden munitions workers: 'This is terrible to think of. Have working men ever been so base[?]' At the end of March she thought 'The Drink Question is the question of the hour. Things are really humming . . . Someone is running an advertising campaign in the papers – just the right thing – a good red "shouter" . . . Heaven send the Cabinet courage (this time!) . . .' She had her doubts, though, when a friend reported travelling in the same railway carriage as the Marquis of Crewe, Lord Privy Seal and a Cabinet member, who 'drank a whole bottle of champagne!' during the journey.[26]

The dream of total prohibition that many saw as the 'great opportunity' proved an illusion. Prohibition seemed just too provocative, potentially causing more dislocation and discontent than drink had ever done. Some thought too that another 'precious opportunity' had been missed – to nationalise the brewing and distilling industry to control drink on the one hand and deal a heavy blow to the Tories on the other.[27] In the end, though, an overwhelming middle-class consensus quickly built up that some move towards temperance was essential and that statutory compulsion was necessary to secure it. So government resolved to tighten further the screw that had already begun to turn when pub opening hours were restricted in the autumn of 1914. During late April and early May 1915 the government steered through the House of Commons amid acrimonious debate a measure to control and restrict the nation's access to alcohol. It came too late to stem the scandal of the shell shortage. The furore over inadequate munitions of war brought down the Liberal government that had been in power since 1908 and forced Asquith and his followers into coalition with the Conservatives on 19 May 1915. That same day the Defence of the Realm (Amendment) No. 3 Act passed into law and orders were made to establish a Central Control Board (Liquor Traffic) (CCB) with potentially draconian powers over the manufacture, distribution and sale of drink. The CCB was made accountable to a newly created Minister of Munitions with a post in the Cabinet. On 25 May the first incumbent was named – it was David Lloyd George.

The CCB moved quickly to enforce temperance, mainly at first by reducing access to 'liquor' in the shipbuilding, steelworking, mining and munitions-making districts and provincial ports. Restrictions on pub opening hours were tightened in these districts from 6 July, including Bexley, Crayford and Erith in south-east London. This same order under DORA prevented 'treating' in any public house: no person could buy drinks for another, not even a husband for his wife. At the end of September 1915 it was decreed that the whole of Greater London, then defined as the Metropolitan Police District, would be considered a 'munition area', and on 11 October the 'no-treating' order was applied to the metropolis – prosecutions for this offence would become a regular feature of London life till the end of the war. From 29 November pub opening hours across Greater London were cut from nineteen and a half a day pre-war to just five and a half and five on Sundays. Pubs could now open only from 12 noon to 2.30 p.m. and 6.30 to 9.30 p.m. (9 p.m. on Sundays). Concessions were made to some 250 named public houses near the London docks and fifty more near the main London wholesale markets at Smithfield, Billingsgate, Spitalfields, Covent Garden, Stratford, Borough, Islington Cattle Market and the Central London Markets to accommodate the needs of dock workers, salesmen and porters in the early morning. The four pubs near the Royal Small Arms Factory at Enfield Lock were purchased by the CCB in January 1916, the state running and improving them while cutting their opening hours even further to four and a half a day. At the same time steps were taken to reduce the alcohol in 'liquor'. Spirits in London were ordered to be diluted from the time of the no-treating order; Lloyd George's tax changes had already weakened the strength of beer from November 1914 and raised the price by 1d a pint to 4d. Further measures to reduce the alcohol in beer and spirits were periodically introduced until the end of the war. The restrictions on pub hours were applied also to hotels, restaurants and clubs.[28]

In Hackney the local paper recorded that the impending introduction of drastically shorter pub opening hours had 'caused quite a commotion'.[29] It didn't go down well in Pall Mall either. The secretary at the Reform Club agreed with a retired Artillery Colonel

> that it seems a real hardship to refuse to serve beer with your Supper, but I am sorry to say I am quite powerless in this matter.
>
> The Club comes under the provisions of the new drink rules and it is causing difficulties day by day – but there are persons of all classes watching the working of the Regulations and the Club is liable to very heavy penalties [a fine of £100 and/or six months' imprisonment] for infringement of them.[30]

The club now closed at midnight (formerly 2.30 a.m.); it could not sell drink after 9 p.m. but there was half an hour's drinking-up time if alcohol was served with meals. And proposals from teetotallers among the members to ban drink from the club during the war had to be fought off from time to time (Herbert Asquith, we might recall, was a member, and so was Rosebery).[31]

Resentment in London at what many saw as class legislation smouldered on. The secretary at the Reform Club made a telling point that club servants (as well as puritans among the members) might well make mischief if they saw their 'betters' getting what working men and women had to go without. There were collective expressions of discontent as well. Protest meetings had been held in working-class areas of London after the earlier closing times were imposed in November 1914. The London Trades Council and the Working Men's Club and Institute Union, their bar takings under threat, loudly opposed the restrictions. Agitation in the working-men's clubs against 'the "killjoys"' and 'teetotalers' was going on in January 1915, even before Lloyd George's Bangor speech. A 'League of the Man in the Street' was formed that month and by April it could boast an office in Great Queen Street, Holborn, with branches across London. In the Commons two London Labour MPs, Will Thorne (West Ham South) and Charles Bowerman (Deptford), with others, opposed the legislation as a libel on working people; and outside Parliament Horatio Bottomley and his *John Bull* railed against such 'ridiculous', 'Grandmotherly Legislation'. Early in 1916 the excitable Thorne felt able to make the spectacular but unverifiable claim that '400,000 Metropolitan trade unionists and club members have protested' against pub restrictions in London, though Lloyd George's Ministry of Munitions denied all knowledge of any protest. Allegations that the CCB was packed with teetotallers (there were certainly some) and complaints about the oppressive misuse of its power rumbled on in Parliament and beyond for the rest of the war. And in London, as no doubt elsewhere, the 'no-beer pub' from Monday to Thursday, the brewing trade plagued by shortages, became a common frustration of working life.[32]

When, in July 1917, commissioners reported on the causes of a wave of industrial unrest that had shaken the Lloyd George government and seemed to indicate that working people had lost the stomach for war, liquor control was top among the 'Minor Complaints' of the Londoners. Restriction on the sale of beer and its high price and weak strength when available had 'produced hardship, ill-feeling, and irritation among the large industrial population accustomed to take beer at their principal meals'. 'There appears,' they continued, 'to be inequality amounting to absurdity in the distribution of supplies, *e.g.* in Woolwich, a place to which there is an enormous daily immigration, public houses are frequently closed for days together on account of want of supplies.' They recommended 'Some relaxation of the existing restrictions', though none was implemented in London as a whole. So the Lloyd George-induced panic over drink and munitions in early 1915 played its part in stoking another over the morale of the industrial worker some two years later.[33] Looking long-sightedly at these events from across the Atlantic, the radical American journalist Arthur Gleason reached a view of this great moral commotion over drink in 1915 that is difficult to resist:

> It was the making of shells that taught England the new synthesis of capital and labour. Suddenly she . . . had to learn overnight how to get a large product. She began in the manner dear to ruling classes: she started an old-time 'personal-morality' campaign of the evangelistic sort, and her most gifted exhorter, Lloyd George, went out to down drink.[34]

Then she found the only answer to suit the circumstances of the war: state control, even state ownership, of production. Whatever part 'the drink' played in the nation's difficulties in producing munitions in the spring of 1915 was exiguous or non-existent. Lloyd George – surely consciously – began a campaign more in the puritan and Liberal interest than in pursuit of victory on the Western Front, furthering the wider concerns of those who saw a nation requiring moral regeneration in 'a war for purity', as the Bishop of London put it.[35]

If the intellectual justification for Lloyd George's campaign was weak its effects were momentous. The drinking habits of Britain and the Londoner were permanently changed. The ubiquitous strong beer which for generations had soothed the strains of the workbench for the London artisan and eased the burden of the labouring poor – for good and ill – had gone for ever. Drunkenness, street rowdyism, domestic violence – none of these disappeared from London working-class life, but the frequency of the first two at least was greatly diminished. There had been nearly 68,000 convictions for drunkenness offences (drunk and incapable, drunk and disorderly) in Greater London in 1914; in 1918 the figure was just over 10,000.[36] Numbers moved up once more with the coming of peace, but never again approached the pre-war level.

Whether DORA did this alone, or whether (as is likely) the reduction in poverty and worklessness and the wartime rise in living standards made a contribution, remains a moot but insoluble point.

The war went on to provoke puritan assaults on many fronts. Some, like nightclubs, gambling, drugs and prostitution, generally arose later in the war and we shall meet them in their place. Others emerged early. Targets were widely spaced, but many pleasures under fire had this in common: they were treasured elements in working-class culture. First came professional football, its season beginning shortly after the declaration of war. The charge was led by Frederick Nicholas Charrington, the 64-year-old scion of an East End brewing family who had renounced his inheritance to pursue the causes of temperance and Christian purity. He had won notoriety (or fame, depending on one's point of view) in the 1880s for his harassment of London music halls and their proprietors. That same decade he built the Great Assembly Hall in Mile End Road, capable of seating 5,000, where he regaled audiences with temperance sermons and gave free teas to 700 poor people every Sunday afternoon. The 'great opportunity' offered by war rallied Charrington and others against any public entertainment that seemed to distract men from the business of killing.

Soon after war was declared Field Marshal Lord Roberts had said that it would be disgraceful if professional football were allowed to continue and in his support Charrington made an early appearance in the cause of puritan patriotism. In early September he published a telegram he had sent the King requesting he cease to be a patron of the Football Association (FA). At Craven Cottage on Saturday 5 September he caused a fracas at the match between Fulham and Clapton Orient. He asked the Fulham officials if he could address the crowd at half-time and after he gave an 'assurance' that he would not condemn the continuation of football during the war they allowed him to do so. Seated in the centre stand, he rose at the interval 'and, removing his silk hat, commenced to speak. "I am here," he began, "to protest against football being played." He got no farther', for he was promptly seized by the Fulham chairman and secretary 'and forcibly ejected from the ground'. He summonsed both men for assault, but the case was dismissed by the magistrate at West London police court.[37]

Charrington the fanatic swept along others in his train. In December 1914 Michael MacDonagh, the *Times* journalist, remarked in his diary how before the war football fans used to be confronted with evangelical posters greatly concerned for our eternal welfare . . . 'Are you prepared to meet your God?' and bidding us 'Repent, for the time is at hand.' In these days the posters carried by a line of sandwich-men, walking up and down before the gates of the Chelsea football ground, ask . . . 'Are you forgetting that there's a War on?' 'Your Country Needs You'.[38]

Some magistrates jumped on the gun-carriage, the elderly Thomas Hedderwick at North London Police Court berating a 26-year-old labourer found drunk and incapable after a football match: '"It is a most contemptible thing for a young man like you to be going to see men kicking a ball."' The issue was inevitably taken up by puritans in Parliament, demanding that cheap train tickets to matches be prohibited, that football supporters not in uniform be somehow hit with 'a tax' and that professional matches be suppressed. The FA, supported by Asquith, at first resisted, though the rugby and hockey authorities quickly gave in. The FA sought to assuage the onslaught with recruitment meetings at matches. But these proved largely ineffectual and, after relentless pressure in the daily and local press, in April 1915 the FA announced that professional football would be abandoned for the duration. The last FA Cup Final till after the Armistice was played at Old Trafford, Manchester, on 24 April between Chelsea and Sheffield United: Chelsea lost 3–0. Three weeks or so later Charrington endeared himself to MPs by entering the Commons chamber in 'evening dress, an overcoat, and a silk hat' and seizing the mace in protest at the members' refusal to ban drink from the House.[39]

Attacks on other forms of public amusement persisted through 1915 and 1916. The music halls, as Charrington's evangelising career testifies, had long been an affront to purity campaigners. Their thirty-year battle with the music halls was redoubled after the declaration of war. To the old objections that the music halls encouraged sexual immorality and licentiousness was now added a new one that brought allies to the puritans' side: that, as in the case of football, frivolity and waste of time and money seemed a moral affront in time of war, especially the all-absorbing conflict of this Great War. That last argument could be – and was – extended beyond the music halls to theatre and cinema in particular.[40]

A frontal attack was launched from early January 1915 at the music halls' weakest point, the Theatres and Music-Hall Committee of the

London County Council (LCC), the licensing body that determined whether their continuing operation was legitimate or otherwise. By refusing to renew an annual entertainment licence, the LCC could close a hall. It had long contained representatives of the 'nonconformist conscience' – Liberal in politics, often evangelical in religion, nominally abstemious and puritan in habits, with a special repugnance for 'liquor', and ever willing to impose their own preferences on others. Pressure came from a wide spread of purity organisations in London. Among them were the London Council for the Promotion of Public Morality – or Public Morality Council (PMC) – formed in 1899. Its chairman almost from inception was Winnington-Ingram, Bishop of London. The PMC's preoccupations in 1915 focused on nightclubs and 'the character of music-hall performances'.[41] They lobbied the LCC on music halls in January 1915, and from that spring the Lord Chamberlain, Viscount Sandhurst, was kept busy dealing with complaints about the 'revues' or topical variety shows that drew large audiences to the Empire, Leicester Square, and smaller houses. In May he met the Bishop of London and explained his efforts at 'squashing as far as possible the salaciousness' of revues, both comic turns and dancing girls. Not himself a puritan – though a mild anti-Semite, it appears, from his frequent references to 'Jew' promoters and managers – he nevertheless had an instinctual upper-middle-class feeling for what was good for the masses, with a nose for the 'beastly' and 'vulgar'. Even so, he was by the standards of the time fair-minded and prepared to reach an independent judgement, not always swayed by the puritan chorus.

> As part of my duty I went to the Empire Revue. It is a bright show and very much appreciated by the audience, among whom were very many soldiers and sailors – nothing to complain of – clever in places, dances and posturing good, [George] Graves [the comedian] very clever and rather vulgar, but no harm. There are however great possibilities of danger in it if in bad hands or not looked after.[42]

The increasing popularity of revues and variety, froth and wit and innuendo more to the taste of wartime audiences in London than serious drama, provoked a first backlash within the LCC: in November 1915 the Council banned drink from theatres that had turned over from plays to variety.[43]

In their battles with the halls the puritans found themselves with other powerful allies, far beyond the ranks of the LCC. One day in mid-March 1916, when Sandhurst arrived at his office,

> I was told I was wanted on the telephone and it turned out to be the King . . . It was about a picture at a music hall shown in an illustrated paper. I sent for the manager, who could not be found. But I had a long interview with [Alfred] Butt of the Empire who promised to alter the particular scene to the extent of leaving more clothes on the Ladies, and I sallied forth on a wet night to see it; excessively tiresome, but the alleged harm was nullified by the change.[44]

Another self-appointed guardian of morals on the stage proved more of a thorn in Sandhurst's side. This was Sir Horace Smith-Dorrien, former commander of the BEF's 2nd Army in France, who returned to London from active service early in 1916. Smith-Dorrien's purity campaign demanded 'the suppression of everything of a suggestive or indecent nature on the stage, at the cinema, and in newspapers, post-cards, and novels'. It was run 'purely from the Army point of view', the soldier's morals his main anxiety, and he was tireless in his attacks. He bombarded the Lord Chamberlain with complaints about the alleged immorality of the London stage. Smith-Dorrien saw indecency everywhere, his targets including one of the great popular hits of the war, *Chu Chin Chow*.

> To His Majesty's Theatre [in the Haymarket] to see the piece which Smith Dorrien says is indecent. He is wrong again. The best way to judge a piece is to observe the audience, in this case an admirable sample of a successful show's audience, most excellent class of respectable people – smart set absent – the house was packed and had been so for weeks. I thought it tedious and felt so ill I went away after two hours [!], but it is *not* indecent. A great show of colour, and it is true some slaves might have more clothes on their backs, but there is nothing indecent or sugges- tive in it whatever. I was bored with the thing, but I am old.[45]

Unsurprisingly, given pre-war concerns and its growing popularity among all classes but especially the poor, the cinema provided the next great purity target. Many organisations took aim. The National Council of Public Morals, for instance, based in Great Russell Street, Bloomsbury, appointed a 'Cinematograph Commissioner', a well-known evangelist, the Reverend James Marchant. And from late 1915 Frederick Charrington

began a '"cinema crusade"', calling for cinemas to close on Sundays
and for the 'suppression of demoralising pictures of crime'. He was also
concerned with the perils of darkness, sending his 'Lady Agent', a Miss
R. Fraser, to report to the police on dubious premises, like the cinema
at 12 Acre Lane, Brixton, where 'The Gallery lends itself to favour
young couples who do not come to see the pictures. Price of seats in
gallery 1/-. Not worth it except for seclusion . . .'[46]

By the spring of 1916 the LCC, the licensing authority here too, was
concerned at the prospect of molestation of unaccompanied children
by men, and a number of credible cases were reported to police (eleven
in London in 1916). From May they required cinemas to appoint a
'children's attendant', conspicuously badged, to watch out for vulnerable children. That was worthwhile though difficult to enforce. But
what exercised Smith-Dorrien and others most was what appeared on
the screen and on advertising posters at the cinema door. Tempers were
not helped by a perceived rise in juvenile delinquency during 1916,
which many linked to crime and violence in the films. By October
1916 government was proposing a state cinema censorship to replace
the British Board of Film Censors established by the industry in 1913.
To avoid this move the Board codified and sharpened its censorship
criteria in 1917. Powers were, however, given to licensing authorities
to take action to remove cinema posters thought indecent.[47]

None of this could constrain the cinema's popularity: weekly attend-
ances rose greatly during the war, probably tripling between 1914 and
1917. This alone was a source of grievance to the 'Die-hards', as Michael
MacDonagh and others called them, who resented any expenditure of
breath or cash on 'luxuries' or pleasures that took time and money
from the war effort. They were supported by a significant portion of
the daily and London evening press and by many MPs in the House
of Commons. The die-hards fortified each other in organisations like
the Crusade of the United Workers for Self-Denial (active in early 1916,
Dean Inge of St Paul's a prominent spokesman) or the Strength of
Britain Movement, associated with the paranoid right-wing MP Noel
Pemberton Billing, formed around November of the same year.[48]

By 1916 almost anything could be classed as a luxury and condemned
forthwith: imported motor cars, furs, public dances, alcohol, billiard
competitions, bridge. Perhaps Mrs Ethel Alec-Tweedie, who had written
a history of Hyde Park a few years before the war, took this further
than anyone else. In an article on 'The Pleasures of Economy', reprinted

in a collection of her essays in 1918, she called for the extermination
of cats and dogs to save food, an end to window-dressing, the prohibition of scents and fancy soaps, oranges and lemons to be restricted to
the hospitals, underwear shops selling crêpe de Chine '"nighties"' to
be closed down, golf courses to be dug up for potatoes and much else
in a list that might appear Swiftian were not irony also an unaffordable
luxury among the die-hards. 'The Defence of the Realm Act goes a long
way,' she concluded, 'but it does not go nearly far enough.'[49]

It was in this spirit that some of the great free pleasures of London,
more popular than ever in the war – the British Museum, the Science
Museum, the Natural History Museum, the London Museum and others
– were ordered for closure in early 1916 as measures of 'national
economy' and puritan severity. The National Gallery and the Victoria
and Albert Museum were notable exceptions, gratefully received by
Londoners, and so was the British Museum Reading Room, open to
scholars but only until dusk.[50]

In this fertile soil it seemed to many in the Christian churches that
London was more ripe for conversion than at any time in living memory.
In early 1916 the Church of England announced preparations for a
National Mission of Repentance and Hope. The council established to
oversee the arrangements was chaired by the Bishop of London. But
its metropolitan message was undermined by an undignified spat over
the role of women preachers in the Mission. The Bishop, a keen supporter
of puritan suffragettes pre-war, we might recall, was reported to have
announced he would 'allow women to preach in churches'. This
provoked an angry reaction among London clergymen as being 'contrary
to the teaching of Holy Scripture', and among many religious upper-
class women within the laity, led by Lady Henry Somerset. Winnington-
Ingram swiftly distanced himself from any movement 'for a woman
priesthood', which he opposed as 'both undesirable and un-catholic'.
He withdrew his 'concession' to 'women messengers' to give Bible classes
in the body of the church, confining them to 'parish halls or school-
rooms'. In October the Mission was launched by the Archbishop of
Canterbury in Westminster Abbey. A few days before, the Bishop of
London had set out his aims for the metropolis in a speech at Guildhall
in the City:

> London a hundred years ago was more godly than it is to-day. We must
> get back to the custom of family prayers; the City churches must be used

daily for private prayer; and we must keep our Sundays for the observance
of public worship . . . as a day for church [and] for rest from daily
work . . .[51]

At a large Mission rally in Hyde Park in mid-October the fighting
Bishop enlisted other Christian warriors, including Admiral Sir David
Beatty, who had told him '"The nation is not even yet roused out of a
state of self-satisfaction"', and General Sir William Robertson, who, when
asked how the Church might help the army, replied, '"Bishop, make the
nation more religious."' That was a large objective. Too large: in early
1917 the Mission petered out amid a gnashing of clerical backbiting.[52]
A resurrection of sorts was tried again in September 1917 but on a
narrower front. Woolwich, virtually the country's only shell- and gun-
manufacturing district before the war, had seen a great influx of young
men and women munitions workers from all over London and far
beyond. The difficulties of providing housing and entertainments for
the new workers in this unlovely industrial town at the south-eastern
edge of London had proved intractable. For two weeks from 2 September
they found themselves the centre of attention. The Archbishop of
Canterbury, six bishops led by the Bishop of Southwark, with a battalion
of clergy and lay people, men and women, descended with banners
flying and bands playing on the bemused factory hands in a 'Woolwich
Crusade', exhorting them to 'uphold truth, honour and purity of life'
while they stuck to the nerve-racking and dangerous task of making
shells and guns for fresh slaughter in France. The crusade received the
'sincere wishes', one might almost say blessing, of Prime Minister David
Lloyd George.[53]
As will have been clear, the towering figure holding high the torch
for puritanism in London was Arthur Foley Winnington-Ingram, the
Bishop of London. He embodied the alliance between puritan and
patriot that had such influence over the life of London and the nation
during the war. His lifelong foes – amounting, as he happily admitted,
to an obsession – were '"Drink and Lust"'.[54] With war he added a
third: his country's enemies. On the first Sunday of Advent, 1915, at
Westminster Abbey, he 'preached what might be regarded as the most
infamous sermon in Anglican history', extolling the nation's 'great
crusade . . . to kill Germans: to kill them not for the sake of killing,
but to save the world; to kill the young men as well as the old . . .
and to kill them lest the civilization of the world should itself be killed'.[55]

Yet Winnington-Ingram had not always lusted so much after blood. On the first Sunday of the war, 9 August 1914, at St Paul's, he had urged 'perfect charity'.

The 25 German school boys who were singing in his garden three weeks ago in English were still the same boys to-day; they were no more responsible for the war than those in this Cathedral. If Christ prayed for His enemies so must they. They must pray against the success of their arms, but they could pray for the people themselves. They should take particular care that the Germans in London on business still received the same kind treatment they had learnt to expect.[56]

Clearly, by the end of 1915, much had changed.

4

THE ALL-INVADING ALIEN

THE excitement and trauma of the first four days of August 1914 took an immediate toll on Germans and Austrians living in London. The excitement faded soon enough, but the trauma for those who remained beyond 4 August endured for the next four and a half years at least; for many it lasted a lifetime.

Some few thousands escaped from London before the gates shut on 5 August. 'Before the war,' a London hotelier recalled, 'there was hardly such a thing as a waitress or an English waiter in London private hotels.' Almost all were German or Austrian 'boys' or young men; a few were Swiss. Many were of military age. In the West End on the evening of 1 August, Ferdinand Tuohy watched hundreds of German waiters and students and others mingle mainly outside the cafés and beer halls of Soho. 'A young German at my side bawled: "They're twelve hundred of us going back to-morrow."' Among those who left were the two German waiters at a hotel owned by the businessman George Cross in Lancaster Street, Bayswater, who 'dodged off' just before Britain declared war. German and Austrian musicians deserted 'every kind of musical ensemble' in London, 'from symphony orchestra to restaurant trio', and in the City entire sectors seemed stripped of brokers and merchants overnight. The London sugar trade, for instance, was largely in German hands: Gordon Hodge returned to his office after the Bank Holiday on 4 August 'to find that the Germans in Mincing Lane, both principals and clerks, had gone home via Holland by every possible boat, including cargo boats, on the Saturday, Sunday, and Monday; some were still leaving on the Tuesday [the 4th]'.[1]

Most had no choice but to remain – men with German or English wives, many with English children, who had long made their home in

London; women governesses in England so long they had no continental refuge to go to; the elderly and the frail for whom a rushed journey across the North Sea was not feasible, even if desirable. Few can have imagined the hardships they would face by staying. On 5 August the Aliens Restriction Act was rushed through Parliament, receiving royal assent that same evening. It required all 'enemy aliens' born in hostile countries, male and female, to register with police. Within weeks, 50,633 Germans had registered nationwide and 16,141 Austrians and Hungarians. Of the total, probably more than 40,000 were resident in London.[2]

The Aliens Restriction Act, together with some DORA regulations against naturalised Britons born in Germany or Austria, provided the framework for restricting the movements of individuals, for preventing access to certain places (like the Port of London) and for arrest and internment as ordered by the Home Secretary or military authorities. This was the statutory basis for an official reign of terror against Germans in London; an unofficial terror would be imposed from time to time by the Londoners themselves.

There was sporadic violence against Germans and Austrians from the very beginning of the war. It was of limited effect and short duration but must have been terrifying for those on the receiving end. On the nights of 5 and 6 August there were attacks, for instance, by an angry crowd against a German baker's shop in Chatsworth Road, Hackney, and on 6 August a crowd said to be 5,000 strong demonstrated outside a butcher's in the Old Kent Road, Southwark, crying, 'Down with Germany'.[3] There is every reason to believe that events like these were neither unique nor even exceptional.

At the same time a spy panic swept the capital and the nation, occasionally fuelling violence in its wake. German spies were suspected and 'discovered' everywhere. As early as 8 August the Kensington lady diarist recorded, 'More German spies are being arrested', and gave a convincingly detailed account she'd heard of a bomb factory in Portobello Road – entirely false. A couple of weeks later, 'Heard that German workmen dismissed from a Garage in North Kensington set fire to the place, saying that if they couldn't work, the British workman shouldn't. Some have been arrested.' And a couple of weeks after that, 'Heard that a German tried to erect a wireless station on top of the Ritz Hotel. He was arrested. The manager & another of the staff of the Ritz have been arrested.'[4]

At Scotland Yard, Harold Brust, a Special Branch officer, reported for duty immediately after the declaration of war 'to find the spy scares flooding in by thousands. Every few minutes huge sacks of mail arrived . . . Offices were seas of paper. Letters were stacked in great heaps on tables, chairs, window-sills, tops of cupboards, under tables, in corners.' Of almost 9,000 allegations received by police in London not one proved to have any foundation. As Basil Thomson, Assistant Commissioner of the Criminal Investigation Department, remarked later, in those first weeks of the war 'it was positively dangerous to be seen in conversation with a pigeon'. This was literally true. Henry Lannoy Cancellor, a new and temporarily credulous stipendiary magistrate appointed on the day war was declared, sentenced a German to six months' imprisonment on the evidence of 'the wife of a first-grade civil servant': she 'believed' she had seen him 'let loose a carrier pigeon on Primrose Hill'. The German was freed by order of the Home Secretary.[5]

Yet it is true enough that there really were German spies in London. During the war twelve enemy agents were executed in Britain, most shot by firing squad in the Tower of London. The first was Naval Lieutenant Carl Hans Lody, but they included Willem Roos, arrested at the Three Nuns public house, Aldgate, and executed with an accomplice in 1915; an observer recalled, 'They bared their chests themselves, but asked not to be blindfolded, and this was respected.' Nineteen more 'bona fide enemy agents' were arrested and otherwise dealt with, like Maria Janotha, a well-known pianist and former pupil of Brahms, living in Holland Road, Kensington, who was deported from Tilbury to the Netherlands by steamer; or Bertha Trost, from Frankfurt, an antique dealer and beauty specialist with addresses in Bayswater, Portland Place and Mayfair, also shipped off to Rotterdam.[6]

Partly because of these genuine risks, partly to assuage the national anxiety, the internment of enemy aliens began in earnest from 28 August. On that date Home Secretary Reginald McKenna told the House of Commons he was arranging for the confinement in 'concentration camps' – both term and concept British inventions in South Africa during the Boer War, though meaning something far worse in the years to come – 'of alien enemies whom the authorities have any reason to think likely to be dangerous', mainly young men of military age. The exhibition halls at Olympia, Kensington, were empty and had already been requisitioned by the Metropolitan Police. From 6 August they were used to hold some suspected spies and the crews of two Austrian ships impounded in the Port of London, but after 28 August Olympia became the main transit camp for the few thousands of those arrested and interned in London in the early part of the war. No official transport was available for this mass internment and pantechnicons and furniture vans 'crammed with Germans' became one of the sights of the London streets, 'jolting along towards Olympia' or moving on to Alexandra Palace, which was soon established as a large internment camp in north London.[7]

There began now a process of eradication of German influence from London life, an influence honourably exerted over many generations that had given much to metropolitan culture. Everywhere German-born Londoners were thrown out of work, from lowly German waiters to Theodore Kroell, popular manager of the Ritz in Piccadilly since 1909, to Prince Louis of Battenberg, First Sea Lord, forced out of the Admiralty by the press, jealous enemies and 'a stream of letters, signed and anonymous', calling for his dismissal. German surnames became anglicised or abandoned: the orchestral conductor Basil Cameron changed his name from Hindenberg, a well-known foreign exchange trader in the City became Robert Kay from Robert Hecht, Ludovic Goetz, a governor of the London Hospital, adopted his wife's maiden name and became Foster, George von Chauvin, managing director of Siemens Brothers, electrical engineers, was quickly granted naturalisation and dropped the von, the Merton-born writer Ford Hermann Hueffer became Ford Madox Ford, and the House of Commons was assured there were no clerks employed in the Treasury of German or Austrian nationality: 'One British-born clerk, who had a name of Teutonic origin, has changed it since the outbreak of War.'[8]

There were adjustments everywhere. In the Reform Club, as in the rest of clubland, notices were posted asking members not to bring alien enemies as guests. In Sainsbury's, 'German sausage', a big favourite with Londoners pre-war, was quickly renamed 'Luncheon sausage'. In Bermondsey, where 'We were not without a large share of aliens in our midst', shop fascias were transformed from 'Schnitzler, et cetera' to '"The Albion Saloon," or "The British Barbers of Bermondsey"'. The study of German was abandoned at Toynbee Hall, the university settlement in Whitechapel. Pubs changed their names, so that the King of Prussia, formerly popular in London, now became a rarity (one in Tooley Street became the King of Belgium); and local residents across the metropolis campaigned for the Teutonic taint to be removed from their street names often, after much delay, with success – Stoke Newington's Wiesbaden Road becoming Belgrade Road, for instance.[9]

All of this resulted in much misery. Among the large number of prosecutions of Germans for failing to register was a trickle of press reports from September 1914 of the suicide of Londoners who overnight had become enemy aliens: Joseph Pottsmeyer, fifty-two, a gramophone packer from Hoxton, sacked from his job and unable to get another, found hanged in his room alongside a note expressing admiration for England; John Pfeiffer, assistant manager at the Holborn Viaduct Hotel, who shot himself in the eye and then, with extraordinary determination, the temple; and four weeks later an Austrian couple, recently married and only in their twenties, who took poison 'it is believed . . . from fear of internment and separation'. There would be many others.[10]

The sporadic violence against German shopkeepers in the poorer trading streets of London remained a constant threat through these early weeks of war and indeed far longer. Before 1914 was out it turned much worse. October saw the first serious outbreak of collective violence by the Londoners, beginning on the 17th at Deptford High Street and Evelyn Street nearby and widely copied in other parts of south London (Old Kent Road, Atlantic Road in Brixton, Tower Bridge Road, Camberwell and elsewhere) for a few nights after. The crowds of 5,000 or so were so fierce and persistent that the police had to call out the military for assistance – butchers' and bakers' shops were wrecked and looted, shopkeepers and their families fleeing to friendly English neighbours for protection.[11]

These terrifying events of October 1914 seem to have had a specific cause. The German shopkeepers before the war had been no less popular in London than any other trader. The German baker, in particular, was an important part of many working-class and lower-middle-class communities and was frequently regarded with affection. War had now brought cold shoulders, boycotts and worse. But news of the German army's atrocities in Belgium, some exaggerated but much convincingly evidenced, had stunned the British public. The first Belgian refugees from Antwerp to be quartered in Deptford, about 800 of them, had arrived early in the evening of the 17th and it was said to have been this first glimpse of their miserable condition, relayed by word of mouth round the streets and pubs, that 'set on fire the ugly portion of the crowd'.[12]

The very first Belgian refugees had arrived in London some weeks before, in early September. Much of the work of registering and billeting was coordinated by the London Society for Women's Suffrage, who, with sixty-two metropolitan branches, had organised many of the meetings, demonstrations and propaganda for Votes for Women before the war. Among the earliest were 300 refugees said to be 'in a pitiful plight' and with 'Harrowing Stories of German Atrocities', received in Dulwich and bedded down in Goose Green public baths. Another 300 around the same time moved into the workhouse infirmary and casual wards in Hackney. With the evacuation of Antwerp from 7 October and its subsequent fall on the 10th, the numbers of refugees leapt up, 3,000 arriving in London on the 12th alone, 1,200 of them sent to south London workhouses, half to the one in Tanner Street, Bermondsey.[13]

By the end of 1914 Belgian refugees were accommodated all over London in empty private houses and public institutions vacated specially for them. No metropolitan district was without its Belgians. They were willingly received by the Londoners. Children were taken into the schools, doctors and dentists gave their services free, hotels charged cut rates and wealthy families took in wealthy Belgians as free lodgers. Workshops for Belgians were opened until men and women could be absorbed into the labour market, a Belgian newspaper, *L'Indépendance Belge*, was published from London, doles and free clothing were given from local relief funds coordinated by the War (later Belgian) Refugees Committee and generously supported by collections as part of the ubiquitous 'flag days' that became such a feature of London's streets during the war. Many wounded Belgian soldiers were taken into the hospitals, 324 at the London Hospital on 14–15 October, the governors buying 100 extra beds from Harrods to meet the emergency, and 130 at St Bartholomew's around the same time. In early 1915 three 'King Albert's Hospitals' for Belgians opened in London, treating soldiers and civilians – in all 57,000 were treated in hospitals in the UK by the end of 1915, including over 9,000 soldiers and officers, the great majority in London. And London undoubtedly took a large share of the 180,000 Belgian refugees thought to be living in the country by late April 1915.[14]

At first, just as for the German internees, though in different spaces presumably, use was made of Olympia and Alexandra Palace to shelter and feed the Belgians before they could be absorbed into London. But early in 1915 Earls Court Exhibition was turned over for use by the Belgians. When Hallie Miles, who ran a choir that performed often for refugee charities, visited it in June 1915 she thought it 'a regular Belgian

Town . . . One enters by the same long subway, but just before emerging into the grounds there is a barricade; behind it there are refugees swabbing the floors with disinfectants . . . Every available building is converted into something useful for the Belgians', with 'little shops' and a 'huge "nursery" for the children. The men's enormous "bedroom" is the auditorium of the great Concert Hall. The velvet seats have been turned into hundreds of little white beds round the Amphitheatre, all in tiers, as the seats are . . . The women's (unmarried) bedroom is the other side of the building.' It was all very well but, she concluded, 'they are virtually prisoners in Earl's Court'.[15]

Few things could have contrasted so sharply between the welcome given to the newly arrived Belgians and the intensifying loathing in which the Germans, so long a vital part of London life, were now held. And yet the engagement and sympathy that the Belgians had first evoked quickly began to pall. The constitutional mistrust, even hostility, with which generations of Londoners had always greeted a foreigner began to surface even as early as 1915. It did so most often privately. 'Everyone was Belgian mad for a time,' wrote young Mary Coules of Acton in her diary some time before September 1915. 'Mother helped furnish a home for Belgians, & gave a monthly subscription', and Mary herself sang in a choir in the streets to raise money for them. 'But the Belgians are not grateful. They won't do a stroke of work, & grumble at everything, & their morals . . . ! It may be true enough that Belgium saved Europe, but . . . save us from the Belgians! As far as I am concerned Belgianitis has quite abated.' Rose Macaulay, in an amusing novel of 1916, had a middle-class mother from Upper Clapton relaying the sort of thing that one imagines must have been common gossip: '"They say those Belgians in the corner house eat ten pounds of cheese each week. Edwards' boy told Florence. Just fancy that. Not that one grudges them anything, poor things."' And Caroline Playne, much later in the war, had a conversation at a Belgian 'at home' in Kensington: 'Met elderly lady who said since the war she had done all she could for Belgians but was very disillusioned concerning them. They dressed smartly on charity & then said we English were dowdy.' But whispered comments rarely broke the surface and never led to any collective protest against the Belgians in London, let alone public abuse.[16]

It was very different for the Germans. That spark igniting Deptford and other parts of south London in October 1914 led within days to a fresh wave of internments of enemy aliens, more a public order measure than to protect national security: 'The action of the Home Office should tend to allay public anxiety', as one local paper put it.[17] Nonetheless isolated incidents of attacks on German tradesmen and their premises continued to find their way into the London police courts through the rest of 1914 and spring of the following year. So too did the prosecutions of enemy aliens for failing to register or for breaking their registration conditions. And so did a trickle of inquests on German and Austrian Londoners' war-related suicides. Tensions bubbled away for some months. And from April 1915 anger against Germans intensified with their use of poison gas against Allied troops on the Western Front, and fabulous stories in the London papers of Canadian soldiers being crucified by their captors.

Then, on the afternoon of Friday 7 May 1915, the great Cunard liner RMS *Lusitania* was torpedoed off Queenstown, Ireland, with the loss of 1,198 lives, including many women and children and 124 US citizens. The sinking shocked and horrified the world. The news reached London with the evening papers. It was received as a culmination of atrocities. Horatio Bottomley, editor of *John Bull* and former MP for South Hackney, issued 'a plea for reprisals', urging 'that the devil must be burnt with his own coals'.[18] Over the weekend of 8 and 9 May serious anti-German rioting broke out in Liverpool, the *Lusitania*'s home port. Next day the papers carried pictures and reports of distressing scenes at temporary mortuaries at Queenstown, with their row upon row of children's coffins. Then, beginning in Canning Town, West Ham, and other parts of east London on 11 May, and building to a London-wide conflagration on Wednesday the 12th, a frenzy of violence fell upon Germans in London.

Over the next six days, every Metropolitan Police division from Harrow to Croydon and Hayes to Romford experienced violent disturbances. The sole exception was the West End, for this enmity was local and personal and did not need to travel to find its targets. At least 257 people were injured, including 107 police officers, regular and special, beaten for standing between the Germans and the crowd. There were 866 arrests. By great good fortune no one was killed. Shops known – or guessed, the Londoners' hostility to foreigners uncomplicated by political geography – to be run by Germans or Austrians had windows smashed and doors broken down. Interiors – staircases, cupboards, ceilings – were 'hacked to pieces'. Provisions and property were carted away by the barrowful. The violence extended to homes as well as

shops. In Poplar, where it was thought the crowds were more destructive and determined than elsewhere,

> in an area of a quarter of a mile half a dozen houses were attacked
> simultaneously by different crowds in the early afternoon. Before the
> constables were able to attempt to disperse the mob, horse-drawn carts,
> handcarts, and perambulators – besides the unaided arms of men, women,
> and children – had taken everything away from the wrecked houses.
> One saw pianos, chests of drawers, dressers, and the heaviest type of
> household furniture being carted triumphantly through the streets. "Here
> is wealth for the taking," said one man who had possession of several
> spring mattresses, and was calmly driving his overloaded donkey-cart
> down Chrisp-street . . . The scene in the streets was amazing. Every man
> seemed to have given up the day to the Anti-German orgy; and every
> other person one met seemed to be in possession of looted property. No
> attempt was made to cover the goods. "Made in Germany" was the
> excuse for possession.[19]

Scenes similar to this took place in many of the working-class shopping streets of London. When the hundreds of people prosecuted began
to find their way into the police courts, working people of all complex-
ions but especially the poor were represented, women and men equally
responsible. In Lambeth and other south London courts there were
dock labourers, housewives, meat porters, metal workers, women flower
sellers, paper sellers, general labourers, youths as young as fourteen. In
Hackney, charges arising out of an attack on Engel's bakery in Lower
Clapton Road, involving a crowd of 'several thousands', led to numerous
charges, including for assaults on police; those accused were a tobacconist, a soap maker, piano tuner, a laundress, a packer, a housewife
and a dressmaker, seven in all including three women, ages ranging
from sixteen to fifty-three, all said to be of previous good character,
swept up in the rage and excitement of the night. Magistrates tended
to be hard on men using violence but were generally lenient to those
charged with affray and theft; at least one thought that more rioting
would have followed 'severe sentences'.[20]

Not everyone joined in the anti-alien terror. Joe Williamson's mother,
living in Arcadia Street, Poplar, pulled two men out of her local German
baker's and helped hold back an angry crowd because the baker's wife
was heavily pregnant. A similar case was reported from south London

and no doubt there were others. Many middle-class observers too were sickened by the violence and some, like Arnold Bennett, were brave enough to write against it. Those few organisations that had established themselves to relieve needy aliens were kept busy dealing with scores made homeless and hundreds stripped of their belongings. The Friends' Emergency Committee was prominent among these 'Hun-coddlers' as they were often called – heroism indeed to appear to be pro-German in May 1915. At the Friends' Meeting House in Holloway some seventy German and Austrian refugees from the rioting made their home for about a month on makeshift beds, installing a communal kitchen: 'the clothing room was besieged by people who had been robbed of everything they possessed – in one case, even to the wet garments which had been washed overnight and hung in the kitchen to dry'.[21]

The general mood, however, was unrepentant and malevolent. After the *Lusitania* sinking but before the riots, members of the London Stock Exchange, old financial grievances perhaps festering in the background, boycotted brokers of German birth even when naturalised. They marched on Parliament in their top hats, 2,000 strong, calling for internment of all Germans, naturalised and alien, men and women alike. Their demand was supported by the national and local London press. On 12 May William Joynson-Hicks, Hun-baiter-in-chief for the die-hards in the House of Commons and a puritan of the most conservative stamp, delivered a petition bearing a quarter of a million signatures praying for general internment. Next day, after the first night of rioting, the government – bearing every indication of panic at the prospect of public disorder capable of setting London and the nation alight – announced that all enemy alien men of military age were to be 'segregated and interned, or, if over military age, repatriated . . .' Women and children would also be repatriated where possible. All this was 'for their own safety, and that of the community', and not otherwise in the interests of national security, though that was left unsaid. Naturalised Germans and Austrians would be left alone unless they presented a proven danger.[22]

Internment, a feature of German life in London since August 1914, now became the common fate of German men and an enduring anxiety and sadness for their wives and children. By 10 June 3,339 more men had been interned and 2,274 repatriated, including all German men resident in the City of London, where victimisation was so remorseless. By 5 July 26,713 were interned nationwide and 4,800 repatriated; by

14 September 4,460 women and 2,924 children had left the country; by 14 October the total interned reached 32,400, nearly 9,000 of them since the *Lusitania* riots.[23]

What was this experience like for the alien enemies of London? In general it was miserable and sometimes disastrous. We might cite the case of Rudolf Rocker, born in Mainz in 1873 and in London since 1895, a non-violent anarchist well known for his agitation among and on behalf of the poor working Jews of east London, though not himself Jewish.[24] In 1914 he was living with his wife and son at Dunstan Houses, Stepney Green. The internment that followed the riots of October 1914 removed many of his German comrades and he anticipated it would not be long before the police came for him too: 'I kept my small case packed ready.' Rocker's turn came soon enough. He was arrested by order of the War Office on 2 December 1914 at 7 p.m., despite the efforts of his seven-year-old son, Fermin, who clung to his father 'with all my might . . . howling and sobbing'. Next day he was taken to Olympia by a Scotland Yard detective.[25]

There he found replicated the class system from which he had been plucked, 'the "best people"' living in what had been the restaurant and paying £1 a week for whatever comforts they could gather; similar arrangements pertained at Alexandra Palace, where, '"What, no feather pillows?" . . . became a stock joke' among the better-off tradesmen interned there.[26] Rocker rejected the privilege and joined one of the twelve camps separated by heavy ropes, a hundred and more men in each. It was all 'grey and drab and miserable'. There was never enough to eat and all in his part of the camp went hungry unless they could get extra food sent in by friends or relatives. Damp clothes hung drying everywhere on string and the 'air was foul with the smell of human bodies' and the five latrines used by 1,200 men and 'always in a filthy state'. No one was allowed outside the hall for exercise. That December the place was freezing cold. Perhaps in part because of this ill-treatment, Rocker was struck by 'the almost hysterical German patriotism of most' of his fellows.[27]

Later in December Rocker was moved to the *Royal Edward*, a prison ship moored off Southend, where his brother-in-law was also held; and at the end of May 1915 he was moved again to Alexandra Palace. There nearly 3,000 internees were partitioned off in the cavernous Great Hall, each given 'a straw pallet, a straw-filled bolster, and three horse-blankets'. Day and night a sentry with fixed bayonet paced a platform erected at one end. Internees were woken each morning by a whistle, had breakfast in a huge dining room and then were lined up to be counted. Exercise was allowed in a compound fenced with barbed wire and watched over by more soldiers. Despite this prison-camp environment something like a civilised, even cultured, existence could be had there. Photographs of Rocker at Alexandra Palace show him at a table surrounded by shelves of books and papers, and he and others were allowed to give lectures in the theatre; visits were permitted monthly and after representations from Rocker the internees were able to hug their loved ones; letters that passed the censor were accepted from home and abroad. Despite an occasional escape that led to temporary reprisals by the army authorities, the place was tolerably and tolerantly run. It was very different from the camp at Carpenters Road, Stratford, whose commandant 'had a dreadful reputation among the internees' and who reputedly passed day-to-day responsibility to chosen cadres among the prisoners, their leader said to be a sadist. Stratford Camp was shut in 1917, when some of the 2,200 occupants moved to Alexandra Palace.[28]

On the other hand, the Islington Internment Camp, in a former workhouse at Cornwallis Road, where 720 or so internees were held from July 1915, was able to develop something like a community. It was established for middle-class internees with British wives, and many others sought to be transferred there when vacancies arose. Some men had private rooms, for which they paid 20s to 25s a week. There were a barber's shop and a steam laundry, an interned dentist offered free treatment to those who had difficulty paying, and there were workshops where surgical instrument makers and others could ply their trades. There were tennis and croquet courts for recreation, which included Swedish drill, gymnastics and skittles. There was waiter service – no shortage of staff, one imagines – in the dining room, paid for from 'camp funds' kept buoyant from rents and other contributions. Wives enjoyed relaxed visiting hours. There was a camp orchestra and a fortnightly newspaper, *Hinter dem Stacheldraht* (*Behind the Barbed Wire*), and reputedly an underground trade in smuggled cigars and tobacco. A drawback was the dietary, heavily reliant on bread and margarine for all meals except midday dinner; yet, in April 1916 at least, the internees had meat every day.[29]

Things were bad for the Germans and Austrians in London but they might conceivably have been worse. We have seen how the shadow of the Zeppelin hovered over London long before the real thing appeared.

In January 1915 the Admiralty became convinced that there was no adequate defence for London against aerial bombardment. Fear of an unpreventable catastrophe for which he would find himself held to account caused the First Sea Lord, 'Jackie' Fisher, to panic. 'He proposed to me,' wrote Churchill some years later, 'that we should take a large number of hostages from the German population in our hands and should declare our intention of executing one of them for every civilian killed by bombs from aircraft.' Fisher threatened resignation if he did not get his way and Churchill had to take his proposal to Cabinet, where it was rejected on Churchill's recommendation.[30] Most Londoners, though, might well have applauded the idea: when raids began on the capital at the end of May 1915, anti-German rioting once more broke out, again multiplying arrests and internments to pacify public opinion.

By 1916 the pre-war face of cosmopolitan London had begun to alter. In its details it would never be the same again. The biggest shift was in the former German quarter of the West End, north of Oxford Street and west of Tottenham Court Road in the district known to later generations as Fitzrovia. The mass internment of men had stripped the trading backbone from the area, with German cafés, bakers', butchers', restaurants and delicatessens all or largely gone, its clubs and meeting rooms closed, its homes broken up, even women and children forcibly removed to a country they had left long ago or perhaps had never visited. When the writer Thomas Burke went in search of 'what remained of the German Quarter' he found it now very mixed: 'in a grey street off Tottenham Court Road we found a poor man's cabaret' in the back room of a coffee bar. 'Two schonk boys, in straw hats, were at a piano, assisted by an anaemic girl and a real coal-black coon, who gave us the essential rag-times of the South. The place was packed with the finest collection of cosmopolitan toughs I had ever seen in one room.'[31]

Burke thought these coffee houses had multiplied since 1914 and that seems likely to have been the case. In November 1916 the local police station in Tottenham Court Road noted some twenty-eight cafés kept by 'foreigners' established in recent months, but now they were run not by Germans but by French, Swiss, Italian, Russian, Romanian and (mainly) Belgian proprietors. This latter influence was also growing in Soho, where Belgians tended to fill the place of Italians after Italy declared war on Austria in May 1915. Hundreds of Italian reservists left Soho and Little Italy in the Warner Street area of Holborn – 700 waiters were said to have gone by October, for instance.[32] One transformation of these years might stand for many. A public house at 49 Dean Street, Soho, had been run as the Wine House by a German until he left in 1914; the business was then taken over by a Belgian, Victor Berlemont, who had been in London some years and changed the name to the York Minster, which soon became famous as the French House.

Burke noted in 1917 that 'two more Chinese restaurants have lately been opened in the West End', together with a 'Chinese café in Regent Street', and for the Chinese community in London the war also marked an important moment. A shortage of British sailors brought more 'coloured' men into the Port of London as they filled empty berths in merchant ships worldwide. Among them in 1915 were some 14,224 Chinamen crewing British ships, though this figure gives no indication of how many might at any one time have been staying in London. There were long-standing Chinese settlements in Limehouse, some fifty years old, and in and around Pennyfields, off the East India Dock Road in Poplar, with roots put down later in the nineteenth century. A degree of permanence in both districts was afforded by many Chinese lodging houses, some 'of a quite superior kind', Chinese restaurants and places for opium-smoking and gambling. These two vices, the first especially deplored by the authorities, frequently brought the community into conflict with the police, as we shall see in a later chapter.[33]

The numbers of Chinese seamen in the East End, said to be displacing British seamen for lower pay, began to provoke questions in Parliament in the summer of 1916. In September the Trades Union Congress expressed alarm at the extent of 'Chinese and cheap Asiatic labour' in the merchant fleet. A *Times* journalist considered the number of Chinese in the East End 'has certainly increased', with lodging houses spreading beyond Limehouse Causeway and Pennyfields – 'the invasion is becoming serious'. The Seamen's Union, partly led by Captain Edward Tupper, a racist ultra-patriot, claimed that the Chinese population had increased by 7,000, though true figures are unobtainable and almost certainly this was a large exaggeration – in 1918, for instance, Pennyfields was home to just 182 Chinamen and it seems unlikely that even in the war years many more than a couple of thousand were living in the East End at any one time in a population that remained highly mobile.[34]

One new departure, however, did become apparent by early 1917, a tendency of employers, desperately short of labour everywhere, to recruit Chinamen into industries beyond the riverside. The London Hospital's attempt to employ Chinese porters and kitchen staff was met with hostility from other workers, who refused to work with them. The proposal was abandoned, though a Chinese chef, Yan See, proved indispensable and was allowed to remain in the hospital kitchens for the duration. Around the same time the Bethnal Green Board of Guardians decided to employ Chinese porters in the workhouse, chosen from men 'submarined whilst in boats carrying provisions to England' and replacing 'old men who used to do the work, but who had since left the House'. The proposal caused a row but seems to have been implemented nonetheless. Later in the war Chinese labour was also used on aerodrome construction for the new Air Ministry. By then there were diplomatic difficulties in the way of boycotting the Chinese workmen – China had declared war on Germany and Austria and so became an ally in August 1917. With these small extensions of the Chinese into London life in both West End and East End the war marked something of a turning point for the community.[35]

The same could be said for black men from Africa and especially the Caribbean. Again, seamen were key. West Indian seamen 'have always formed part of our marine, and many of [them] are married to English wives and domiciled in the Port'. They were noted as men of 'good character' and regarded as 'good comrades' by 'white seamen'; they made up much of the small black community in Canning Town before and during the war. But by 1917 they had been joined by a 'much less desirable' element – this the judgement of a Charity Organisation Society worker in the Port of London – of 'young unsettled men who come over on banana boats and as emergency hands and get discharged here'. They 'have no very keen desire' to go back to the Caribbean and 'loaf about the Port, sponge where they can, and are a cause of trouble and disorder'. This latter migration, bolstered by West African seamen, seems likely to have been the origin of the black lodging-house and café district in Cable Street, Stepney, which became so notorious after the Second World War. There was also a small harbinger of the anti-black rioting that affected many dockside areas of the country, including east London, not long after the Armistice. Houses where black men lived were stoned for some nights and blacks were attacked in Victoria Dock Road, Canning Town, in June 1917; the row was said to have been caused by sexual jealousy – 'White Girls and Black Men' was how the papers put it.[36]

Away from these small corners of London, right across the metropolis the remnants of the German community continued to suffer abuse, discrimination, even violence. Local Unionist clubs threw out members born in Germany or Austria, whether naturalised or not; the LCC withdrew scholarships offered to children of enemy alien parents; resolutions circulated around metropolitan borough councils and Boards of Guardians calling for yet more internment and repatriation; hapless and obscure individuals had the details of their lives picked over on the floor of the House of Commons; City brokers identified by the Anti-German Union, one of a number of organisations self-appointed to harass enemy aliens, were blacklisted by the Stock Exchange; rumours abounded in the City about the 'Unseen Hand', a Whitehall conspiracy said to be protecting Germans for traitorous ends; British wives of alien enemies were snubbed by families and neighbours and thrown out of work by employers; and suicides continued among those facing internment or deportation. The pressure was unrelenting and pitiless. And some of the anti-German violence after air raids approached that seen in the *Lusitania* riots of May 1915 – not so widespread but sharp and destructive nonetheless.[37]

Internments also continued, with internees able to have their applications for exemption referred to an Advisory Committee, which seems to have operated fairly in all the circumstances. At the end of June 1916 4,931 German men and 4,418 women, and 3,796 Austrian men and 2,654 women, 15,799 in all, remained at large in London, including some 5,000 men of military age, mainly 'persons of friendly race or sympathies', such as Czechs, Poles, Slavs and natives of Alsace-Lorraine.[38]

From the summer of 1916 and right through 1917 another alien population emerged to share in the fury of metropolitan hostility. These were the Jews, especially the working-class Jews of the East End of London. Conscription into the fighting services, implemented for single men from 10 February 1916 and then extended to all men aged eighteen to forty-one from 25 May, provided the spark.

Up to that point the relationship of East End Jewry to the war had been complex. Some British-born Jewish East Enders had volunteered at the outset, responding among other things to a call for patriotism drummed up by the Anglo-Jewish aristocracy of the City and West End. But many young men from the Jewish East End were foreign-born, including some enemy aliens born in Austria's eastern provinces, like Galicia, though mainly hailing from European Russia and therefore 'friendly aliens'. They had fled economic dislocation and religious persecution, even pogroms, in an empire in which they were plainly unwelcome. The parents of some had migrated purposely to avoid compulsory service in the Tsar's army, where Jews were universally ill-treated: when a young Jew was conscripted, the prayer for the dead was said as he left home. Britain's alliance with Russia from 4 August 1914 left a sour taste in the mouths of most East End Jews.[39]

There matters generally stood until early 1916, East End Jews sharing in the prosperity of wartime London, with the occasional police raid on anti-Tsarist organisations in which Jews were often involved, and sometimes no doubt having to live with jibes in the streets against young Jewish men of military age who other East Enders thought should have been in khaki. Conscription brought this anomaly more clearly into the open. It applied only to those born in Britain. But it also redefined the position of those other young Jews who could not be forced to fight but who were well placed to take economic advantage, it was thought, of those called away. Londoners who were hostile to the Jews – and they were many, of all classes – now seemed to have just cause for their prejudices. Local military tribunals were established across the nation to hear appeals against conscription. In Stepney it was noted that Jewish applicants were sometimes noisily supported by family, friends and neighbours in a way that was unusual elsewhere. Tens of thousands of men made applications for exemption from service across London from 1916 till the end of the war. But what looked like, or could be portrayed as, communal opposition to military service was grist to anti-Semites in the East End and beyond. So too the case of every young Jew in hiding to escape the call-up was magnified, obscuring the fact that many other young men were doing the same. When British-born East End Jews were classified physically unfit to serve, as many were, it was interpreted as official favouritism in action. And one of the most damaging allegations, that foreign-born Jews were left at home to step into English businesses while their owners were fighting in France, began to reverberate across London, even in areas where there was not a Jew in sight.[40]

Government plans to remove this anomaly by requiring Russian men of military age to return 'home' or join the British Army became a matter of diplomatic discussions with Russia by July 1916. There were thought to be over 20,000 Russian Jews in Britain potentially affected by such a policy should the Tsar's government agree to it. But the move was vociferously opposed by a Foreign Jews' Protection Committee (FJPC), claiming 120 local affiliated organisations nationwide. A government scheme to encourage Russian Jews to volunteer for the British

Army – put in place by Home Secretary Herbert Samuel, the first ever practising Jew in a British Cabinet – met with only modest success. And in the House of Commons some of the die-hards now turned their fire away from Germans and Austrians living in Britain and against the Russian Jews of the East End.[41]

This ill-feeling against the Jews produced a bad-tempered response from police and military authorities in the East End. In May 1917 a Friday night 'round-up' seeking Jews dodging conscription in dance halls, billiard saloons and restaurants was carried out with, it was alleged, some savagery by police and Australian soldiers in large numbers; a few were said to have been armed with knuckledusters, though this was denied by the authorities. Some 640 young men were detained, sixty of them under sixteen, so well below conscription age in any event; just nine were discovered to have contravened the Military Service Act.[42]

The position of Russian-born Jews of military age shifted considerably during 1917. News of the first Russian Revolution of February and the downfall of the Tsar was greeted with jubilation in the East End as the termination of so many years of oppression. The prospect of a return to Russia now held fewer terrors and Britain soon after concluded negotiations with the new Russian government to accept the repatriation of Russian citizens not exempted from military service in Britain. The Military Service (Conventions with Allied States) Act 1917 became operative towards the end of July. Applications for exemption from service were to be heard by a Special Tribunal established solely for 'friendly' aliens.

Some foreign-born Jews now viewed a return to Russia with equanimity and made arrangements to go back. Many others did not. Their reasons were understandable. Most had been in the East End ten years or more, before the Aliens Act of 1905 had deterred many potential migrants from choosing Britain as a refuge. The FJPC continued to oppose compulsory enlistment despite the changed circumstances. A movement of Jews from the East End to Ireland, where conscription did not apply, became discernible. And the knowing sneers of the anti-Semites grew louder: the 'Russian Jews in the East-end of London', announced *The Times*, 'have prospered during the war' and 'do not want to fight.' 'Meanwhile feeling in the East-end among the British residents is strongly in favour of the adoption of firm measures to ensure that the Russian Jews shall serve.' On 30 July 1917 the FJPC offices were raided under DORA and Abraham Bezalel, its secretary, was arrested on suspicion of conspiracy to subvert the operation of the new Act. Bezalel was interned and two months later deported to his native Romania.[43]

The East End that summer of 1917 was in a highly excitable state. Over 8,300 Russians appealed against military service and the repatriation or service in the British Army that would follow. A local magistrate who heard charges arising out of the tribunal's proceedings recalled some years later:

A few solicitors specialised in this work. Subtle legal devices of many sorts were used to deflect the operation of the Military Service Acts. Conflicting and misleading accounts of what had taken place before the Special Tribunals were given in the police courts. Exemption certificates were passed from one member of a family to another. Forgery and mutilation of such documents became common . . .

Some who opted for the British Army absconded when their call-up papers arrived; some to be repatriated failed to board the trains for Liverpool, where they were to take ship; some claimed to be over conscription age, their cases before the magistrates supported by 'wonderful documents in foreign characters' and 'aged patriarchs' who 'covered their heads and swore that they had been present at the site of circumcision at places in Russia and Poland over forty years ago . . .' For one reason or another, often for medical reasons, many Russian Jews were indeed exempted from service by the tribunal.[44]

While all this was going on many thousands of British applicants were putting their own cases for exemption to tribunals across London. Some used the threat of their businesses being taken over by what London's local press were calling 'The Alien in our Midst' or 'The All-Invading Alien'. Their arguments gained little credence with tribunals but wide support and publicity in the papers: 'The alien question has ceased to be a problem,' intoned one; 'it has become a public scandal. No sooner have our commercial Tommies stepped into khaki than foreigners with unpronounceable names have stepped into their jobs and businesses.'[45]

From June 1917 there emerged one more reason to be hostile to the Jews. That month a daylight bombing campaign by German aeroplanes caused many casualties in the East End and other working-class districts of London. These were terrifying events for people of all classes and backgrounds. But an enduring myth, surviving the war, had it that Jews in London, in the West End as well as the East, were uniquely panic-stricken by air raids, seizing at all costs the best place of safety, to the detriment and discomfort of their stoic British neighbours. Many digs were aimed not just at the cowardice but at the personal hygiene of the 'aliens' with 'their none too clean and somewhat odoriferous carcases', as a resident of Clapton, Hackney, put it in a letter to the papers. It became convenient for many to scapegoat the Jews as the only cowards in London: 'As to that one blot, the fevered scuttle for shelter in the Tube, the Londoner can tell you, with his hand upon his heart, that the scuttlers were mostly aliens.'[46]

Unsurprisingly some of this hostility spilled onto the streets of the East End. When three Russian Jews protested against repatriation outside the Aliens' Registration Office in Commercial Street in early August, they were surrounded by an angry crowd and had to be arrested for their own safety. And in mid-September the worst communal violence between Jew and Gentile in the East End since the early years of the century erupted in Blythe Street and Teesdale Street, off Old Bethnal Green Road. A fight one Saturday evening between Jewish and Gentile soldiers – Jews were frequently not well treated in the London regiments – escalated on the Sunday when a crowd of 2,000 or 3,000 stoned houses occupied by Jews.[47]

Late in 1917 and especially in 1918, a move away from the capital to escape the bombers by those who could afford it became much remarked upon. Once more, the Jews were said to be the scuttlers, even though it is plain this was something affecting all strata of the London middle classes and above. Anti-Semites fastened gleefully on the issue, naming Brighton 'Brightchapel' or 'Jerusalem-by-the-Sea', submerged in a tide of 'foreign Jews who had no loyalties and no traditions . . . Everybody loathed these people . . .' The government, after inquiry, declared these reports of a new alien invasion 'much exaggerated', but that did not stop Londoners, MPs and the press believing otherwise. Much press comment was indeed vituperative, though J. B. Booth, a popular Fleet Street man, found room for a gentler satire in his spoof letters of Miss 'Billie' Tuchaud, published in 1918. 'Brighton yet again for the week-end,' Billie reports, where the 'Entertainment Committee are seriously considering the addition of two perfectly brand-new synagogues to the list of attractions.' There she finds Mossy Gutsberg held up

by some coarse military persons as he left the pier . . . Of course Mossy
has *heaps* of papers – doctors' certificates, exemptions, appeals pending,
serious hardship, hammer toes, etc., etc., etc., and, as a rule, his valet
follows him, at a distance of six paces, carrying the precious documents
in a pig-skin suitcase (with the monogram M.G. in diamonds) . . .[48]

It cannot have been an easy time for London Jewry during the First
World War, and the East End remained tense from early 1916 till the
Armistice. Even so, the rows and stone throwing over one weekend in
a tiny corner of east London were as bad as things got in terms of
communal violence; and Mossy Gutsberg reminds us that people could
often get a smile out of the war and what it had brought them. The
London Germans, however, were beyond satire. And they continued to
suffer remorselessly to the end of the war and after.

The astonishing success of the German offensive on the Western
Front that began on 21 March 1918 put the outcome of the war on a
knife-edge. For the British people, nearly four years of blood-soaked
sacrifice seemed to promise nothing of reward, even reparation. In April
the panic-stricken authorities raised the conscription age to fifty-one
and fresh rounds of tribunal appeals began once more. The shock and
desperate anxiety of these weeks did not at first result in a further wave
of anti-alien feeling, perhaps in part because German bombers were
flying at full stretch in France and left London alone. The tide of the
war eventually began to turn, though with agonising slowness for those
living through it. But by the summer, with the Germans pushed back
and the limitless resources of the Americans at last decisively helping
shift the balance of power in France, a mood of triumphant vindictiveness swept the British people. From July 1918 'Intern them all' became
the incessant, insatiable cry.

The lead came from the die-hards in Parliament (where Pemberton
Billing, for instance, had called for all born in enemy countries, whether
naturalised or not, to 'wear distinguishing badges in their button-holes')
and from what many called 'the "stunt" Press' or 'Yellow Press'. The
national mood, though, was not manufactured. The anger was manifest
and unappeasable. On Saturday 13 July in Trafalgar Square the 'biggest
crowd seen in the square since the outbreak of the war' demanded '"the
immediate internment of all aliens of enemy blood, whether naturalized
or unnaturalized"', women as well as men. Messages of support were
read out from Rudyard Kipling, Harry Lauder, the music-hall star, and

others; speeches were made by peers and MPs, mayors and bishops, socialists and labour men and women from England, Scotland, Wales and America. One of the loudest cheers of the day greeted the mayor of Bury St Edmunds when he called the Germans 'an accursed race. Intern them all. Or, rather let us leave out the letter "n" and say "Inter them all".' More giant meetings followed in Hyde Park on Sunday 21 July and at the Royal Albert Hall on the 30th. 'Committees of public safety' were established by the town council of Ealing and doubtless elsewhere to keep a close watch over 'every known enemy alien in the district'. Local agitations were organised across London at town meetings demanding internment of all born in Germany or Austria, whether British citizens or not. On Saturday 24 August a monster petition calling for internment without exception and said to contain 1.25 million signatures, was carried from Hyde Park to 10 Downing Street on a lorry accompanied by bands playing and flags and banners flying; the marchers included discharged soldiers and sailors, Dominion soldiers on leave, companies of the British Empire Union, trade union branches, City men in 'silk hats and frock coats' and 'a long array of the general public, men and women'.[49]

By then the petitioners were getting what they wanted. Stung by the furore and with a general election plainly not too far away, the Lloyd George government decided to give the public the blood it demanded. A new Enemy Aliens Advisory Committee was established in July under Mr Justice Sankey to inquire yet again into the circumstances of those Germans and Austrians exempted from previous internment drives. It met frequently, even daily at its busiest, and for the first time published the names and other details of those now at last to be interned. Philip Freund, baker's roundsman of Stoke Newington, forty-eight, twenty-seven years in England, German wife, three British-born children; John Hennig, living in Camberwell, forty-five, in England since he was seven, British-born wife and three British-born children, formerly a head waiter but now making cardboard boxes; Charles Fetterol, a stoker of Canning Town, fifty-two, thirty-eight years in England, British-born wife and seven British-born children. The litany of misery seemed endless. In September a Naturalization Revocation Committee was established to investigate the cases of all gaining British citizenship since 4 August 1914, and the mayors of the metropolitan boroughs agitated (unsuccessfully) to strike enemy-born British citizens from the electoral roll to stop them voting in forthcoming elections. As an alternative to internment, the machinery of repatriation was oiled afresh, shipping now more available than previously to transport men and their families to neutral Holland. By the middle of October it was reported that 200 people a week were being shipped out, with 1,650 having left since August, and the government was actively exploring ways of preventing their return after the war.[50]

Some voices were raised against this fevered victimisation. 'The treatment of these poor people in England to-day,' complained Colonel Josiah Wedgwood in the House of Commons, 'is a blot upon Great Britain', and indeed it was.[51] But the vast majority saw it differently and the cause of humanity, even of reason, was set firmly to one side.

We might let just a few cases stand for many. Take Henry Carle, who could be called a cat-and-mouse alien: he was interned on 7 November 1914, released on 11 January 1915; interned again on 23 August and released again on 17 March 1916, the day his wife died, leaving three small children under ten; interned again on 24 March 1916 and released again on 29 April 1917; interned again on 29 July 1918 and finally released on 23 December that year, when he was granted permission to reside in Britain.[52] Then there was Georg Sauter, a German artist who had married John Galsworthy's sister Lilian in 1894. The following year they had a boy, Rudolf, to whom Galsworthy was very close. By April 1916 Sauter had been taken from the family home at 1 Holland Park Avenue and interned. Galsworthy agitated tirelessly for his brother-in-law's release. This well-known and respected novelist, writing journalism on behalf of the war effort, could obtain personal interviews with the Home Secretary and senior civil servants and gave evidence in person to the Advisory Committee hearing Georg's appeal but could not secure his freedom. Some time after the German offensive of 21 March 1918, 'Rudo' was arrested and also, despite Galsworthy's best efforts, interned, being sent to the huge concentration camp on the Isle of Man. He was not released until August 1919. Georg had already been repatriated to Germany two years earlier; he never lived with Lilian or Rudolf again. And Rudolf Rocker, whom we left in the camp at Alexandra Palace, suffered the same fate around March 1918, when he was shipped to Holland en route to Germany. He, however, was lucky enough to be joined there by his wife and son.[53]

These were three stories among many thousands in London alone. In 1911 the census had recorded 31,254 German-born residents of the County of London, so excluding all or most of the outer suburbs; in

1921 the number had fallen to 9,083. The comparable figures for Austrians were 8,869 and 1,552.[54]

In one direction at least this relentless wartime victimisation of Germans and Austrians proved something of a self-inflicted wound. German nurses employed at the London Hospital and no doubt elsewhere were forced or chose to leave and proved hard to replace. Great difficulties arose when the German egg-graders at the Port of London's Tooley Street egg market, the largest in Europe, were prevented from entering the wharves by DORA. Ton upon ton of rotten eggs presented the residents and business-people of Bermondsey with a new 'Great Stink' from September 1914 to the very end of 1915. More worryingly, many Germans had worked in chemicals or glass or metals manufacture, now vital to munitions production. Here, in order to safeguard the war effort, compromises had to be reached. So at the Carl Zeiss optical instrument works at Mill Hill three skilled German-born workers were exempted from internment so they could remain at the bench; and there were fifteen Germans at the Fairfax National Gauge Company in Kilburn.

When it came to the business of making munitions in London, no hand could be spared, for from the spring of 1915 London had begun to transform itself into one of the greatest killing machines in human history.[55]

5

WORK, WORK, WORK

One of the most startling of the early results of the war was the closing of the Napier Motor Works at Acton Vale, the machines in which have been silent throughout the week. Messrs. Napiers employ many hundreds of men, and the closing of these works alone is a big blow to the industrial life of Acton.[1]

AT first the body blow dealt by the war to the industrial life of London as a whole was felt in every corner. In Hoxton, 'which is able only by desperate efforts to live in a state of famine in times of peace', people were 'threatened by a very disaster of distress under the shock of war'. Workshops making walking sticks, fancy stationery, cheap furniture had all closed; charwomen who scrubbed City office floors for a pittance found their services no longer required. Thrown out of work, parents and children suffered alike. That August the journalist Robert Lynd watched a procession of 700 or 800 Hoxton children march from a local mission to a communal kitchen for dinner:

It is to their feet you have to look . . . if you would see the symbol of their poverty. One or two of them go barefoot . . . One little boy wears an old sandal on his right foot, the ruins of a boot on his left. Another clatters along, his feet corded into boots three sizes too large for him . . . This mockery of boots and shoes is more pitiable than nakedness.[2]

If the poor suffered most, anxiety and real trouble might strike anywhere. The war, it has been said, 'was the worst thing that ever happened to the City of London'. Much of the international capital market passed from Lombard Street to New York, and City men struggled to make good in a world where money flows across Europe had been staunched to a trickle or brought entirely to a halt. The trade in sugar and some other commodities was effectively nationalised, with profits capped and businessmen's hands tied by regulation. Eventually merchants and bankers and financial advisers to government would do very well out of the war, but the dislocation was nonetheless shocking and took time to mend.[3]

Similarly, Fleet Street's publishers, writers and printers were knocked badly off course. It was said that within a week of the outbreak of war some fifty journal titles folded and those that remained often suffered 'Drastic pruning of the number of pages . . .' Authors found their publishers' lists cut or mothballed: J. A. Hammerton had an Argentine travelogue in the press in August 1914 but it wouldn't see the light of day for two more years; and the novelist Marie Belloc Lowndes saw the cheap edition of her latest book postponed and publishers only interested in material with a war theme. In the summer of 1915 some 600 compositors were said to be unemployed in London, and even as late as Christmas 1916 the publisher J. M. Dent was 'hoping still that the war will be over before we have to shut down'. We might spare a thought too for Queen Anne's Gate, St James's Park, in 1914 a street full of architects whose work came to a dramatic standstill; at No. 17 Edwin Lutyens found fees forfeited, commissions cancelled and building stopped virtually overnight from 5 August – he fled to the still-buoyant construction market in India that December.[4]

Architects and related professionals never properly recovered their business until building picked up again some time after the Armistice. But it would not all stay bad news. The men and women of Fleet Street made a recovery of sorts in the publication of war magazines, and some popular playwrights and novelists such as Arnold Bennett could make a fortune in war journalism, war fiction and war escapism of one kind or another. The nascent film industry of Wardour Street, well established before 1914, experienced a wartime boom that brought great prosperity to the Soho property market. And City merchants struck gold in trading commodities made precious by the needs of war – in nitrate of soda, for instance, or tallow, copra, palm oil and byrites.[5]

Far more remarkable was the recovery of London manufacturing. It was astonishingly swift and, with the exception of some small-scale luxury trades, universal. As early as September 1914 commentators were noting a decrease in unemployment. The 'tide of emergency orders for overtime' especially affecting workshops employing women was leading to different concerns in the East End over harsh working condi- tions, low rates of pay and long hours, the traditional features of 'sweating'. By October unemployment in Shoreditch, including Hoxton, was fast disappearing: 'Even the walking-stick trade is looking up again!' and good tailoring machinists, men and women, were 'at a premium'. The furniture industry had not recovered, but some hundreds of local cabinetmakers were employed at good wages building huts for soldiers all over southern England. The recovery was not yet comprehensive and its effects on individuals were uneven – 44.4 per cent of women nationally, for instance, were thought to have been out of work for some of September 1914. But we must remember that irregularity of employment was a weekly feature of London workshop life in almost every trade. And although the depression noted in Hoxton and elsewhere in August 1914 was sharp and painful for those made hungry by it, any 'abnormal' distress proved thankfully short-lived.[6]

Nowhere in these early months did the enterprising capacity of London's workshops show better than in the garment industry. Clothing factories and workshops, and countless needlewomen taking in 'outwork' at home, were clustered especially in the East End but were a feature of London industry all over the central districts. Before the war the trade was characterised by irregular employment and pitiful pay for long hours. At first many workshops closed their doors on the outbreak of war. But demand for 'the khaki', military clothing of all kinds, swept over the workshops of east and central London like a tidal surge. The East End trouser makers, formerly producing ready-made garments for the wholesale trade, couldn't get enough hands – 'They were begging you to come in and work.' London's shirt makers had to meet an inexhaustible demand – one employing 200 workers found itself needing 1,000 more workers; they recruited unemployed blouse makers and dressmakers and trained them up to speed in 'about three weeks'. Just as workers had to adapt their skills, so employers had to change their lines. A big theatrical costumier employing nearly 200 switched to War Office khaki and shirts and didn't have to lay off a single worker. High- class furriers took on contracts for winter coats for soldiers and officers. A Dalston factory working on fine embroidery for court dress and stage costumes turned to machine-embroidered naval and army badges 'on huge Swiss embroidery machines'.[7]

Indeed, great changes to machinery and processes began to affect the

London rag trade more widely: Hoffman presses replaced the heavy pressing irons that there were now too few male pressers to lift; the band-knife enabled women to penetrate the mysteries of cutting; the subdivision of labour, long a reality in London's garment workshops, was taken as far as it could go. And in the East End the demand for factories filled empty premises in the workshop districts of Whitechapel, Spitalfields and Bethnal Green even before the end of 1914. These conditions persisted in the rag trade throughout the war: on 14 November 1917, for instance, in what before the war would have been the dark days for the East End garment industry just after the annual Lord Mayor's Show, we find advertisements in the local papers clamouring for thousands of tailoring machinists – forty needed by a firm in Albion Road, Stoke Newington, 100 in Cowper Street, City Road, another 100 for Goldstein in Bishopsgate, 200 for leather jerkins and tunics in Bunhill Row and so on. As the novelist Esther Kreitman, a Jewish Belgian refugee in London from 1914, makes the elderly wife of an East End trouser maker truly say, '"The war's been a miracle for us!"'[8]

The extraordinary versatility of London's workshops, coping with everything thrown at them by the demands of total war, was demonstrated in every borough in London. We might take two instances to stand for all. In the great workshop district of Islington, even before the end of 1914, scores of firms were employed on war work, making bandoliers, jackets, belts, haversacks, horse rugs, mess-tin covers, needle-cases, ration bags, sleeping bags, trousers, shaving brushes, gloves, dressing gowns, shirts, overcoats, motor fur rugs, kit bags, hairbrushes, 'bomb slings' and 'cannon cleanser'. Even Islington's artificial-flower makers were prospering as German competition quickly dried up, a feature soon to be shared by piano and toy makers London-wide. And south of the river in Bermondsey, world-famous for its leather industry, though with a surprisingly diverse manufacturing base in addition, a chemical works made the most effective 'neutraliser' of poison gas until a new type of mask was introduced in 1917; sawmills produced bulk timbers for bridgework and mahogany sheeting for aeroplanes; a single shirt maker produced 274,000 flannel body-belts and 339,000 shirts for officers and men, besides much else; a factory in Long Lane made most of the army's white tape for use on night patrols in no-man's-land; Hallett and Sons made brittle antimony for shrapnel; the food producers made biscuits, pickles, jams and marmalades, calf's-foot jelly, lime cordial, bottled fruits, baking and custard powder, and soup squares, all for the troops in France; and Bermondsey's great industry made Sam Browne belts, bootlaces, saddles, boots, straps, wallets, harness, stretcher bindings, machine-gun case straps and much else besides for a war machine still kept in place by leather.[9]

London's enormous industrial boom – for such it was, and so it was called at the time – created a demand for labour surely without parallel at any previous time in its history. The problem of unemployment quickly gave way to its opposite. Labour shortages became acute by the early weeks of 1915. They were felt directly by everyone in London. On 22 January a heavy snowfall blocked streets and pavements but the 'impossibility of finding casual labour' meant that many borough councils could not keep the streets clear, as they had done in past years.[10]

That same month Michael MacDonagh counted thirty steamships in the river 'waiting their turn to be unloaded', held up in 'inextricable confusion . . . due to the scarcity of labour. Not enough labour available at the London docks! What an unprecedented state of affairs.' Indeed, the Port of London had provided for generations a daily showcase of the capital's casual labour problem in all its ragged misery. Twice every morning the 'call' for men at the dock gates presented men literally fighting one another for the right to earn a day's, even half a day's, work. Within four months the war had accommodated them all, not generally in the army, which was at this stage able to be choosy about the physical condition of men selected, but in the bottomless sump that London's labour market had now become.[11]

The Port of London, like many other ports in Britain, entered a period of unexampled busyness. In the early months shipping was diverted to London by the blockade of many continental ports. The Port of London Authority responded by building an additional 2 million square feet of storage space in 1915 and that same year an improvement scheme at the East India Docks, Blackwall, made them accessible to larger cargo steamers of deeper draught. Average daily employment of labourers at the Port rose from 7,846 in 1914 to 11,149 in 1915. To supplement the labour supply boys of fifteen and sixteen were taken on and so were older men unfit for army service. From 1916 Transport Workers' Battalions, soldiers who were often former dockers, boosted local labour at times of shortage. Tonnage entering the Thames declined later in the war as government took control of British ports and evened out shipping between them, and as submarine warfare took its terrible toll of ships in 1916 and 1917. But from the summer of 1918 the value of shipping in London and the number of labourers employed once more exceeded pre-war levels. In all that time it proved generally difficult to keep the number of men the Port required, labourers frequently leaving, whether enlisted to work in French or Belgian ports or tempted by 'dazzling wages' in other employment.[12]

The demand for labour had some strange, almost dramatic effects in London. The Salvation Army night hostels for homeless men and women emptied as if by sorcery. So did the London workhouses for the able-bodied poor. In Lambeth forty-eight inmates of Princes Road Workhouse had left by March 1915 to work at Woolwich Dockyard – forty-one of them were over sixty years old and a further four over seventy. At Wandsworth an institution built for the able-bodied became essentially an old people's home by early 1916. Space could be rationalised to free up workhouses for other purposes, like the internment camp at Cornwallis Road, Islington, or for Belgian refugees or as overspill military hospitals. Similarly, despite the stresses of war and a probable rise in London's population, the number of 'certified lunatics' in metropolitan mental hospitals was lower by almost 16 per cent between 1914 and 1918. Even more dramatically, the number of men received in the London prisons fell by nearly 63 per cent between 1913 (33,776) and 1918 (12,631). The Commissioners of Prisons, while making a predictable genuflexion to liquor control, concluded that 'the prisons of the country may be largely emptied of the petty offender when the conditions of labour are such as to secure full and continuous employment for all . . .'[13]

With even these remarkable supplies of labour virtually exhausted the needs of the army for men left employers constantly struggling to keep their workforces up to strength. The problem persisted throughout the war. Bermondsey's street-sweeping contractor was left with just thirty-seven out of 160 men, the rest having enlisted or found more congenial work elsewhere by the spring of 1915; he was having to pay old men twice what the young men had received pre-war. A Hampstead builder complained to a client in 1917 that he had only eleven men out of forty and they were 'all old and not venturesome on high ladders'. That same year when Georgina Lee moved house in Kensington the removal men arrived four and a half hours late: 'But my anger was quickly disarmed at the sight of the 4 decrepit old fellows, knock-kneed and splay-footed. They could barely struggle under the chests and chairs they had to carry.' Shortages of grave diggers, coffin makers and carriage horses combined to cause backlogs in funerals in south London in 1917, and the delivery of domestic coal supplies across London was disrupted because of insufficient labour. Besides old men, some employers called on children. A Stoke Newington milkman was fined for employing a boy of nine in 1915, for instance, while others made lawful arrangements to take children early from school: at Pinner, a baker unable to get a roundsman persuaded a local JP to release his son from school at thirteen to deliver bread for him, and a girl at the same school was allowed to leave early to make syringes at a local glassworks.[14]

She was not alone. From the first weeks of the war women had stepped into the breach left by men joining the services. At Sainsbury's grocery chain, for instance, a rush of young shopmen to the colours had induced managerial concerns within a month of declaration: 'they are not all wanted at once', managers were sharply told, and measures were put in place to stop men joining at the drop of an apron. It was not enough, and the first week of September saw the start of many advertisements for women shop assistants that heralded a revolution in the grocery trade. 'The woman grocer's assistant is a product of the war,' noted the *Daily Mail*, reporting that Sainsbury's had advertised for 200 'single young women'. By the spring of 1915 women were serving in all the big London stores and 'lift girls' were a notable feature of the popular Army and Navy Stores in Victoria.[15]

From these earliest days women began to penetrate virtually every aspect of working life in London, seemingly in ever greater numbers as the war progressed. The movement was noticeable everywhere through 1915 and became pervasive with conscription of men to the forces from February 1916. One of the most obvious changes was in London's public transport, where both male trade unionist and political prejudices against women's employment took some time to overcome. The railways proved most innovative. By June 1915 women ticket collectors were employed by South London Railways, and at the newly opened Maida Vale station on the underground's Bakerloo Line extension the entire staff were women. By November the LCC had begun employing women tram conductors and that month the first women bus conductors were employed by Thomas Tilling's. The huge LGOC did not follow suit till March 1916, but by the end of the year they had over 1,700 and the company would eventually employ 3,500 women 'clippies'. For many Londoners the woman bus conductor became the most visible, even lovable, face of female wartime labour, fondly featured in fiction and journalism.[16]

Women also extended their role in London's hospitality industry. Waitresses were well known in tea shops and cafés but not much seen in hotels, restaurants and clubs before the war. The early demise of the German and Austrian waiter combined with later army recruitment to draw men in shoals from waiting at table. The newly renamed British Empire Hotel in De Vere Gardens, South Kensington, employed 'quite a beauty chorus of waitresses. It was a novelty then', in 1915. The clubs of St James's seem to have resisted change as far as they could but eventually had to give in. The first waitress was apparently employed at the Athenaeum, 'Of all places', as Michael MacDonagh put it. At the Reform Club, where many staff joined up at the outbreak of war, as we have seen, advertisements for waiters, 'Tall. Good Appearance', in September 1914 gave way by November to plain 'Coffee Room waiters' of any description as long as they were men. But by April 1915 continuing complaints of poor service led to women being hired to serve lunch at one of the dining rooms: 'It is impossible to get trained waiters and all the Clubs in London are experiencing difficulties and even employing waitresses,' the secretary lamented.[17]

By then other employers had also succumbed to the inevitable. Postwomen began to appear in south London in September 1915. That same month the South Metropolitan Gas Company was employing women gas fitters to install and maintain domestic meters – local housewives were reportedly very pleased with the change, the women neater, quieter and quicker than the men. The company agreed and within two years nearly 2,000 women were employed in every aspect of the business, maintaining gas stoves and fires, lighting street lamps, even making gas in the retorts and humping coke. From 1916 women and girls were working almost everywhere they had never worked before – driving delivery vans (both motor and horse-drawn), portering in workhouses, carrying messages in every institution in London, boiling sugar in refineries, emptying dustbins, combining in all-female orchestras and staffing every aspect of stage management in the London theatres.[18]

Some male bastions held out. Despite the shortage of taxis on London's streets there was great resistance among the drivers to the licensing of women. They were supported by several home secretaries and by Sir Edward Henry, Commissioner of Police. When, in February 1917, after much debate, women were allowed to study for the knowledge and apply for a licence the men's union threatened to call out ten men for every woman employed. It is unclear whether any woman actually drove a cab in London before the end of the war. Men in some professions also proved tenaciously resistant to the employment of women. The London Hospital, for instance, whose medical men had successfully kept out 'coloured' doctors, allowed a girl messenger to replace a boy in the Almoner's Department in May 1915 and employed 'lady dispensers' in the pharmacy a year later, but in early 1916 concluded that taking on women medical students 'would be most inadvisable'. Seven women doctors were, though, accepted at the end of 1916 into those 'firms' 'which approve of women residents'. Women medical students were not entered onto the hospital's books until a month before the Armistice.[19]

The greatest impact of all the many extensions of women's labour in the war years was made in the production of munitions. The scandalous shortage of shells that brought down Asquith's Liberal government and led to Lloyd George's reign at the new Ministry of Munitions from May 1915 brought about a revolutionary re-evaluation of women's labour in the national economy. It was plain to government that without women making munitions Britain would lose the war and lose it quickly. The enormous transformation of British industry that followed depended both on nationalisation and on women, not only to take the place of men but to do jobs that men had never even been asked to do in such numbers before.

Confronting the extended male prejudices and protectionist instincts of the Amalgamated Society of Engineers was a fight that the leaders of the pre-war suffrage movement were eager to take on. For Emmeline and Christabel Pankhurst and their supporters this was to wage the suffrage campaign by other means. On a cold wet Saturday, 17 July 1915, a great 'Procession of the Women' or 'Women's War Pageant', said to be 50,000 strong, marched along the Embankment. At the rear of the Ministry of Munitions in Whitehall Gardens a platform was built so that the Minister and his officials could watch the march troop past, bands playing. Organised by the Pankhursts and other suffragists in collaboration with Lloyd George, banners proclaimed that 'Women's Battle Cry is Work, Work, Work' and 'Shells made by a Wife may save her Husband's Life'. 'We're going to do our bit,' a marcher told a young man 'in mufti' watching from the pavement, 'are you going to do yours?' Lloyd George received a deputation from Mrs Pankhurst, Christabel,

Annie Kenney and others who made it plain that 'They desired to make no bargain for serving their country in the making of munitions.' During July 193,000 women were employed nationwide in munitions; a year later there were 487,000.[20]

Why did so many women answer the call for 'Work, Work, Work' and what had they been doing before? Clearly, many were motivated by the desire 'to do our bit' to win the war, to kill Germans and save British lives, those of their fathers, sons and brothers among them. The relatively high wages – nearly a quarter of women at Woolwich Arsenal in 1917 earned over £3 a week – pulled in women from other industries and gave them the chance to take a larger share in the general prosperity. And despite the well-known dangers of the work, its long hours and unsocial shift patterns, there were the satisfactions of independence, of being someone in the world and of having a valued status in society. The munitionettes were indeed someone. They were much written about and photographed, songs were sung about them and they starred, in fantasy at least, on the stages of London and elsewhere: a variety bill at the Hackney Empire in the summer of 1917 featured '"Smith, V.C.," a merry little munitions sketch, in which Miss Edith Carter appears as the Yorkshire munition lass'.[21]

Many women, of course, had been employed in workshops of all kinds before the war, though none at all had worked in munitions: of a survey of 444,000 women in manufacturing nationwide in January 1917, 31 per cent had worked in the same trade before August 1914; but 22 per cent had been housewives and 17 per cent domestic servants. This last group, especially prominent in the London labour market outside the East End, were thought to make up about a quarter of women working in munitions. In other work the proportion could be even higher: 43 per cent of 1,700 women becoming LGOC conductors by the end of 1916 were former domestic servants, for instance. Once Alice Kedge, twenty in 1915 and in service to 'a nice American lady in Golders Green', heard the call for women to work on munitions she 'shot down' to Camden Town labour exchange and was soon making shell fuses in Gray's Inn Road. A 'lady' similarly told a friend in September 1915 that her housemaid, moved by Lloyd George's appeal, had left to make shells; and 'Our late parlourmaid has gone to make aeroplanes,' recorded Viscount Sandhurst in March 1918. The impact on middle-class households in London was often painfully and personally felt. 'Not a parlourmaid to be had,' complained Virginia Woolf in

1917, while Mrs Alec-Tweedie thought that 'Servants are not hit by the war' in contrast to 'Women with brains and education'.[22]

Before the war London's outer suburbs had contained the nation's main armaments-manufacturing districts. First in origin and importance came the Royal Ordnance Factory at Woolwich Arsenal, making the country's shells, artillery and gun carriages and employing some 10,000 men at the outbreak of war. The Royal Small Arms Factory (RSAF) at Enfield on the River Lea – the famous Lee-Enfield rifle was the stock weapon of the British infantryman – employed 1,800 men and boys making rifles and ammunition. And at the Royal Gunpowder Factory at Waltham Abbey 900 men made explosives for shells. These government establishments were supplemented for small arms by private manufacturers in Birmingham and in London, where the London Small Arms Company at Victoria Park produced 250 rifles a week compared to the RSAF's 1,000 new and 1,000 repaired, with additional numbers from Eley's in Angel Road, Edmonton. Machine-gun manufacture was principally in private hands, with Vickers at Erith and Crayford, down-river from Woolwich, capable of making just ten or twelve a week. London was also in 1914 'the national centre of the aircraft industry', its various private manufacturers adding to those produced at the Royal Aircraft Factory at Farnborough.[23]

All of London's 1914 armaments centres grew hugely during the war. In May 1917, at its peak, the Royal Arsenal at Woolwich was employing 75,000 workers, over 25,000 of them women. That year the RSAF had 10,000 workers, including 1,544 women and girls, and the Royal Gunpowder Factory had 5,300, over 2,100 of whom were women. Vickers, in greatly extended factories, was producing 5,000 machine guns a month as well as other munitions. Even more dramatic growth was seen in the provinces. The pre-eminent position in armaments manufacture once enjoyed by London did not survive the period of production for total war that began in the spring of 1915, when the resources of the nation were turned into one vast killing machine. Even so, much of the rest of London manufacturing was requisitioned for this superhuman struggle. And the formerly anonymous suburbs of west and north-west London – Park Royal, Perivale, Greenford, Hendon, Hayes – would now play as vital a part in waging war as did the trenches of the Somme.[24]

When Lloyd George took on the Ministry of Munitions he had envisaged that the infinitely adaptable small-scale engineering works scattered like iron filings across London's central districts would play a leading role in component manufacture for shells. He was right in part. Certainly backstreet industries everywhere in London turned their hand to the new demands of war-engineering. George Cross, now running the British Empire Hotel in De Vere Gardens, Kensington, but eager to do his bit for the war effort, made aeroplane parts and chemical warfare components in a small engineering works off Baker Street; Thomas Glover's gas meter factory at Tottenham, employing 800 before the war, was soon putting 2,000 to work on radiators and aeroplane and gun parts; Klinger's famous blouse makers in Tottenham and Hackney made gas masks, London dominating in that aspect of war manufacture; W. F. Watson, a skilled engineer before the war, worked from 1914 at Woolwich Arsenal and other places before settling at a newly established workshop in stables off Pentonville Road, Finsbury, making crank cases for aeroplanes; the General Electric Company's factory making electric light fittings at Union Street, Southwark, switched to bomb-dropping gear, aeroplane gun sights, trench periscopes and other necessities of scientific warfare. Across London perforated-music makers, printers, candle makers, cinematograph and photographic equipment workers, organ builders and stationers and many more turned over to munitions components of one kind or another.[25]

As well as this swift adaptation of London's multifarious engineering or electrical concerns, even by 1915 the role of London in munitions had begun to expand. Munitions factories were planted in gasworks and waterworks and in municipal buildings across London, at empty LCC schools and tram-repair depots, at the workshops of Claybury and Horton mental hospitals, at borough lighting departments and at empty warehouses in the Port of London. These larger works were generally employed in filling shell cases with explosives. And largely because of its position as the nexus of the nation's railway network, but also because of the huge labour resources available, London was rapidly marked out for a giant expansion in its munitions-manufacturing role.[26]

Important developments took place in 1915 along the eastern reaches of the Thames close to the great expansions at Woolwich and Erith and Crayford: so Siemens cable works at Woolwich were enlarged to make telephone equipment, much of it for the trenches; chemicals and explosives works were added to existing centres from Silvertown to Rainham; national cartridge-box factories were set up at Dagenham,

Deptford and Woolwich. Similarly the long-established works at Enfield and Edmonton were supplemented by new factories making photographic lenses, trench mortars and cartridges. The east and north-east expansions were added to in 1916 with a National Projectile Factory at Hackney Wick, employing some 4,500 workers, a third of them women; a National Filling Factory at Abbey Wood, Greenwich; and a national factory making gas shells at Walthamstow. There was also a National Filling Factory built on vacant land at Sumner Street, Southwark, in late 1915.[27]

But it was west London that saw the most extraordinary industrial expansion for manufacturing a huge variety of war materiel. Engineering had been no stranger to west London before 1914. In particular, London's motor and aircraft industries had found a congenial mix of cheap land and suburban housing attracting skilled workers to places like Acton, Chiswick, Fulham and elsewhere a few years before the war. That labour pool was now extended by the servant girls and working-class housewives of west London, who generally lacked the work opportunities and traditions offered by the clothing trade and small workshop industries of the East End. There was one more factor in west London's favour. London was the railway hub of the nation; but most feeder lines, railway termini and junctions lay on the western side of the capital, connecting it to the engineering districts of the Midlands and the North-West, and in the South-West to the main ports sending men and munitions to France. King's Cross, St Pancras, Euston, Marylebone, Paddington, Victoria, Charing Cross and Waterloo enmeshed west London in a network of steel. Within it, especially in the north-western suburbs, munitions factories quickly took root.

Most important of these developments for posterity was at the disused Royal Agricultural Society showground of Park Royal and the land adjoining it in North Acton, Harlesden and Willesden. The empty showground had been part-developed as a stadium for Queens Park Rangers football club, but this was commandeered by the army when professional football folded in 1915. By the end of the year a giant National Filling Factory was opened on a 120-acre site, making fuses, detonators and gaines (explosive-filled triggers connecting shell nose caps to the TNT filling). By mid-1917 it was making 1.8 million shell components each week; at its peak that year it employed 5,250 workers, 4,850 of them women. In the nearby suburban towns and villages other munitions factories were quickly planted: a cartridge-filling factory at

Hayes employed 10,600, over 80 per cent of them women; the former White City exhibition ground was turned over for munitions production; a gas-shell filling plant at Greenford employed 1,000 workers; a factory making liquid oxygen for weaponry was established in Willesden; tank engines were built by the Aster motor company at Wembley; and a trench-mortar bomb-filling factory was established further south at Fulham.[28]

West London also proved especially fruitful for the expansion of London's aircraft industry. Napier's motor factory at Acton Lane developed a large aero-engine plant besides building army lorries and motor ambulances: despite the closure of the motor works in the war's first week, 'Never had the company had such business' as in these years of total war. Nearby, aircraft were built by the Aircraft Manufacturing Company (Airco) at Hendon, the site of London Aerodrome from around 1911, with Geoffrey de Havilland taken on as designer just before the outbreak of war; the Fairey Aviation Company had their London factory at Hayes and tested planes at the Royal Flying Corps (RFC) aerodrome at Northolt; Handley Page were based at Cricklewood; Hooper and Company of Wembley made wings for the Sopwith Camel, assembled at Sopwith Aviation Company on the river at Kingston; there were aircraft component works at Barnes, Feltham, Dollis Hill, Colindale and Kilburn. In addition, a National Aeroplane Factory was opened at Waddon in Croydon. Most of these munitions, vehicle and aircraft factories, were entirely new additions to the industrial landscape of west London north and south of the Thames; even those that were there before the war were now operating at such a completely different capacity they were essentially new enterprises.[29]

The wartime consequences for individual workers were pretty momentous too. 'When I ran away from my difficulties in 1909' and joined the army, recalled the engineer James Royce,

bands of unorganized workless men wearing hitched-up corduroy trousers and carrying picks and shovels on their shoulders were marching around the streets of London singing, 'What will become of England if things go on this way?' In 1917 I came back to a new world. Men with the slightest knowledge of handling tools were worth £4 a week any day. During my first preliminary survey of the surrounding North West London districts, dingy factories were buzzing till late at night, and even brand new ones were springing up in the outlying fields.[30]

Before the war Rose Neighbour's mother had been a laundress in Acton Green, 'Soap Suds Island', as it was locally known. By the end of the war she had brought her married sister from Battersea to live with her in Acton and the women took alternate shifts making munitions at White City and sharing house rent and childcare. Benefits spread wider than the workers alone. Edith Hall's mother, living in Southall, with her husband in France and later a prisoner of war, boarded girls working in a shell-filling factory at Hayes, most from the East End and up to three girls in a room. And despite the dangers and social disadvantages of munitions work, most munitionettes seem to have had the time of their lives. 'Laughter, anger, acute confusion, and laughter again' was how Naomi Loughnan, a middle-class munitions worker, described being thrown in among East End girls: 'Once, when several of us had been standing on the tables [in the works canteen] dancing hornpipes to the accompaniment of numerous penny whistles and hundreds of strained vocal cords, the Superintendent arrived quite pale to request a little less din.' She thought that 'Munition life is the grandest chance that has ever come to us women.' Sylvia Townsend Warner, admittedly no ordinary munitionette, made ammunition for Vickers at Erith, where she found her fellow workers 'coltish' as they 'cast down their tools' for their dinner break on the night shift: 'as they ran through the shop, dodging between the machines and curvetting over stray shells with awkward exaggerated leaps, they nuzzled each other with the unthinking affection of animals let loose.'[31]

This affectionate comradely zeal in the collective endeavour of total war is much in evidence in a literary archive that has come down to us from at least one London war factory. *The Aircraft Rag*, later *Air-Co Rag*, was produced by workers at the Aircraft Manufacturing Company works at Colindale Avenue, Hendon. It had started as an informal bulletin 'known as the Rag', typed or handwritten and drawn, circulated from bench to bench. The management approved of it and from May 1917 the *Rag* became a lively witty news-sheet of factory life, professionally printed, published monthly and selling 1,800 copies at a penny – an arrangement it thought 'almost unique' among other 'employees' magazines'. It gave news from every corner of this giant factory that employed designers and draughtsmen, skilled engineers and hundreds of detailed process workers. Airco fielded six teams in the various divisions of the London Munitions Football League – 'we went off with a bang' – and two elevens in the London Munitions Cricket League. The company had a harriers club and a hockey section. Less strenuously, there was an Orchestral Society under the leadership of 'an old Army musician'; some thirteen strong, it performed at a 'Concert Party' in April 1918 which revealed 'a vast store of latent talent available throughout the Works'. Summer outings took staff to West End restaurants and – a favourite of the Bolt Inspection Department – a Thames boat trip from Windsor to Marlow and Medmenham Abbey. The factory canteen, run by the Young Men's Christian Association, proved a source of complaint and satire over standards of service and food shortages: an optimist, it was said in May 1918, 'is a man who stirs his cup of tea in the Y.M.C.A. Canteen'.[32]

The *Rag* generally kept clear of the downside of factory life in these years – its dangers. Accidents happened everywhere. But the greatest risks of all were faced by those handling toxic chemicals and explosives. Industrial poisoning from substances thought vital to the war effort had begun to appear by early 1915. Toxic jaundice – among many symptoms, the skin turned a yellow-green, hence the popular term for munitionettes of 'canary girls' – was caused both by tetrachloroethane in the dope or varnish used to treat aeroplane fabric and by trinitro-toluene (TNT), which quickly became the main explosive ingredient of shells. Two deaths from 'dope poisoning' at a Crayford aeroplane factory, one of a 'young girl', were brought to the attention of MPs in March 1915. Reckless exposure of workers in some factories – poor Ellen Clark was working twelve-hour days at Silvertown on the 'dope-varnishing' that killed her in early 1916 – led to a dozen deaths before tetrachloroethane was banned from dope in September. Dope continued to be a problem in ill-ventilated works till the end of the war, though no longer the killer it had been.[33]

The first fatality from toxic jaundice caused by handling TNT also occurred in early 1915. The effects were cumulative: first, dermatitis; second, diarrhoea and vomiting; third, anaemia, putting a strain on 'heart, liver, kidneys, and circulatory system generally'; finally, if exposure continued, destruction of liver cells causing generalised jaundice and proving fatal in 25 to 30 per cent of cases. In 1916 there were fifty-two deaths (thirty-one of them women), forty-four in 1917 (forty-two women) and ten in 1918; 404 cases of toxic jaundice were reported over these years. Yellowing of the skin seems to have arisen more commonly with exposure and was belatedly identified as a warning sign that workers should be put on other tasks. The change in skin colour, though a badge of pride for some, was generally loathed by the women; it proved a barrier to recruiting to shell-filling works in west London and no doubt elsewhere.[34]

In addition to these insidious health risks from industrial poisons there was the ever-present risk of explosions. Familiarity with the production process sometimes led to foolhardy behaviour: there was a trickle of prosecutions of men and women in the London police courts for smoking in munitions factories, for instance. But even with careful handling catastrophe was always a threat. Three workers, two men and a woman, died in an explosion at a munitions factory at Camberwell in July 1916; and during Lloyd George's period at Munitions 'several women' were killed in an explosion while filling gaines at a factory in Hayes.[35]

The value of munitions workers to the war economy was everywhere recognised – in principle. Adequate rewards, and safeguards to preserve women's health and efficiency at work, were often only tardily introduced. Wages could vary and even the best generally compared badly to those of men: at Napier's in early 1916, women were reportedly receiving 15s 6d for a fifty-four-hour week on a drilling machine for which men received nearly twice as much. Hours at some factories were inordinately long, tiredness adding to the great dangers presented by the work itself: from the spring of 1916, for instance, the night shift at Vickers in Erith was ten hours long, six days a week.[36]

Many women also, of course, had the burden of childcare adding to their hours of labour once they returned home, making the best arrangements they could, like Rose Neighbour's mother, to ease domestic duties. Not all coped so well. A sad case of neglect came to public attention at Hoxton in September 1917: Rose Johnson, twelve, was picked up by police, not for the first time, and charged with 'wandering' at night; her mother was a munitions worker on night shifts and Rose was afraid of the dark, made worse because they lived in a 'condemned' house where all the windows were boarded up. She was remanded for inquiries.[37]

The huge demands made on manufacturing in London, with its insatiable hunger for men's and women's labour, was matched by the demand for office workers. Some replacement labour for young men volunteering and later conscripted was met by the return of men from retirement: in the witty way of the time, they were often referred to as 'dug-outs', an apt wartime pun. But there was also a great deal of replacement by young women, indeed women of all ages. It happened everywhere. In local government, for instance, where Bermondsey Borough Council took on its first 'lady' typist in March 1916 to replace a man who had joined up and a first woman telephonist a year later, and Wandsworth Board of Guardians employed female assistant relieving officers from October 1915. In banking, where the Bank of England had recruited 350 women clerks by the spring of 1915 and 'well over a thousand' by the war's end, while at Baring's over half its clerks were women by the summer of 1915. And in the offices of every large firm where men could not fill the gaps made by war service. Indeed, nationwide 'there were more women replacing males at work in banking, finance, and commerce than in the metal and chemical trades put together'.[38]

It was in these years that the City of London became truly feminised, the masculine black of so many pre-war days now giving way to brighter colours and with women themselves showing an entirely new sense of freedom. Women had worked in the City before 1914 but never in such numbers. Michael MacDonagh noted at the cancelled Bank Holiday of August 1916 'how enormously the short skirt has conduced to the great and ever-growing part that women are taking in general business and War work', offering 'freer personal movement and increased equality with man . . .' And office work opened up a new world for young women, who could raise their sights above anything their mothers could have imagined. In the East End, it was said that

> Jewish girls discovered that there was a great demand for office workers. One can learn shorthand and typing in six months, so even the poorest of mothers saved their last ha'pennies, and didn't send the girls into workshops when they left school at the age of fourteen; instead of making sweatshop workers out of them, they aspired to make them into office 'ladies', working with their brains instead of their hands.[39]

New vistas were indeed opening. The war created whole new vast office undertakings of its own. Government offices took on more functions than ever before as the public sector seized directive sway over private enterprise. They became bloated with staff, many of them necessarily women. The demand for government office space around Whitehall and the Houses of Parliament became so great that London's existing buildings were inadequate to satisfy it. Whole townships of hutments spread like mildew over nearby open spaces, obliterating a good deal of the Victoria Embankment Gardens and removing acres of St James's Park from the Londoners' recreation ground. The War Office was the greatest propagator of this mushroom growth, but the Admiralty and others were not far behind. The huts were filled with clerks and typists, most of them women, so that Whitehall, once another black-coated male preserve, became even more of a female domain than the City: every evening 'Whitehall, Trafalgar Square, Northumberland Avenue, or the Strand, are, with their dense, quick-moving throngs of women, like rivers in spate.'[40]

Some of these government offices were wholly new war creations, like the Ministry of Food, the Ministry of Information, the Ministry of Health and the Air Ministry, or the smaller establishments, numerous as minnows, like the propaganda department at Wellington House in Buckingham Gate, or the censor's office. This last grew big enough to spawn small fry of its own: it outgrew its original base at the General Post Office, ending up with a staff 2,000 strong at Strand House, Carey Street, with suboffices at South Kensington for prisoner-of-war letters and a separate Cable Censorship Office. Most imperious of all was the Ministry of Munitions. Its aggrandisement knew no bounds. Beginning modestly enough at 6 Whitehall Gardens, it soon spread to Whitehall Place, then requisitioned the nearby Hotel Metropole, effectively turning Northumberland Avenue – and later Kingsway – into extensions of Whitehall; it took over the Grand Hotel at Charing Cross and planted satellites at the Hotel Victoria, at Storey's Gate (Explosives), at St Ermin's Hotel in Caxton Street (Priority Department), at Princes Street (Inventions) and others besides. In all it acquired between May 1915 and November 1918 seventy-four central London buildings. Between July 1915 and January 1916 its London headquarters staff grew from 668 to 3,082; by November 1918 there were 25,144. Its male clerks and other staff came from every background – novelists, composers, theatrical managers, clergymen, lawyers and many underused clerks from the Railway Clearing Office at Euston. But just as in the filling factories, a high proportion of women were employed: it was 'One of the outstanding features of the Ministry' compared with permanent departments of state.[41]

What was this new world like for the young women coming fresh to these extraordinary opportunities? We know something of the miseries because complaints that promotion among women clerks at the War

Office was 'dependent rather upon influence and favouritism than upon merit, efficiency, and length of service' reached even the floor of the House of Commons from 1917; and the heartfelt though veiled recollections of Rose Squire, Director of Women's Welfare at the Ministry of Munitions from March 1918, 'that if jealousies and gossip are steadily ignored by the head of a Department' staff would either pull their weight or 'make room for another', tell us a lot. More positively, we know too about the glamour of it all: for instance, the 'painted girls' in the Ministry of Information who shocked Arnold Bennett by their forward, even predatory, behaviour towards male colleagues; or the women clerks at Adastral House, formerly De Keyser's Hotel on the Embankment near Blackfriars Bridge, by November 1916 headquarters of the RFC. Michael MacDonagh observed them watching that year's Lord Mayor's Show:

> At every window were clustered flower-like groups of the girl clerks. There is rivalry between the Government Departments as to which can boast the most beautiful corps of shorthand writers and typists. I think the palm, or the apple, or the biscuit, would be given to the girls of the Flying Corps. As the Anzacs and the Canadians marched past they slowed down, and it was not 'eyes front' with them but 'eyes left' – though I heard no order to that effect from the officer in command. The wonder is that the men did not stand still transfixed by that blaze of feminine loveliness. It almost dazzled even my eyes.[42]

But for the sheer fun and joy of life, in the midst of so much agony, we might turn to some letters that have survived from the girlfriends of Edie Wensley, a typist in Park Buildings, the War Office hutments at St James's Park. Edie, daughter of Frederick Porter 'Weasel' Wensley, one of the most famous Metropolitan Police detectives of his day, was born in 1897 and lived with her parents at 22 Powys Lane, Palmers Green, an aspiring middle-class suburb in north London. Letters from Edie have not surfaced, but she had a number of correspondents among friends she knew from school and young women she met at work. All were typists or clerks at a variety of private and public offices, every one taking advantage of the burgeoning opportunities for girls from her background.

Edie, from all we can tell, was a lovable girl. Alice Stockwell, a workmate, thought of her as the 'little girl who, directly one's back was turned' in one of the typing rooms at Park Buildings, 'put bars of chocolate and other nice things on my machine, and when the question was asked, "Who put this on my machine[?]" just kept a profound silence. No such little luxuries here, dear, I can assure you.' 'Here' was Strome and Co. Ltd, of Bridgewater Square, Barbican, in the north of the City, a firm of import and export commission merchants trading with the Far East. Alice was kept busy:

> there is plenty of work, at times I am inclined to call it 'real hard grind,' but am getting to better know the business and am now finding it some-what easier . . . Do I ever wish I was ever back at Park Buildings. Well, honestly, there are times when I wish I was, for we did have some real nice times together, did we not. And 5 o/c. tea time was a real good break. However, the money is more and hours considerably less, so after all, being War time, we <u>have</u> to take into consideration the <u>financial</u> part of the question.
>
> Kindly convey my love to <u>all</u> my friends in both Rooms. Am hoping to come over one evening in June, without fail, so please understand you are <u>not</u> to get off early <u>that</u> evening.
>
> Was surprised to hear Miss ['Baby'] Lee had left, but knew that Miss Shanahan was going.[43]

Turnover was indeed hectic. Freda Creighton, a few weeks into a new job in a City bank in the cold wet spring of 1917, told Edie, 'I am just about getting used to it now . . . You will be surprised to hear that I have not done any shorthand or typewriting yet, they have put me on pass books etc. and I am surprised to find myself getting quite keen on figures . . . Of course the work is rather simple but most office work is once you have got your hand in.'[44] 'Bobbie' Kaine seemed to be having a more exciting time of it, writing of her new position after leaving Park Buildings:

> I am now at the Canadian Record Office as Shorthand Typist (Swank) . . . the only Stenographer in this Branch . . . I shall always remember you and your sweetness to me during my stay at the Park. I very often think about the silly manner in which I carried on. Although I have not altered a tiny bit. In fact I am worse if anything. (The girls here say that they are longing for the Summer holidays to come so that they will be in peace for a week.) You wouldn't say that would you kipper? . . . I don't get nice TEA here and whats more I don't get a chance of making it.

But work had its compensations:

> There are a good many soldiers, but of course, I do not take much notice
> of them, and they don't take any notice of me. (And when I told them,
> they didn't believe me, . . .) . . . Wait a minute I must just go and give
> one of our girls here a smack, she has just tried to strangle me, because
> I am singing. She tells me the cats at night time make a better tune. Isn't
> that rude? Yes, don't argue Edie, it is rude.[45]

And a similarly irrepressible Daisy Parsons, by 10.30 a.m. just arrived
at 'biz.' at 9 Mincing Lane, a multi-occupied City office building with
dozens of tenants, gets a note off to Edie to thank her for a weekend
spent in Palmers Green: 'You should see my matter-of-facty appearance
now – fierce countenance, "Plain Jane" clothes, nobody to laugh at or
with, work staring me in the optics, telephone buzzing, the constant
tramp of many a man's feet, &c.' Not all those feet kept on walking.
Though describing herself as 'a fat, bewhiskered, ungainly old-maid',
just a year later Daisy writes that 'you will be surprised to hear that I
am shortly to become engaged to the General Manager at my office &
I am going away to Rayleigh [in Essex] this weekend as he is staying
there for part of his holiday'. By that time, the spring of 1918, Edie
too had left Park Buildings, probably for the Women's Army Corps.
We shall meet some of these young women again.[46]

The vivacity and exuberance of munitionettes dancing on the canteen
tables, or of office girls' laughter spilling onto every page of their
correspondence, marked a big change in the life chances of London's
young women. No doubt something of this had gone on before. But
the great difference was that it was happening to so very many. Change
had begun from that first full day of war on 5 August 1914. By 1915
it was in full flood and affecting every sinew of London life.

6

ZEPPELIN NIGHTS: 1915

Thank God that 1914 is dead and done with! It has been a year of misery and world wide disaster. May we never see such another year in our day![1]

H. Rider Haggard's feeling of good riddance to a year of 'so black a record' seems to have been widely shared. It had ended with torrential rain and strong winds, causing destruction of property, flooding in the Thames Valley and even loss of life in London, a harbinger of the filthy weather that would play so large and so dire a part in the fortunes of war for nearly four years to come. Happily no one could tell what 1915 would bring. It was generally welcomed in with parties, music and dancing in the West End hotels, nightspots, clubs and restaurants. Crowds gathered outside St Paul's as its bells, and thousands more across London, rang in the New Year – Virginia Woolf, in lodgings at The Green in Richmond, at first 'thought they were ringing for a victory'.[2] Roland Leighton, a brilliant schoolboy due to start at Oxford but now in the uniform of a 2nd Lieutenant of the 11th Sherwood Foresters, stood under a bright full moon with the crowds around Eros at Piccadilly Circus to see the New Year in:

I had that feeling of extreme loneliness one is so often conscious of in a large crowd. There was very little demonstration; two Frenchmen standing up in a cab singing the 'Marseillaise'; a few women and some soldiers behind me holding hands and softly humming 'Auld Lang Syne.' When twelve o'clock struck there was only a little shudder among the crowd and a distant muffled cheer and then everyone seemed to melt away again, leaving me standing there with tears in my eyes and feeling absolutely wretched.[3]

There was a resoluteness about the Londoners' welcome to 1915, for Leighton and the crowds melting away knew that they had a war to get on with. Despite the uncertainties that all felt lay ahead, and with little belief that the war's end was near at hand – betting among City men at Lloyd's was three to one against it being over by the end of 1915 – there grew a sense that Londoners were learning to live with the war. Frederick Robinson, the City merchant, felt in January that people were getting used to it. He thought things were going on pretty much as usual, with brisk shopping in the January sales. The streets, thought Michael MacDonagh, were 'as full of traffic as ever. Omnibuses and motor cars abound. The pavements are thronged with pedestrians.' Some things could indeed be relied upon: two weeks after New Year Arnold Bennett journeyed to town from Thorpe-le-Soken in Essex, taking the train to Liverpool Street – 'Train late. I have never known the 10.7 not late.' A few months later, in London with his wife, Marguerite, he too found 'Crowds of women in Oxford Street and Regent Street just as usual, and shops just as usual'.[4]

This appearance of normality during daytime in the West End up to May 1915 was reassuring to some but an affront to many. 'Not a theatre has been closed and the restaurants seem to be doing a greater business than ever,' noted R. D. Blumenfeld in March. 'The general complaint is that people are taking this war altogether too easily . . . altogether life, particularly in the metropolis, is calm and easy.' And there were those in the metropolis, and doubtless many more beyond, for whom the war was really an irrelevance, at worst an inconvenience. In early 1915 it hardly touched John Middleton Murry and Katherine Mansfield, a more unworldly couple even London could not offer. In March, or thereabouts:

I got great satisfaction from painting and preparing our new rooms at Elgin Crescent. I took a simple pleasure in making them beautiful against her return [from France], and considering how little money there was to spend, I did it pretty well. Since we could not afford to have our bits of furniture removed from Rose Tree Cottage [in Sussex], it had nearly all to be done again. I bought the scrubbiest pieces of furniture if I saw they were soundly made, knocked them to pieces and reconstructed them, crudely but effectively; and I paid for it all by living chiefly on porridge and bread and butter . . . I lived entirely to myself, not unhappily, for when Katherine was happy I was never ill-contented.[5]

There were other indications that, despite the war, London was going on 'as usual'. It continued, for instance, to modernise, in some ways at least. In February, Dr Johnson's house in Gough Square, off Fleet Street, saved from demolition and restored by Cecil Harmsworth, was opened to the public. That same month, after much debate stretching back years, the new London Ambulance Service was started by the LCC, the first motor ambulances operating from Fulham with five other stations established at Bloomsbury, Shoreditch, Newington, Lee and Brixton; its arrival could not have been more opportune – in 1915 it received 2,405 calls, in 1918 15,911. On the London Underground, escalators made their first widespread appearance in the new stations opening on the Bakerloo Line extension from Paddington to Queen's Park. And between Paddington and Waterloo construction continued underground on the Post Office railway, despite attempts to kill the scheme by MPs worried about the cost.[6]

Other less wholesome aspects of London life continued 'as usual' too. On New Year's Day an inquest in north London reached a verdict on the death of Mrs Margaret Lloyd. A bride of just one day, she was found dead in her bath on 18 December 1914 at 14 Bismarck Road, Highgate – now Waterlow Road, the name changed in 1917 for patriotic reasons. The jury's verdict of death by misadventure seemed to rest Mrs Lloyd easily in her grave. But the unusual circumstances resulted in a paragraph in the *News of the World*. It was read by the father of a young woman, Mrs Smith, who had suffered a similar fate at Blackpool a year earlier. He contacted his local police station at Aylesbury, who referred the matter to Scotland Yard. In early January it came to the notice of Detective Inspector Arthur Neil of Y (Highgate) Division, then busy with other inquiries and 'in the thick of interning aliens'. 'Mr Lloyd' had left Bismarck Road immediately after the death and could not easily be found. But after careful watching for several days in that bitter February he was arrested in Shepherd's Bush and eventually charged with murder. While in custody a third case came to light of a new bride drowning in her bath at Herne Bay, Kent, in 1912.

The trial of George Joseph Smith for what the press quickly dubbed the 'Brides in the Bath Murders' was a sensation. The case filled newspaper columns that spring and crowded the Old Bailey and the streets around from 22 June, when the trial opened. Smith, originally from Bethnal Green, his father an insurance agent, was a villain in a classic tradition of English murder, his victims killed for their money rather than sexual gratification. His trial proved the most complex murder hearing in English legal history to that point, requiring 112 witnesses brought from over forty different towns of whom eighteen were solicitors or their clerks and fourteen were bank officials. A strong element in the sensation was Smith's attractiveness to women, seducing so many with astonishing ease. Women flocked to the trial by bus, tube, train and taxi: 'never in the whole of my life,' Arthur Neil later recalled, 'have I seen so many women present. Women of all ages clamoured, crowded and surged the public entrances to get into the Court, many were turned away.' Smith was convicted and in August duly hanged.[7]

Such interest in the fate of one man when so many were suffering and dying daily was an irony that struck observers at the time and after.[8] Perhaps, like West End shopping, there was comfort in the distraction offered by London 'as usual', of a return to the 'normal' preoccupations of the city before 4 August 1914 changed everything. For so very much of normal London life had been taken away. 'There will be no London season this year as it is known in its acceptable form,' noted R. D. Blumenfeld. 'Hospital visits take the place of luncheon-parties . . .' There was no opera or ballet at Covent Garden, closed for the duration and used as a furniture store by the Office of Works, and no street musicians to delight children in the backstreets, the vanished 'German bands' now followed by the organ grinder more gainfully employed elsewhere. The end of professional football after the FA Cup was followed by no Derby at Epsom, no Ascot, no Goodwood, no Boat Race on the Thames and a summer with no cricket – 'It seems almost impossible,' thought Blumenfeld.[9]

Indeed, normal life had altered in so many ways. London at night was alien and dangerous, even Whitehall 'so dark now in some places' that government ministers leaving their offices had to feel for the pavement's edge 'with one's foot'. Those things that rich Londoners had once relied upon as paragons of service now proved distractingly inefficient. 'Sharp skirmish with Harrods on telephone about my skirt,' Cynthia Asquith, the Prime Minister's daughter-in-law, complained to her diary in April. 'Had hair waved at Emile. Went to Harrods – found it closed and skirt just dispatched to fictitious address in Conduit Street.' At the Reform Club, hit as was everyone in London by food prices 45 per cent higher at the end of 1915 than before the war, by coal at its most expensive yet and by staff shortages, many members resigned and could not be replaced: 'Candidates are not coming forward to join this

1. Outside Buckingham Palace, around 11pm on Tuesday 4 August 1914. At first the London crowds were muted and far from enthusiastic for war. But Germany's invasion of Belgium made British intervention an inescapable matter of honour for most. Here a jubilant crowd demonstrates solidarity with King and nation at the moment war is declared.

2. Anti-war feeling hardly survived the invasion of Belgium but had been popular and vociferous for the few days before. Here the veteran socialist Keir Hardie addresses workers and others in Trafalgar Square on the Sunday before war breaks out.

3. Young men queue to volunteer, Whitehall, August 1914. Some 107,000 Londoners had been recruited to the colours by mid-November, one of the highest proportions of the population in the country: clerks, shop assistants and school teachers were prominent among them.

4. Khaki in the London streets. Overnight, soldiers seemed to be everywhere as reservists and territorials were called to the colours. They were a startling sight at first, as here in the Strand in the first few days of war.

5. Soldiers entraining for France, Victoria Station, late 1914. Vast numbers of troops travelled to London from all over the country to take trains to the Western Front. This, for many, would be their last contact with the capital.

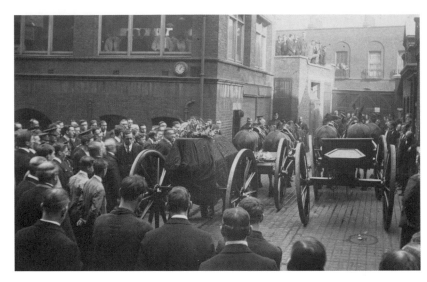

6. Funeral of Belgian soldiers, London Hospital, late 1914. Wounded Belgian soldiers were quickly shipped by British forces to London's hospitals. They were soon followed by thousands of Belgian refugees, received with considerable sympathy and generosity in London.

7. German internees' beds, Great Hall of Alexandra Palace. Ally Pally was turned into the largest internment camp for German men arrested in London, not because they imposed a threat to the war effort but because their presence was deeply resented by the Londoners.

8. Anti-German riots, May 1915. Following the sinking of the liner *Lusitania* which saw the loss of over 1,000 lives, rioting and looting broke out all over London, the worst of it in the East End, as here on Chrisp Street, Poplar.

9. We Are Russians. Any foreign-owned shop ran the risk of attack during anti-German rioting. Here an East-End shopkeeper has sought to maintain immunity from the Londoners' fury.

10. Zeppelins on their way to bomb London, 1915–16. The picture shows L32 on its fatal last flight to London. It never reached the city, as it was brought down in flames over Billericay, killing the crew of twenty-two.

11. The Gotha bomber. This was the most destructive weapon in the German armoury against London, operating from May 1917 to May 1918. In all, 668 Londoners were killed in the raids by planes and Zeppelins and 1,938 were injured.

12. Odhams printing press disaster, Long Acre, 28 January 1918. Many industrial premises were used as air raid shelters, as here where some 600 were huddled when a 300-kg bomb exploded in the street outside, killing thirty-eight and injuring eighty-five.

13. Seventh Avenue, Manor Park, May 1918. It was not only central London that suffered from the bombing. Damage proved indiscriminate and occurred right across London's vast built-up area, as here in suburban East Ham.

14. Methuselah doing his bit. No one and nothing was immune from enrolment in London's total war effort, as here at London Zoo, where a tortoise reminded visitors of the country's need for armaments.

15. The Women's War Pageant, Saturday 17 July 1915. This great march, said to be 50,000 strong, demanded that women be allowed to play their full part in the war effort, especially in making munitions. Here 'Belgium' reminds the crowds what the war is being fought for.

or any other Club', a judge who had tendered his resignation was told. Others stayed and complained, like Sir Walter Runciman, outgoing President of the Board of Trade, who called the coffee room 'inferior to a fourth-rate cafe'.[10]

For ordinary Londoners too daily life brought multiplying frustrations as 1915 wore on. The standard of street sweeping and refuse collection deteriorated through labour shortages and transport problems, with foul-smelling accumulations at depots. Councils put up posters to warn that snow shovelling would be impossible so householders should themselves clear the pavements in front of their premises. Road maintenance in Stepney got so bad that the London Hospital formally complained about the discomfort to wounded soldiers brought in by ambulance. 'Economies' became general practice across London government, dominated as most boroughs were by conservative (Municipal Reform) politicians. From May 1915 a party truce and coalition at the LCC enthusiastically embraced economy, despite the vocal opposition of the newly formed London Labour Party and its active young secretary, Herbert Morrison. The City of Westminster, for instance, closed some libraries, reduced opening hours, cancelled newspaper subscriptions and shut 'news rooms'. And Hackney Council caused such a furore by proposing to close public gardens on winter Sundays – at a weekly saving of just £2 – that the idea was abandoned. The government, though, pressed ahead with a charge of a penny entrance fee for Kew Gardens on the grounds of 'national economy'.[11]

Added to these inconveniences were the limits imposed on daily life by DORA and other war regulations involving hundreds of prosecutions in the London police courts for infringements of the drink and lighting restrictions. And there was a steady trickle of offences stimulated by the circumstances of war: crying false news of 'Great British Victories' so that newsvendors could sell more papers; wheedling money by false pretences from war charities for soldiers' and sailors' families or for Belgian refugees; and there was the nerve-racking prospect of being passed false £1 or 10s notes, that new currency required by the disappearance of gold since August 1914. Some 60,000 forged notes were thought to be circulating in London in 1915. The printing works were eventually traced to a backyard workshop in Vartry Road, South Tottenham; three men from Stoke Newington and Finsbury were sent to prison, but not before the works were visited by the Chancellor of the Exchequer, who turned the printing-machine handle to utter a forged note, watched by the secretary of the Bank of England, whose 'signature' each note bore.[12]

These domestic aggravations of war were added to from February when the industrial peace that had so surprisingly broken out in August 1914 seemed to fracture. The rising cost of food and other necessities, and long hours and high-pressured labour in many industries, failed to secure adequate reward in the eyes of many workers and their trade unions. Pay claims bombarded employers in both private and public sectors. Employers too often proved parsimonious in their response, bolstered by the demands of 'economy' and fuelling mistrust that already some capitalists were 'making fortunes' out of the war.[13] In London the worst disruption was caused by a strike on the LCC's tramways that began to shut down the network from 14 May. The strike was over pay and conditions and the inequitable distribution of a cost of living 'war bonus' that only applied to better-off employees. There were serious repercussions in Woolwich, where munitions workers depended almost entirely on the trams for their journey to work. Much patriotic pressure was brought to bear on the strikers, many of whom drifted back. The LCC sacked strikers of military age and hired new men, leading to some violence and stoning of 'blackleg' trams. By 1 June the LCC conceded the main demands and the strikers returned to work, though the position of sacked men was still unresolved. It was around this time too that ominous signs of disaffection began to appear in the Metropolitan Police: three Greenwich PCs were fined by the Commissioner for recruiting to 'an unauthorised association styling itself the National Union of Police and Prison Officers'.[14]

But most unsettling of all was news from the front. The Battle of Neuve Chapelle from 10 to 12 March, a British offensive bringing only marginal gains but large numbers of casualties, broke open the political unity that had marked the months since the beginning of the war. It was followed by the first German poison gas attack, at Ypres on 22 April. British losses this spring were horrific – 24,500 casualties in March, 31,000 in April, nearly 66,000 in May, the worst single month of the war from the outbreak to July 1916. Indeed, May was a month of general crisis: the anti-German riots following the sinking of the *Lusitania*; a report by *The Times*'s war correspondent that the shortage of shells was a 'fatal blow' to the British Army's chance of success; rumours of division in the Cabinet; the *Daily Mail* burned at the Stock Exchange for criticising Lord Kitchener's performance as war minister – all combined to unleash 'an orgy of political intrigue as Great Britain had not seen in living memory'. It was merely stifled not quenched by the formation of a coalition government under the continued leadership of Herbert Asquith at the end of the month.[15]

The nerve of many Londoners was badly shaken by these events and others this May. The young men of London suffered greatly in attacks at Aubers Ridge and Festubert. These battles engaged for the first time large numbers of Territorials and New Army volunteers. The 13th, 23rd and 24th battalions of the London Regiment, with others from the Middlesex Regiment and the Surreys, sustained large numbers of casualties from 9 May till nearly the end of the month. Even worse was to come at the Battle of Loos in September, when once more the London Territorials were 'squandered' in a fruitless and badly led but heroic offensive against intact barbed wire and countless machine guns.[16] British losses through September and October totalled 85,000. Philip Gibbs watched the 47th (London) Division move to the battle lines at Loos, 'men whose souls had been shaped by all the influences of environment, habit, and tradition in which I had been born and bred' and who 'did freakish and fantastic things of courage'. As they went into battle it was reported that a 'London Irishman' dribbled a football across no-man's-land and 'held it for 1,400 yards': 'Some of them were blowing mouth-organs, playing the music-hall song of "Hullo, hullo, it's a different girl again!" and the "Robert E. Lee," until one after another a musician fell in a crumpled heap.'[17]

Early in May, Cynthia Asquith, up from the country and staying with a friend in the West End, noted a different feeling about the place. 'London, I think, looks distinctly more abnormal now – more soldiers, more bandages and limps, and more nurses – quite a sensational sense of strain.' It was at this point that the private diaries so many Londoners had resolved to keep since the outbreak of war became peppered with a tragic litany of loss. 'In May we heard that Geoffrey Butcher had been killed by gas,' noted Mary Coules of Acton; 'he died in hospital after suffering fearful agonies . . . Two of the sons of Mother's cousins in Cambridgeshire were also killed in May.' Georgina Lee, in South Kensington, fortunately placed with a husband too old to serve and a son still in his cradle, nonetheless had to record the loss of friends and acquaintances: 'I was shocked to hear that Alastair Dunsmure had been killed, a boy of 20, in the Cameron Highlanders' (February); 'We heard today of the death of another young officer, Captain Johnston, Eugene

Crombie's first cousin' (April); 'Heard today that another young relation of the Wason family, Walter Andrews, has been killed in the war' (April); 'The second son of [her husband's] partner Henry Bolton, a boy of 18, just out of Dartmouth has been killed at the Dardanelles. It's terrible. He had been out there barely a month. All the boys are being killed' (June); her husband's 'first cousin Dick Lee, who was in the 10th Suffolk Regiment, has just been killed in Flanders' (November). Edith Bunbury of Camberwell noted 'Hart's death in the Casualty List on Saty. – for June 16th . . . Have written to his mother.' She took some comfort when she heard that he died 'leading a charge. Grand. A man of nerves – musical.' But in September she noted two more, one dear to her, 'Shot by a German air machine gun' and 'Geoffrey Strahan killed – Dardanelles.' That month too the Mayfair socialite Duff Cooper mourned the loss of friends at Loos and just after, one of them Yvo Charteris, Cynthia Asquith's beloved younger brother, only nineteen; John Kipling, the writer's boy, was also killed at Loos, though reported 'missing' in that dreadful no-man's-land of not-knowing faced by so many families at the time.[18]

Large numbers of the wounded from the Western Front and beyond were sent to London for treatment at the city's general hospitals, the growing number of military hospitals and the innumerable private hospitals for officers set up in the homes of the London rich. Frederick Brittain, who enlisted in the Royal Army Medical Corps in 1914 aged twenty-one, was a nurse at the Military Hospital, Chelsea. He and his comrades were quickly hit by the shockwaves of any great engagement. After Neuve Chapelle, 'About 60 wounded arrived at midnight, so we got to bed about 2 a.m.' After Aubers Ridge and Festubert, 'A trainload of wounded arrived including many lifeguards. Eleven came to our ward, one with a foot blown off'; other injuries included 'shrapnel wound in leg (red lotion), shell wound in the small of the neck (red ointment), and a wound in the top of the back (carbolic gauze)'. London's hospital system was at breaking point by May. The War Office told the London Hospital that 15,000 wounded were lying at Boulogne for want of beds in England and begged the hospital for help – it was unable to offer any.[19]

Indeed, the war's shock waves reached London from further afield. On August Bank Holiday Monday Brittain noted, 'Australian wounded arrived from Dardanelles', and similar shipments continued throughout the year. One ANZAC officer, Captain Ralph Ingram Moore, for instance, invalided from Gallipoli with enteric fever, arrived by ship at Bristol and was taken by casualty train to Paddington, coming in at 5.30 a.m. at the end of October: 'Train journey very cold,' he noted in his diary. At Paddington he had to wait till 8 o'clock for the discharge officer but found some comfort in the station buffet for sailors and soldiers. He was taken by 'private limousine', 'beautifully fitted out', to 3rd London General Hospital at Wandsworth: 'Glad my 1st sight of England was on fine day.' Moore and the many other ANZAC soldiers and officers in London came under the care, for medical and other matters, of their HQ quickly established at Horseferry Road, Westminster.[20]

The private agony accumulating in diaries and the suffering of individual soldiers hospitalised in the capital were reflected in new ways of registering public grief in London during 1915. Names of fallen old boys were read out at school assemblies and in February it was said that head teachers of 'Most of the elementary schools throughout London' were displaying names on rolls of honour. In London's town halls the names of staff dead or wounded were similarly read out at council meetings and recorded in the minutes; rolls of honour commemorating all the fallen of the borough began to appear outside council buildings also from around February. Some of those killed were special enough to be commemorated in different ways, chief among them in 1915 Nurse Edith Cavell, executed by firing squad for assisting British soldiers behind German lines – 'Edith Cavell, DAWN, Brussels, October 12, 1915', as her statue near the National Portrait Gallery puts it. She had obtained her London nurse's ticket at the London Hospital in 1895–6 and then been assistant matron at the Shoreditch Poor Law Infirmary from 1903 to 1906. At the London Hospital a nursing home was named after her at Queen Alexandra's personal request and at the Infirmary a plaque was later unveiled in her memory. A memorial service was held for her at St Paul's at the end of the month; Cynthia Asquith thought the crowd outside 'disgusting, just like Derby Day'.[21]

Most moving for everyone, perhaps, were the rolls of honour published in some (not all) London weekly newspapers giving local names and, by regiment, in national dailies. The journalist Sir Henry Lucy of *Punch* thought that these 'lengthening columns' in September 1915

form a chapter in the history of the war whose sadness no victory by land or sea can assuage. Every entry, whether recording the death of distinguished officers or obscure privates, is a tragedy blighting a home. The very multitude of names of killed, wounded or missing does something to blunt the sharpness of sympathy. Death on the battlefield has become so much a matter of course as to deprive it of some of its terrors.[22]

Not for all, though, did these rolls anaesthetise sympathy. C. F. G. Masterman, a former MP for West Ham (North) and South-West Bethnal Green, now Director of Propaganda at Wellington House and a man naturally plagued by misery, 'used to say that he felt, if only the war would end, he would never feel melancholy again. Every list contained the possibility of a friend killed.'[23]

Things would only get worse. And for the Londoners they did so with dramatic effect that very May. For on the night of Monday the 31st the people of London found their homes and themselves on the war's front line. They came under fire from aerial bombardment.

The threat posed by Zeppelins had been recognised from the very beginning of the war, as we have seen. The German navy's intention to bomb '"those parts of London which are of military importance"', especially the riverside from Woolwich to the London Docks, became known to British Intelligence by the end of 1914. On 1 January 1915 Churchill warned the Cabinet of 'an attack on London by airships on a great scale at an early opportunity'. He was not reassuring: 'the Air Department of the Admiralty must make it plain that they are quite powerless to prevent such an attack if it is launched with good fortune and in favourable weather conditions.' Within days, this official nervousness had infected the whole of London. A rumour that Zeppelins had reached Colchester caused consternation in the East End as early as 3 or 4 January. On the 10th the London Hospital received a warning from the War Office to expect air raid casualties. A week or so later, Marie Lowndes dined with relatives of Reginald McKenna, the Home Secretary,

> where I was told that Mr. Gatty [a London historian] had heard from the Duke of Westminster that Winston Churchill says he expects a fleet of a *hundred Zeppelins* to leave for England on the eve of the German Emperor's birthday, January 26th! He expects seventy to be destroyed, but believes that thirty will reach London and he estimates the casualties at 10,000 to 12,000! Several people are so affected by this tale that they have already sent their children away into the country.

Not to Great Yarmouth or King's Lynn, one hopes, where next night, the 19th, the first air raid on Britain took place, two Zeppelins dropping bombs that killed four people and injured sixteen more. 'God grant they may never reach London,' Hallie Miles selflessly confided to her diary. The *Hackney and Kingsland Gazette* reassured its readers that 'Experts are practically unanimous that a raid on London will be attempted within the next few weeks, but it is consoling to find them equally unanimous in the opinion that it will be doomed to failure.'[24]

Consoling or otherwise, the January scare faded away. The Zeppelins seemed to have other targets, especially on Tyneside and the Humber, and again in East Anglia. The irksome darkness in London, the city's only effective defence in the eyes of the Admiralty, continued under protest. The unrelieved winter gloom and a steady rise in street accidents encouraged many to press for a relaxation of the lighting restrictions, without success. Comforting rumours began to circulate that led some to wonder whether the threat had been exaggerated: Cynthia Asquith picked up a 'rather interesting titbit of war gossip – that the only reason why there has been no Zeppelin raid on London is that the Kaiser absolutely refuses to countenance it on account of all his relations there'. Others, such as Hallie Miles, continued to prepare their own defences should the Kaiser change his notoriously unsteady mind: 'all the basements and cellars' at her house, probably in Bloomsbury, 'are being got ready to flee to', with 'a lot of furs and rugs and blankets'; 'Our house-maid has had a course of "first-aid" so she is in charge of the wounded, should there be any.'[25]

But in May, that anxious month, Londoners again had cause to steel their nerves. On the 10th, 17th and 26th Zeppelins bombed Southend and other places on the Thames Estuary. These seemed like preparations for a raid on London, and so they were interpreted in the metropolis. Yet perhaps partly because of the far from catastrophic results of bombing elsewhere, and partly because there was so much else to worry about, these warnings failed to produce the near-panic of January. Rather, it seemed like time for gritted teeth. By the third week in May town halls in London were warned by the Commissioner of Police that attacks were now 'probable'. The papers reported his advice that people should stay indoors during raids and keep lower doors and windows closed to shut out poison gas.[26]

On the last night in May what had been feared for so long now arrived. A single Zeppelin, LZ38, approaching from the east and with the aid of a full moon, reached London at around 10.50 p.m. and for some forty-five minutes looped over the inner north-east suburbs of Stoke Newington, Dalston, Hoxton, Shoreditch, Whitechapel, Stepney, West Ham and Leytonstone. From a high altitude, unseen and barely heard, it dropped eighty-nine incendiary bombs and thirty 'man-killing grenades'. The first bomb known to have been dropped on London hit 16 Alkham Road, Stoke Newington; it was an incendiary, quickly put out and causing no casualties. But shortly after this another incendiary hit 33 Cowper Road nearby, killing poor Elsie Leggatt, not four years old, and her sister May, who died in hospital of burns a few days later. There would be other fatalities that night, seven in all, including a couple burned to death in a house at Balls Pond Road; and in Christian Street, Stepney, two Jewish children on their way home from the cinema were killed sheltering in a doorway. The Londoners met the raids with that unpredictable mixture of sangfroid and blind terror that characterised their response to aerial warfare throughout the First World War. Three incendiaries hit the roof of the Empire Music Hall in Shoreditch High Street, causing damage but no fire; the manager made an address from the stage to calm nerves and the band 'played lively airs while the audience left the house in an orderly manner'. Not far away, in Hoxton, where there was considerable damage, and in other parts of the East End, according to Sylvia Pankhurst, 'Panic ran rampant.' Next day there were attacks on German bakers' shops, their owners assaulted in the streets; crowds of sightseers flocked from west to east to assess the damage done by this new form of warfare; and crowds of children roamed around 'picking up shrapnel' and digging bomb fragments out of the roadway.[27]

There were four further Zeppelin raids on London in 1915, each of increasing severity. Around 10.30 on the clear starlit night of 17 August a lone Zeppelin killed ten people in Leyton and Leytonstone with a mix of incendiary and explosive bombs. Then for two nights running there were raids causing considerable damage and loss of life. On the night of 7–8 September, two airships, one a Zeppelin and the other an elderly wooden vessel, raided the riverside. A sailing barge, the *John Evelyn*, working the coastal trade between London and Suffolk, was hit by an incendiary, its master and mate both dying in hospital from extensive burns; there was a sustained attack on the industrial districts of the Isle of Dogs, Rotherhithe and Deptford; and a dreadful tragedy in one of London's poorest and roughest slum streets where, at 34 Hughes Fields, Deptford, five members of the Beechey family, mother, father and three children, were wiped out by a high-explosive bomb. In all, eighteen people were killed by just forty-five devices. The London Ambulance Service, on war duty for the first time, sent four ambulances to numerous incidents, ferrying patients from the *John Evelyn* and elsewhere to Poplar Hospital and to Guy's on the South Bank.[28]

The next night's raid on 8–9 September brought the war to the heart of the City of London. A single Zeppelin, L13, commanded by the intrepid and determined Heinrich Mathy, carried incendiary and high-explosive bombs including one weighing 300 kilos, the most destructive weapon to be deployed against London to that point. His first bombs were dropped on Golders Green, then two more near Euston Station fell with little damage on Bloomsbury, where Hallie Miles spent the night in her basement. The first fatality was in Lambs Conduit Passage, Red Lion Street, where the Dolphin public house and a nearby bank were damaged: the Dolphin proudly showed off its clock, stopped at 10.49 and never to go again, for a generation to come. Major fires broke out in Holborn in which a fireman lost his life. Mathy's haphazard trail of destruction then turned south towards the City. Just before 11 p.m. four young children were killed in a tenement block at Portpool Lane, Clerkenwell Road, and shortly after two men were killed leaving the Admiral Carter public house in Bartholomew Close, Smithfield. It was a night of intense drama, with the London sky reddened by fire, a dozen searchlights seeking and at last holding Mathy's ship showing yellow in the glare, hundreds of thousands of Londoners (including Prime Minister Asquith from a window at 10 Downing Street) staring spellbound and anti-aircraft guns opening up all around, including the great 8-inch naval guns at Woolwich. The hunted Mathy decided to head for home and so turned east towards the sea. As he passed over Liverpool Street Station on the eastern borders of the City, he let go four bombs, one hitting the railway lines but three dropping to the west and north of the station. Two of these, as ill luck would have it, hit motor buses still working their routes, killing nine crew, passengers and bystanders between them. In all, twenty-two died that night from the bombing and eighty-seven were injured; twenty-nine fires were started.[29]

The devastation in the City, more accessible to most middle-class observers than Hoxton, Leyton or Deptford, was much visited and marvelled at over subsequent days. Mary Coules and a friend, sightseeing from Acton, saw 'half a house hanging across a passage in Coleman Street, with chairs & a sofa mixed up in the beams. In Moorgate there was not a window whole – in fact, the windows everywhere have come off very badly.' Streets in the City were reportedly two inches deep in broken glass and 1,200 panes were smashed at St Bartholomew's Hospital. 'People in London appear much excited,' thought Viscount Sandhurst, 'and there is a great rush to get into the insurance offices for houses, property, etc.'[30]

There then followed a hiatus, more by luck than forethought because at least two German attacks broke down before reaching London in September. But the fifth and final raid of 1915 proved the most destructive of all. On the night of Wednesday 13 October, beginning just before 9 p.m., three Zeppelins made separate attacks on London. One dropped bombs on East Croydon, causing extensive damage to houses and killing nine people; another, L13, again commanded by Mathy, hit the riverside from the Surrey Docks to Woolwich, where one person was killed at the Arsenal and a dozen injured. The third, L15, a new machine commanded by Joachim Breithaupt, approached London from the north-west, its main target the Admiralty between Whitehall and the Mall, just south of Trafalgar Square. Breithaupt overshot and his bombs fell mainly on the theatre district along the Strand and Aldwych before he turned north along Chancery Lane and Gray's Inn Road and then eastwards across the City to the coast. Seventeen people were killed when a bomb struck the roadway in Wellington Street, the Strand, either pedestrians or in buildings nearby. In all thirty-eight were killed in central London. It could have been worse. The theatres were crowded as usual that night. None sustained a direct hit. Even so, in some 'disorder reigned', in others the show went phlegmatically on, the performers calming nerves in the auditorium. Outside, though, according to Rose Macaulay writing soon after, Chancery Lane and no doubt other places 'had been the scene of that wild terror and shrieking confusion which is characterised by a euphemistic press as "no panic"'. Viscount Sandhurst was dining that night in the Ritz and felt the same: 'It is said they create no panic; I've only witnessed one raid – lots of women in tears and almost in hysterics running about not knowing what they were about.' He reported, probably from others' accounts, 'panic in the tube stations'. Now the former irritation over lighting restrictions was replaced by the popular conviction that they did not go far enough: 'A lighted cigarette-end was enough at this time to gain a man a blow.' And in working-class districts those few street lamps left burning were smashed by anxious residents during and after raids.[31]

The air raids of 1915 understandably provoked fresh adverse comment about the German way of waging war. 'Another Example of German "Kultur"' ran a headline in one local paper after the very first raid of 31 May – 'this pre-eminently German spectre', as Violet Hunt and Ford Madox Ford put it in their fantasy novel of the time, *Zeppelin Nights*. The horror of babies burned in their beds recalled and amplified the stories of German atrocities in Belgium that had been so prominent an element of press coverage earlier in the war. On the other hand, German propaganda that London was a 'fortress' and so a legitimate war target was hard to gainsay. We have seen how London's industries and hundreds of thousands of its 'civilians' were making munitions of war or carrying out other essential tasks that made the Western Front capable of fighting at all. Virtually the whole of the nation's war effort worked through, often travelled through, London. The smooth operation of its myriad communications systems and the unfettered energy of its productive power were both indispensable to the purpose of total war. In these circumstances, London as a fortress was not inapt. And in attacking this most powerful of all British fortresses the primitive bomb-aiming equipment of the time (and for many decades after) meant that 'military' and 'civilian' targets could never be satisfactorily distinguished.[32]

But how closely was this fortress guarded? This was the great doubt raised by these first raids. None had been repulsed. None, as far as Londoners knew, had been deterred. The noisy response of naval guns had been on the face of it ineffective. The British airmen had proved incapable of bringing down what, from the ground, seemed very fat sitting ducks. Criticism was vocal, near-ubiquitous and increasingly exasperated as raid followed raid. In Parliament many MPs pressed for the War Office to take London's air defences away from an apparently supine Admiralty; the latter's new arrangements, involving a single up-to-date anti-aircraft gun brought over from Paris and a fresh leader, Admiral Sir Percy Scott, seemed too little too late to many. In any event, even his hands were fettered: the red tape that beset so much wartime administration seemed to be throttling initiative at London's expense. As Scott wrote to Arthur Balfour, who had replaced Churchill at the Admiralty after the Gallipoli fiasco:

> Up to last week, I was led to believe that the Admiralty had ordered guns for the defence of London. On Friday, the 15th [October], you informed me that they had not done so. I at once ordered some guns. The firms with which I placed the order wrote to the Admiralty for confirmation. The Admiralty have not confirmed the order.

And this, in any event, was after the Zeppelins had bolted for 1915, the last raid of the year having taken place two days earlier.[33]

New forces, though, did come in. On 15 September there were just twelve guns protecting London's built-up area, all at fixed points; on 13 November there were twenty-four, nine of them mobile. Each gun had accompanying searchlight crews, frequently manned by special constables. A handful of guns were paraded at the Lord Mayor's Show in November to reassure the citizens. It was not without effect. Despite dangers from anti-aircraft shrapnel and despite any tangible results against the enemy, the Londoners unsurprisingly found their guns a comfort. Bermondsey residents christened their local gun – rather astonishingly perched at the centre of the upper crossing of Tower Bridge – 'Barking Charlie'.[34] And from 1 October London's lighting restrictions were made more stringent, with draconian penalties for defaulters, whether householders, shopkeepers or motorists. For many it merely added to the terrors: 'the blackness that envelopes London is a sort of nightmare,' thought Hallie Miles. 'I get home as early as I can, for the darkness horrifies me.'[35]

The most vexed question of all was whether there should be public warnings of raids. Scotland Yard was alerted by telephone when Admiralty coastal observation stations detected Zeppelins apparently headed for London. The London Fire Brigade and Woolwich Arsenal were then alerted and some private warnings given by telephone to important firms, prominent politicians and others. It was all very hit and miss. St Bartholomew's Hospital, for instance, received their warnings from 'Miss Simmons, sister of chief of London Fire Brigade' and a good friend to the hospital. 'She gives the notice and the nurses are got out of bed and hurried into a cellar.' Despite agitation in press and Parliament, however, government resisted telling the public that a raid was impending: 'the dangers of issuing warnings far outweigh any advantages there might be,' Sir John Simon, Home Secretary, told the House of Commons in October after the raid on London's theatre district. The reasons were not for fear of panic, he said – though it is hard not to see in the official stance that mistrust of working people that had so characterised class relations before and during the war – but because intelligence of raids was unreliable and would lead to false alarms and wasteful disruption, and because people would fill the streets from curiosity and thus cause more casualties. Simon's views followed the advice he had received from the Commissioner of Police, Sir Edward Henry.[36]

Not all Londoners were satisfied at being kept so literally and meta-phorically in the dark. In Hackney, and no doubt other places, the dark streets and night fears – so reminiscent of eighteenth-century London, as a number of commentators remarked at the time – resurrected old traditions of self-help by 'watch and ward'. As early as the end of June a 'street patrol' of fifty-five volunteers was sharing 'the watch' in Rendlesham Road, Clapton, prepared to 'call out' residents who had responded to a leaflet asking if they wanted to be alerted in the event of a raid. Other streets were soon similarly organised. Despite some criticism of the move in the local paper as 'evidence of blue funk', the idea 'caught on' and received a fillip with the raids of early September, notwithstanding a cool response from the Metropolitan Police. From October these local initiatives were common in lower-middle-class streets of clerks, artisans and shopkeepers across Hackney. In the event, no more raids were launched against London that winter, although the Zeppelins were active elsewhere over England. It seems possible that the deployment of a small number of fighter aircraft near London, spotted by the Zeppelin crews on 13 October, did something to deflect pressure from the capital for a time.[37]

The Zeppelin raids, though leaving many people badly shaken, seem to have done little by themselves to dent Londoners' morale. But there were signs in London, and in the nation as a whole, that the appetite for war manifested in the first four or six months of the conflict could no longer be sustained. The news from the Western Front from March, and from Gallipoli after lengthening casualty lists among London Territorials in August, brought home the risks and sacrifices of volun-teering for the forces as nothing else could do. From April, at Kitchener's behest and as part of the 'Great Patriotic Fortnight' that same month, the mayors of London boroughs were urged to create local battalions of infantry and if possible artillery. These 'pals' battalions' – the term seems not to have been much used in London at the time – were locally recruited through the town halls and the money for at least some of their equipment, food and billeting was raised by local subscription until the War Office was ready to take over. By June the Shoreditch Battalion, for example, was 500 strong, with plans to recruit a further 850. The Borough of Hampstead, unable to find enough men for the infantry, formed an artillery battalion instead – 'Happy Hampstead Howitzers' they were dubbed by the mayor.[38]

In fact the results of these initiatives proved disappointing for the authorities. The war's demand for young men was now insatiable after the many reverses and great losses of 1915. A '"monster recruiting rally"' on 2 October, with 6,000 troops marching behind bands along five different routes in central London and the suburbs, tried to revive metropolitan volunteering under the banner 'Wake Up, London!' The weather was 'grey and damp' and Michael MacDonagh in his article for *The Times* confessed that the immediate results of the rally in the recruiting stations were 'meagre'. Privately, in his diary, he noted more worrying signs of division. The marches were accompanied by recruiting sergeants who approached any 'likely young man' in the crowd to cheers and shouts of '"Fall in!"' from the soldiers. 'Some, however, showed an ugly temper. I heard cries of execration hurled at young fellows who turned away, as most of them did, from the recruiting-sergeants.' A few days later a recruiting meeting at an amateur football match in the Clapton Orient ground in Hackney was addressed by the mayor of Bethnal Green, who had lost a son in the war; he called it '"Disgusting"' when 'crowds of young men surg[ed] out of the gates' while he was speaking. That same month, October, saw a revival of the white feather stunt that had made an appearance before the end of 1914.[39]

For some months already there had been talk of the necessity for conscription if too few volunteers came forward. The prospect revived for some middle-class observers those class fears that August 1914 had done so much to ease, for a time at least. Viscount Sandhurst, for one, thought conscription would be very difficult to implement 'in London, with its thick and shifting population, where I hear very bad accounts of that seething mass being ready for any mischief . . .' But towards the end of 1915 conscription began to look a near-certainty. In August a National Register was made of all men aged between fifteen and sixty-five not serving in the forces; in late October Lord Derby, in charge of recruiting, introduced a scheme for men not employed in essential war work to 'attest' their readiness to serve in the forces if called upon. The threat of forcible enlistment should insufficient men come forward could hardly have been plainer.[40]

The emerging shift from a war fought by volunteers to one fought by pressed men now revived the anti-war dissent that had stayed quiet, or nearly so, since August 1914. Anti-conscription provided a broader platform for criticism than pacifism or international socialism. It made it easier to mobilise public feeling in London to question, if not openly oppose, the war by the end of 1915. The rising number of anti-conscription meetings provoked a vicious response from conservative die-hards, whipped up by the 'Yellow Press', the *Daily Express* (with R. D. Blumenfeld as editor) publicising meetings of organisations like the Union of Democratic Control (UDC) and other groups as an incitement to direct action by partriots. A UDC meeting at the Memorial Hall, Farringdon Street, at the end of November was 'broken up with violence', and so was one in Ilford a week or two later where Ramsay MacDonald was a speaker.[41]

By the end of 1915, then, some cracks had begun to open in the united front that had so far characterised London's response to the war. The early signs of a return of industrial strife; the breakdown of public discipline and respect for property during the anti-German riots; the advantage being taken by some to reap unearned profit from war charities and war necessities; the unease caused by the Zeppelins and the inability of authority to deal with them; the frightful unending casualty lists and the caution they engendered among potential volunteers; and the political divisions in government and beyond over the way the war was being waged – all these pointed to an anxious and uncertain future.

The strain showed everywhere. Perhaps it was at its most expressive at the great railway stations of London, with their swirling torrents of men – on stretchers, on crutches, on leave with the mud of war still caked on their boots, on their way back grim-faced or devil-may-care as they took train once more for France. Around them all were the grieving and welcoming Londoners, women most visible of all. Many came not to see loved ones but merely to take it all in. Everyone knew this was a sight unique to this generation, this time, this city; and Londoners were drawn to it in droves, if only to witness.

At Victoria Station, a great centre for leave trains, 'There are people who have gone there every day to gaze at scenes which bring home to them as nothing else can the realities of war.' Hallie Miles lived close to Euston and felt the pulse of London at war almost through the soles of her feet – 'We always know when there is a great movement of troops taking place' because of the activity there: 'We hear an incessant muffled roar of trains all night; it is like the roaring of the sea.' Even so, she too visited Victoria for the spectacle and pity of it all, 'moving scenes that people can hardly speak of for their pathos'. A few felt more patriotism than pathos. Ella Bickersteth, a clergyman's wife, saw her son off from Victoria in November, one of '1,500 men and officers returning to the Front after leave'. She noted in her diary that 'What struck me most was the cheerful bravery of the women who sent their men off almost invariably with smiles.'[42]

But many found the experience too heart-rending to face. Sergeant-Major Rixon of the London Irish Rifles, a South Lambeth man with a wife and young son, would not let his family see him off from Victoria after a week's leave: 'May bore up like the brick she is until I had to say goodbye . . . I am glad she did not come to Victoria, as it would have been too much for her there, and if she had cracked up then I would not answer for myself . . .'[43] Nor was it all smiles for those wives who did see their husbands off. So many partings must have been overshadowed by loss or worry or regret or just the terrible strain of the moment. Lady Ian Hamilton said goodbye to her husband at Charing Cross Station on 13 March: General Sir Ian Hamilton was leaving to take command of Allied forces at Gallipoli.

> At the last moment I went up to Ian . . . and he turned hastily and kissed me through my veil, and I pulled it up and said: 'Not through my veil, darling, it is unlucky.' He kissed me again, but it had vexed and put him out, and he said impatiently: 'Why do you say that – too bad to say unlucky.' I felt awful and put my head in at the carriage door to say: 'I only did not want you to kiss me through my veil,' and he said rather crossly: 'Well, if it is unlucky you should not have said it.' This saddened me terribly . . . Frances Horner seized me, and said: 'Don't watch him out of sight, it's not lucky.'[44]

It was the mainline stations that perhaps made Londoners most of all seem 'as if we were in a garrison town', as Lucy Masterman put it some time that year. There were other signs too. Khaki was everywhere on the streets, especially round Whitehall and the West End, where, by the Christmas of 1915, London seemed to be marching to the soldiers' tune. Thousands were home on leave, thronging the stations daily in the run-up to the holiday – 'Turmoil at Victoria,' noted *The Times* on 23 December. The shops too were offering 'A Feast for Children and Soldiers', toys and the table this year's focus, with 'Parcels of Christmas fare' for those unlucky enough still to be in the trenches. Particular care was taken to welcome those many ANZAC soldiers on leave in London or in the hospitals, where great efforts were made to bring 'good cheer' to the wounded. Soldiers and sailors figured too on Christmas cards and calendars for the New Year, although there was a slump in sales that surprised the GPO – 'Christmas cards were not the vogue this year,' reported the *South London Press*. In the West End theatres the martial note was continued, with *Babes in the Wood* at the Aldwych Theatre dressing Robin Hood in khaki. In the event, more foul weather, together with the enforced darkness and lurking fear of the Zeppelins, led to a quiet Boxing Day – 'almost characterless', the only 'manifestations of the season's merriment to be seen in the streets were due to soldiers on leave'.[45]

This soldiers' Christmas was not enjoyed by all who should have been there. We left Roland Leighton at Piccadilly Circus seeing in the New Year of 1915 with tears in his eyes. Since then he had served in France and last saw his girlfriend, Vera Brittain, in August, when he bought a new pipe at Dunhill's and 'restocked his medical case with morphine', a 'good supply', at Savory and Moore's in New Bond Street. Leighton was due home at Christmas for a week's leave. In preparation Brittain spent her half-day's holiday from nursing at the 1st London General Hospital, Camberwell, shopping for '"some really nice mufti"' to welcome him home: 'a neatly cut navy coat and skirt, a pastel blue blouse in soft crêpe-de-Chine, an unusually becoming fawn felt hat trimmed with crimson berries, and a black taffeta dinner-dress with scarlet and mauve flowers turned into the waist'. Leighton was due to arrive in London on Christmas Day, but he didn't telephone and she assumed he'd been delayed.

> The next morning I had just finished dressing . . . when the expected message came to say that I was wanted on the telephone. Believing that I was at last to hear the voice for which I had waited for twenty-four

hours, I dashed joyously into the corridor. But the message was not from Roland but from Clare; it was not to say that he had arrived home that morning, but to tell me that he had died of wounds at a Casualty Clearing Station on December 23rd.[46]

Another two victims, Roland and Vera, had been added to the interminable sacrifice exacted by this most rapacious of wars. There would be many more sacrifices to come.

7

COME HOME, COME HOME,
YOU MILLION GHOSTS

THE outbreak of war prompted an epidemic of giving in London. It infected all classes. For the rich, giving was public duty, appeasement of conscience and insurance policy. We might recall those first anxious days when the temper and patriotism of the working classes were still open to question, with £2 million given to the National Relief Fund in the first month of war, £3 million by the end of the second. As the conflict progressed the giving scarcely abated. The Charity Organisation Society (COS) estimated that in the first two years giving to war charities exceeded the extraordinary sum of £30 million. By then the causes had multiplied a hundred-fold with 'Tipperary Clubs for the soldiers' wives, Comfort Funds . . . for troops of every sort, Refugees' Funds, Bread Funds, Prisoners' Funds, Wounded Funds, war libraries [and] ambulance corps'; the RSPCA trumpeted the needs of war horses, and even the preservation of historic buildings could be given a patriotic twist.[1]

It was not only the rich who put their hands in pockets and purses. A large proportion of all who could give something joined in this collective generosity. John Galsworthy, for instance, a left-leaning writer from the comfortable middle class, was said to have given away some three-quarters of his income during the war years to one cause or another. And the anonymous millions of London gave in their own way what they thought they could spare whenever the occasion arose or resources allowed: when shopping at Sainsbury's, perhaps, with its '50,000 shillings appeal', where John Sainsbury himself had pledged to add 6d to every bob donated; or when passing Bermondsey Town Hall, where over £2,000 had been dropped off, mainly in coppers one imagines, by the end of October 1914.[2]

Over time, the methods of extraction became both inexhaustible and exhausting. There were whist drives, dances, house-to-house collections, cinema collections, theatre collections, town hall and church bazaars, 'war teas' and 'in-aid-ofs' for every imaginable cause. But most of all there were flag days. They were local and they were national but all demanded money from the Londoners. In the summer of 1916, for instance, there was Dr Barnardo's Homes Flag Day, justified by the extra calls of war orphans, Russian Flag Day for wounded Russian soldiers, the Church Army War Fund Flag Day, France's Day (French Red Cross Flag Day), Kensington War Hospital Flag Day, YMCA Flag Day to fund soldiers' 'huts', while plans were announced for a Kitchener Flag Day in November.

Londoners were unsparing in their giving – charity the only item of expenditure in which thrift was not urged – so that, for instance, 80,000 flags were sold in Hackney alone for St George's Flag Day that spring, and Russian Day was so well supported in Bermondsey that a 'Bermondsey bed' was to be provided 'in perpetuity' in Petrograd Hospital with the borough's coat of arms above it. 'Flag Day Frenzy', as Bermondsey's mayor dubbed this unwonted call on the public's purse, was so importunate that it met with some adverse reaction in the spring and summer of 1916. 'Some good-natured fun is being indulged in just now in regard to the swift repetition of Flag Days. Even the best intentioned efforts can be overdone,' a Holloway furniture store noted in its advertisements. And by July at least one local paper was calling for 'a Truce': 'Flag Days, like Tennyson's brook, are evidently going on for ever.'[3]

The call went unheeded. Flag days continued to abound, not just because of the insatiable needs of total war but because they were so much fun to take part in. The 'head of a women's bureau', frustrated by her inability to recruit women to 'useful work', deplored 'the number of women immediately available when a flag-day with its possibility of amusing adventures and lunch and tea at rich patrons' houses, is announced'. There were other compensations too for society women, like the frisson of seeing one's name in the newspapers. 'Many well-known women helped yesterday' at the Church Army Flag Day. 'Lady Gort took charge of Victoria and neighbourhood; Lady Huntingdon sold flags at the Ritz, the Carlton, the Piccadilly, and other hotels . . .' And flag days gave such an opportunity to look good. Cynthia Asquith helped at Claridge's for Mesopotamia Flag Day: 'I wore my lovely old black-and-white cloth dress and my aigrette hat.' This aspect of flag days struck J. B. Booth's creation Miss 'Billie' Tuchaud as 'so *fearfy expie*. No self-respecting girl can wear the same kit twice . . .'[4]

Flag days gave other opportunities too. One of the volunteers keen to sell at the Bulldog Residential Club for Soldiers and Sailors Flag Day in June 1917 was Ada Jones, forty-eight, needlewoman, of Warlock Road, Paddington, found to have a 'secret pocket' in her blouse in which she had squirrelled 3s 9d in flag money: it cost her three months' imprisonment. Indeed, the scope of charity fraud widened considerably as the war went on. 'The swindlers who prey upon the benevolent public have reaped a large harvest since the war began,' complained the COS. 'We read of spurious agencies for tracing missing soldiers, of funds collected for the sick and wounded and confided to the care of a procuress, of non-existent homes for Belgian babies, of bogus officers in uniform requesting loans to enable them to return to the front'; of the Westminster Entertainments for Wounded Soldiers and the Red Star Society for relieving air raid victims, both frauds run by convicted confidence tricksters; of fraudulent subscription lists to benefit a soldier's widow; and, as perhaps every war in London's history had done, we see the appearance of crippled 'soldiers', one double amputee falsely claiming to have lost his legs in the trenches; and so on.[5]

The street-collecting regulations were tightened up in London by the Commissioner of Police in August 1915 and prosecutions were duly brought. A year later, it proved necessary for a War Charities Act to suppress the more dubious enterprises at source, but in 1917 a journalist scoffed at its ineffectiveness, especially in restricting exorbitant overheads like 'editorial salaries' for those devising the charities and advertising them:

There have been any number of 'honorary' secretaries of war charities up and down Fleet Street these last two years. The extraordinary thing about them is that, although they receive no salaries, and were in comparatively poor circumstances before the war, their achievement of this honorary position has allowed them to blossom forth into astrakhan coats, to smoke shilling cigars and to spend much time and considerable money entertaining their friends.[6]

Yet despite this blatant breach of public trust and goodwill the flow of giving never abated, the reservoir of charity seemingly bottomless.

When cash was deemed insufficient or hard to raise, then attics and storerooms were ransacked for something to give to some useful cause. The otherwise depleted social calendar was enlivened by brilliant Red Cross sales where antiques, paintings, precious books and hoards of jewellery were auctioned to aid the wounded and the maimed. The sale at Christie's over two weeks in April 1915 realised £48,000 for the Red Cross – treasures in the 'English and Continental porcelain and pottery, objects of art, arms and armour' sale days included a 'Spode writing set fetching 200 guineas (Lady Wernher's donation)' and a Sèvres cover and stand given by Leopold de Rothschild and knocked down at 150 guineas; prices generally were 'ruled distinctly high'. And for one of the last sales of the war Matthew Arnold's daughter was rooting out the poet's manuscripts for auction and the 'Red Cross pearl necklace' assembled from 2,500 single pearls donated by rich women was sufficiently astonishing to be displayed at the Grafton Galleries, Mayfair, in June 1918. In between these charity spectaculars were a host of sales and auctions for the war effort that must have gladdened collectors' hearts and been a boon for private investors: a sale of toys, automata, puppets, games and curiosities for St Dunstan's Hostel for blinded soldiers and other institutions, and Whiteley's Red Cross sale of antiques, coins, curios and Oriental shawls, both in July 1916, for instance. And then there were ceaseless collections of articles deemed useful to the war effort, from sheets, pillowcases and towels for military hospitals, to limousines, given or loaned for the duration, for the transport of wounded soldiers – or, rather, wounded officers.[7]

Some could afford to give even more. Many of the London rich gave up their town houses to the war. They did so for a variety of uses. Mrs Arthur Sassoon, at 2 Albert Gate, Knightsbridge, turned some of her rooms into 'a luxurious-looking tailor's showroom, trying-on department, reception office and so on' for the Men's Clothing Branch of the Officers' Families Fund, organising charitable donations to the struggling middle classes; John Galsworthy handed over the family home at Cambridge Gate, Regent's Park, for a wounded soldiers' club, fitting it out at his own expense; and Lord and Lady Lamington gave up their house in Wilton Crescent, Belgravia, as a home for deafened soldiers.[8]

But the most popular and prestigious use of a London home donated to the war effort was as a hospital for wounded officers. Two-thirds of officers' beds were in these private houses, most in the rich West End districts from Mayfair to Knightsbridge, where about twice as much was spent on caring for each wounded officer as for a man in the ranks, and where one nurse was provided for four beds compared to one for sixteen in military hospitals and one for forty-four in converted poor law workhouses. Some became celebrity hospitals, much praised in the press, their patients visited by the greatest in the land, including royalty. One of the most stylish and luxurious was said to be Mrs Freddie Guest's at Park Lane, but there were many others, like the Duke and Duchess of Rutland's and Lady Manners's, both in Arlington Street, Piccadilly; Lady Ridley's in Carlton House Terrace; Lady Pamela Lytton's in Nottingham Place, Marylebone; the Marquess of Londonderry's in Park Lane; Lady Mary Mennell's in Lennox Gardens, Chelsea; Mrs Gwynne Holford's, for amputees, at Roehampton; or Sir Alfred Mond's at Highgate, 'reputedly the best hospital in London', according to Captain Robert Graves, who was a patient there.[9]

At the beginning of the war these places opened at the owners' expense with prodigal panache, but as time wore on, and as the costs and burdens of war mounted, keeping private hospitals going became a source of considerable anxiety, even to the rich. By the end of 1916 the Honourable Mrs Rupert Beckett's hospital was costing her '£90 a week in food, medicine, and nurses, for twenty beds. She only got down to this figure by going to Lipton's for her groceries,' buying wholesale at 'about a quarter of shop prices'.[10] And the strain began to show by late 1915 at Lady Evelyn Mason's Officer Hospital, 16 Bruton Street, Mayfair. Historians have tended to stress the luxury lavished on wounded officers in comparison to rankers, and so it seemed first to Captain Roland Pelly, son of the Canon of West Ham. He was wounded at Gallipoli, shot in the mouth: 'Jaw broken, tongue torn, cannot swallow or speak'. He found the Bruton Street hospital 'v. swell. Very nice & comfortable . . . only fear that it may be too swagger & one may get fussed. One girl nurse had the impudence to say "Poor wee kiddy: he looks fourteen" & I unable to answer back!' Pelly got on well with nurses and his medical treatment was first class. But within two or three weeks those fears of swagger and fuss had flown, and the mere-triciousness of Bruton Street, 'the abominations of this place', had begun to get on his nerves: 'everything done for Economy & Comfort not thought of, nurses' quarters a piggery etc. Why not do 20 beds (instead of 40) decently?' There were problems over the cold ('No fire again – O Lady Evelyn!'), over provisions ('bought some brown sugar which Lady Economy cannot run to giving me'), and over the autocratic way 'this ridiculous house' was run. 'Clogg [his surgeon] gave me leave to go away for Sunday but Lady E.'s rule is if anyone goes away they stay away – so "that's that".' It was 'quite a wrench leaving Bruton Street' a couple of weeks before Christmas, but this was due to friendships he had forged with some nurses and not regret at leaving Lady Economy and her aristocratic style.[11]

Lady Evelyn, no doubt, thought she was doing her best, and the responsibilities must have been a strain on both her purse and her nerves. There was some compensation, though, in feeling that 'her bit' for the war effort was not insignificant and some satisfaction that this was recognised in the society pages and court circulars and in the conversation of her friends.[12]

Whether these pleasures outweighed the anxieties of giving for Lady Evelyn is unknowable but for many others there is little doubt that sacrificing time and money could be fun. Some might even turn a personal passion into patriotism. 'My own particular War-work was the Choir,' recalled Hallie Miles, 'which I inaugurated immediately the War broke out, for giving Concerts in the Hospitals, and "Patriotic Teas", and Concerts to the wounded and others, in the Salons of the E.M. Restaurant', her husband's business at 40 Chandos Street, Trafalgar Square. Poets found congenial war work in occasional poetry readings, time given free and entrance fees donated to war charities – Walter de la Mare, W. H. Davies, Laurence Binyon, Henry Newbolt, W. B. Yeats and Hilaire Belloc read for the Star and Garter Home for disabled soldiers at Richmond in Lady d'Erlanger's Piccadilly mansion in April 1916, for instance. More onerously, some painters gave rights in their work for the war effort, Sir John Lavery giving the London Hospital in June 1915 reproduction rights to a fine picture of wounded soldiers, officers it seems, on one of the wards; and the Royal Academy's War Relief Exhibition of January 1915 gave the artists a third of the price their paintings fetched, the rest going to the Red Cross.[13]

Others indulged a hitherto unrequited passion for the stage, Lady Paget and Lady Essex among others putting on charity matinees in West End theatres. Members of the cast included professionals with a sprinkling of society beauties, some less enthusiastic than others, although it was fun and celebrity for all nonetheless. In the bleak February of 1916 Cynthia Asquith went with some friends with a view to borrowing clothes for me to wear at the performance Lady Essex has let me in for in such a high-handed American way. It is going to be at the Gaiety and we are to be lady buyers looking at a parade of mannequins in a dressmaker's shop. Lady E. had my name printed on a large poster without asking my leave: I suppose I ought to be angry, but I'm not really. Diana [Manners] told us there was a music hall skit on her in which she is amusingly 'taken off'.[14]

For those with stage fright there were still bit parts that might get one noticed: 'Mrs Bingham and Lady Astor selling flowers and flags' at one Alhambra matinee, and 'looking very pretty'. It was all grist to the satirist's mill:

Lady Dinky told me that she and the Pont girl have been absolutely compelled to divide their day into three parts: all morning they spend with the dressmaker, and all afternoon they sell programmes at some matinée or other, for every matinée means a new dress, as of course you know. Their evenings they spend with the Society paragraphists.

No, dears, women are *not* negligible factors in war time.[15]

For the comfortable middle classes and above, 'all usual activities, social duties and established standards of life being dropped, everybody *had* to get busy on some "war work" or other'. From the earliest days many society women, at first unsure of their potential capabilities, waged war with their needle. About twenty ladies were invited to a 'sewing party' at Onslow Gardens in the early days of the war, but their work was 'so bad' that Georgina Lee spent 'half my time . . . unpicking and correcting mistakes', while the shirt she herself made had an opening no man could get his head through. Not everyone, it seemed, could sew shirts for soldiers, but some women 'were working like professionals' and all presumably improved with perseverance.[16]

The need for armies of 'lady volunteers' declined as industry stepped up to the enormous demand for khaki, but some volunteer workshops were run on a large scale and continued throughout the war, at middle-class Woodberry Down, for instance, where 189 'ladies' on war work laboured at the Stoke Newington Hospital Supply Depôt in 'a beautiful house' loaned for the purpose; or at the Wimbledon War Workers' Depôt, where men and women volunteers spent time on 'carpentering, surgical dressings, bandages, splint-padding, and garment making'. Some moved restlessly from task to task. Georgina Lee, the upper-middle-class housewife in her forties from South Kensington, immersed herself in war charities (visiting poor families for the Ragged School Union and for a children's care committee in Hackney, and visiting middle-class families for the Belgian Refugee Fund) and in numerous volunteer workshops, including making and packing bandages and other surgical requisites at a depot in Chelsea, where she became a supervisor. These activities continued till the Armistice and after.[17]

In 1915, unsurprisingly given the munitions crisis that year, 'Shell-making is the latest Society craze; a ghastly sport indeed!' Even Cynthia Asquith worked an occasional two-hour shift making respirator compo-nents, giving her an insight into manual work that seemed to do some-thing to heal the class divide, to her satisfaction at least: 'It is such fun feeling a factory girl and it gave one some idea of how exciting it must be to do piece-work for money . . . [But] I was very glad I hadn't got to do a twelve-hour day – it is quite tiring.'[18]

Opportunities for war work opened in every direction, involving men as well as women, the very young and the aged. The Boy Scouts, for instance, were on duty in police stations every night from around June 1915 till the end of the war to assist as messengers during air raids; they used their 'trek carts' to move furniture for Belgian refugees, to collect sugar bags, waste paper and bottles for recycling, to move khaki garments from the clothing manufacturers to the depots, to collect eggs for the wounded under the National Egg Collection scheme; they distributed handbills, acted as guides for troops and as patients in first-aid classes.[19]

Older men, 'dug-outs', filled the ranks of the Specials, the supple-mentary force in London assisting the Metropolitan Police, depleted of young men by army recruitment and overwhelmed by the new duties of war, not least DORA and aliens restriction. The Metropolitan Police Special Constabulary were formed on 8 August 1914 and within some twelve days all 20,000 constables and senior ranks had been appointed. They were 'attested' at great festivals of patriotic fervour – 2,000 at a time in the Royal Albert Hall sworn in by Sir John Dickinson, the chief metropolitan magistrate. All sorts and conditions of Londoner were taken on: no 'civilian force created by the war was more representative of the varied citizenship of London', from courtiers to costermongers. Nor was age a barrier. 'My father at 77 became a Special Constable in London,' recalled William Beveridge, then a senior civil servant at the

Board of Trade, 'and was sent to guarding gas and water works at Shepherd's Bush.' It involved him in a two-hour train journey from Hindhead in Surrey to Waterloo and a two-mile walk to and from home to the station. 'Secret intervention with the police authorities enabled me to secure that after a few months my father was placed honourably on the reserve list and told to keep his truncheon so as to be ready for a call.'[20]

The Specials had no uniform to speak of until after the anti-German riots, when some were taken for rioters by the regular police and whacked accordingly. But uniforms were a bonus wherever they were to be had, proclamation that one's bit was duly being done. Georgina Lee's Uncle Gerry was taken on by the Royal Naval Volunteer Reserve anti-aircraft division, manning a gun on the Crown Agents' Office roof in Whitehall: 'They are all gentlemen on his post, twenty-four of them', but they got 'to wear a dark blue uniform, like a yachting suit' as compensation for six-hour shifts in all weathers.[21]

Uniforms were important in women's war work too. The YMCA huts, where soldiers could get a cup of tea or coffee and perhaps a meal, and which were often funded by a single benefactor – Mrs Alec-Tweedie established one in memory of her officer son, killed in France in early 1917 – were staffed by uniformed lady volunteers. So were the railway station buffets for soldiers and sailors which opened from mid-1915, the first at London Bridge and then at Euston, Victoria, Liverpool Street, Charing Cross and Paddington. Waterloo was the last to open in January 1916 because it was thought the throughput there of 10,000 men a day was just too large to handle. Around the autumn of 1917 Victoria soldiers' buffet was catering for 42,000 men a week. Each was operated by uniformed 'ladies' under the general supervision of titled women, like Lady Limerick at London Bridge or Lady Brassey at Waterloo. All costs came from voluntary subscriptions and donations from wealthy supporters. It made for some interesting class interactions, Lady Bee Pembroke tickled by being addressed by soldiers as '"my girl"' or '"waitress!"' and flummoxed when asked for '"two Zepps. and a cloud-burst"' (sausages and mash). Among many society women working at the soldiers' buffets was Katharine Asquith, daughter-in-law of the Prime Minister – 'her canteen' was at Euston.[22]

But the most glamorous of all the uniformed women in London were the nurses and helpers of the various women's Voluntary Aid Detachments (VADs). The nurses were solidly middle class or above and could

genuinely claim to be in the front line of civilian warfare. The great
wave of casualties following the push at Neuve Chapelle created a
pressing need for more nurses: 'If only I could help in this way!' sighed
Georgina Lee. 'I am longing to do some useful work.' She was not
alone. In the first two months of war, the London Hospital in unfash-
ionable Whitechapel received 1,479 applications from 'would-be [Nurse]
Probationers'. The Hospital's matron, Miss Eva Luckes, was dismissive:

> I need hardly say that a considerable number of these applications were
> from totally unsuitable Candidates. Large numbers of 'Society' ladies
> were inspired with the desire to come for one, two or three weeks, under
> the impression that this brief insight into Hospital life would qualify
> them to go to the Front to nurse wounded soldiers.

But even Miss Luckes found some encouragement, hoping that this new
interest in nursing 'may result ultimately in a more adequate supply of
educated Candidates than has been forthcoming in recent years'.[23]

She would not be disappointed. A stream of '"Society" ladies', bluestockings and university students did indeed rise to the challenging
work of nursing in wartime. Lady Diana Manners, one of the greatest
beauties of the day, nursed working-class patients at Guy's and wounded
officers at her mother's hospital in Arlington Street; Vera Brittain temporarily abandoned her studies at Oxford to nurse at Buxton and in
London, at the 1st London General Hospital, a military extension of
Bart's at Camberwell, and the 2nd London General Hospital in converted
school premises at World's End, Chelsea; Enid Bagnold, upper middle
class, beautiful and bohemian, gave up the world of letters to nurse
officers at the Royal Herbert Hospital, Woolwich. The other ranks of
VADs, so to speak, worked in humbler stations in 'general service' as
kitchen hands or ward helpers, and as clerks, telephonists, pharmacy
and laboratory assistants. Many of these were paid, but many society
women shouldered these domestic burdens too: Winifred Tower helped
with parlourmaid duties at an officers' hospital in Park Lane, delighted
to be known as 'one of "the Fairies of Londonderry House"'; and
Cynthia Asquith did 'pantry work' in her friend Lady Pamela Lytton's
hospital at Marylebone, finding compensation in wearing a 'pure white'
uniform supplied by Harrods; none appears to have voluntarily done
without parlourmaids at home, it seems.[24]

The nursing duties of VADs on London's hospital front line were fearfully onerous. Soon after the declaration of war Diana Manners began to learn her trade on the women's surgical ward at Guy's, where she found the terrors of the operating theatre nothing to dressing wounds of patients recovering back on the wards:

> I was called behind the screens by Sister to watch a dressing on a woman who had had a kidney removed. She had a biggish hole in her side, and as Sister squeezed and pressed her stomach and flanks a stream of green pus oozed slowly into a kidney-dish. I felt sick and weak.

Despite her cosseted background, her determination and sharp intelligence were readily valued and she found herself and other VADs 'very well received'. She attended lectures but was not eligible to take exams. Even so, in a few weeks, apart from dispensing, she was doing everything trained nurses did, 'giving injections, intravenous and saline, preparing for operations [and] cutting abscesses . . .' After a spell nursing wounded soldiers at a hospital in France she came to Arlington Street, where, on a visit there, Cynthia Asquith thought her 'wonderfully efficient'. But for Diana it all 'seemed soft and demoralising after spartan Guy's', with a maid 'arriving from Rumpelmayer's laden with chestnut-cream cakes and sherry for our elevenses'. In May 1918 she returned to Guy's: 'I've had it out with Mother . . . She thinks Guy's is a penance. For what? Too much life? Too much love, or too much suffering?'[25]

Hospital life was indeed a penance, even a sacrifice. There was some satisfaction to be taken in one's own personal discomfort when so many others had suffered so much: 'O the pain of the bones of my legs and feet,' complained Diana Manners; 'they send shivers down my back and a dull sickness as I walk the wards. My hands too would frighten tame bulls, and my neck is like the man they couldn't hang though they tried to six times – from the collar's sharp grip.'[26] And Enid Bagnold lamented:

> My ruined charms cry aloud for help. The cap wears away my front hair; my feet are widening from the everlasting boards; my hands won't take my rings. I was advised last night on the telephone to marry immediately before it was too late. A desperate remedy. I will try cold creams and hair tonics first.[27]

For many of these deeply committed young women inconveniences vanished in the satisfaction they had in serving men who had risked or had suffered everything, just as many of their own loved ones had done. 'Their world is often near me,' Bagnold recorded from the outer reaches of Woolwich, 'their mud and trenches, things they say when they come in wounded. The worst of it is, it almost bores me to go to London, and London was always my Mecca.'[28] And Vera Brittain recalled a few years later how

> It never then occurred to us that we should have been happier, healthier, and altogether more competent if the hours of work had been shorter, the hostel life more private and comfortable, the daily walks between hostel and hospital eliminated, the rule against sitting down in the wards relaxed, and off-duty time known in advance when the work was normal. Far from criticising our Olympian superiors, we tackled our daily duties with a devotional enthusiasm now rare amongst young women . . .[29]

For when all things were balanced out, it was the men and women in London's hospitals, including Manners, Bagnold, Brittain and the rest, of everyone on London's home front, who came closest to knowing just how much suffering this war was causing.

> No. 22 was lying flat on his back, his knees drawn up under him, the sheets up to his chin; his flat, chalk-white face tilted up to the ceiling. As I bent over to get his untouched [meal] tray his tortured brown eyes fell on me.
>   'I'm in pain, Sister,' he said. No one has ever said that to me before in that tone. He gave me the look that a dog gives, and his words had the character of an unformed cry.

Nurse Bagnold told sister that the officer in bed 22 was '"in great pain"'; '"I know", she said, quite decently, "but I can't do anything. He must stick it out."'[30]

In this emotional hothouse of hospital life, with so many young men and women thrown together, romance blossomed. Captain Basil Robinson, a patient on Charrington Ward at the London Hospital, agreed to pay the hospital £25 4s in compensation when he took Sister Agnes Graham as his bride. Other hospital trysts proved less fruitful. Lieutenant Roland Pelly, with those dreadful facial injuries sustained in Gallipoli, won much sympathy with his boyish demeanour and the self-deprecating charm and good humour that gleam through his diary. But a staid Christian upbringing, nurtured in innocence, rendered him fatally priggish in matters moral, proving a barrier when he and Nurse Browne at Lady Mason's Bruton Street hospital fell for each other. He was shocked when she told him she was a good deal older than he. 'Thought & prayed a good deal for Brownie (Browne). I like her very much – dare say I shall recover.' In a couple of months things had not moved much further forward:

> I have helped her & must help her, over faith, in the future but she must not be led to think I am 'smitten' with her. Ought I to write plainly & say we are real friends but no more? A boy & girl corresponding piously can be such a risky thing. Supposing she was unmarried in 10 years & I felt it might be due to me . . .

Pelly's surviving diary ended a day later on New Year's Eve 1915 – but things didn't look hopeful.[31]

All these young people, like every last Londoner around them, lived in the shadow of death. Some, like Pelly, had missed it by an inch or less. Others, like Enid Bagnold, smelled it festering in front of them. Everyone had acquaintances, friends, close relatives and loved ones they would never see again but would remember for the rest of their days. When, two generations on, historians came to question former munitions workers about their war, the dominant memory veiling all that freedom and fun was the bereavement suffered for the lives cut short by war.[32]

We might take the experience of one unexceptional middle-class household to stand for countless others. The Palmers Green family of Frederick Porter Wensley, the Scotland Yard detective, entered the war with three children. Perhaps because of their father's many years in the public service, the Wensleys were fortified by strong ideals of duty, both to country and to God – all three children were committed Christians in the High Anglican tradition. Edie, the War Office typist, we've met. She had two brothers. The elder, Frederick Martin, received his teacher-training certificate from Culham College, Oxfordshire, enabling him to become a schoolmaster from 1 August 1914. He was then eighteen. On declaration of war he promptly abandoned his plans, enlisted, and was commissioned a 2nd Lieutenant in the Lincolnshire Regiment in March 1915. Frederick's posting to France was delayed until February 1916 when he was injured in training, a grenade having accidentally exploded, killing another soldier. Once there he joined the preparations for the British attack on the Somme. On the first day of battle, 1 July, Frederick's battalion, the 10th Lincolns, were virtually massacred, losing some 421 killed and wounded out of 500 men. Relatively unscathed, he was then engaged in fierce fighting over the next few weeks of German counter-attacks. On 5 August he was leading an advanced bombing party when he and his men came under heavy shellfire. Frederick was 'instantaneously killed', according to his commanding officer, employing a phrase that must have given comfort to so many families at home.

The fateful tattoo of the Post Office telegram boy's knock reached 22 Powys Lane, Palmers Green, on 9 August: 'Deeply regret to inform you that 2nd Lieutenant F.M. Wensley 10 Lincoln Regiment was killed in action 5 August the Army Council express their sympathy – Secretary War Office.' Frederick's death was felt beyond his family, among army comrades and former school and college friends; he also left a fiancée, Lillian, whom he had met while training in the Midlands: 'Oh Edie you cannot imagine what his loss means to me. I loved him so much, but now I am just longing for the day when we shall be reunited never to part again.' Among numerous letters of condolence was one to Frederick's young brother, Harold, from the boy's former headmaster: 'And it is a proud thought that even of those close to us some have made the supreme sacrifice in the greatest conflict in which Englishmen have ever been called to fight. But that is no complete solace – and the pain must be sharp.'[33]

Harold, the youngest Wensley, was then seventeen. When Frederick had left for France, Harold enrolled at the Royal Military College in Sandhurst, some thirty-four miles south-west of London. He was a clever and conscientious schoolboy and came tenth out of over 300 successful candidates in his year. He remained at Sandhurst till graduating in April 1918, when he was nineteen. Over that period, not only had Edie lost her older brother, but death had become a common experience among her acquaintances too. It crops up casually in her friends' correspondence. Daisy Parsons had to break off a social engagement when her boss's son was killed in training and a fellow former typist was widowed with a young daughter, for instance. But at least while Harold was at Sandhurst he was safe, and Edie clung to him: 'I have not received my usual Monday letter from you, so I suppose that you have severed negotiations till I answer the last thirty or forty you sent me,' he wrote in August 1917.[34]

Yet Harold must have been grateful for the contact, because not everything about Sandhurst proved congenial to him. He wrote to his father complaining that 'the fellows here on the whole are a rotten lot. Out of the 60 odd in our Company I should be ashamed to bring 55 home.' He worried about their language, blasphemous and obscene, their gambling, smoking and drinking: 'My first feeling when I came into contact with words I had not heard since I was at Dempsey Street School [in Stepney, where his father had been stationed for many years] was one of absolute disgust with fellows, who call themselves gentlemen and behave like brutes.' Other things worried him too, for in October 1917 he joined the Alliance of Honour, pledging himself to 'Purity and a chivalrous respect for womanhood'.[35]

From Sandhurst Harold joined his dead brother's regiment and was posted to Cork, in south-west Ireland. In July 1918 a letter home noted there had been an outbreak of influenza in his battalion. In Ireland Harold languished frustrated, eager to get to France, until October. At that point, disappointment turning to anger, he asked his father for help. 'I don't intend to be the first Wensley to fail in his duty, all the more since I have your example and Fred's before me.' His father pulled the necessary strings. Harold was granted seven days' home leave on 15 October and left for France on the 22nd.

In the early part of November his main duties appear to have been supervising army traffic at Berlaimont, on the French–Belgian border, in the immense task of forwarding the final British advance. He was struck by the irony of it all – 'Now I am no more than a common or garden PC on point duty . . .' But a letter to Edie, probably written on 1 November, showed him reconciled to his mundane role:

So surely as a man does his duty in this world, or woman, so surely he will be rewarded on the other side & in most cases in this; & those who have been parted by death if they have done their duty will most certainly meet again beyond the grave.[36]

On 10 November 1918 Edie wrote yet another affectionate letter to 'My Dear Hal': 'I am glad you are keeping merry and bright, for theres nothing like it.' Her letter would eventually be returned unopened. By now Hal was far from merry or bright. On the night of 11–12 November he went sick with influenza. On 13 November the Post Office at Palmers Green delivered a telegram to 22 Powys Lane: 'Regret 2 Lt. H.W.

Wensley Lincolnshire Regiment Dangerously ill Influenza at No. 3 Casualty Clearing Station now Twelve further news sent as soon as received Secretary War Office.' Just after 12 noon on 16 November the Metropolitan Police passed on a telephone message from the Red Cross at Boulogne reporting Harold 'too bad to be removed to Hospital'. Four hours later the family's dreadful wait was over. Harold had in fact died the day before, 15 November, of bronchopneumonia. He was nineteen. A telegram from Buckingham Palace – 'The King and Queen are deeply grieved to hear that you have lost yet another son' – did not arrive until 12 December.[37]

The confusion of those final conflicting messages and the clutching at any straw offered were part of the agony of bereavement experienced by many. It was frequently compounded by the news that a loved one was 'missing', with no body ever found, no grave ever to visit. Often there was nothing but memories or carefully husbanded letters to remember him by. 'Come home, come home, you million ghosts' was Stella Benson's fitting, haunting, cry for so many of her and Edie Wensley's generation.[38]

As the count of ghosts mounted the public's efforts to share in the grief of loved ones took new forms. The rolls of honour that began to appear in schools and outside town halls during 1915 were added to by almost every London institution. Some were only completed at the end of the war – at Birkbeck College, where a plaque remembering ninety-three staff and students was eventually erected; or at the LCC, whose 1,065 officers and workers killed were marked by a sumptuous memorial volume.[39]

The working-class streets of London began to honour their collective sacrifice well before the war's end. Tiny local 'shrines' or 'rolls of honour' emerged after the slaughter at the Somme, from July 1916. In some streets large families could have many sons in khaki – the Carpenters of Hanover Gardens, Kennington, had six and so did the Hammonds of Branksome Road, Brixton, and doubtless there were many such, often living near to one another, sometimes in the same house. It was not long before individual streets could boast of large numbers of men in the army, proclaiming their residents' patriotism and shaking up shirkers. Trafalgar Street, Walworth, had reportedly 175 enrolled in the services by the end of July 1915, 200 by mid-September that same year – all volunteers – and 300 by October 1916, when a list of the fallen, handpainted and framed in oak, was fastened to a house wall to commemorate the street's casualties, seventeen dead, twenty-seven injured, with one prisoner of war. Many other streets, north and south of the river, were similarly equipped by the end of the year. The idea was taken up too in middle-class suburban housing estates, among business people in the City wards, and by the Church of England, whose bishops and clergymen were keen to 'bless' or 'dedicate' publicly the street shrines and created their own for London parish church-yards. The Bishop of London, unsurprisingly, was active among the appropriators.[40]

This clerical opportunism helped bolster feeling in the churches by the end of 1916 that the time for a religious revival might be ripe. That, as we have seen, proved not to be the case. But for some Londoners the war unquestionably added zest to a spiritual hunger and revived old ways of satisfying it. The churches were uneven beneficiaries. A few could record 'a sort of spiritual revival', collections at the Wesleyan Church in Mayfield Road, Dalston, for instance, the largest for twenty years at mid-1917. The consolations of spectacle and ceremony, and an influx of Belgian refugees, ensured that many Roman Catholic churches in London were also packed; St George's Cathedral, Southwark, had real difficulty squeezing the congregation in on Christmas Day in 1915, many soldiers on leave among the worshippers. A similar phenom-enon affected Anglican churches in central London where many soldiers from all over the country were temporarily garrisoned or in transit, as at St Martin-in-the-Fields, for instance, which made soldiers especially welcome under its pastor, the Reverend Dick Sheppard. Elsewhere the story was more patchy, some parish churches modestly thriving with others reported to be stubbornly empty except on watchnight, that special evening in the London calendar. Perhaps parish leadership, as at St Martin's, was key to progress or decline, affected as was everything else by the war and the loss of young men at the Front.[41]

Even so, for many religious people some aspects of the war offered spiritual consolation. They might find it anywhere. H. Rider Haggard thought 'the goodness and protection of God' had 'preserved this country . . . from reaping the fruits of ruin' that it had been busily 'sowing for over a generation'. Thomas Hancock Nunn in Hampstead could console a friend who had lost two sons that 'God draws to Him this mighty host of our best spirits to build our New Jerusalem. Be assured He will lead them – in love and joy – to right the wrongs of the world, to triumph over hatefulness in high places – and to be always

ours.' How much consolation that and similar reassurances gave is
unclear – some, it seems, because the letter survived. And Nunn was
not alone in finding a higher cause in others' loss. Caroline Playne
talked in November 1916 with a Miss Dare, who 'clung to the idea
that the young men giving their lives was a splendid sacrifice like the
death of Christ'. It 'should be made even if it achieved nothing . . .
Sacrifice had intrinsic merit apart from all the evils it produced . . .' 'It
was a regular glorification of cruelty,' Playne thought.[42]

Others sought relief in older, less sophisticated forms of superstition.
We might recall Sir Ian and Lady Hamilton at Charing Cross Station,
burdened by what might prove 'unlucky', and 'luck' was fortified by
what has been called a 'folk threnody' of 'charms, mascots, [and]
amulets' released by the war. This could sometimes combine with a
hugging attachment to more orthodox religion: in Bermondsey, and
probably elsewhere, people crowded into a local mission hall on air
raid nights, thinking its religious connection offered special protection
over their own homes or other places of shelter.[43]

Organised religion proved more wary of the wartime revival of
spiritualism. There were so many dead, so long before their time, that
it was no surprise that families and lovers sought to reach them. The
extraordinary success of the scientist Sir Oliver Lodge's *Raymond, or
Life and Death*, published in November 1916 and describing his soldier
son's short life and recent death, and the contact his friends had maintained with him since, had powerful resonance when so many had
suffered similar bereavement. 'I have been reading again,' the publisher
J. M. Dent told an American friend, 'that book of Sir Oliver Lodge's,
Raymond . . . I know him, and I know that he is a completely sane
man, and he loved his boy. I do not know whether I shall not try myself
to get into touch with my boys [one killed at Neuve Chapelle, one in
Gallipoli] as he has with his.' Sir Arthur Conan Doyle, who was also
a friend of Lodge and whose brother-in-law had been killed in the
retreat from Mons, became famously convinced by spiritualism and a
credulous believer in other matters psychical around this time.[44]

The churches in London treated spiritualism with suspicion. Its
overtones of the miraculous, and its long-term association with fraudulent mediums, rendered many Anglican clergymen sceptical, even
hostile. The Bishop of London turned a withering fire on Lodge and
the spiritualists as enemies of true faith, while commending the tradition of remembering the dead on All Saints' Day. Nonetheless the

spiritualists drew large numbers to their London meetings. Dean Inge, in early 1917, heard Lodge speak at the Religious Thought Society to a room 'full of women in mourning, and of wide-eyed cranks'. Spiritualism also held a fashionable appeal for 'Society people', as Caroline Playne put it, who 'had recourse to certain ancient superstitions to distract their minds and relieve their fears'. Like Lady Cynthia Asquith, for instance. She was an occasional dupe of quacks, having herself injected at great expense in mid-1916 with 'seawater collected off the coast of Ireland!' for 'stagnant blood' causing 'speckles on my face'. Intrigued when told that her dead brother Yvo had relayed messages at a table turning, she accompanied her mother to a seance at Tavistock Square to try to contact Raymond, her brother-in-law, recently killed. She was not, however, convinced: 'The poor man got hopelessly on the wrong track about me, thinking my husband had been killed.' Duff Cooper visited a medium, Mrs Fernie, to try to contact dead friends but was also 'most disappointed'. It started well when she said 'there was a spirit of a young man standing by me and after one wrong shot said his name was John. This was remarkable', but when 'John' spoke directly to Cooper

> everything he said and every word he used were so utterly unlike him that with the best will in the world I could not believe. Then she mentioned other names but they were all wrong except George but the description of him did not answer. I came away very sceptical of the whole business.[45]

Mrs Fernie and her ilk could make a fortune out of credulous Londoners. Almira Brockway, fifty-nine, an American 'psychic' and fortune-teller in Linden Gardens, Notting Hill Gate, was said to have received £115 in thirty-four days when her case came to court in December 1916. And at the other end of the social scale, Philip Marks, an eighteen-year-old travelling showman and casual dock worker from Stepney, was fined 40s for telling fortunes at a penny a punt to a crowd in the Broadway, London Fields; he operated with a 6-foot-high figure he called 'The Gipsy Queen'.[46]

Yet perhaps, in this world of suffering and anxiety, Almira Brockway and her kind, even Philip Marks, might have offered solace to some whose friends or relatives had paid 'the ultimate sacrifice'. And perhaps too in the public mind there were worse ways to turn the war to account. For from the outset, gaining strength as the fighting wore on, a consciousness steadily grew that not all were sharing equally in the nation's agony. We have met instances of this disquiet already: the white feather torment, the angry hissing from soldiers who watched young men turn away from recruiting sergeants, the disgust of fathers mourning dead sons who failed to get a hearing when urging enlistment, the fury of 'English' Londoners at Germans and Russians apparently avoiding the obligations demanded by their adopted country. The affectation of national unity in fact masked a fine mosaic of divisions in which many weighed up their own or others' sacrifices and found them wanting. Thomas Hancock Nunn, offering comfort for his friends' 'great sacrifices', found himself and others like him 'standing farther from the altar with our lesser gifts'. Ford Madox Ford's fictional army officer Christopher Tietjens was affected with 'the slight nausea that in those days you felt at contact with the civilian who knew none of your thoughts, phrases or preoccupations'. 'My one deep regret is that I personally am suffering so little when others are giving all,' Georgina Lee noted in her diary, and the journalist G. S. Street, an 'over-aged buffer', felt 'the shame of being alive at all'.[47]

This desire for an equality of sacrifice was, of course, unobtainable. Everyone was differently situated and some had more to give (or lose) than others. But it was no wonder that those who appeared to spurn the cause of sacrifice attracted special loathing. As the war went on two special categories grew more sharply defined. The first was the profiteer, that shady figure who had been present from the beginning of the food panic of early 1914 but whose depredations, real or imagined, took a pinching hold towards the end of the war. The other was the conscientious objector and his pacifist allies. And he emerged in the next great dark year of total war: 1916.

8

IN IMMINENT FEAR OF AN
EARTHQUAKE: 1916

THE foul weather that stifled Christmas pleasures at the end of 1915 persisted into the New Year with heavy rain and gales. There was a thick snowfall at the end of February and a blizzard at the end of March: snow and slush disrupted traffic and pedestrians for longer than normal because, outside the City, the shortage of labour meant there was no one to shift it. A day or so later one of the worst storms to afflict London in living memory brought down thousands of trees, including around a hundred ancient elms in Kensington Gardens; people from the poor streets of North Kensington and elsewhere gratefully lopped off branches for firewood. Around this time emerged 'the beginning of the great macintosh epoch' among women in London, even fashionable women, some sporting 'transparent macintoshes of pink, yellow or green, as scornful as military officers of the effeminate umbrella, whose use was being confined to clubmen and old dowdies'.[1]

Somehow the weather seemed to suit the increasingly grim turn of the war, the heavens and millions of Londoners marching in step to the same beat of the drum. Conscription, the forced enlistment of eligible men of military age, came in with the New Year. This would no longer be a war of volunteers but of men who had no choice but to fight. The first Military Service Bill was introduced into the House of Commons on 5 January 1916 and was in force by 10 February, calling up all single men between the ages of nineteen and thirty that March. But this call on the nation's young men proved quickly as inadequate as all previous recruitment drives and in May a much more far-reaching second Military Service Act conscripted all men, married and single, aged from eighteen to forty-one and ordered the re-examination of all those previously rejected on medical grounds. This draconian extension of compulsion revived once more old doubts about the patriotic convictions of the London working class: soldiers were placed in readiness to quell anti-conscription disturbances expected in the East End and guards at the palaces were doubled. The precautions proved unnecessary.[2]

Men content to be called up duly reported to the local recruitment offices as ordered by the War Office. It could be a shocking experience for some. Richard Church, a sickly civil service clerk from south London, reported for his medical at Chelsea Barracks and found himself among 'men of every kind, including the dregs of our urban civilisation. I stood in my place amongst them, loathing the stench of unwashed bodies and filthy clothes . . . At last, overcome by physical disgust and the strain of standing so long, I began to feel the ominous signs of faintness' until a recruiting sergeant allowed him to sit down.[3]

Those men wishing to claim exemption from call-up had to present their case to a Military Service Tribunal. These were established in each local authority area and were composed in the main of elderly middle-class council worthies – the mayor, aldermen, former town clerks – who chaired the tribunals alongside a War Office nominee (retired senior officers) and frequently a local representative of organised labour. In the early days many tribunals were made up of adamant patriots who stead-fastly refused to grant any exemptions all, regardless of the grounds on which a case was founded. These grounds were various. No complete statistics of the tribunals' work exist, but it seems likely that eight out of ten applications were based on domestic grounds or for essential reasons of employment, equally split, with another 10 per cent a combination of the two. Just 1 or 2 per cent claimed exemption because of a conscientious objection to war, mainly based on religious scruples opposing all war or socialist objections to this 'capitalist' war in particular.[4]

Most of the thousands of applicants for exemption in the early weeks of the tribunals found themselves talking to a brick wall. 'Nearly All Appeals Refused at Hackney,' reported the local paper on 1 March, and a similarly marked refusal to use discretion to grant an applicant even temporary exemption was a feature of many tribunals in south London too. Doubtless some tribunal members took pleasure in saying no: Lieutenant-Colonel Hamilton, the military representative at the Chelsea Tribunal, reportedly dismissed one conscientious objector with the words, 'You cur, you ought to be whipped round the streets!' But dissatisfied applicants could take their case to appeal tribunals which had a firmer grip of both the law and fair play and slowly the system settled into a more reasonably minded routine of careful attention to the applicant's case. Colonel Repington, then *The Times*'s war correspondent, a man of the world but a world tightly restricted to West End drawing-room life and country house weekends, found his work on the Hampstead Tribunal a revelation: 'It is very interesting work, for one gets an insight into the home life and the circumstances of numerous people and classes whom one never mixes with.'[5]

As experience grew, even the war dissenters received a measured if rarely sympathetic hearing. Efforts were generally made to accommodate them in work at least removed from the mechanics of killing, while still contributing generally to the 'war effort'. Walter Southgate, a socialist founder member of the National Union of Clerks, had his conscientious objection accepted at Stratford Tribunal and was sent to labour in the potato fields at Dagenham Marshes; similarly, Herbert Morrison, secretary of the London Labour Party, whose blind right eye could anyway have secured him medical exemption, appealed to the Wandsworth Tribunal as a conscientious objector and was directed to work on the land at Letchworth in Hertfordshire, where he absorbed himself in his party duties and in making a detailed study of London history.[6]

Those who refused these alternatives or who were not offered them while still refusing to fight had a much harder time, spending much of the rest of their war in prison. Stephen Hobhouse refused the Shoreditch Tribunal's offer of service in the Quaker Ambulance Unit as 'entirely unacceptable', was arrested and sent to the 10th City of London Regiment (the 'Hackney Rifles'), where his non-cooperation landed him in Wormwood Scrubs on hard labour. R. M. Fox, the socialist engineer and anti-war campaigner, had his conscientious objection rejected by a north London tribunal and after court-martial at Mill Hill Barracks served two years' hard labour in Wandsworth and Brixton prisons. Fenner Brockway took a similar route to Wormwood Scrubs and Walton Gaol in Liverpool and was only freed some five months after the end of the war. These men were not alone: Brockway reckoned that by July 1916 some nineteen members of Bermondsey Independent Labour Party were in prison and the number grew as older men were called up.[7]

Despite the loss through banishment or imprisonment of these leading cadres of the anti-war opposition, the dissent that had begun to show itself at the end of 1915 over the threat of conscription redoubled with its arrival. It began to develop too into a movement for a negotiated peace. And, just as at the end of 1915, the anti-war campaigners provoked a violent collective reaction from patriots.

The campaigners themselves were not helped by their differences. The socialist organisations were a world apart from genteel liberal opponents of conscription on the one hand and Christian pacifists like the Quakers on the other. All, though, took bravely to the field on their chosen terrain. The British Socialist Party opposed the war at the traditional street-meeting pitches of Leighton Road in Kentish Town, King Street in Camden Town, and in Regent's Park and on Parliament Hill at Hampstead Heath; Sylvia Pankhurst and the Workers' Suffrage (later Socialist) League braved open hostility to meet outside the East India Dock Gates or march to Victoria Park; the ILP were active in organising street meetings and marches at Bermondsey; the middle-class intellectuals of the Union of Democratic Control put the case against compulsory enlistment at indoor meetings; the North London Herald League continued to campaign against the war at Finsbury Park; and the Christian socialists of the Brotherhood Church in Southgate Road, on the Islington and Hackney border, played ecumenical host to many different anti-war dissenters.[8]

But with the two Military Service Acts in operation from May 1916 the No-Conscription Fellowship (NCF) began to play a leading role in anti-war dissent. The NCF had its origins in late-1914 pacifism, opened a London office in early 1915 and 'really came to life' with its first National Convention as conscription began to appear a near-certainty in November 1915. It had a national membership and organisation, though its business was necessarily metropolitan in focus, if only because of its daily engagement with the War Office over the treatment of conscientious objectors by the tribunals and the army. In London, as least, it occasionally acted as an umbrella organisation linking separate local anti-war groups – helping form a South London Federal Council Against Conscription by April 1916, for instance. The NCF was never suppressed by the authorities, though its publication, *The Tribunal*, was shut down, its printing presses seized and many members were arrested and imprisoned. But it lived in the shadow of suppression and had a secret duplicate organisation ready across the nation in the event of government moving against it.[9]

The NCF and the other dissenting organisations in London lived in interesting times in those first months of conscription in early 1916. Coupled with the fear of arrest came the danger of a beating from those resentful Londoners who viewed pacifists as not only undermining the war effort but negating the sacrifice of so many loved ones on the battlefield. Public meetings in the parks were broken up by hostile crowds, street speakers were hustled and silenced, meetings were cancelled when local authorities and others discovered that their rooms were to be used by pacifists. It was said that men and women leaving NCF meetings were 'roughly handled', 'pelted with stones and struck on the head with sticks'; the police, Metropolitan and City, were accused of joining in the abusive language and doing nothing to protect the dissenters from violence. Fights broke out on the floor of the Brotherhood Church, the opposition frequently led by soldiers in uniform there to give the pacifists a bashing. Most famously of all, at an anti-conscription march and rally in Trafalgar Square on 8 April, the plinth was stormed by ANZAC soldiers and speakers unceremoniously bundled, women and men alike, to the ground.[10]

With the draconian conscription arrangements of May 1916 actually in place, the meetings of the NCF and other pacifist organisations appeared less of a threat to the practical conduct of the war and attracted less public opprobrium and violence. It was still, though, not an easy time to be a pacifist in London's working-class districts. Stephen Hobhouse and a partially lame friend were collecting signatures for a national petition pressing for 'peace by negotiation' in Hoxton that summer when a rumour went round that they were Germans; they managed to escape a crowd 'somewhat the worse for drink' who were intent on throwing them into the canal only by jumping on a passing tram.[11]

Towards the end of the year the Military Service Acts had begun to spawn a different sort of violence in London with the 'round-up' or 'comb-out' of crowded places where young men congregated. These were carried out by police and the military, the latter seeking inappropriately to impose an unwonted discipline on the civilian Londoner and frequently by all accounts overstepping the mark. At the Chiswick Empire Music Hall in September, for instance, army officers took the stage at the end of the performance and ordered all men of military age, broadly interpreted, to remain behind while their call-up papers and exemption certificates were checked: 'An entirely unnecessary roughness was shown by some of the army officers in cross-examining perfectly innocent persons, while the police behaved with consideration and courtesy.' That same month, a round-up at the Ring, the south London boxing venue in Blackfriars Road, led to exciting chases over the Southwark rooftops. And in November a raid on a Soho working-men's club, said to have involved police and 200 soldiers, led to complaints of watches, rings and other valuables being pocketed by the military. It was around this time that the production of false exemption and medical certificates became a prosperous and ingenious backstreet industry in London.[12]

The tensions involved in the introduction and operation of conscription darkened the public mood in the capital from the outset of 1916, a mood blackened further by the ceaseless extension of 'war economy'. Constant invocations to save for the war effort and to spend less on clothes, fuel and food bombarded the Londoner on posters and advertisements in the newspapers. 'The drabness of civilians is very noticeable,' thought Michael MacDonagh that summer: 'Trousers with baggy knees and frayed edges indicate that you are, as the saying is, "doing your bit" to win the War.' The Bank Holidays at Whitsun and August were cancelled by royal proclamation and the Mondays treated as normal workdays. From June petrol rationing took its toll on private motoring whether for business or pleasure: Frederick Robinson's 'very moderate' request for twenty to twenty-five gallons a month ended up as permission for twenty-five gallons a quarter, leaving him to walk sometimes to the station for his City train. Public services like street watering were curtailed by London's borough councils that summer, the LCC ceased taking children under five years old into their elementary schools, and as we have already seen the Londoners' daily pleasures were hit by the closure of museums earlier in the year, also ostensibly in the interests of national economy.[13]

A more welcome innovation that proved permanent was the introduction of 'daylight saving' or British Summer Time from Sunday 21 May 1916. That evening Christopher Addison, Lloyd George's parliamentary secretary at the Ministry of Munitions, had supper in the garden at his Hillingdon home: 'one's first impression is to wonder why it had not been done before.' Far less welcome, the darkness of impending winter was made darker still by tighter lighting restrictions from 1 September, the 'sepulchral gloom' added to from 30 October by an early-closing order that shut almost all shops from 7 p.m. six days a week and 9 p.m. on Saturdays. The impact on traders catering to working-class Londoners, used to working long hours and nipping out for tobacco and other essentials in the evening, seemed to spell ruin, though no doubt people adjusted.[14]

Yet despite all this belt-tightening, public and private, the Londoners fought hard to take their pleasures and enjoy their opportunities for fun and entertainment as best they could. Some found it easier than others, but now more or less all had money in their pockets and some of the old privileges of the leisured classes had begun to be straitened, even tarnished. Club life, for instance, had lost much of its pre-war lustre.

Members were said to be spending half the money in clubs that they had spent before the war, with the Reform Club's annual income down by £1,500; resignations were frequent because of lack of time or other calls on cash (the Reform lost twelve members in May alone); and the amenities continued to decline – no game was served at the Reform that autumn because 'it was so very costly'. Some clubs closed altogether for the duration, the mid-priced National Liberal Club in Whitehall Place (6,000 members) and the Constitutional Club in Northumberland Avenue (6,500) both commandeered for government offices in 1916.[15]

Other aspects of London high life, however, continued to flourish as ever. In July Sir Henry Lucy noted:

> Dining last night at the Savoy Hotel I was struck by the appearance of the dining hall. Except that at small tables here and there khaki uniforms were displayed, there was no sign of the circumstance that the country is in a state of war. I have not seen in the same place in piping times of peace a more crowded or more animated scene. Every table was allotted.

And in November a high-life scandal erupted over the goings-on at Ciro's Club or Restaurant in Orange Street, behind the National Gallery. This place had sufficient resonance in the public mind to give its name to a revamped French farce called *The Girl from Ciro's* at the Garrick Theatre from September. But a month or two later real life copied fiction in a dramatic raid by police to check whether drink was being sold after hours. They found champagne served in jugs and called 'ginger-beer' and lined up on tables round which clustered the social elite of London. The club was struck off the register and heavily fined. *The Girl from Ciro's* suffered no loss of custom as a consequence.[16]

Different attractions, still in the West End, appealed to a more democratic audience. One of the great theatrical successes of the war opened in April 1916 at the Alhambra Theatre of Varieties, Leicester Square. This was *The Bing Boys Are Here*, a revue produced by the theatre's impresario, Oswald Stoll. It starred the music-hall comedians George Robey and Alfred Lester and contained one sensational hit number, 'If You Were the Only Girl in the World', an enduring legacy of this war so memorably punctuated throughout its duration by popular music. *The Bing Boys* played to packed audiences through 1916, on some nights experimenting with an all-female orchestra, and almost every adult Londoner seems to have seen it at least once. The Lord Chamberlain went 'at duty's call' in late October and found it 'in places vulgar and, to my mind, tedious to the last degree and idiotic', its popularity showing 'how decadent is public taste'. But the Alhambra was packed as usual, 'Lots of soldiers in the stalls, and in the galleries or circles crowds of excellent second-class people, all enjoying it hugely'. Indeed, the nightly crowds were so great, and Leicester Square so crammed every evening, that a local tobacconist won a high court injunction against Stoll and the Alhambra requiring them to keep access to his shop clear of people.[17]

The Londoners' appetite for entertainment had never been so insa-tiable and their numbers were swelled beyond parallel 'every night with thousands of soldiers on leave from the front'. These men 'were not seasoned London playgoers', according to George Bernard Shaw, and even those few who were found themselves 'thirsting for silly jokes, dances, and brainlessly sensuous exhibitions of pretty girls', where 'Trivial things gained intensity and stale things novelty.' The West End rose to the challenge from the spring of 1916. And audiences elsewhere drained every drop of consolation on offer, whether from Sir Thomas Beecham, knighted that year, and his opera company at the Shaftesbury Theatre; or piano recitals by the eccentric Vladimir Pachmann at Queen's Hall that spring; or in the cinema, where Thomas Holding in *The Spider* became a heart-throb among Edie Wensley's girl-clerk coterie; or at exhibitions in small West End galleries or at the National itself, which remained open to grateful crowds throughout the war.[18]

But the war was never far away. When Michael MacDonagh left the Alhambra after seeing *The Bing Boys* one night the evening had some glitter quickly knocked off by 'red-capped military police' at the doors who stopped every eligible man 'for proof that he was not evading military service'. And the Londoners' year continued to be punctuated by occasional military spectaculars. The first ANZAC Day on 25 April involved a march from Waterloo to Westminster Abbey, and from there to the City, of ANZAC Gallipoli veterans, among them Captain Ralph Ingram Moore. After the brief service attended by the King and Queen, by Kitchener and the ANZAC commander General William Birdwood, 'I felt I wd. liked to h. got away & had a cry, especially at end when 16 bugles blew the last post f. all those poor chaps we left behind.' It was a day, he thought, 'that will live in [Australia's] future history'. There were other causes for celebration at the Lord Mayor's Show in November, 'a stirring pageant of the Empire's Forces'; and at the mooring of a captured German submarine at Temple Pier on the river for a fortnight from the end of July, though Frederick

Robinson for one thought the admission price of 1s 6d a fraud on the public given how much they had already paid for the war.[19]

But in general the war news through 1916 was bleak, even threatening. The Easter Rising in Dublin came as a shock to the superstructure of wartime unity created in August 1914: there were repercussions in London, with raids on the Gaelic League's London premises in May, and on Irish clubs in Hackney and elsewhere in July and August; and in August Sir Roger Casement was hanged for treason at Pentonville Prison. In spring too an invasion scare swept London and the South-East, taken sufficiently seriously for thousands of troops and volunteers to dig trenches to protect London from the east and south, some 14,000 men digging trenches in Essex alone. Worst of all in that first half of 1916 came news of the sinking of HMS *Hampshire* and the drowning of Lord Kitchener. London heard on 6 June, and when 'Lord Kitchener Drowned!' appeared on the news-stands the traffic in the main streets stopped and drivers and pedestrians thronged to buy a paper. The blinds were drawn at the War Office and flags across London were lowered to half-mast. Many in the crowded streets thought it wasn't true, perhaps some sort of war ruse to befuddle the enemy, and rumours in the streets that he was saved 'roused cheers, again and again'. As certainty dawned the loss of this man, revered by so many as a saviour of his country from the beginning of hostilities, dented the Londoners' morale as few things had done in nearly two years of war: 'Frightful depression about Lord Kitchener's loss,' the pacifist Caroline Playne noted in her diary on 7 June.[20]

It was not long after this staggering event that other rumours began to percolate through London. Talk of a great British push in the offing became common currency, fuelled by visible troop movements and by military gossip. Georgina Lee noted 'a general feeling of suspense in London' from 23 June, and Viscount Sandhurst picked up 'Rumours about the town of our advance in the west' on the same day or a day before. He was a former military man and found the talk troubling: 'I cannot help doubting our intention to advance, as it has been advertised in London for a fortnight.' Soon enough there was no doubt, for at the end of June the London hospitals were urged or ordered to prepare themselves for an unprecedented wave of casualties. St Bartholomew's had orders 'to evacuate every possible bed to the extent of 80 per cent' and was asked how many surgeons it could ship to France for ten days at twenty-four hours' notice; and at Camberwell the 1st London General Hospital was ordered to clear out all convalescents and to expect a 'great rush of wounded'. At Camberwell too Nurse Vera Brittain 'could feel the vibrations of the guns' as the Battle of the Somme opened with its bombardment of unendurably sustained ferocity.[21]

News of the 'Great British Offensive' reached the afternoon editions of London's newspapers on the fateful Saturday the battle opened, 1 July 1916. The first news, as so often, gave false hope of a 'successful advance'. Caroline Playne noted on the day how 'people in street & train looked all happier with a tinge towards mafficking', or jubilant celebration. Success or not – and in the absence of accurate information no one could tell – the effects of the Somme offensive were very quickly felt in London, and the Londoners soon saw how monstrous the consequences were. The hospitals were informed on Monday that casualties were on their way, and even those like the London Hospital, who had not received wounded for months because the War Office had capacity elsewhere, were quickly put on alert. The full weight of the burden was felt in the hospitals especially from Tuesday 4 July. 'There were so many wounded the day before,' Vera Brittain wrote home to her parents, 'that there were not platforms enough at Charing Cross to land them and they had to be taken round to Paddington.' 'I felt very depressed,' Playne now recorded in her diary, 'saw ambulances driving down to meet the trains for wounded – part of the days routine!' This was indeed the first day of what would now become the dominating reality of London for the next five or six weeks, 'immense convoys' of ambulances from the stations to the hospitals and back again, almost it seemed without intermission. At the railway stations in these first hectic days of the Somme, grief and worry seem at times to have come close to losing all control. Captain Robert Graves, at first reported dead, was one of the wounded arriving at Waterloo in July.

> The roadway from the hospital train to a row of waiting ambulances had been roped off; as each stretcher case was lifted from the train, a huge hysterical crowd surged up to the barrier and uttered a new roar. Flags were being waved . . . As I looked idly at the crowd, one figure detached itself: to my embarrassment – I recognized my father, hopping about on one leg, waving an umbrella, and cheering with the best of them.[22]

The Somme marked a qualitative shift in the war experience of the Londoners – on their streets, at the railway stations and in the hospitals, where Vera Brittain at the 1st London General became conscious of a new and interminable strain:

Day after day I had to fight the queer, frightening sensation – to which, throughout my years of nursing, I never became accustomed – of seeing the covered stretchers come in, one after another, without knowing, until I ran with pounding heart to look, what fearful sight or sound or stench, what problem of agony or imminent death, each brown blanket contained.[23]

July 1916 was the most destructive month of the war for the British on the Western Front, with 196,000 men killed or wounded. The battle did not end there. It went on with hardly a pause to staunch the flow of blood as the fighting raged back and forth until the winter rains made more 'offensives' impracticable: 75,000 casualties in August, 115,000 in September, 67,000 in October, 46,000 in November. The implications for London continued to be unremittingly dire. Month after month the stations were daily filled with wounded. 'I do not think I am addicted overmuch to the emotional,' wrote R. D. Blumenfeld in October,

but I do not mind admitting that certain features connected with the war grip me with an inexplicable intensity. I cannot pass the gates of Charing Cross station at any hour of the day without a choking sensation in the throat. There, day by day, during these 'big push' operations, you see a deep double line of people, mostly women, standing mutely and hourly from the doors of the station to the Strand entrance and even beyond, watching the outpouring motors and ambulances filled with the wounded . . . There is no cheering. Just a little waving of handkerchiefs from women with tear-stained faces, and as each motor goes down the line the women gently fling roses.[24]

Sir John Monash, soon to become commander of Australian forces on the Western Front and at this point training in England, relayed in a letter to his wife and daughter – in part to persuade them not to hazard the perilous voyage to join him – 'the terrible feeling of the people in London' that October. 'Whenever there is a rumour of any London unit being engaged, the railway stations at Charing Cross, Victoria, and Waterloo are besieged day and night by dense crowds of parents, wives, children, straining to catch a glimpse of the wounded as they come in.' He thought it a city of 'hysterical anxiety and strain', not least because so many local London units were engaged and decimated: in autumn 'The casualty lists were very heavy,' lamented the LCC's *Record of Service*, and there were terrible losses for the Bermondsey Battalion in the attack on Flers in September, for instance. The very large numbers of wounded soldiers now in London provoked reactions among the public and the authorities, some more bizarre than others. In August the infinitely flexible DORA regulations were extended to make it a criminal offence for Londoners to emit a shrill whistle in the time-honoured way to call a taxi at night in case the rest of soldiers in hospital or elsewhere be disturbed. More generously, a movement began in the spring of 1916 among the residents of many London squares to open their private gardens as 'Squares for the Wounded'. Most of the residents of the West End squares had joined the campaign in time for the influx of wounded and disabled from the Somme.[25]

Besides its impact on London streets, stations and hospitals, the Somme overran the London cinemas too. On 21 August *The Battle of the Somme*, a five-reel film made by Geoffrey Malins and J. B. McDowell and running for seventy-two minutes, opened in London at thirty-four cinemas. It combined real footage of the fighting with some reconstructed battle scenes made at British Army training schools in France. These purported to show men falling dead as they left their trenches, often the most memorable moments for spectators, though the film's authenticity seems to have gone unquestioned at the time; certainly, film of the wounded was genuine and many found it shocking. Just as with *The Bing Boys* at the Alhambra, almost every Londoner seems to have turned out to see it. In early September queues to book tickets were seen throughout the day outside leading London cinemas and halls. Audiences were intensely involved, often emotional, sometimes exclaiming as a soldier chum or relative was apparently glimpsed on screen. Cynthia Asquith found it 'Very thrilling and moving'; H. Rider Haggard's patriotism was predictably stirred by 'the marvellous courage and cheerfulness of our soldiers'; Frederick Robinson, usually so jaded by official war exhortations, marvelled at it and thought it in 'excellent taste'.[26]

The Battle of the Somme, from 1 July through till November 1916, provided a deeper engagement between London and the war than even the first two years of conflict and suffering had so far forged. And now, three days or so after the Somme film opened, the Londoners found themselves once more directly in the line of fire as air raids began again towards the end of August.

There had not been a raid on London for over ten months, since mid-October 1915. But the threat of raids, and the anxiety they caused in the mind of the Londoner, had never gone away. Hallie Miles waited a week or two into the New Year before she 'had courage to go out in the evening since the cruel raids. But as there is a moon' – thought to deter the Zeppelins – 'I am venturing. I don't think we have any of us loved the moon as we do now.' At the end of January a Zeppelin raid on Yorkshire and the Midlands set London nerves jangling, especially because it took place 'in bright moonlight and in broad daylight. So now there seems *no* protection and *no* respite.' Metropolitan apprehensions went unappeased by the absence of attacks on London, it seemed only a question of time before the raids returned: 'I actually met a man this week,' recorded R. D. Blumenfeld in February, 'who confessed that the Zeppelin raids made him feel so much afraid that he had decided to go and live far inland', though the German spring air offensive that sent airships across the North-East, Midlands and Scotland must have given him pause for thought. On 1 February rumours of an attack on London, officially credited, brought suburban trains to a halt from 6 p.m. till nearly midnight; fifty ambulances were said to be 'lined up along the Embankment'. Faith persisted in the deterrent effect of a full moon – concerts and theatrical performances were advertised as taking place on moonlit nights, 'which means no chance of Zeppelins'. But attempts to bomb London only narrowly failed to reach Woolwich on 31 March and 25 April, and a few bombs were dropped more or less harmlessly on Waltham Abbey on 2 April. These events were not widely publicised, but for those in the know it seemed certain that the Zeppelins would sooner or later get through to London.[27]

The Zeppelins' difficulties in spring and early summer were compounded by a strengthening of London's air defences. In London itself most faith was put in the lighting restrictions, and the Commissioner of Police steadfastly resisted any system of public warnings. Even so, the police undertook to warn key locations, such as hospitals, by telephone and the Post Office issued warnings from February that subscribers should not use their phones during raids to allow the network to be devoted to official business.[28]

More significantly, responsibility for air defences was transferred from the Admiralty to the army's home command under Sir John French, now brought back from the front. London became his responsibility from 16 February, the rest of the country following somewhat later. On the same day an ill-tempered debate in the House of Commons voiced criticisms of the country's air defence services, the main critic being Joynson-Hicks, the puritan ultra-conservative Hun-baiter who had been a thorn in the Asquith government's side since the outbreak of war. Lloyd George thought the government got a deserved beating and had been 'very remiss' in its neglect of air defence. Joynson-Hicks would soon be joined – indeed replaced as chief air critic – by Noel Pemberton Billing, whom we have met before. Billing was a wealthy aviator born and raised in Hampstead who had resigned from the Royal Naval Air Service to pursue in Parliament the development of military aircraft. He was narrowly defeated at a by-election in Mile End in January, and then in March stood as an independent in East Hertfordshire. He succeeded resoundingly despite a coalition against him of Liberals and Conservatives, his candidature noisily advocated by the *Daily Mail*, Horatio Bottomley's *John Bull* and what Liberals thought of as 'the liquor interest'.[29]

Billing's views on air defences could not be ignored despite his insolent, impetuous, even eccentric interventions on the floor of the House. How much influence on policy he had in practice is dubious, but it is clear enough that London's air defences were strengthened during the first six months of 1916 by better coordination, more guns (sixty-four, though the desired number of eighty-three was never reached), more searchlights and – most important of all – a reorganised London home defence squadron of at least twenty aircraft, at first BE2cs, at ten stations. Their headquarters were at Hounslow, with the most active stations at Sutton's Farm (Hornchurch) and Hainault Farm (near Romford) on the busy Essex approach to London. By the end of July these aeroplanes were equipped with a new combination of incendiary and tracer bullets for their machine guns.[30]

Knowledge of these arrangements was unsurprisingly not widely shared and so could do nothing or little to quell any public unease. This continued to grow despite a lull in Zeppelin attacks against the British mainland, raids by the slow-moving craft being ill-suited to the short nights around midsummer. Whether the offensive on the Somme, so productive of fears and anxiety for the fate of the British Army, itself generated worries over German reprisals or merely added to the apprehensions of the moment is hard to determine. But General Sir John Monash, in London during July and writing home to Australia, gave a striking portrait of a city in the grip of dread:

> The Zeppelin scare is just as if the whole place was in imminent fear of an earthquake. At night the whole of London is in absolute darkness, every window heavily screened, no street lamps, no lamps on vehicles, all trains with windows closed and blinds drawn, constant street accidents and traffic blocks, and a bewildering pandemonium of confusion in the streets.[31]

London's long wait ended on the night of 24–25 August. Heinrich Mathy in a new 'Super-Zeppelin', L31, penetrated the London defences on a windy night of heavy cloud cover and rain, dropping bombs on south-east London around Woolwich, killing nine and injuring forty more. The raid overall was a failure; twelve airships had set out and although a few bombs were dropped on coastal towns only Mathy reached the main target.[32]

With hindsight the dissolution of that August raid came to be seen as a turning point, the end of the beginning of the air war against London and even Britain itself. For it was followed by an even worse disaster for the German naval air command a week later on 2 September. Sixteen Zeppelins attacked London. Not one penetrated the city's augmented defences, though some bombs were jettisoned on the far outer suburbs causing no casualties and minimal damage. Worse still for the Germans, Lieutenant W. Leefe Robinson of 39 Squadron at Sutton's Farm achieved the first victory of London's air war by bringing down around 2.30 a.m. SL11, a wooden airship, which fell in flames close to the village of Cuffley in Hertfordshire. The rest of the Zeppelins dispersed. Leefe Robinson's feat won him a Victoria Cross and provided a memorable spectacle for the Londoners. John Galsworthy watched the burning vessel fall from his flat in the Adelphi: 'Glad to say that enthusiasm did not *quite* prevent feeling for the thirty men roasting in the air. We went out and talked a few minutes to some policemen; the great cheering in the streets was over and they were empty.'[33]

Nonetheless the German airships regrouped and mounted another large-scale attack on London some three weeks later on 23 September. Out of eleven Zeppelins taking part, three new vessels were deputed to attack London and two got through, one of them once more commanded by Mathy, who bombed Streatham and Brixton; another airship bombed Poplar, Bethnal Green and Shoreditch. In all they killed twenty-six, injured seventy-three and started thirty fires, some of them serious in the East End. Although Mathy lived to fight another day, the other two airships attacking London were brought down: one, damaged by gunfire from both ground and air, landed near Chelmsford and its crew were captured; the other was destroyed by 2nd Lieutenant Frederick Sowry near Billericay in Essex, burning up and killing all on board.[34]

There was a bizarre sequel, so revealing of the transnational solidarities of class that even the ostensible unity of war could never quite overcome. On 27 September the German aircrew were buried with full military honours at Great Burstead. Twenty-two men had died, including the commander, Peterson. The bodies were brought to the graveyard in coffins loaded onto two lorries, twenty-one on one and Peterson on the other. His was the only coffin to bear a brass nameplate.[35]

Even these victories, trumpeted in the newspapers and plain for all to see, did little to settle Londoners' nerves. Some papers predicted a 'gigantic Zeppelin raid on London' by no fewer than eighty airships in the last week of September, causing considerable alarm; and Zeppelins were said to be dropping poisoned sweets in the hope that children would eat them. Then, on the night of 1–2 October, the Zeppelins provided one of the great spectacles of London's war that lived in the collective memory for generations. The daring Heinrich Mathy was brought down in flames at Potters Bar, just north of London. His was one of eleven airships, those targeting London kept out by fierce gunfire; even Mathy was forced to jettison his bombs over Cheshunt, damaging only the market gardeners' greenhouses and injuring one person. He was then attacked in the air by 2nd Lieutenant W. J. Tempest and set alight by incendiary bullets. The L31 fell with the loss of all its crew, the scene watched open-mouthed by hundreds of thousands of Londoners. It was a moment of terrible beauty, made more terrible still by the response of the watching crowds. Michael MacDonagh was among them, on Blackfriars Bridge walking home after work at the *The Times*, and wrote it up in his diary a few hours later:

> Looking up the clear run of New Bridge Street and Farringdon Road I saw high in the sky a concentrated blaze of searchlights, and in its centre a ruddy glow which rapidly spread into the outline of a burning airship. Then the searchlights were turned off and the Zeppelin drifted perpendicularly in the darkened sky, a gigantic pyramid of flames, red and orange, like a ruined star falling slowly to earth. Its glare lit up the streets and gave a ruddy tint even to the waters of the Thames.
>
> The spectacle lasted two or three minutes. It was so horribly fascinating that I felt spell-bound – almost suffocated with emotion, ready hysterically to laugh or cry. When at last the doomed airship vanished from sight there arose a shout the like of which I never heard in London before – a hoarse shout of mingled execration, triumph and joy; a swelling shout that appeared to be rising from all parts of the metropolis, ever increasing in force and intensity.[36]

This was effectively the end of the Zeppelin war against London, and of the first phase of the German air bombardment, though there would be one final fling about a year later. There was a harbinger of what was to come. In the early morning of 28 November a single German LVG biplane dropped six bombs in a daylight raid that had the Admiralty as its target. Ten people were injured in the streets around Victoria Station, but there was little damage done. London would remain immune from raids of any kind for six months or so to come.[37]

The Londoners, then, had weathered the aerial storm of the late summer and autumn of 1916. But they didn't know it and they did not know what, if anything, was round the corner. And though their nights were relatively undisturbed, their days continued to be of unremitting worry, new concerns arising with relentless frequency.

Most intrusive of all were the shortages of various domestic commodities and consequent rising prices. From January, Georgina Lee had noted the virtual disappearance of methylated spirits from the shops at anything other than exorbitant prices and soda crystals for washing up couldn't be had at all. The quality of many commodities still available tended remorselessly downwards, with the Reform Club soap unpleasant to the touch, its corona cigars distasteful to many members, its bread rolls shrinking in size and its bread made from 'inferior flour' with 'very little substance in it'. It was the increasingly effective submarine warfare against British merchant shipping that had the most worrying impact, and that was on food supplies. In the House of Commons some shortages were said to be affecting the working classes worse than others. Will Thorne, MP for West Ham South, complained that small London butchers could not obtain New Zealand lamb, for instance, allegedly reserved for more favoured customers in the West End. In April it was said that songbirds were being killed for food and sold in West End butchers' shops, though larks had long been a legal London delicacy. In the Wandsworth workhouses and infirmary granulated sugar was so scarce by March that it had to be replaced with 'yellow crystals', in July sausage replaced salt beef on the dietary (proving a popular change) and in October rabbit replaced mutton. It was indeed the food supply that worried Londoners most – declining quality, periodic shortages and, worst of all, rising prices. There were steep price hikes in January, April to May and October to November 1916, with food prices rising 26 per cent during the year, and they combined with a general deterioration in both the quality and the range of food available.[38]

For those with foresight the food problem seemed an impending social and political crisis some months before government eventually acted. It was Winston Churchill, now a backbencher after the Gallipoli fiasco, who first melodramatically called for government action to ration food by need and not leave it to the market to ration by price: 'a more cruel or more unfair way' could not be devised because it 'would simply starve the poorest classes out of existence'. That was in August 1916. But the need for action only tardily stirred those in government and civil servants, including William Beveridge, were tasked with devising a solution only some three months later.[39]

By then many Londoners had begun to take matters into their own hands by growing food for their and their neighbours' consumption. This was a movement with uneven beginnings in the semi-rural districts at London's southern edge. As early as August 1914 in Croydon a landowner made empty development sites available as allotments, and an Agricultural Committee was established in Wimbledon in December 1915, with thirty-seven plots 'on the Sewage Farm' worked by early 1916. Through the spring the idea caught on, with a campaign for the compulsory use of vacant land for growing food finding some support in the House of Commons. But it was the deepening food shortages from late autumn 1916, with all their potential for disgruntlement and unrest in the working-class districts of London, that at last provoked official action by government on the coat-tails of popular action. In December 1916 an extension of DORA, the Land Cultivation Order, enabled the acquisition of empty land by local councils for use as allotments. From then local authorities formed committees across London, putting recreational land to other uses, with the flowerbeds in Bermondsey's parks turned over to vegetable-growing, church lands in Clapham and Norwood and elsewhere cut into allotments, and 'large parts' of Hampstead Heath used for growing food. As so often during this war, there was a tendency to puritan hysteria in this new commitment to economy and total war, some MPs proposing unsuccessfully that Hyde Park and Regent's Park be ploughed up for potatoes. But by the end of the year the fruits of the allotment movement were becoming apparent everywhere in London. 'I visited various districts,' recorded Michael MacDonagh on Boxing Day 1916 – 'Greenwich, Tooting, Clapham, Dulwich, Wimbledon, to mention only a few – and saw in all of them groups of people busy with spade and fork.'[40]

Despite Churchill's far-sighted intervention in August 1916, sharply rising food prices did not receive full government attention till November.

Its inaction seemed to typify once again a reluctance wholeheartedly to commit the resources of the nation to the task of winning the war. At every turn since August 1914 it seemed to many that the Asquith governments, both Liberal and coalition, had been behind events, dragged, prodded and poked into action only when circumstances had become intolerable – over interning enemy aliens, for instance, over munitions, over conscription, over London's air defences and now over the availability of staple foodstuffs at a price ordinary people could afford to pay. Dissatisfaction that autumn combined with the continuous bloodletting of the British Army on the Somme, all – it seemed – literally for nothing. But it was the food question that became the ultimate test of the credibility of Asquith's leadership, indeed of the usefulness of what looked like an outdated creed of Liberal individualism that was now threatening, through scruples and niceties, the very survival of the nation itself.[41]

Lloyd George offered the dynamism that most of the political classes now thought they needed in a war leader. His demands for a refashioning of the War Cabinet, not led by Asquith, who would nonetheless remain prime minister, was at first accepted by Asquith. But the humiliation of such a position was brought home to him by a *Times* leader and he changed his mind. Lloyd George promptly resigned from the Cabinet. His government tumbling around him, Asquith offered his resignation to the King on 5 December. Bonar Law, the Conservative leader, was asked by the King to form a government, but was unable or unwilling to do so. With nowhere else to turn, the King sent for Lloyd George. He became prime minister on 7 December. These were days of intensely dramatic events and bitter political manoeuvring in the Commons, the Lords and the great London clubs, but little of this spilled out to ruffle the Londoners, all struggling to deal with problems of their own. On 8 December Asquith and Lord Grey called a meeting of their Liberal Party supporters, still a large number, in the Reform Club, where Asquith complained of 'a "well organised and carefully prepared conspiracy"' against him, with Lloyd George the chief plotter. Michael MacDonagh waited with other journalists outside in Pall Mall. There were no crowds. 'It is remarkable,' he thought, 'what little public excitement the crisis has aroused . . . Asquith and Lord Grey left the Reform Club together. They took no notice of us.' Most Londoners probably looked on the change as inevitable and desirable. But for those who saw Asquith as a reluctant warmonger, representing traditional Liberal verities, it was one more bleak moment in a year of tragedy:

'Political crises loomed large,' noted Caroline Playne in her diary. 'I felt very depressed. Foggy, wretched day.'[42]

One of the new government's first acts was to appoint a Food Controller, Lord Devonport. It was an appointment promised over three weeks before by Asquith but nothing had happened, a failure symptomatic of the old coalition's near-paralysis. The Londoners felt the Controller's impact within days: restaurants and club meals in London were confined to two courses at lunch and three at dinner.[43]

With Christmas just two weeks away, the Food Controller's exhortations and restrictions merely added to the misery. The weather gave every sign of turning into a savage winter. Exiguous street lighting made any attempt to go out at night hazardous, even deadly as street accidents and fatalities seemed to multiply. On his way home from the Oxford and Cambridge Club in Pall Mall the Lord Chamberlain found it so 'dark coming back I tumbled over low rail by flower beds in front of Buckingham Palace and ran into a pillar-box'. 'To wish each other "Merry Christmas",' thought MacDonagh, 'is almost a mockery. Of such is the prevailing gloom.' Celebrations at the West End hotels were cancelled in response to Lloyd George's clamouring for economy and the Food Controller's strictures about overeating and waste. The foul weather capped it all. Caroline Playne charted it almost daily: 'Cold, dark day'; 'Snow on ground'; 'Very wet early'; 'Very bad fog'. The 'thick, dank fog' stifled almost all public entertainment over the holiday. 'Very few people were abroad,' *The Times* reported of London's Boxing Day, 'and most of those appeared to be bound for the shelter and warmth, as well as the entertainment, of music-halls and picture-houses.'[44] Even when people did venture out, Playne thought, their mood was bleak. A few days later she noted how

> Everyone looked sad & depressed over the Christmas time in the tubes and streets, with very few exceptions. Only some young people were sometimes happy. The soldiers coming & going look sad, just those who have evidently been met by wife and children had glad expressions. Some dressed up, dissolute couples – soldiers, officers and got up ladies were enjoying pleasure of a kind.[45]

Those 'got up ladies' offering 'pleasure of a kind' would come to play an increasingly lurid part in London life in the year ahead.

9

HARLOT-HAUNTED LONDON

WHEREVER men had come together in London prostitutes had always been on hand to receive them. Now there were more men gathered in the metropolis than ever before in history. In all the circumstances that had combined to bring them there it was small wonder that they should seek excitement and solace from women and no surprise at all that some would pay for the sexual comfort they received.

Who were the women who catered to their needs? They were of all kinds and by no means all professional prostitutes. Indeed, trying to clarify just who was a 'prostitute' was always difficult , and especially so in these exceptional times. That did not, however, prevent moralists, social workers and others substituting prejudice and ignorance for fact or plain common sense. Disentangling myth from reality, truth from fiction, in these circumstances is impossible, not least because no one seems to have talked to the women themselves.

Many observers were struck by the change in the London streets brought about by the war: 'You have vast numbers of soldiers on leave, and you have a large number of young women living a more independent life than they were in peace time', so that 'the streets are very much more crowded now'.[1] Among the crowds of women, those concerned with the changing morality of wartime London thought that

since the war, and perhaps for some years before the war, there were considerable numbers of young girls who were, if not adopting the profession of prostitutes, at any rate leading immoral lives. There is a very much larger number now of young girls on the streets than there were, say 20 years ago – quite young girls of 15, 16 and 17 years of age.

Challenged to provide evidence for this confident assertion, Sir Ernley Blackwell, a junior Home Office minister, offered the experience of a man about town:

> I would arrive at it simply by walking along the streets and taking notice myself. I see that there are. I do not think anyone who has known the London streets for the last 20 or 30 years could avoid being struck by the fact that, whereas 20 or 25 years ago the streets of the West End between 8 and 12 o'clock were full of women, professional prostitutes, but women of considerable age, well over 25 years of age, now I should say there are far fewer of these regular professional prostitutes and many more quite young girls, whom you did not see in old days; at any rate, they would not be there alone. [2]

A somewhat different view of the same phenomenon was given by Miss Elithe MacDougall, a Scottish social worker who knew the girls of Lambeth well and who in October 1918 was 'Lady Assistant' to the Metropolitan Police. She agreed that the age of prostitutes in London had come down since the start of the war but on the other hand thought 'a great many young girls do not take money at all if they go wrong' with soldiers: 'They are simply out for a lark.'[3]

These larks took place pretty much everywhere in London County and no doubt beyond. But the war brought with it new fields of action and intensified familiar theatres. The streets around the London railway stations, for instance, had long presented opportunities for sexual encounters, but the war, with its extraordinary demands, thrust out new marketplaces in every direction. So around Victoria Station, for instance, traditional soliciting walks at Terminus Place and Vauxhall Bridge Road and the cheap lodging district of Pimlico were extended into Horseferry Road, encouraged by the ANZAC headquarters there. It was said that 'the evil is to a large extent foreign to the locality, and has sprung up there since the beginning of the war'; by early 1917 it was 'a hot-bed of immorality, undisguised and unchecked', where 'Prostitutes of all types and ages, but noticeably in most cases young and rather showily dressed, parade the streets and loiter at the corners with the same effrontery' as in the traditional street-walking districts. Around this new local trade 'convenient "lodgings" abound in every direction' and public houses happily tolerated the women and their clients.[4]

In the West End, in Soho and Fitzrovia, streets long used by prostitutes continued to hold their own. In March 1916 Arnold Bennett dined at the Reform Club alone and wandered into the West End: 'London very wet and dark and many *grues* mysteriously looming out at you in Coventry Street.' In June 1917 he strolled out again: 'Walking about these streets about 10 to 10.30 when dusk is nearly over, is a notable sensation; especially through Soho, with little cafés and co-op clubs and women and girls at shop doors. It is the heat that makes these things fine.' And perhaps the war-enforced darkness too, as on

> the north side of Coventry Street, where officers, soldiers, civilians, police and courtesans marched eternally to and fro, peering at one another in the thick gloom that, except in the immediate region of a lamp, put all girls, the young and the ageing, the pretty and the ugly, the good-natured and the grasping, on a sinister enticing equality.[5]

Although there were very large numbers of men in London in these years, however, it is impossible to determine whether the numbers of prostitutes on the streets rose in proportion. What figures we have are for arrests and convictions for soliciting and associated offences. Both declined significantly during the war years, arrests falling from 9,406 in the two years 1913–14 to 5,843 in 1917–18, despite the public furore over prostitution rising to a fever in 1917 and despite the operational strength of the Metropolitan Police rising by 10 per cent or so over the course of the war. Although the police had many new wartime obligations that must have squeezed out routine duties these figures hardly suggest any rise in full-time professional street prostitution of the traditional London kind. Similarly, convictions for brothel-keeping fell away from an average of 249 a year over the five years before the war to 191 in 1914–18.[6]

Nor does there seem to be much evidence for a rise in the numbers of foreign prostitutes on the streets of London, though they were frequently complained about at the time. Known German prostitutes were removed under the restrictions imposed on enemy aliens at the outset of the war, though it is likely that the place of some would have been taken by French and Belgian women.[7] When Belgian and other continental entrepreneurs moved into the old German quarter north of Oxford Street, taking over abandoned cafés and restaurants and starting up new ones, continental freedoms allowing prostitutes the run of their places quickly brought them trouble from the police. 'I beg to report,' the Sub-Divisional Inspector at Tottenham Court Road police station wrote to the Commissioner in November 1916,

> that a large number of Cafe's kept by foreigners have sprung up on this Sub-Division during the past few months and I have received information that drink is sold in several of them, and that gaming is also carried on. Disorderly conduct is prevalent, prostitutes and other undesirables are harboured, and the establishments are much frequented by British, Colonial, and foreign soldiers. Most have Automatic Pianos which are playing almost continuously till late at night.[8]

Of twenty-eight places listed, twenty-two were said to be used by prostitutes, their proprietors Belgians, French, Swiss, Russians and Romanians. Prosecutions for harbouring prostitutes were duly brought against the Café d'Alliés in Rathbone Place, the Au Roi Albert Café in Tottenham Street and the Café Franco-Italian in Windmill Street, the last two (run by a Belgian and a Frenchman respectively) described as brothels. Reports of foreign-run brothels appeared frequently too in the London press, as indeed did the home-grown variety, run by women and men alike throughout St Pancras, Holborn, Westminster and Marylebone. Even so, not all the prostitutes using these places can have been foreigners, even where the proprietors were: the police at Bow Street, for instance, charged 211 'known prostitutes' with soliciting and similar offences during 1916 – one was Belgian, one Danish and 209 were British.[9]

In all the excitement of the times maybe it was the girls and women 'out for a lark', or 'amateurs' over whom 'the police have no control', who were the dominant figures in London's lively street life, and who also benefited from the trade in casually rented cheap lodgings around the railway stations in particular. We might get closer to this reality by looking in more detail at the district around Waterloo Station.[10]

No area drew greater press interest or produced more sensational rumours than this congested district of North Lambeth. Its notoriety as a place of prostitution in London went back generations, even pre-dating the railway station, but the trade was greatly extended when the terminus of the London and South Western Railway and other companies was planted there from 1848. Waterloo Station's rebuilding was begun in 1909 but delayed by the war and not completed till 1922.

Even so, as the main terminus for Southampton and Portsmouth, the station handled trains carrying hundreds of thousands of soldiers and sailors on leave or injured. The station's connection with the armed services in fact went deeper. The largest military hospital in the country, King George's, opened in June 1915 in Stamford Street, occupying what was formerly the huge HMSO and Office of Works store; from here walking wounded in their 'hospital blues' would take the air and meet comrades at Waterloo Station. And there was an earlier famous connection in the Union Jack Club, a great clubhouse with restaurant, billiards room and hostel accommodating 335 men for a night or two and opened in Waterloo Road in July 1907. The Union Jack Club cemented the district's connection with prostitution too: for servicemen and no doubt others, the area around Waterloo Station was known as 'Whoreterloo'.[11]

It was this unlovely London neighbourhood that encapsulated in a few streets the anxiety of the nation, even the Empire, over the sexual morality of its servicemen during wartime. It is possible, with caution, to pick out some of the reality of 'prostitution' in its various forms from the sensationalism that began to paint the district in such lurid colours during the winter of 1916–17.

First, the numbers. They seem to have been generally very large. In late 1915 'the scandal of young women frequenting Waterloo-road' was remarked on locally, with weekend soliciting charges at Tower Bridge police court alone on a Monday morning routinely seeing a score of women in front of the magistrate. That year 'upwards of 800 women were charged' at Kennington Road police station 'for offences of indecency soliciting &c.', mainly in Waterloo Road and around. This seems to have continued throughout the war. 'Night after night the short stretch of road between Stamford-street and the "Old Vic." is thronged by women who are unmistakeably pursuing the traffic of prostitution', it was said in February 1917. 'The whole district is so infested by prostitutes that no one could walk a hundred yards from the station in any direction without passing scores of them.'[12]

The ages of women prosecuted ranged generally from eighteen to twenty-five but with a minority of older women into their forties. By no means all of the young women were 'common prostitutes' known to the police. 'Two, who said they were only "larking", were remanded for inquiries; a third, who said she was going to be married next week to an Australian soldier, was also remanded.' And 'Ann Newman (25), milliner, took a soldier by the arm and invited him to go for a walk with her. She had been in regular work for 11 years. – The magistrate remarked that she was beginning to play the fool with soldiers and bound her over to be of good behaviour.' 'Playing the fool' and 'having a lark' laid women open to arrest, a night in the cells, a lecture by the magistrate and their names in the papers, although some women were indeed looking for a treat and a payment for their time:

> Alice Brown (43), independent, and Nellie Taylor (36), no occupation, were walking arm-in-arm and stopping soldiers. Brown was overheard to say to one 'Are you coming for a walk with us, dear?' They were each ordered to find a surety in £5 to keep the peace, or to undergo six weeks' imprisonment.

Among many hundreds of the more professional sort we might cite Jessie Tate, twenty-four, of Tenison Street, leading 'an immoral life' for two years and just out of prison; or a girl of nineteen, formerly in service at Bath, who told the magistrate 'she "was prepared to go to the devil her own way"'; or one Madge Thatcher, twenty-one, no fixed abode, fined 30s for soliciting in Waterloo Road or twenty-one days' imprisonment. And other women were attracted to the area less for the personal services they might render in time of war – doing their bit, perhaps – than for the ready plunder offered by drunken men only too glad to be home from the front: Louisa Gifford, forty-two, and Charlotte Williams, twenty-five, from the roughest part of Hoxton around Essex Street, were given hard labour for pocketing money and a paybook in the Lord Hill public house on Waterloo Road and stealing from a soldier in the street in September 1916, for instance.[13]

In and around this thriving trade a distinctive housing market had been constructed for generations. Some were 'brothels' where more than one prostitute lodged, perhaps complete with maids and 'bullies' to protect them. More were 'disorderly houses' where prostitutes could take a client for a 'short time' or longer. This housing market was likely to have been extended in every direction during the war. There was a hierarchy that rested on some private nuance of respectability: '"we never take ins and outs"', a 58-year-old packer explained to the magistrate of the disorderly house run by himself and his wife at 85 York Road in early 1917: '"They must stay the night."' For the ins and outs the profits were potentially very large. Maud Yates, forty-three, was said to receive 8s 6d for every man taken to her house in Brook Street, Newington, where two prostitutes lodged, for instance. Of whatever variety, houses like this were all over the Waterloo Road district and leached out in every direction. The main roads around Waterloo Station were peppered with such accommodating residences, in Waterloo Road itself of course, but also in York Road, Belvedere Road and the places off to the south-west of the station, and Stamford Street, notorious for generations, to the east; and then through Kennington to Brixton south-wards and through Bermondsey and beyond downriver, all shearing the uniformed sheep of Waterloo. The trade was so profitable that many took advantage of this special housing market by letting prostitutes use their premises, at a price: a dentist in Waterloo Road, second-hand furniture dealers in Lambeth Walk, music-hall artistes finding a lucrative sideline for a flat in Cranworth Gardens, Brixton; and it attracted women and men of all ages and conditions, like Sarah McGann, eighty years old, convicted of running a disorderly house in Chicheley Street, York Road, and fined £10: "'I'll lose my Lambeth and old age pensions and have to go into the workhouse."' Or Emily Woolougham, eighty-one, fined £15 for running a disorderly house at Kennington Park Road; she paid by cheque, confessing to a private income: 'Well-to-do Octogenarian Brothel-keeper' was the headline in the local paper.[14]

Inevitably this was a trade whose pleasures could not fail to arouse the prurient and the prudish. The most sensational claim made against London prostitution in general and the Waterloo Road district in particular was that women were drugging soldiers and then robbing them of everything they had. Stories of this kind had circulated in late 1915 about Victoria and Euston stations and were said to originate from one helper at the YMCA 'Hut' for soldiers in Seymour Street, Euston.[15] A couple of months later this canard was driven to Waterloo by the Reverend Frederick Brotherton Meyer, Baptist minister of Christ Church, Westminster Bridge Road. A tireless self-publicist, Meyer was brought up in Clapham and had been a leading light in the social purity movement: in an earlier spell at Westminster Bridge Road, from 1892 to 1907, he claimed to have closed over 700 brothels in that area of Lambeth alone. He was a long-standing vociferous opponent of drink and public houses. Sixty-seven when war broke out, he sympathised with peace campaigners while never himself taking an anti-war position; and from 1917 he led a movement preparing the nation for the imminent second coming of Christ.[16]

It was F. B. Meyer who first publicly made the claim that women were drugging soldiers, to the Surrey licensing bench at Southwark Town Hall in February 1916. During his night-time investigations into the Waterloo Road district, and in conversation with soldiers at the YMCA's Waterloo Hut, of whom 'some two-thirds had been under the influence of drink', 'I have met with many cases of men who have been drugged and who have been at the mercy of any harpy who desired to plunder them.' Soldiers, especially colonials from Australia and Canada, had lost not just substantial sums of back-pay, 'but they lost more than that. They lost self-respect and purity, and those great thoughts of London which had brought them there.' 'Dr. F. B. Meyer's Startling Statements' were immediately picked up by the press. His supporters among local evangelicals were quick to bring forward 'proof' that individual soldiers known to them had indeed been drugged. But when the police asked Meyer for details of any cases, none of which he had brought to their attention before making his public statements, they all proved too vague and insubstantial to be investigated. The police thought the men referred to were merely drunk, sometimes on home-distilled alcohol or 'Pot Sheen' (poteen), sold to them in backstreet shebeens.[17]

It was around this time that the state of the streets near Waterloo Station became a national scandal, taken up by the daily press and leading to official protests from Dominion representatives over the risks posed to their young men on the streets of London. Cases of robbery and assault on colonial troops, better paid than home-grown Tommies, were given special prominence in the newspapers and there seems little doubt that some among the residents of this notoriously tough district saw these colonial men as easy pickings. So we read of two women and a man imprisoned with hard labour for robbing an Australian convalescent soldier whom one of the women met in Waterloo Road. He asked if she knew of lodgings and she took him to a tenement flat nearby, where he slept in the kitchen. After drawing £7 10s back-pay, he handed over the exorbitant sum of £4 in advance for his lodgings; when he fell asleep next night he awoke to find the rest of his money gone. Saying he was going to the police, the three promptly attacked him. Two young women, nineteen and twenty-four, were given hard labour for robbing a soldier of the Canadian Mounted Rifles of £8 in a pub in Waterloo Road – it was his first visit to London. And a 38-year-old cook was imprisoned for stealing £13 from an Australian soldier she had met in Waterloo Road – she had lived with him for some days in Oswin Street, Elephant and Castle; there were numerous others.[18]

Things might get more serious. On 8 November 1917, Private Oliver Imlay, a Canadian soldier, met a comrade at the Waterloo YMCA Hut. Out for a stroll, they got chatting to two Australian soldiers, one of whom was with some girls. The four men decided to go in search of a drink and fell in with a local dock labourer, Joseph Jones, who promised to get them some 'whiskey'. In a dark passage, Valentine Place off Blackfriars Road, both Canadians were hit over the head, probably with truncheons and probably by Jones and one of the Australians. The Canadians were robbed as they lay in the street. Imlay's skull was stoved in and he never recovered consciousness. All three stood trial for murder and Jones was hanged at Wandsworth jail in February 1918.[19]

Women were in even greater danger during these murky transactions. In February 1915 Alice Jarman, about forty, a prostitute then living in a woman's common lodging house in Crescent Street, Notting Dale, one of the poorest and roughest districts of London, was found dead in a ditch in Hyde Park. 'There was a terrible gash in her throat, and wounds in her abdomen, arm, and chest,' apparently inflicted with a bayonet. She had last been seen in the company of a soldier in the Uxbridge Road. Despite 'an old sword-bayonet in [a] scabbard' being found in a sewer nearby, and despite 900 troops put on identity parade at White City barracks, Jarman's killer was never found.[20]

Amid all the talk of a '"harlot-haunted" London' by half-hysterical moralists like Arthur Conan Doyle, or the 'orgy of licentiousness existing in London' reported by the Chaplain of Holloway Prison, it is difficult to look behind the sensationalising of wartime prostitution and uncover what it might have meant for those involved at the time. We come closest to the yearning and pity of it all from the rich observations of Sylvia Pankhurst, who visited Waterloo Road with some companions during the height of its scandalous notoriety one biting-cold Saturday night. She crossed over Waterloo Bridge from the north.

In one of the alcoves of the bridge sat a merry party – two sailors and two women – opening packets of sandwiches and cake, with quip and joke. In another a man and woman were together silent, hand clasping hand, in the moveless throes of sorrow.

Over the bridge the people were denser; policemen and special constables met one almost at every step. Sometimes a woman stood by the

curb, or hung back close to the wall. Just as one chose, one could deem
her a 'harpy,' or merely a respectable woman waiting for a 'bus or a
friend. Two soldiers went by us together, and behind them two girls,
giggling noisily – to attract the attention of the men, one might judge if
one pleased, or just with the jolly unconsciousness of youth, enjoying its
night out.

A poor, battered creature, of sixty years or more, drunk or demented,
railed dismally to the unheeding void: 'You, you, you'll be getting me
locked up! You'll be getting me locked up!'

A crowd had gathered, helmeted policemen in the centre, special
constables on the outskirts, urging the people to move on. 'Get away
from me! Get away from me!' a man's voice shouted. 'I've lost a leg at
the Front, where *you* ought to be!' Women and girls were wringing their
hands with cries of protest: 'They are treading on him! He has got eight
wounds and only one leg! Oh! Oh! They are treading on him!' A one-
legged soldier lay on the pavement. The police had taken his crutches;
they lifted him to an ambulance, and wheeled him off. No one could tell
us why.

A group of soldiers and women tumbled out of the public house at
closing time. The men were rolling drunk; the women approximately
sober. 'Good night! See you to-morrow!' they chorused cheerfully. A stout
woman patted the cheek of one of the sailors with a loud guffaw. The
men reeled off round the corner, shouting some ditty, the women went
together by the main road, chatty and jovial.[21]

Perhaps we get closer too, though from a different direction, through
'Robert Hutton', 'a homosexual and an alcoholic', whose memoirs were
published many years later. In 1914 he was sixteen years old, living at
home in 'a South London suburb' and studying at an engineering college.
Sometimes he would skip lectures and take the train to Victoria and
then bus or tube to the West End just to watch the 'men in uniform,
hucksters, prostitutes and people like myself, killing time and enjoying
the crowds . . .' Victoria Station was well known during the war and
probably before as a pick-up point for men – so much so that Cecil
Chapman, a new Westminster magistrate from early 1917, was surprised
by the numbers of men brought before him for 'solicitation'. Hutton's
first homosexual encounter was in a summer house at Belgrave Square;
the man who picked him up at Victoria Station bookstall had a key to
the square's overgrown gardens. Some time later, probably in early

1915, Hutton was hanging around an entrance to Piccadilly Circus tube station.

> I was just inside the entrance, on the Circus side, when I saw a young officer approaching. Our eyes met as he approached and he looked back. He turned and without the slightest hesitation, came up to me.
> 'Are you waiting for someone?' he said.
> 'No one in particular,' I replied, with my heart in my mouth.
> 'Come and have some tea then' . . .[22]

After going to the theatre they spent the night together. Hutton telephoned home to say he'd missed the last train home and was staying with friends. Some three years later he heard the officer had been killed in action. By then Hutton had become acquainted with 'certain recognised places where homosexuals gathered' in the West End: a bar in Shaftesbury Avenue, 'more like a club', run by a former actor; Sunday mornings at the Trocadero Long Bar; Alex's Hotel, Covent Garden, and no doubt more.[23]

The 'orgy of licentiousness' said to have been brought on by war elicited an immediate response among guardians of the Londoners' morals. One long-lasting consequence was the creation of an entirely new extension of London's policing arrangements. This was the first appearance of a women's police force. It originated in puritanism and class superiority – a matriarchy of the elite, we might call it – and unsurprisingly was an offshoot of the suffrage movement now directing virtually all its considerable energies to one aspect or other of the war effort. The architects of a women's police force in London included Nina Boyle and Mary Allen, former suffragettes who had both been imprisoned before the war; Margaret Damer Dawson, a leading campaigner in the puritan National Vigilance Association; and Adeline, Duchess of Bedford, Mrs Louise Creighton (another purity campaigner) and Mrs M. G. Carden of the National Union of Women Workers (NUWW), despite its name an organisation run mainly by upper-middle-class women.

Dawson seems to have been the first to approach the Metropolitan Police Commissioner, Sir Edward Henry, soon after the outbreak of war. Making arrangements for Belgian refugees at the London railway stations, she 'had been struck by the number of women loitering there, whose presence and whose object seemed unexplained . . .' After consultation with the Home Office, Henry gave Dawson permission to organise what became the Women's Police Volunteers (WPV) from among 'women of similar calibre, social standing and education, mentally and physically above the average'. Nina Boyle was her deputy, though 'an intransigeant' according to the Commissioner. Boyle split from Dawson in late 1914 over the WPV's readiness to enforce a night-time curfew against women in Grantham, a military town in Lincolnshire, where the first women police outside London were deployed: most of the Volunteers followed Dawson, who was willing to implement the curfew, into a new Women's Police Service (WPS).[24]

By the middle of 1915 there were three women's police organisations active in London. The Women Patrols of the NUWW, some 236 women wearing no uniform 'save an amulet' like special constables and carrying a numbered badge on their left wrist; Nina Boyle's WPV, which, though in uniform similar to the WPS, were not recognised by the Metropolitan Police but patrolled in London without interference nonetheless; and Margaret Damer Dawson's WPS of '"Ladies in Blue"', dressed in jacket and long skirt of blue police serge and a blue felt hat bearing 'WPS' in silver letters; none carried any weapon. Like the NUWW, the WPS worked with the official sanction of the Commissioner and were reluctantly tolerated by the rest of his force.[25]

The WPS and NUWW patrols were deployed in munitions factories from 1916, both in London (the royal factories, national filling factories and large works still in private hands) and beyond. Their duties were to serve industrial efficiency – combating 'Habitual loitering' and flushing out 'girls hiding away from their work in all sorts of strange places'; and to strengthen morality, remonstrating for instance against 'frequently appalling coarse' behaviour and 'the most profane language', preventing 'petty thefts' and so on.[26]

But the presence of the various women's police organisations was felt most in London's streets and parks. Their object was to deter or disrupt immoral behaviour rather than to prevent crime. Just what constituted behaviour worthy of intervention was very much in the eye of the beholder. The women police usually patrolled in pairs and, in troublesome districts with large numbers of professional prostitutes likely to resent intrusion, as in Waterloo Road, they were often accompanied by a police constable. In general, though, they left prostitutes alone. Their target was more the larking girls of the amateur variety, their purpose to discourage promiscuous mixing of the sexes, their tactics unsubtle and no doubt found objectionable by many. Mary Allen of the WPS recalled with satisfaction how 'The number of loiterers around Edgware Road and Marble Arch (often middle-aged well-dressed men) was considerably reduced. Finding themselves watched at every turn by policewomen, they would soon tire and move off.' We get a closer look at their methods on the ground from the police at Vine Street, C Division:

> I beg to report that for some time past about six women have been seen nightly, some in blue uniform, others in private attire wearing detachable badges on the arm and working jointly, patrolling various thoroughfares on this Division. No in-timation has been received by Police here from any source as to the object they have in view, or under what authority they are acting . . .
>
> They usually patrol in Piccadilly Circus, Coventry Street, Leicester Square, and Charing Cross Road, between the hours of eight pm and twelve-thirty am. They work in double patrols and appear to have a superior patrolling officer who has been seen to visit them from time to time.
>
> On seeing a woman who probably appears to them to be a loose character they follow her a few yards behind, and if she stops and speaks to any other person, whether male or female, they sidle themselves as near as possible apparently to overhear any conversation that passes, and by their ostentatious action and persistent gaze compel the parties to occasionally separate or move away.[27]

Unsurprisingly, there were complaints: about the women patrols 'flashing electric torches in the faces of respectable persons sitting on the seats in Hyde Park after dark', for instance; and a 'lady' in Wimbledon complained to a magistrate that two of the WPS had told her fourteen-year-old daughter that 'she "ought not to crimp her hair and must put her hat on straight"; also that she was "dressing herself up and walking about to attract the attention of men"'.[28]

This new machinery of surveillance and control over the behaviour of women in the streets was supplemented in 1916 by the revival of an old issue that had long vexed puritans, the place of the central London music halls in metropolitan prostitution. Prostitutes gathered outside the music halls as unaccompanied men left and, more provocatively, attended in force as customers. The 'promenades', open foyers between the back of the dress circle and the bar, were notorious pick-up places at the Alhambra and Empire theatres in Leicester Square. A noisy campaign to close the promenades in the early 1890s, led by a feminist puritan, Mrs Laura Ormiston Chant, she and her supporters vilified in sections of the press as 'prudes on the prowl', had some temporary success in suppressing the Empire's promenade, though it subsequently reopened in 1895.[29]

Arnold Bennett noted in March 1916 how prostitutes were 'allowed to sit in back row of dress-circle' at the Alhambra, but it was what went on behind that most troubled campaigners. The 'restless Promenade' was a popular place, thronged by 'programme girls, the cigarette girls, the chocolate girls, the cloak-room girls, the waiters, the overseers, as well as the vivid courtesans and their clientele in black, tweed, or khaki . . .' The young Robert Hutton picked up an officer at the Empire promenade and was fascinated by what went on around him:

> The prostitutes, for the most part, remained seated, and a luscious lot they were . . . They were meticulously turned out and elaborately hatted . . . There was one lady, tall, blonde and Scandinavian, who charmed me; by any standards she was extremely good-looking. She sat, always, on the same banquette and I never saw her make the least gesture of offering herself to a passing customer. Most of the other women would smile at any likely prospect, but the Scandinavian merely waited, surveying the scene with a rather haughty stare. If a man addressed her, she would look at him for a moment before she nodded, or, as occasionally happened, averted her eyes . . . Apparently she was in a position to choose her clients.[30]

Complaints about the promenades were revived and made to the LCC, the licensing authority for the halls, during the spring of 1916. The Council was sympathetic to these purity representations – perhaps influenced by the Bishop of London, who pressed clergymen to stress to their local county councillors 'that they would watch their votes and expect to find that they were sound on [the] great moral question' of closing the promenades. In July the LCC resolved to put the onus on the music-hall managers. Rather than order the promenades to close, it was made a condition of the licence that '"prostitutes shall not habitually use any part of the premises for the purpose of prostitution"'. Representations continued to flow into the Theatres and Music-Halls

Committee about other places, but by the autumn of 1916 the Empire and Alhambra had shut down their promenades.[31]

It was around this same time that the question of prostitution generated something like a national panic, this time over its role in spreading venereal disease. The temperature was raised by colonial politicians in London for the Imperial Conferences held in London in 1917 and 1918. Some used 'very strong language', Sir Robert Borden, the Canadian premier, publicly stating 'that in no future war would he or any Prime Minister of Canada allow any troops to come to this country, because of the dangers which lie before them and the reckless disregard of the health of the troops'. It was not the dangers of the trenches he had in mind but the 'women on the London streets [who] are the real cause of the downfall of their men'.[32]

The official reluctance to promulgate prophylaxis through the use of condoms and post-coital treatments – thought to be a threat to the nation's morals – left the suppression of prostitution and punishment of individual prostitutes as the only acceptable policy available, together with improved treatment of those who had already caught the disease. This last had been made easier from 1913 by the development of an effective treatment for syphilis: the arsenical compound 'salvarsan' or '606'. Unfortunately, it was discovered by Dr Paul Ehrlich, a German Jew, and its manufacture was in enemy hands until alternative supplies could be generated in Britain and France a year or so after the outbreak of war.[33]

A Royal Commission on Venereal Diseases had been set up immediately after Ehrlich announced his discovery to the world at an international medical congress held in London; it reported finally in 1916 and among many recommendations proposed that salvarsan be made freely available to sufferers through local authority clinics, which should also take on health propaganda to warn of the dangers of contracting VD. The means to avoid catching the disease, however, were ducked, the Royal Commission relying on 'more careful instruction in regard to self control generally, and to moral conduct as bearing upon normal relations . . .'[34]

Others, though, held to a more robust approach, advocating greater, even draconian, control over women as the main source of infection and demoralisation. F. B. Meyer in early 1917 called for young women found 'interfering with soldiers' in the streets to be 'shut . . . up to work in munition factories'; and Arthur Conan Doyle pressed the government to take severe action 'to hold in check the vile women who prey upon and poison our soldiers in London':

> These women are the enemy of the country. They should be treated as such. A short Bill should be passed empowering the police to intern all notorious prostitutes in the whole country, together with brothel keepers, until six months after the end of the war. All women found to be dangerous should be sent to join them. They should be given useful national work to do, well paid, kindly treated, but subjected to firm discipline at the hands of a female staff.[35]

Government did not go this far. But a week or so later, in February 1917, it sought to increase penalties for keeping disorderly houses and soliciting, and proposed to make it a criminal offence for anyone infected with VD to have sexual intercourse. This last proposal was said in the House of Commons to have provoked fury among 'All the women of the country', with its suggestion of resurrecting the old Contagious Diseases Acts that had allowed the state to compel the intimate examination of women's bodies, and had seemed to treat women so much less favourably than men.[36]

While the Criminal Law Amendment Bill was being considered in the Commons, some magistrates in London, caught up in the hysteria of the time, began to take the law into their own hands. In April 1917 magistrates at Brentford remanded to Holloway Prison two women charged with soliciting to ascertain whether they were suffering from VD – the hospital's male doctor duly examined them, claiming they had raised no objection, and when found free from infection the magistrates acquitted them. The case raised a storm and generated anxious questioning of the bench by the Home Office. It was not the only case: in December a stipendiary magistrate at Westminster allegedly 'sentenced' a girl to the infirmary '"until cured"'; Cissie Green, seventeen, refused to have a medical examination until her mother said she would take her home if she was found not to be infected.[37]

The Criminal Law Amendment Bill stalled, but the idea of a more restricted power to control women who might infect servicemen with VD took root. The use of DORA to protect soldiers against women began to be urged from late 1917, the pacifist leader Ramsay MacDonald being one keen advocate among many. And we see something of the popular hostility to women over this issue in two cases arising at the turn of the year.

In early January 1918 police were called to a second-floor back room in Great College Street, Camden Town, where they found Gladys Canham dead in bed. She had been shot with his service revolver by her husband, Private Henry Canham of the Machine Gun Corps. Gladys had deserted Henry and their baby and set up as a prostitute. When he returned on Christmas leave she had telegrammed him to press for a reconciliation and they spent the night together. While in bed she allegedly told Henry she had contracted venereal disease, she thought from an officer, and Henry shot her: '"I consider I only did my duty as I did in France,"' he told police. Others thought he had done his duty too. At the trial at the Old Bailey the Crown accepted his plea of manslaughter and the judge bound him over to keep the peace for two years in the sum of £5. Whatever the truth of the matter, Canham was examined and found not to be suffering from 'the horrible disease'.[38]

Also in January, Phyllis Earl, 'an unfortunate' with three children and a husband in France, was found dead under a railway arch in Hackney Downs with her throat cut. George Harman, a local man who had migrated to Canada and was now a private in the Canadian Corps, admitted to murdering her but claimed in his defence she had infected him with VD: she had indeed been infected about a week before her death, according to Bernard Spilsbury, the Home Office pathologist. Harman was sentenced to hang, though the jury recommended mercy. A large petition was gathered in Harman's favour and he was reprieved in March 1918.[39]

That same month DORA Regulation 40D made it an offence for a woman with VD to solicit or have sex with a member of the armed forces. It was not an offence for an infected soldier to have sex with a woman, though it had been a disciplinary offence since 1889 to conceal VD. In the unlikely event of a woman complaining to a soldier's commanding officer that she had been infected, the soldier would be examined and court-martialled if appropriate. Regulation 40D quickly became notorious. A woman could not in theory be examined against her will, but an examination was frequently the price of freedom, women being remanded to Holloway, where in most cases an examination was submitted to. This unequal and intrusive treatment of women, turning the clock back to the 1880s, provoked much resentment nationwide. Petitions calling for the repeal of 40D were gathered from June 1918, with more than 600 of them by the end of October. But the regulation survived the Armistice and over 100 women were convicted under it after the end of the war. Among all this high anxiety, one fact seems to have escaped attention: that despite 400,000 British troops estimated to have contracted VD at home and abroad at some time during the war, the percentage of soldiers infected was lower than at any time since 1866, when figures were first collected, and lower than among the civilian population as a whole.[40]

London's 'orgy of licentiousness', or rather its representation, showed itself in other places and other ways. One was the 'drug craze', which became something of a national panic, overladen as it was by fears of race degeneracy. The old connection between the Chinese community and opium had been highlighted in the early years of the war but not as a problem in the backstreet 'opium dens' of the East End. Britain was a major manufacturer of morphine, so opium became a precious resource in the war effort. Its export was banned and tightly supervised, but an illegal opium trade from Britain to China and the Far East, where it was used for recreational purposes, usually smuggled out by Chinese sailors and port-side traders, became a problem in London and other seaports, especially Liverpool.[41]

Taking morphine for pleasure grew among the British elite through 1915 and 1916. It was freely taken in Diana Manners's set, one of her sisters thought to be 'a regular *morphineuse*', with little parties assembling at night to inject themselves with the drug. It was openly sold in liquid form in packs of capsules for officers to have handily available in the trenches: we might remember how pleased Vera Brittain was that Roland Leighton had restocked his medical case in this way before leaving for his final tour of duty in 1915. He was supplied by Savory and Moore, who, with Harrods, were successfully prosecuted in February 1916 for infringing the Pharmacy Acts. In June 1916 DORA Regulation 40B made it unlawful to sell morphine or cocaine in any form to members of the armed forces. The trade in cocaine, probably originating from doctors, dentists and pharmacists, moved underground, traded mostly in the West End by pimps (hotel porters) and prostitutes. The quantities must have been tiny, but they were stimulating enough to spark noisy talk of a drug craze in the popular press and to make police and government jumpy. It helped foster those wild stories of soldiers drugged around Waterloo and other London stations through 1916 and into 1917. But cocaine use seems largely to have been confined to that lively but restricted mix of elite and demi-monde that took its pleasures in the West End and nearby.[42]

More sensational still was the revival of the Chinese opium den as a lurid incubus on the Occidental imagination. Opium-smoking among the Chinese in Limehouse was a permanent feature of life there, provoking official reaction from time to time as particular cases became scandalous. With the drug craze anxieties of 1916 and 1917, police attention moved east. In July 1917 a drug dealer's premises in Poplar High Street were raided and Ching Foo Jack and four other Chinamen were found cutting and weighing opium for sale; Ching was fined £10. There were similar prosecutions of 'opium dens' in Limehouse Causeway, Pennyfields and Poplar High Street through 1918, all involving Chinese dealers. That year the connection between the East End Chinese and West End drug use was firmly established. In August William Gibson, thirty-six, a shipping merchant who lived in South Kensington and traded in the City, was found dead in a flat used for opium smoking at Portman Mansions, near Baker Street. His death was due to choking while unconscious from 'opium poisoning'. He was a frequent visitor, it was said, to Limehouse and a Chinaman had called at his office in Finsbury Street, where Gibson refused to see him.[43]

The most sensational case of all came to light a few weeks later. On 21 November 1918 Miss Billie Carleton, a former chorus girl at the Empire from 1915 and by now a promising stage actress, was found dead in her flat at Savoy Court, an annexe of the Savoy Hotel off the Strand, apparently from an overdose of cocaine. She was just twenty-two. The inquest uncovered astonishing stories, relayed with relish and at great length in the newspapers, of 'Doping Parties' held for some months past at Notting Hill Gate, Long Acre and Dover Street, Mayfair, of drug traffickers in Soho and of visits to Chinatown, where Carleton and various friends smoked opium together. There followed over the next four months prosecutions for offences connected to supplying Carleton with opium and cocaine – Ada Lo Ping You, a Scottish woman married to a Chinaman at Limehouse Causeway, who had prepared opium at some West End parties, was given five months' hard labour and her husband, an opium smoker since the age of eleven, was fined £10. A friend of Carleton, Reginald De Veulle, a dressmaker and designer, was pursued with particular vindictiveness, at first charged with her manslaughter but acquitted, and at last convicted in April 1919 of the novel charge of conspiring to supply cocaine; despite poor health, he was imprisoned for eight months. By then, 'wholesale drug-taking'

seemed to represent the canker at the heart of a West End society
demoralised by the experience and legacy of war.[44]

The apparently endless strains of wartime London, which sought
some release in a '"sniff"' of cocaine for those who could both afford
it and knew where to find it, discovered other outlets. Drink, of course,
was denied for far more hours of the week than it was allowed, though
efforts to get round this were indefatigable – or incorrigible, depending
on one's point of view. London, according to the journalist C. Sheridan
Jones, 'has become an underground city' of 'clubs, of secret rendezvous,
of meeting-places that are known only to a comparatively few habitués',
with unlicensed early-morning drinking places around Piccadilly Circus,
Leicester Square, Fitzrovia and 'the other side of the water', where
back-parlour shebeens and out-house stills seem to have been common
enough in the Waterloo Road area.[45]

Jones thought too that London now had 'a larger number of gambling
establishments run for men of all classes' than 'perhaps for . . . over a
century'. Certainly police raids and prosecutions were frequent from
late 1917 through 1918 all over London: in Hackney and Whitechapel,
for instance, gambling became a famous 'vice' among the Russian Jews;
in Soho and Fitzrovia, where most gaming clubs seem to have been run
by Frenchmen, Italians and other migrants; and in unlikely parts of the
West End such as south Belgravia – Madeline Nereshiner, otherwise
Morton, thirty-one and said to be the wife of an American, did so well
out of her Ebury Street premises, where *chemin de fer* and poker were
played for high stakes by 'persons of good standing', that she had
£3,000 invested in War Bonds by February 1918. High-stake poker
'was very largely played in houses and clubs' locally, the police thought.[46]

By this late stage in the war it seemed to many that London really
was in the grip of a moral decline. Arnold Bennett, though no prude,
began to be shocked by the tone of the London stage – perhaps spiced
with a little professional jealousy. Attending *As You Were* at the Pavilion
Theatre, Great Windmill Street, in October 1918, he found that 'Every
scene turned on adultery, or mere copulation. Even in the primeval
forest scene, an adultery among gorillas was shown. This revue is the
greatest success in London at present, and is taking about £3,000 a
week.'[47] And among the 'sniffing' classes of the West End there was a
taste for something even stronger than lustful gorillas:

Alex called for me at four and we went off to see a play given by the

Pioneer Society. It's a ridiculous bit of chicanery – the censorship being dodged by calling themselves a 'Society' and having tickets on the subscriber system. The performances are always on Sunday. Found Oggie there and she told me *La Femme et le Pantin* was an unspeakably improper book . . . As a matter of fact, it turned out not at all bad – threatening in tone, but nothing actually very shy-making. The scene where the girl dances naked was very well managed with a screen. She acted extraordinarily well and I enjoyed the play. The clothes were good and the sunny guitar-twanging sort of atmosphere well suggested. The huge theatre was *packed*.[48]

For most Londoners, though, pleasures of the 'underground city' were either undiscovered or undesired. Different ways of finding release had to be etched out of the steeling adversities of daily life during the war. Most popular of all was dancing: 'never before in the history of England had there been such a craze for movement; such a gliding and hopping, such a swaying and clinging; such a stamping and clapping and grabbing of food. Two mouthfuls and then: "Come on, let's have a turn!"'[49]

The dancing craze was first noticed by the newspapers as a growing feature of the big West End hotels and restaurants around February and March 1917. No doubt it had set in before, but not long before because in the summer of 1916 'it is only through the advertisements that we learn of dancing here, or dining and wining there'. For many moralists, dancing too was a sacrilege, condemned as '"Enjoying the War"'. But it quickly became plain that soldiers themselves were as active on the dance floors as any civilian. The *New Survey of London*, looking back on the changes war had brought to the capital, acknowledged that 'the invasion of American dances' began 'immediately preceding the war' but noted how dancing 'was powerfully generated by the psychological and emotional conditions generated by the war'.[50] And, we might add, by the sheer gruelling toughness of it all: for 1917, the year so many 'crazes' began or matured, would prove the most difficult year of London's war by far.

EVERYONE IS SO WAR-WEARY!
1917

THE New Year crept in – shamefaced, gloomy, laden with foreboding. No bells were rung, no sirens sounded on the river, 'no cheering, no one stirring' in the streets 'save for a few revellers, and those wending their homeward way from watchnight services'. In north London 'Two shrill railway whistles gave one shriek each on midnight – it may have been chance that they sounded at that moment – this was all the sound that broke the dull quiet.' As morning dawned, 'Few wishes were exchanged. The few that were took the form of "a happier year" or "a better year".'[1]

Hopes of that were quickly dashed. On the night of Friday 19 January, pitch-black at 7 p.m., Michael MacDonagh was waiting on Blackfriars Bridge for his tram home to Clapham and fumbling for a halfpenny to buy his evening paper from a newsboy.

There was not even the light of a muffled gas-lamp near by and the newsboy, to help me in my search for a copper, turned on the little electric-torch with which they are all provided. Then suddenly a golden glow lit up the eastern sky, making everything clear as day; and looking down the Thames I saw a high column of yellow flames rising, as I thought, from the river. This quickly died down, and the sky immediately became overspread with the loveliest colours – violet, indigo, blue, green, yellow, orange and red – which eddied and swirled from a chaotic mass into a settled and beautiful colour design. Dazzled and awestruck, I saw that London, so dark a few moments before, was made glorious as if by a marvellous sunset the like of which had never been seen before. The phenomenon lasted, I should think, several seconds. Its disappearance was accompanied by a terrific explosion, riving and shattering and dying away with an angry growl. I had the sensation that at the same moment a vibrating tremor ran through London.[2]

The Silvertown explosion was seen, felt or heard by every single Londoner. The noise reached the King at his Sandringham estate in Norfolk, 100 miles away, and a dozen miles to the south at the edge of London the shock made every house in Croydon tremble. Amid suspicions of a giant Zeppelin raid or some great gasworks blast, the truth became clear: it was the Brunner, Mond & Company's TNT factory at Silvertown, a formerly disused caustic soda plant pressed into service for the exigencies of war despite the company's reservations over locating such a dangerous business in a heavily populated district. The damage was enormous, at first incapable of being grasped. Nothing was left of the factory, three terraces of houses were reduced to rubble, neighbouring works including an acid-making plant and one of the biggest flour mills in England were largely destroyed; the blast leapt the river, causing a gasometer near Woolwich to sink in the ground and then explode. With rumours of 4,000 dead, the numbers of casualties slowly became clearer though never definitive. They were miraculously small, just some forty dead and around 120 seriously injured. Fire engines – with bad luck the local fire station was also destroyed by the explosion – ambulances and lorries carrying hundreds of soldiers, police and special constables, hospital doctors and Red Cross nurses, converged on Silvertown that night to do what they could for the wounded and the homeless.[3] At the London Hospital in Whitechapel,

Injured people soon came up in Motor Lorries, Butcher's carts – all sorts of vehicles. Treated about 60, then a lull. Some very bad cases, and four died during the night. Injuries very terrible. Brought up on doors, shutters, etc. Children brought up, not always injured but dazed. One child of eight, with baby in arms and leading a child of 4. Could not find Mother. Kindly driver picked them up in destroyed streets . . . Little dog came up with one fearfully injured woman. It would not leave her. We let it go into the ward with her.[4]

Next day Nurse Enid Bagnold, drafted in from her Woolwich hospital by train, found fires still burning at noon and the site covered in fine ash

so that it looked like an old ruin, something done long ago . . . the soil
of the earth turned up; a workman's tin mug stuck and roasted and hardened into what looks like solid rock – a fossil, as though it had been there
for ever. London is only skin-deep. Beneath lies the body of the world.[5]

In the immediate aftermath there was some ugliness:

during the week [after] the streets leading from the scene of the explosion
were filled with lorries, vans, and even donkey barrows laden with
household goods. Unfortunately there was a great deal of looting, and
many families were found to be still huddling together among the ruins
of their homes, afraid to leave for fear of losing what little remained of
their possessions. The whole area was guarded by the military, and, as
no one was allowed through without a permit, one can but suppose that
they were the victims of their neighbours' unscrupulousness.[6]

And when government examined claims for compensation – the Ministry
of Munitions paying in full – many for clothing and possessions proved
fraudulent. The cause of the explosion was probably accidental. But
understandably rumours of sabotage found many believers, could not
be conclusively scotched and persisted long after the war.[7]

The Silvertown explosion added to the gloom besetting London for
much of the first quarter of 1917, made miserable as ever in this war
by the weather. It was bitterly cold, with spells at the end of January
and early February when the temperature never rose above freezing,
the thermometer falling as low as −10°C. People reached back into
history for comparisons: 'It is alleged to be the coldest spell since the
sixties,' recorded Cynthia Asquith; 'the hardest winter I remember since
1880–81,' thought Charles à Court Repington of *The Times*; 'The
weather in town . . . has, I think, been the worst that I remember during
the whole of my life, and the intense darkness of the streets added to
its misery,' H. Rider Haggard, who had known London since the early
1880s, complained to his diary. All that was in January, but things did
not get markedly better in a winter that seemed to last half a year or
more. In February there was 'black fog'; in March, 'We have plunged
into winter again! 9 degrees of frost and biting east wind. The wind
has been east for months now and we don't seem able to shake off this
worst of all winters'; and in April, 'Heavy, heavy snow has been falling
all the morning and the streets are thick. No sound of traffic is to be

heard. What a winter! It has been relentless since last October, always damp and bitterly cold.' At 31 Bedford Square, wickedly dank, Emily Lutyens, with her architect husband working in the heat of India, found the servants' rooms 'so damp that their clothes were wet in the morning', and despite 'several hot-water bottles and a dog and a child for company' in bed she found it 'too cold to sleep. "Words will never describe to you the awful coldness of this house",' she wrote to Edwin.[8]

All classes suffered because all classes were affected by a shortage of coal in London, civilian supplies having been depleted by the unprecedented requirements of every department of war. Perhaps for the first time, wealth was no protection, for coal was not to be had for a purse full of sovereigns. Visiting a friend for dinner at a house near Buckingham Gate in early February, Cynthia Asquith found 'Alas, great domestic crisis – poor Frances' cellar quite empty and no coal to be procured for love or money . . . We all shivered and had goose flesh . . .' Next morning, 'Breakfasted in fur coat'. A lady with a sick mother living in a 'house large and old-fashioned', found herself without coal and her mother's illness getting worse: 'I drove round London in a cab with a laundry basket begging just a few lumps from this friend and that.' City offices, similarly unable to get supplies, made do by keeping fires burning in a single room. 'At last we are beginning to feel the pinch of the war in material things,' mused Cynthia Asquith. 'What a long time it has taken!'[9]

But fur coats were not available to everyone. The poor, as ever, felt the pinch hard also. They had shivered every winter of their lives and to some degree could draw on experience to help them cope. 'At Shoreditch, crowds of patient women have waited at the coal wharves with sacks, barrows, hand-carts, bassinettes, go-carts, sugar-boxes on spidery wheels, and other contrivances' to carry coal. That was in February, but such scenes were common at railway stations and canal- or riverside coal wharves throughout London into April. Working people too had support from their local councils, using their purchasing power to buy cheaply in bulk and selling on to poor families at cost. And government sought to regulate matters in favour of working-class consumers, less through equity than anxiety: in April the Coal Controller called on wholesalers

to load any poor people who should come to their Depot or Wharf for supplies in small quantities, and . . . if the position becomes threatening

by the assembling of large numbers of people, they must cease to deliver
to the better-class houses in order to cope with the demand made by
these poor people.

Nevertheless, the suffering and death toll from this dreadful winter
was incalculable though surely large: on 16 February alone a south
London paper reported eight inquests of sudden deaths of persons aged
five to seventy attributed to the intense cold. In October a rationing
scheme for London limited coal sales by the number of rooms a household occupied, ranging from 2 hundredweight a week for four rooms
or less to 2½ tons for sixteen rooms or more. This mechanism, though
hardly equitable, seems generally to have avoided the worst effects
caused when rationing by price.[10]

Just as worrying to government, and similarly inconvenient to the
Londoners, food shortages also caused great disruption to daily life this
winter. The need to conserve wheat supplies meant that more of the
grain had to be used in flour milling, and materials other than wheat
had to be introduced. The white loaf accordingly disappeared from
shops during January and was replaced by 'war bread' or 'standard
bread' of 'a dirty grey colour'. The standard loaf caused many complaints,
especially at first when millers and bakers were adjusting to the new
flour; although nutritionally an improvement on white bread, it remained
unpopular and seemed to hit directly at working-class living standards,
bread still being the staple food of the poorest. To counter waste, from
March bakers were forbidden to sell fresh, newly baked bread: now all
bread had to be at least twelve hours old before it could be put on
sale. It also cost more, 11d for a 4-pound loaf, double the 1914 price,
leading to protest meetings organised by trade unions in Lambeth and
doubtless elsewhere.[11]

March also saw the worst of the shortages at this time: potatoes
almost disappeared from the shops. It was now that the first food
queues materialised everywhere in the metropolis. They were so long
and slow-moving that police had to regulate them in every working-
class district from Edmonton to Peckham. In Walthamstow, Harold
Walker, a schoolboy of eleven, earned extra pocket money taking the
place of busy housewives in the queues. In the East End, fish and chip
shops ran out of potatoes. A horse-drawn van taking supplies to Cooke's
eel and pie shop in Kingsland High Street was surrounded by a crowd
of housewives said to be a thousand strong; a sack disappeared and

later 'women were seen dancing on the pavement, waving hands holding potatoes, and singing music-hall songs'. Even in polite Hampstead, Caroline Playne observed 'Quarrel at the greengrocer's over potatoes[.] Women swarming in & one at least very abusive'; and a couple of days later, 'Great ructions at greengrocer's. Everyone wanting & trying to get potatoes and being very jealous of anyone else getting any.'[12]

The Food Controller, Lord Devonport, who had been appointed by the new Lloyd George government just before Christmas, proved unable to do anything about the potato shortage. In February he had announced 'voluntary rationing' for bread, meat and sugar. The scheme 'had no scientific basis and bore no relation to the facts of life for three-quarters of the population'. It recommended bread be restricted to 4 pounds a head per week, too low for working-class families, and meat to 2½ pounds a head, which was far too high for working-class consumers, who never ate 'anything like that quantity even if it were available'. London's walls were plastered with preposterous posters, such as 'Eat Less Bread and Victory is Secure'. Yet this first rationing was taken very seriously by many middle-class families, despite the reductions in meat and sugar consumption it meant for most. It was adopted in the royal household, this being the second 'pledge' by the King, and many seem to have followed suit. In May, the King issued a royal proclamation urging reduced flour consumption, read in the time-honoured way from the steps of the Royal Exchange and printed on a form which people were urged to sign. Loyal Edie Wensley and her parents in Palmers Green duly pledged to reduce bread consumption by a quarter and avoid using flour in pastry and foods other than bread. Just how many Londoners took it quite that seriously is unclear. On Empire Day people were enjoined to wear a purple badge to show they were 'keeping the "King's pledge" about food restrictions'. But Rider Haggard recorded that 'Neither in London or on the way down here [Ditchingham, Norfolk] have I seen a single purple badge!' He didn't say whether he sported one himself.[13]

In April compulsion was applied to restaurants, hotels and clubs by a Public Meals Order. The manufacture of 'light pastries, muffins, crumpets and tea-cakes' was prohibited – the muffin man disappearing from London's streets, where he had been a fixture for generations. Cakes and buns to the value of 1s 9d per person could be had after 6 p.m. – those who indulged to the last penny were known as 'Bun hogs' and Lyons and other tea shops were known as 'Rhondda-vous' after the new Food Controller, Lord Rhondda, appointed in June. In restaurants, hotels and clubs Tuesdays were proclaimed compulsory meatless days, with potatoes served only on Tuesdays and Fridays, and meat, sugar, bread and flour restricted at all meals: at Rider Haggard's club, the Windham, 'I was only furnished with one tiny lump for my morning tea', a serious blight on a sugar-gulping nation. Despite these restrictions food shortages periodically continued throughout the spring and summer, as unrestricted submarine warfare hit Britain's imports desperately hard: 'Bananas have become unprocurable, and with oranges at 3d each and small apples 4d, it is difficult to obtain fruit . . . We never realised till now how England's market supplies were so dependent on foreign lands.' And the efforts to prevent shortages of some commodities by fixing the maximum price at which they could be sold hardly helped matters, retailers refusing to pay over the odds for stock. Some retailers paid and then charged too much: each week in the London police courts shopkeepers were prosecuted for offences like only selling sugar or potatoes if customers bought other items, overcharging for potatoes, and so on.[14]

Amid all the disruption of food supplies the allotment gained ground in every sense. Allotments were said to be a special feature of metropolitan life and particularly 'a passion in suburbia'. The LCC provided 3,160 allotments in its parks by the spring and another 3,000 by the autumn – in 1918 there would be over 13,000. Some 70 acres of Richmond Park were ploughed for allotments and large quantities of vegetables were grown by allotment holders in Bermondsey's parks and gardens for donation to local hospitals. Pig-keeping returned to inner-city areas like Rotherhithe, whence the tradition had been banished for generations and taken up with gusto in the suburbs – the Polo Field at Wimbledon Park was turned into a piggery, for instance. Some schools gave up their playing fields to growing vegetables. To encourage the movement, and undeterred by paper shortages that put up the price of newspapers, cutting many in size and taking newsbills off the London streets, many local papers gave weekly advice on growing food, on raising chickens and on cooking, nutrition and the avoidance of waste. In the same spirit a number of National Kitchens opened in London as cost-price restaurants to showcase these new public virtues, the first in Westminster Bridge Road, Lambeth, in May, with Maud Pember Reeves on the management committee.[15]

The food question was the largest single cause of the industrial unrest that shook country and government in the spring of 1917. By May food prices were almost exactly twice what they had been in July 1914 and they continued to rise until they peaked at an increase of 106 per cent in September. The various shortages and uneven supply added to the discontent, and with it all went a feeling that some at least of the price rises were due not to genuine difficulty in securing supplies but to 'profiteering', a word assuming large importance during the year. With wage rates generally failing to keep pace with this rise in the cost of living, many workers agitated for more pay and struck when they didn't get it. The London bus workers came out in May for changes to union recognition and a 10s weekly increase for drivers and conductors, with 5s for garage staff. For three days London was virtually without buses: 'any travelling is done by underground. Imagine the crush there,' Georgina Lee complained to her diary. Interfering with public transport for munitions workers was a wartime offence and the risk of legal action was one influence on the unions to settle; under the strain some ill temper was shown to working busmen, one driver in East Ham assaulted, for instance. After government intervention the strikers went back on the promise of an industrial conference and consideration of the pay claim as a war bonus.[16]

More worryingly for government, this same month unofficial strikes of munitions workers in Lancashire spread all over the north of England and then to the London munitions-making districts. Wage rates were one important grievance and so were threats by management to withdraw exemption certificates from military service for men not considered to be pulling their weight. There were strikes of skilled engineers in Crayford, Erith and chiefly Woolwich, bringing out thousands of workers who, though not on strike, depended on toolmakers to keep their machines running. Eight of the strikers' leading shop stewards were arrested under DORA and brought to Bow Street, where they were remanded in Brixton Prison, and there were police raids subsequently on trade union premises in London. Under this formidable pressure the strike was settled and the men returned to work with a promise of no further victimisation. Things continued tense among the munitions workers at Woolwich well into the summer.[17]

Government inquiries into the causes of industrial unrest this spring made worrying reading. The inquiry into London and the South-East concluded that 'The unrest is real, widespread and in some directions extreme, and such as to constitute a national danger unless dealt with promptly and effectively. We are at this moment within view of a possible social upheaval or at least extensive and manifold strikes.' The primary causes were first the cost of living, aggravated by concerns over profiteering, and second the daily hard grind of wartime labour. There was, though, some relief at hand on the cost-of-living front: wage increases were recorded in London from the spring of 1917 in all the building trades, among cabinetmakers, printers, bakers, dock workers, shoemakers, tailors, indeed practically everyone taking home a weekly wage packet.[18]

There were deeper anxieties for government in the spring and early summer of 1917 that perhaps made industrial unrest, at least in London, seem more threatening than it was in reality. The pressures of war had begun to have a destabilising impact on the social and political system of combatant nations and one victim had already fallen. News of the first Russian Revolution and the abdication of the Tsar reached London on 16 March. It gave heart not just to British democrats but to all those who opposed the war and its continuation. On 31 March a 'vast' rally at the Royal Albert Hall 'to rejoice' over the Revolution was filled with an audience of nearly 12,000; a further 5,000 were turned away at the doors. On the streets of London the Tsar's departure seemed to make people a little more cheerful, Caroline Playne thought, until the potential consequences for the Allied war effort began to sink in. That did not take long. 'The war would probably be over this year if those wretched Russians hadn't let us down,' Georgina Lee fumed some six weeks later.[19]

On the home front the Revolution was fancifully seen by many in authority to be irritating, if not directly causing, the industrial unrest that spring. Yet while there were more than enough domestic provocations for industrial strife, it is clear that the Russian experience was one buttress of working-class self-confidence after March 1917. When Christopher Addison, Minister of Munitions, and General Sir William Robertson, Chief of the Imperial General Staff, addressed a meeting of 2,000 engineers, all men it seems, at Woolwich Arsenal in July, they were met by a chorus of 'The Red Flag' sung from the back of the audience.[20]

While the pacifist movement also unquestionably took strength from the events in Russia, here too the influence of 'revolutionaries' was given far-fetched credence by almost all in power. Pacifism and anti-war dissent had both been greatly bolstered by conscription in the first part of 1916. Anti-war meetings continued into the New Year, frequently attracting violent opposition: a Union of Democratic Control meeting at Walthamstow in January where Ramsay MacDonald was billed to speak was broken up by a group of Canadian soldiers, and there were disturbances at a suffrage meeting in Victoria Park in which a speaker had called for peace. The Royal Albert Hall meeting welcoming the Russian Revolution heard a speech from George Lansbury of the Herald League that similarly proposed peace negotiations and large peace rallies began to be organised in London from the spring.[21]

But the Revolution proved a two-edged sickle. Fears of communism and of importing the social and political anarchy prevailing in Russia provided a shot of adrenalin to powerful forces among the die-hards and their supporters. A 'Peace Procession' at Victoria Park in April was broken up with great violence and 'considerable blood-letting', with Australian soldiers vigorous fighters on the pro-war side. In late June, a debate in Finsbury Park between the Herald League and Havelock Wilson, the Seamen's Union leader and a fanatical spokesman for the pro-war faction in the Trades Union Congress, saw the pacifists swept bodily from the park; the forces against them were spearheaded by 200 'torpedoed' sailors brought from merchant ships in the Port of London by Captain Edward Tupper, Wilson's henchman in the union. 'After that I sent men Sunday after Sunday' to disrupt 'the pacifists' gatherings' in Finsbury Park and elsewhere, Tupper boasted years later: 'The Seamen became the national champions against pacifism.' Pro-war politics were also bolstered by a new grouping on the far right. This was the National Party, formed at a Queen's Hall meeting that August and led by 'Never-Endians' or die-hards like Lord Charles Beresford, General Page-Croft and Havelock Wilson.[22]

It says much for the resilience of the peace movement in London that its meetings and propaganda continued throughout the year despite intolerable levels of violence – including an attempt to set the Brotherhood Church in Southgate Road on fire when a meeting was in progress there in October. And a month later, in the aftermath of Lenin's Bolshevik coup in Russia and amid growing fears of revolutionary influence paid for by the same 'German gold' that helped bring Lenin to Petrograd, a state crackdown on pacifist headquarters in London led to extensive police raids and arrests. More than a dozen London organisations were raided under DORA, including the Fellowship of Reconciliation at 17 Red Lion Square, the No-Conscription Fellowship in Duke Street, Adelphi, the Peace Society at 47 New Broad Street in the City, the National

Council of Civil Liberties and the Indian Home Rule League. A planned Herald League meeting in Finsbury Park was prohibited amid fears of 'grave disorder', leaflets and printing presses were impounded, and E. D. Morel of the UDC was arrested and imprisoned under DORA.[23]

It took peculiar courage to be an anti-war propagandist in 1917 and some sort of desire for a negotiated peace probably found more supporters than were ready to announce themselves in public. News from the main theatre of war itself hardly justified confidence in either the politicians or the generals. There was, though, one piece of good, even truly joyous, news. On 6 April the USA declared war on Germany and on the 20th public celebrations of the event in London centred on St Paul's Cathedral, where Bishop Brent 'preached an aggressively democratic sermon, which made me a little uneasy, with the royalties present,' Dean Inge recorded in his diary. It was indeed a democratic moment, with crowds of Londoners filling the streets, hundreds of street hawkers selling tiny American flags for buttonholes and the Stars and Stripes flying over government offices, hotels and the Houses of Parliament. Within weeks London seemed to fill with Americans, the Reform Club (and doubtless its brethren) making honorary members of visiting US scientific men, army officers and diplomats. In July, extraordinary to think of, 8,000 people, 'fully half' Canadians and Americans, turned out to watch a baseball match at Lord's Cricket Ground between these new North American allies: the Canadians won easily. Most important of all, on 15 August American troops paraded for the first time in London, marching past the King at Buckingham Palace en route to Waterloo Station. Jubilant crowds of Londoners, astonished by the soldiers' striking physique – 'tall, slim, athletic, with long, clean-shaven faces' – at long last had something to cheer about.[24]

There was in truth little else. War losses from April through October never fell below 20,000 a week, with April and October each accumulating 120,000 dead, wounded and captured, second only to the first month of the Somme battle in July 1916. The terrible slaughter in the mud of Passchendaele left lasting scars on the memories of all who endured it and all who shared the agony from afar. Londoners in their millions dealt with individual loss in many different ways. So Harry Lauder, the music-hall comedian, his son just killed, had to go on singing 'a sort of "when the boys come home" patriotic song' on the West End stage; when Cynthia Asquith heard of a great friend missing at the front her first thought was to visit Teresina, a 'palmist', to discover what she could; Duff Cooper, lamenting nine dead friends including one just killed, 'dined alone at the Junior Carlton. I drank the best champagne – Pommery 1906 – because I felt that Edward would have wished it and done so had I been killed the first'; H. Rider Haggard, who lost a nephew in November, and Rudyard Kipling, still lamenting his son John, consoled themselves at the Athenaeum with the thought that there could be no Germans in heaven. The war shrines or 'Calvaries' continued to multiply, the convoys of ambulances to the hospitals and the pleas for hospital doctors to be sent to the front never ceased, and at the railway stations, those great waiting rooms of destruction, scores of thousands of premature endings were unconsciously enacted: like Barbara and Captain Jack Wootton, newly married in early September, their honeymoon cancelled after he was called to France, who spent just a single night together at Rubens Hotel, close to Victoria Station, where they parted early next morning.

> Five weeks later the War Office 'regretted to inform me' that Capt. J.W. Wootton of the 11th Battalion Suffolk Regiment had died of wounds. He had been shot through the eye and died forty-eight hours later on an ambulance train; and in due course his blood-stained kit was punctiliously returned to me.[25]

The cumulative effects of all this suffering crept up on people with a generally anaesthetising effect, a deadened reaction to others' losses now mounting to unimaginable numbers. In April, during the disastrous British offensive at Passchendaele, Caroline Playne noted in her diary:

> Heard of Theo Brown being killed leading regiment to attack. Theodor – gift of God – just massacred in his prime . . . Said to one or two that I had had a cousin killed. No one said – how sad – but each began telling of some relative or other of theirs who was wounded or killed.

A month or two later she saw a sight that at first filled her with 'sickening horror', but even this had ceased to move those who had to live with it day after day:

> At Brighton for week end. There the legless soldiers are sent for treatment. A Lady said at first you were horrified when you saw four or five

men who had lost a leg. Now that every part of the town, the front &
the piers has swarms of such men getting about on crutches, you have
got to the stage of talking about it all quite naturally.[26]

Even so the war could still provide shocks for the Londoners. After
November 1916, throughout the following six months or so of that
melancholy winter, they never faced directly the enemy's firepower.
Raids, even rumours of raids, died away. But on Sunday 25 March
nerves were badly shaken by an extraordinary rumour of a different
kind – that a German invasion had begun on the east coast. It was
given credence by the 'news' being splashed in special evening editions
of the Sunday papers. This 'hysterical Sunday', as William Sandhurst
called it in his diary, involved appeals for officers to report for duty
flashed on cinema screens across London, trains kept empty to move
troops and ambulances held back for 'invasion' casualties. Wild talk of
'risings in the east' among the never-quite-to-be-trusted workers of the
East End was not just believed but spread by Sir Francis Lloyd and
other general officers in charge of London's home defences. Next day,
as calm returned, the *Manchester Guardian* reported from London on
'Our Week-End Rumours', 'the craziest' since snow was spotted on the
boots of Russian troops said to be moving through England early in
the war.[27]

Although no one could know it at the time, the almost forgotten
raid by a single aeroplane in November 1916 had signalled the end of
one phase of the air war against London and its replacement by another.
The night of the Zeppelin had passed, or nearly so, and the day of the
aeroplane had dawned. Desultory aeroplane attacks on and near the
Thames Estuary towns, often by a solitary machine, marked the resumption of air hostilities in February 1917 and continued sporadically
through March and April. But in the spring the development by Germany
of heavy bombing planes had been slowly perfected, the first of these
being the mighty Gotha, a two-engine biplane with a wingspan of
around 72 feet, which had a payload of thirteen bombs, seven of 50
kilos and six of 12.5. By early 1917 twenty-three were in service.[28]

The first experimental attack on London by a lone Gotha flying at
night on 6–7 May released six bombs on Highbury and Stoke
Newington, killing one person at Newington Green Mansions and
injuring another. The raid was judged a failure by the Germans, the
difficulty of navigating at night over the darkened city confirming that

the best prospect of destruction was to bomb from a great height in daylight. That was tested on the afternoon of 25 May, when twenty-three Gothas took off for a mass bombing raid on the Kent coast, causing very heavy casualties of ninety-five killed and 192 injured; Folkestone, an important military transit port, was especially badly hit. Despite dozens of fighter planes taking to the air from Royal Flying Corps and Royal Naval Air Service airfields, most British planes couldn't reach the height attained by the Gothas and just one seems to have been damaged on its way home to Belgium, though not destroyed. On 5 June twenty-two Gothas again attacked the Thames Estuary but caused much less damage.[29]

These bombing raids, kicking and scuffing on London's doorstep, indicated to those in the know – not that many, because the truth was greatly obscured by press censorship – that it was only a question of time before the capital itself would once more be targeted. There was not long to wait.

The bombing raid of Wednesday 13 June 1917 would live long in Londoners' memories. It was a beautiful sunny day. Fourteen Gothas reached London around 11.30 a.m. and bombed without interruption, out of range of anti-aircraft fire. High-explosive bombs were dropped from East Ham and Stratford in the east to Holborn in the west, and from Bermondsey and Southwark in the south to Stamford Hill in the north. Most damage was done in Poplar and the eastern edge of the City. In terms of lives lost, this was the most destructive raid of the war, not just in London but in Britain as a whole. In all, 145 Londoners were killed and 382 injured. The most devastating loss, a bewildering atrocity to contemporaries, occurred early in the raid. Eighteen children were killed and thirty-four injured when a bomb penetrated the roof of the Girls' Department of Upper North Street LCC School in Poplar, passed through the Boys' Department and exploded in one of two rooms in the Infants' Department, killing everyone in it except the teacher. This was terrible luck, but an attack by several Gothas deliberately targeted Liverpool Street Station, where sixteen died, and Fenchurch Street Station, where nineteen were killed. Most of the remaining victims were clustered in this eastern portion of the City and its neighbouring suburbs of Bethnal Green, Whitechapel, Hoxton and Shoreditch. The confusion and horror were never forgotten by those who lived through the raid. Bill Goble, a fifteen-year-old shipping-office clerk in Jewry Street, recalled:

We should have had the sense to stay under cover and in fact as the youngest of all present this is what I was told, but like a typical teenager I rushed out into the street behind the others.

A cloud of dust or smoke drifted down Fenchurch Street, the whole glass frontage of the Albion Clothing Store which then stood between Jewry Street and Minories had been blown out. A bus conductress lay on the pavement – her leg appeared to be severed from the knee. A policeman sat on a chair, his trouser-legs ripped away and one leg covered in blood. To add to the horror of the occasion, a number of window dummies had fallen out into the pavement amongst the bodies of the dead and injured. A No. 25 bus stood silently by the kerb, every window shattered, a solitary figure of a man was hunched up in the seat immediately behind the driver's seat. He sat motionless, a piece of glass was said to have pierced his neck and we were told he was already dead.[30]

This terrible raid, especially the news from Poplar, 'was a fearful shock' to the Londoners. Caroline Playne remarked 'great grief & sadness on all faces. Girl sobbing in tube this afternoon', and that evening found a 'girl coming back to house in our gardens, sobbing in an hysterical & heart-broken way'. Later she noted 'indignation' and 'hatred aroused' by the raid. There was some anti-German aggression in Shoreditch – where a Dutchman was mistaken for a German in one case – and elsewhere, and there was great emotion as many of the Poplar children were buried a week later. Understandably people were jumpy: false alarms in central London workplaces drove staff into the cellars; and for a few days rumours of impending raids were rife.[31]

In fact the next raid took place over three weeks later. If the one on 13 June was the most deadly of London's war, that on Saturday 7 July was the most destructive of property and most humbling of all to the civic pride of the Londoners and the reputation of the authorities. Once more it was in broad daylight and executed with brazen panache. Millions watched a flight of twenty or so Gothas in fan formation approach from the north-east, unmolested by gunfire or attack from the air. No one imagined they were enemy aircraft until at last the guns in the central London parks began to fire. It was not till then that police shouted, 'Take Cover!' and people rushed for shelter in all directions, those who could heading for the tube stations. The planes targeted the City, although the greatest loss of life from a single bomb was in the roadway of Boleyn Road, Stoke Newington, where nine people were

killed; eight were also killed in Tower Hill, just outside the City, when
a van in the street was hit. The worst damage was shared between the
City and Hoxton on its north-east edge. In all fifty-three were killed
and 182 injured, but the physical destruction amounted to nearly twice
the value of property lost on 13 June at over £200,000; ironically it
included the partial destruction of the former German Gymnasium at
King's Cross, now used by the military.[32]

The sheer effrontery of the raid and the ineffectiveness of London's
defences led to a furious response, in two directions. Popular anger was
vented against those enemy aliens still at large or sometimes against
any 'alien' at all. In North Lambeth, though untouched with just two
bombs falling south of the river in Southwark and no casualties
sustained, businesses owned by Germans, Russians and Italians were
fiercely attacked; Russian businesses were also the target of anti-alien
rioting and looting in Bethnal Green, Hoxton, Dalston and London
Fields, where the opportunity was taken by two soldiers and a professional receiver of stolen property to remove an iron safe from a German-
owned shop in the Broadway.[33]

More productively, fury was directed at the inadequacies of the
capital's air raid precautions – plain for the whole world to wonder at
– and the increasingly unreasonable refusal of the authorities to give
warnings of raids, despite having clear knowledge of them as planes
approached or crossed the coast. St Bartholomew's Hospital, for
instance, which took many casualties from the Liverpool Street bombing,
received just five minutes' warning of the 13 June raid; in the ensuing
chaos, when the King visited unannounced on a journey to the north,
he found the floor of the outpatients' department 'covered with blood'.[34]

The raids on the Thames Estuary had already caused queasiness in
Parliament. A week before the disastrous attack of 13 June, Noel
Pemberton Billing – that wilful, mischievous but often prescient critic
of government air policy – highlighted the inadequacy of fighter cover
for London's airspace and the obstinate rejection of any air raid warning
system. He was right on both counts. Sir Douglas Haig had persuaded
government to move some planes from home defence to the Western
Front in the teeth of Sir John French's objections. And even after 13
June the Home Secretary, following the advice of Sir Edward Henry,
held to the position that warnings would not be given because they
would not save lives. Despite protest meetings up and down London
pleading for air raid warnings, Sir George Cave announced in Parliament

on 28 June that he was satisfied it was 'neither practicable nor desirable to give warnings' to schools or the general public of 'possible air raids' which may 'never materialise'.[35]

The humiliating raid of 7 July changed all that. A prompt volte-face was announced by Cave just five days later. The decision to issue public warnings caused consternation among those who had 'regarded the official mind as the repository of superior wisdom' and duly defended the authorities against their critics, but now found 'their confidence has not been a little misplaced'. On such muddle would the pebbles of cynicism begin to construct a mighty bulwark in the minds of millions of Britons during the course of the war and after. Indeed, this confusion over air raid warnings that might have saved lives in London rankled for years to come. After various trials the new arrangements for public air raid warnings were communicated to police stations from the Executive Department at Scotland Yard on 21 July. The system was based on two maroons ('sound rockets' or 'sound bombs') to be fired from selected police and fire stations; these were supplemented by policemen blowing whistles and sporting 'Take Cover!' notices, sometimes carried on bicycles and cars; the 'all clear' was sounded by special constables ringing handbells or by bugle calls, often played by Boy Scouts. These alarms were sounded in daytime only; at night no public warning would be given.[36]

That proved to be yet another fatal mistake. For the Gotha raids continued with unwonted persistence until the end of the year, but they all took place in darkness. On the moonlit night of 4–5 September a raid by nine Gothas killed fourteen and injured forty-eight in a random path of destruction from Kentish Town to Blackheath: a bomb falling on Victoria Embankment destroyed a tram, killing three and permanently scarring the plinth of the Sphinx close to Cleopatra's Needle. 'Great depression everywhere in consequence of raid,' Caroline Playne noted in her diary next day. 'Rumours of more raids to follow were current' for some days.[37]

In fact there would be a lull. But what followed shook the nerves of the Londoners more severely than anything that had gone before: 'Probably no aspect of the raids is more vividly remembered by Londoners,' it was said some twenty years later of the 'Harvest Moon raids' of 24 September to 1 October, with raids on five nights and alarms on six. On 29 September too the attacking aircraft comprised both Gothas and the new Giants, driven by four, five or six engines with a wingspan of 138 feet, larger than any plane bombing London in the Second World War and carrying a payload of bombs weighing almost 2 tons.[38]

In all, the five Harvest Moon raids killed forty-seven and injured 226. But it was less the damage they caused than the relentless disruption and accumulating strain, built up night after night, that people found so intolerable. There were also some major tragedies. Thirteen were killed on 24 September outside the Bedford Hotel in Southampton Row, most said to be watching the raid from the street; four were killed among many sheltering in the Eaglet public house on Seven Sisters Road, Holloway, on the 29th; eight died in separate incidents at Glamorgan Street, Pimlico, and Hows Street, Shoreditch, on 1 October, the most destructive raid of the week in terms of property, with some 770 houses damaged in Shoreditch alone. Property was damaged in other ways too: when Florence Lockwood, visiting from Yorkshire and staying at the Thackeray Hotel in Bloomsbury, visited the site of the Bedford Hotel tragedy next morning she found 'the shops had been looted at once – tobacco, shoes, fruit, etc., taken. I noticed a wig shop that had been looted.' And reports from south London also complained of looting and pilfering and pocket-picking in the darkened tramcars during or after the bombing.[39]

For those caught up in them the raids were terrifying, the growling Gotha engines as the planes flew lower than before becoming a marked and disturbing feature. Lydia Peile, a young woman from Margate who had experienced some bad raids there, came up to London on 19 September for treatment at St Saviour's Hospital, Osnaburgh Street, just north of the Euston Road. She encountered the first of the raids from her hospital bed:

At about 8.15 last night I heard guns in the distance. They came as rather a surprise as somehow one did not expect them so early in the evening . . . The firing came nearer & nearer & I began to feel scared. Then a fearful crash of a bomb came & the Sisters came hurrying up . . . Some of the bombs, or aerial torpedoes made a horrible noise: the echoes were so terrific – By this time nearly all the traffic had stopped & we could hear the roar of the aeroplanes as they came nearer & nearer – The guns from Regent's Park began blazing forth & as we are quite close to them they made a fearful noise & the shrieking of the shells was terrific – Then we heard the bombs falling & we were very relieved when they began to go further away – A lot of bits of shrapnel came rattling down by my window, with pieces of slate & Nurse & I thought it must get broken, but all was well. After about 35 mins: all was quiet again, but none of us slept much as we expected them to return. It is a perfect day again & we are very much afraid we shall have a return of them tonight.[40]

Fear of the bombers' return drove more Londoners than ever before to seek shelter wherever they could find it. They did so every night, whether there was news of a raid or not. The absence of consistent night-time warnings made this situation worse, and local arrangements like night patrols, still implemented unevenly by residents in many London districts, were haphazard and decried by the police. People resorted to the tube stations if they were in reach, their depth a great comfort. Some 5,000 used Elephant and Castle nightly even before the Harvest Moon raids, for instance, and perhaps as many as 300,000 a night across the system by the end of September. The crush at that time was intense, with a woman dying in a stampede on the Central London Railway tube at Liverpool Street Station on 28 September. Queues formed before dusk and by 6.30 p.m. on 1 October, some hours before a raid might reasonably be anticipated, William Beveridge 'found people ensconced at Notting Hill Gate station'. Even on the rainy night of 27 September, when the weather made a raid unlikely, Arnold Bennett found the tube, probably at Aldwych, full of 'Very poor women and children sitting on the stairs'. In the lift people quarrelled with the operator, provoking an irritated response from 'middle-class women saying to each other that if the poor couldn't keep to the regulations they ought to be forbidden the Tube as a shelter from raid'. 'Once people were admitted into the stations,' recalled Caroline Playne, 'it was almost impossible for passengers to get up or down, from or to the trains', and some platforms were made impassable and noisome by shelterers bedding down for the night.[41]

There were not enough tube stations to accommodate all who sought safety. Rotherhithe Tunnel, closed as a public roadway and used for government purposes only since the outbreak of war, was opened as a shelter; it was accommodating up to 30,000 nightly by early October. Blackwall Tunnel took a further 10,000 to 12,000 and the Greenwich and Woolwich foot tunnels some 3,000 between them, with many turned away. Sanitary conditions in the tunnels remained primitive until the end of the year, when 'canvas decency screens' were installed around the buckets of sand and disinfectant that were given to shelterers as toilets. No doubt all was spruced up and hosed down for a visit of the King and Queen to East End shelters on 18 October. Away from these places, any large building was brought into commission: industrial premises like the Wenlock Brewery in Shoreditch, for instance, or church crypts, Whitehall ministries and town halls across London (two boys of twelve and thirteen were knocked down and killed by a motorbus when crowds milling about Stratford Town Hall spilled into the roadway). At the London Hospital shelterers were so disruptive that they spilled into the wards. Aliens were blamed and from mid-July the hospital refused to give shelter from raids but reopened at police request during the Harvest Moon crisis; the Hospital treasurer reported that the crowds now were orderly but 'indescribably filthy, both in their person and their habits'. And despite the disaster at Upper North Street the LCC opened some 330 schools as shelters at night, which took in around 127,000 people between them.[42]

The Harvest Moon raids also provoked an impromptu evacuation of London. All classes of Londoner took part. Waterloo Station was 'crowded with families, poor mothers and children, who are leaving London' on 2 October, people were reported sleeping out in Richmond Park, and others moved right away as far as Devon and other places if they could. When the moon went dark in early October they returned to London.[43]

In all, 'This was undoubtedly the worst week' of the whole war for the Londoners, according to the historian of East Ham writing some sixteen years later. While not knowing what was to come, that was how people felt at the time too. 'Fear, real physical fear overcame more people than before,' Caroline Playne recorded on 29 September.

> Though everything went on as usual the atmosphere was very excited . . .
> The worked up condition of most people was like the mental condition
> in a family where some serious, alarming fatal accident has happened.
> The feeling was more like that which would be produced by an earth-
> quake or natural cataclasm [sic]. Many children suffered from shell shock
> as well as grown ups.

A couple of days later, 'Men even (at Committee) looked pale, and nerve-racked'. Hallie Miles agreed but thought the malaise went deeper, putting it in the context of the raids since June and perhaps much else:

'Everyone is so War-weary! That first wonderful spirit of patriotism seems to have died down. In some ways it is very nearly gone; this is largely owing to the terrible blunders and heart-breaking mistakes that have been made by "those in power".'[44]

From 2 October Londoners were given a respite for over a fortnight. The dark nights without a moon and with deteriorating weather gave cause to expect this situation to continue for some time to come. Then on 19 October there was a great and most unwelcome surprise. The Zeppelins were found to have a sting in their tail-fins. On a dark foggy night, flying high above the clouds with no sound of its engines detectable on the ground, a single vessel, L45, rocked London with massive explosions that seemed to come from nowhere. This, the 'Silent Raid', caused considerable loss of life, thirty-three in all, with forty-nine injured: fourteen were killed at Glenview Road, Lewisham, and twelve at Albany Road, Camberwell, but the most shocking was a high-explosive bomb that fell without warning in Piccadilly around 11.30 p.m. just outside Swan and Edgar's drapery store, killing seven and leaving a crater that stayed a visitor attraction for some days. There were then three Gotha raids on 1 November and 6 and 12 December, killing a total of twenty-two and injuring ninety-nine more, with most casualties in outer south London and Clerkenwell, north of the river; four were killed on the Victoria Embankment on the last raid before Christmas.[45]

In the late summer, with rumours rife that the Germans had a plan to set London ablaze with the night-time Gotha raids – rumours for once well informed – something had been done late in the year to improve London's defences. DORA required the coordination of over ninety local fire brigades in outer London under the general direction of the London Fire Brigade from September; more guns and searchlights were deployed around the southern edge of the metropolis; and on the east 'a broken line of balloons' began to be installed from Edmonton to the river at Woolwich. A steel curtain or 'Apron' was strung between each set of three balloons, ten aprons in all, to force planes to a height vulnerable to anti-aircraft fire. That fire itself, though, was made less effective by the 'astounding' decision taken around September to replace high-explosive shells with shrapnel; in the damning judgement of Commander Rawlinson, for a time in charge of London's defences, 'many lives were lost and much damage done' by shrapnel on the ground, far more deadly there than it ever was 'to the enemy'.[46]

Amid all these moments of terrifying drama, upsetting the capital in the second half of the year in particular, important elements of daily life grew ever more difficult to endure. The weather didn't help even in this year's short summer. On 20 May a violent thunderstorm flooded low-lying districts of south London and nine days later a storm with hailstones the size of peas brought more flooding, while lightning set fire to the Deptford Cattle Market. On 16 June a severe thunderstorm struck North Kensington; 4½ inches of rain fell in minutes, sewers surcharged by 5 feet and basements flooded so quickly that families could not move furniture and possessions to safety, adding to the long-standing miseries of Notting Dale – the mayor established a relief fund, spent mostly on replacement bedding.[47]

Weather aside, getting around London also became distinctly more challenging this year. Private cars were deprived of petrol from April. effectively putting an end to driving for the civilian population. Some bypassed the problem by running their cars on methylated spirits, also hard to get, or on coal-gas carried in huge car-sized bags of balloon fabric strapped to the roof or towed behind in a trailer. The conversion cost £30, a large sum. A few seemed favoured: Herbert Asquith had a 'motor *without* a gas-bag', Cynthia complained to her diary. 'How? Why?' And the common sight of naval and army officers, many safely berthed on the general staff, sporting in motors around London with their girlfriends led many to feel that the burdens of war did not always fall equally on even middle-class Londoners.[48]

Taxis too were becoming harder and harder to find. Things were made worse by a dispute with some railway companies, which tried to charge a fee to drivers who plied from station forecourts. 'At Liverpool Street today I found it impossible to get a taxi and had to ask the porter at the hotel to send my things by messenger,' H. Rider Haggard groused in June; the quarrel was still dragging on in November.[49]

The consequences for overcrowding on public transport were dire. 'Strap-hanging has become a habit in England, where it was formerly unknown,' the American R. D. Blumenfeld noted in September. 'Life in a London omnibus has ceased to be a joy.' Daisy Parsons found herself one of a quartet, two girls and two boys, travelling to the station to get home to Woodford from Palmers Green late one evening in April. The tram they boarded was 'somewhat crowded' and the two girls, climbing to the top deck, 'were pushed, punched, had our toes trodden upon, all sort of things . . . The number of people on that tram almost squashed us to death', though Daisy seems not to have minded the squeeze too much. But at tram and bus stops crowding had become intolerable by the end of the year:

> Getting home during rush hours was a daily terror, especially on dark winter evenings in London. The crowds of office workers were vastly increased and the scramble to get into some of the longer distance trams and omnibuses constituted a bear fight out of which those of both sexes, who were worsted or driven off the overladen vehicles by the conductors, retreated to the pavement with hats bashed in, umbrellas broken, shins and ankles kicked and bruised, in a dazed and shaken condition . . . The dread of the evening struggle in dark streets hung over many workers all the time, adding considerably to the strain of life.[50]

The disorder in the streets was so bad, and disabled or wounded soldiers were treated so badly in the melee, that the London local authorities agitated for the enforcement of queuing at bus and tram stops, that courtesy entirely foreign to the rush-hour Londoner. In December 1917 the LCC organised a conference on how best to achieve this new departure.[51]

Despite these worries and strains, and despite DORA's restrictions on what restaurants could offer their customers, the Londoners defiantly took their chances to enjoy themselves. Some took them further than others. 'Brenda was there in an outrageous dress,' recorded Cynthia Asquith of a summer dinner party, 'shorter than anything I have seen off the stage and drawn tight under her outlined behind.' For most the stage would be as far as they would go, or the silver screen. The cinema remained a great favourite, this being the year of a second major war film, *Tanks*, of D. W. Griffith's *Intolerance* and of Charlie Chaplin as the main draw in anything at all; tragically, though, and so typical of this year, four children were trampled to death when someone shouted, 'Fire!' at the Electric Picture Palace, Deptford High Street, in April.[52]

On the stage it was the musical revue that continued most of all to capture London audiences' allegiance. *The Bing Girls are There* opened at the Alhambra in February, its main writer that great late-Victorian favourite George Grossmith offering a feminised take on *The Bing Boys are Here* and celebrating the wartime independence of young women. And *Chu Chin Chow*, which opened the year before at His Majesty's Theatre, Haymarket, embedded itself in metropolitan culture during 1917. It became a show that everybody had to see and indeed everyone seems to have seen it. 'The music is delightful, the colour captivating and the acting superb,' enthused the journalist Sydney Moseley, taking 'sweet little Minnie' with him on 1 April; he went twice more that month. It drew even the self-denying Wensleys too: 'Fancy, you folks going to see Chu Chin Chow – horrid, selfish, unpatriotic, spendthrifty lot!' Daisy Parsons ribbed Edie.[53]

As usual, men in khaki provided a good share of the West End audiences. At Chelsea Barracks, young Lieutenant F. H. Ennor, in training with the Grenadier Guards, spent every evening he could in the theatre, his taste ranging from Shakespeare to revue, inevitably seeing *Chu Chin Chow* in February ('beautifully staged & acted, and we enjoyed it very much'). That same month he saw *Three Cheers* with Harry Lauder at the Shaftesbury ('awfully good & we enjoyed it immensely'), *Zig Zag* at the Hippodrome, Irene Vanbrugh in *The Land of Promise* at the New Theatre, *Under Cover* at the Strand ('most thrilling & well acted detective play'), *Maid of the Mountains* at Daly's Theatre, Cranbourn Street; and in March he saw *The Bing Girls* but 'did not care for the play very much', *Zig Zag* again, *Antony in Wonderland* with Charles Hawtrey at the Prince of Wales's, and *General Post* at the Haymarket ('awfully good'), and so on until his last visit, to *Smile* at the Garrick in late July. He shipped to France from Waterloo Station on 10 August.[54]

Besides all this huge variety in the London theatres it was during the war, according to Stephen McKenna, that the 'love of music, ceasing to be the foible of the few, became the craving of the many'. He singled out Sir Thomas Beecham, 'owed the gratitude of thousands' for his opera seasons at Drury Lane Theatre, opening unpropitiously in 1917 just before the Harvest Moon raids with Rimsky-Korsakov's *Ivan the Terrible*: Cynthia Asquith was there on 4 October and enjoyed it – 'I like noisy operas.'[55]

Operas, plays and musical revues offered the only brightness in an otherwise unprecedentedly bleak midwinter. The Christmas season shepherded in a return of the food crisis, now more marked and threatening than ever before. Queues for sugar had been common since the autumn, made more miserable by the prevailing bronchitis and influenza – people were in line for four hours to get served in Bermondsey in October, when a man collapsed and died as he waited. But by December there were queues for what seemed like everything – butcher's meat, bacon, tea, cheese, butter, margarine – with food 'the one topic of conversation' by Christmas. Rumours that a shop might be taking in supplies caused queues to assemble before daylight in the bitter December fogs. Some were 1,000 people long, 2,000, even 3,000, far too long in many cases for commodities to last in most shops, even if they had been there from the outset. Anger found expression in anti-profiteering agitation in working-class districts, the Victoria Park Anti-Profiteering League being one among many local organisations calling for government action against '"all persons . . . forcing up prices of necessities of life"'. As Christmas approached the queues grew even longer and the spectre of a hungry holiday haunted many. The Food Controller was bombarded with pleas for action, a telegram from the Lewisham Food Control Committee, part of the nationwide network established to assist in the distribution of supplies, insisting that 'very grave issues hang on the meat shortage in particular'. Calls mounted for compulsory rationing and the nationalisation of supplies. Invidious (and not always accurate) comparisons were made between long queues in poor areas with few or none in the wealthier districts: shoppers from Southwark, women, boys and girls – 'Girls of elementary school age actually carried babies in their arms' – tramped over the bridges to queue at shops in the City, where tea and margarine were reportedly on sale, for instance.[56]

'It is the fourth Christmas of the war, and for many it is going to be a very quiet, if not a sad one,' the *Observer* mused on Sunday 23 December: 'For the first time, though we are all making the best of things, Christmas has lost its festive air . . ' The paper caught the mood of many. Caroline Playne, an *Observer* reader, also reported that 'this Christmas is an extremely sad one. There is a great deal of a grin and bear it spirit but the vast majority of men & women look worn out & deeply sorrowful.' The feeling was shared by the City merchant Frederick Robinson, whose diary had grown to 2,000 pages by April 1917; he remarked that every Christmas of 'this awful war' had been less joyous than the last. And those few who were moved to send Christmas cards now had to struggle with the added complication of fixing numbers to the London postal districts, a new system introduced that March.[57]

So it proved for most people. Christmas 1917 was a 'subdued shadow indeed of the joyousness and revelry that used to mark the season in the roaring times of peace', according to *The Times*, 'the most chastened Christmas that London has spent for many years'. There was, however, some last-minute relief on the food front. Supplies of meat did at last get through to the shops by Christmas Eve. 'The abundance of meat and poultry this fourth Christmas of the War is amazing,' thought Michael MacDonagh. 'Everything was dear, of course. But the price did not matter.'[58] That was true. For despite the general gloom, most Londoners now found themselves with money in their pockets as never before.

THE CURSE IS BEING REMOVED

DESPITE the flurry of wage rises secured in many industries by the industrial militancy of 1917, it seems clear enough that throughout the war the cost of living generally outpaced any gain in wage rates. Most workers' hourly pay, men and women alike, struggled to play catch-up in an economic climate where, measured by wages alone, the prices of food and other commodities made ever bigger claims on family resources. The one very important exception to this general picture is the case of unskilled London men in previously overstocked industries like the building trades and on the docks, where the huge pool of available labour had traditionally kept wages cripplingly low. But during the war the wages of the poorest paid dock worker in the Port of London more than doubled from a daily rate of 5s 10d in July 1914 to 11s 9d in October 1918; and a bricklayer's labourer earning 6½d an hour in 1914 was getting 1s 3d by the end of the war. Both these increases outstripped the rise in the cost of living over the same period, which approximately doubled. As the journalist Arthur Gleason truly remarked in 1917, England 'now paid a living wage to people who had never had it before . . .'[1]

By the measure of wages alone, then, it seemed that most London workers except the poorest breadwinners were worse off at the end of the war than at the beginning, and that this held good for each year of the conflict because wages consistently lagged behind prices. But wages alone do not tell the full story. For earnings were frequently augmented by overtime, staff shortages meaning that those who were left had to work longer hours. Alfred Grosch, his German surname from forebears who had come to London well over a century before, was a 26-year-old clerk in the GPO's telephone service when war was declared. 'I came on duty one evening to find sixteen of the staff absent . . . and myself the officer in charge. Instead of 54 hours I worked 85 hours a week', doubling his weekly wage packet from 35s to 70s. Overtime seems also to have been a feature of munitions work, with women volunteering for extra hours or an additional Sunday shift, 'the increased comfort of the home being weighed in the balance against the additional strain of the factory'. These exceptionally long hours probably accounted for the exaggerated stories in the papers of sensational munitions wages for women. On the other hand, not everyone took the chance to work extra hours or made the effort to earn more. '"Why should I work any harder?"' one munitionette asked Naomi Loughnan. '"My mother is satisfied with what I take home of a Saturday."' Those takings were, Loughnan thought, unprecedented:

> there is no doubt that we do earn more than women have ever earned before. We 'pick up' our three pounds a week, and fall into a rage because we were expecting three pounds and tuppence. At the same time living is so very expensive in these days that three or four pounds are not what they seem.[2]

But even more than rising wages, even more than earnings from overtime rising faster still, it was the effect of full employment on the London working class that had the greatest impact on the standard of life during the war. All families, especially those with children over the school-leaving age of fourteen, could expect to generate a household income from many sources, with each often earning well and regularly. Even where mothers did not work they usually had a separation allowance if their man was on active service. So H. J. Bennett, a schoolboy in Walworth, saw how 'the family finances improved somewhat' during the war: 'My father benefited from the overall wage increases given to engineers who became the cream of the labour force with the demand for more and more munitions of war'; his elder brother was a clerk in the City before joining up in 1918 and his elder sister was packing backache pills from the age of fourteen. Even the chaotic Jasper family from Hoxton – father a drunken timber porter before 1914 – now had money coming in from all directions. Father upgraded to a timber salesman boasting his own horse and cart, and also had a sideline selling screws and glue stolen from a Bethnal Green workshop where his son-in-law made munitions boxes; mother made clothes at home and sold them from a stall in Hoxton Street; one daughter also made munitions boxes; her married sister, sharing accommodation with her parents, bought a sewing machine to make bandoliers at home; and an older brother in the Merchant Navy was always flush with money when on shore leave. In all or many of these trades the war not only expanded the choice of work on offer but ironed out the pre-war fluctuations of demand dictated by fashion or the seasons that had long kept London earnings both low and irregular. There are no comprehensive unemployment figures for London in these years, but rates for two significant trades are suggestive: in engineering, unemployment for the first seven months of 1914 averaged 3.9 per cent, while in the last seven months of the war (May to November 1918) it was 1.3 per cent; for building the figures were 9 per cent and 0.8 per cent.[3]

The impact of higher wages and even higher earnings, and most of all of full employment, on working-class living standards in London was astonishing from 1915 onwards. The poorest felt the improvement most. In 1913–14 the LCC had fed an average of 35,000 poor schoolchildren with 146,000 dinners each week; by 1915–16 the number of children being fed had almost halved and in 1918–19 it had dropped to 9,500 children receiving just 22,500 dinners each week. In 1918 the proportion of 'poorly nourished' schoolchildren in London was 'considerably less than half the percentage in 1913'. And nationwide it was thought at the end of the war – despite shortages, rationing, declining quality of foods like bread and a possible rise in adulteration – that the families of unskilled workers were 'slightly better fed' than four years before.[4]

As with food, so with clothing. Although in late 1915 schoolteachers in Bethnal Green continued to appeal, as they always had, for donations of children's clothing, especially boots, by 1918 the LCC's school '"clothing cupboards", from which exceptionally necessitous children used to receive garments before the war, are no longer resorted to . . .' Alfred Grosch, the GPO clerk, found that a 'very few weeks' of overtime 'not only put us on our feet, but rigged us out in new clothes . . . For the first time since our marriage [around 1912] we were able to breathe freely, even though we had two children to support.' R. M. Fox noted how in a north London engineering works, 'The younger, flashier machine men appeared wearing gold rings, which were soon dented and knocked to pieces in the shop.' This conspicuous consumption drew the envy of some and the disdain of others. John Gray, confined to a wheelchair by a spinal problem and a keen observer of life from the windows of his father's pub in Finchley, 'could tell a munitioner anywhere . . . There was no mistaking the flashy fur coats and the fashionable high-legged coloured boots of the women, or the gaudy suits and caps of the men, and the money-to-burn manners of both'.[5]

Few things aroused the wrath of the workers' social superiors more than this flaunting of money to burn from high wartime wages among the previously poor of London. It wasn't just showy clothing that rankled but what people knew or suspected was also happening in the workers' homes. Working-class comforts had suddenly been put on a par with the lower middle class, even with those enjoyed in the homes of struggling professionals. 'The British piano dealers have never been so prosperous as they are to-day,' thought R. D. Blumenfeld in April 1916. 'You cannot buy a cheap piano for immediate delivery. They have all gone into the cottages of the workmen, who have never made so much money.' Mrs Alec-Tweedie, that fearless class-warrior, adopted a harsher tone:

> The servant-maid is chiefly obsessed with the fact that her married sister (whose husband has one of the overpaid jobs) has bought a piano which she cannot play, has invested in an American carpet – these carpets are coming into this country in thousands – and is the proud possessor of a fur coat, which she forgets to keep clean . . .[6]

The piano was such an often-quoted emblem of the new luxury that some historians have doubted the very existence of this troubling instrument as 'folklore'. In fact, though, the lavishing of comforts on the homes of the London working class did indeed include pianos, both new and second-hand. The British piano trade, with domineering pre-war German competition removed almost overnight from the outbreak of war, stepped into the breach. Early in 1917 a Stamford Hill piano manufacturer sought exemption from military service because his firm 'was doing a large business in the piano trade, which was formerly in the hands of the Germans', and later in the year the federation of piano makers was keen to train young workers in the LCC's evening institutes. Indeed, 'but for the war', a speaker at the Scientific Products Exhibition claimed in September 1918, 'it would have taken twenty years to convince the public that British pianos were best'. We know that at least some of these got into the homes of London's workers, because Lambeth County Court criticised a Hatton Garden piano dealer for trying to recover a piano bought on hire purchase from a south London wounded soldier who failed to keep up the payments. And auction rooms in working-class districts were said to be crowded with 'those made wealthy by the war' keen to 'pounce on pianos' and 'plush armchairs'.[7]

These new possessions in the homes of the London workers gave great joy. Florrie Roberts from Camberwell, her father a carman and stableman and her mother a coster's daughter, worked with her sister making boxes after she left school at fourteen:

> I used to spend my money as soon as I got it. I was all for making the house look nice. I bought something each week: curtains, a new blind, an aspidistra to put in the window, carpets on the floor – Little things to make the place look right.[8]

Dolly Scannell's mother in Poplar, whose husband was at the front but with three daughters at work, two of them in the City, bought so much new furniture that her husband complained of her extravagance when he returned home. She got it mainly on hire purchase from Killwick's in Stepney, most memorably furniture for the parlour:

> a green plush sofa and two matching armchairs. They had mahogany curved arms and legs and beautiful cream roses on the seats of green plush. A carved mahogany occasional table, a rug by the marble fireplace and a mahogany over-mantel with many mirrors on it completed the furnishing of this luxury room.[9]

Even the poorest homes were affected. Indeed, it was there that the expansion of home comforts was most noticed. And to show that Mrs Alec-Tweedie's scornful gaze did not represent the sum of polite opinion, we might cite a more sympathetic view from a Miss Middlebrooke, 'an unpaid Health Visitor' who had undertaken voluntary work with the Woolwich Public Health Department since before the war:

> With better financial conditions, many of the homes I almost despaired of have become improved almost beyond belief, which goes to prove very emphatically that if we want to eliminate the slum type of human being and the slum type of home, the surest and quickest way is to give the

workman a good living wage . . . With more wages coming in, all [these] difficulties disappear as if by magic, and the housewife begins to buy comforts for her family and home which never could have been afforded before. She gradually improves in health and spirits and is anxious to make her surroundings correspond with her own improvement.[10]

There were many comparable signs too in the sharp fall in London of those workers having to rely on the poor law to keep body and soul together. 'No one, we think, could have predicted that the war would have had such a remarkable effect in reducing pauperism as it has had,' noted an editorial in *Charity Organisation Review* in January 1916. By then the London workhouse casual wards, providing one or two nights' accommodation for vagrants and unemployed looking for work, were almost empty; and for that same class the war saw the beginning of the demise of the privately owned common lodging house or 'doss-house' in London, numbers in the County falling from 308 in 1914 to 211 in 1918. Even among the aged poor many were somehow magicked out of the workhouse, taken back by relatives who could now give them a home, or winning once more an independent existence through work. As the war went on, that movement out of the workhouse by aged paupers over seventy years old, and their relinquishing of poor relief altogether, steadily continued, with 14,800 relieved in London in January 1914, 13,400 in January 1916, 11,100 in December 1917 and 9,900 in December 1918. Some of the statistics of pauperism had begun to move in this direction before the war: casual wards were less resorted to from 1913, for instance, the numbers relieved in their homes from about 1912 and workhouse numbers from 1911. Nonetheless, the decline of pauperism – not a measure of 'the poor' but only those turning to the state for subsistence – was remarkable, falling by about a third in all forms of relief during the war, with under 47,000 'indoor paupers' in London workhouses in August 1918 compared to over 69,000 four years before.[11]

The general transformation was remarked on by all with eyes to see. Michael MacDonagh, always a sympathetic observer of London life, witnessed the traditional working-class holiday at "Appy 'Ampstead', Whit Monday at the end of May 1917:

The great thing is that there was no sign in the crowd of the old ugly squalor of poverty. More has been done for the social betterment of the

16. Munition Education Class, Brixton School of Building, 1915. This was not just a soldiers' war but an engineers' war too. Men continued to be needed on the home front, with the most skilled munitions tasks still the preserve of men rather than women.

17. Women making army petrol cans, Fulham, 1916. Women made every conceivable war requisite, here taking on an indispensable task for an increasingly mechanised army.

18. Women munitions workers' football team. Camaraderie among women war workers was legendary and took on many guises, as here at the AEC munitions factory at Beckton, East Ham.

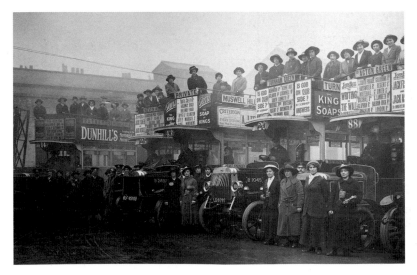

19. Women Clippies with London General Omnibus Company B-type Buses. Women bus conductors became one of the most noticeable and fondly regarded features of the wartime London streets. Here new recruits pose with their vehicles.

20. Charing Cross Station, July 1916. Within twenty-four hours of the opening of the Battle of the Somme, silent crowds in large numbers gathered to watch the endless stream of ambulances taking wounded men to London's hospitals.

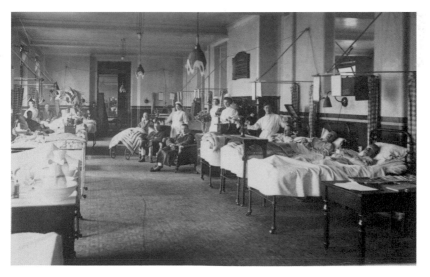

21. Turner Ward, London Hospital. A large burden of caring for wounded troops fell on the capital's general hospitals, as here in an officers' ward at the London Hospital in Whitechapel.

22. Wounded and maimed soldiers entertained in the West End. Many West-End theatres arranged matinee shows especially for the wounded in their 'hospital blues', an increasingly common sight in London as the war dragged on.

23. Remembrance. Shrines commemorating the fallen began to appear in the poorer areas of London in 1916, listing those who had died from individual streets. Here a memorial service is being held at a shrine outside St Agnes Church in Acton Lane. This local movement of remembrance gathered strength and was soon appropriated by the established churches.

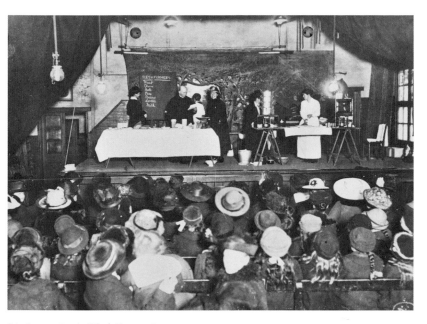

24. Instruction in 'Flesh Formers'. From 1917 unrestricted German submarine warfare put Britain's food supplies under great pressure, with major shortages at the end of the year and rationing for many foodstuffs shortly after. Here a lecture on making the best of a bad job is held at St Augustine's Hall, Victoria Park.

25. *Chu Chin Chow*. This was a musical war, punctuated by memorable songs and spawning some great West-End stage hits. None was bigger than *Chu Chin Chow*, opening in August 1916 and running well beyond the Armistice. The costumes revealed rather too much flesh, many thought at the time.

26. Silvertown explosion, Brunner Mond's TNT Factory, 19 January 1917. The destruction of this giant works was perhaps the most shocking event of London's war. Rumours circulated about sabotage but it seems to have been a tragic accident. Miraculously only some forty people were said to have lost their lives.

27. Munition workers' hutments. The London housing problem was greatly exacerbated during the war by a virtual stoppage in housebuilding and an influx of workers to the munitions areas. Here temporary huts provide some relief for Woolwich engineers and their families.

28. Coal queues, King's Cross, 1917. Coal shortages hit London hard from early 1917. For once they hit the middle classes and wealthy; coal merchants were instructed to favour poor customers, especially if trouble looked likely, though these children clutching their receptacles look patient enough.

29. Armistice Day, 11 November 1918. Never before or since did London enjoy such an outpouring of relief and joy as at news of the Armistice at 11 o'clock that morning. The crowds were unparalleled and immense and gathered all over the capital, with Nelson's Monument in Trafalgar Square one of the most popular destinations.

labouring classes by three years of this frightful War than by the garnering
of the harvests of peace for many generations!

A few months later he thought that 'there is now no such word as
"poor" in our social vocabulary'. Chartres Biron, the magistrate at
Lambeth police court during the war, recalled how 'the war seemed to
have abolished poverty'. And Arthur Gleason, another middle-class
celebrant of this most surprising feature of London's war, summed it
all up with a biblical ring: 'Comfort and well-being, the margin of
leisure, the elements of happiness, are greater for the mass [of] people
than at any other period. A sullenness and despair have gone from the
earth. The curse is being removed.'[12]

Not all middle-class people felt that way, though, if only for the
understandable reason that their own living standards during those four
or five years of war had moved in the opposite direction. That was not
true for everyone, of course, because many manufacturers prospered as
never before from war contracts and many others found work in the
government service. This white-collar salariat class grew in these years
faster than ever before, and those at the lower levels found that at least
from 1916 wages and overtime kept them more or less abreast of the
cost of living. Senior staff, however, had salaries pegged at pre-war
levels until 1918 – all part of war's 'sacrifice' – their households burdened
by at least a 60 per cent increase in the cost of living. And there is
evidence that the salaries of commercial clerks, at least in banking, did
poorly when compared to the cost of living, their position not made
easier by the employment of female labour, invariably cheaper to the
employer.[13]

Whether they earned well or badly, however, it was the middle classes
who carried the large burden of wartime taxation. Income tax was
doubled in November 1914 from 1s 2d to 2s 4d in the pound, and
various purchase taxes (affecting everyone) increased at the same time.
Income tax rose again in September 1915 to 3s 6d and more workers
were brought into its lowest band; supertax was raised to 7s; and an
'excess war profits tax' was introduced for entrepreneurs from the same
time. By the end of the war this last had risen to 80 per cent, more
earners had been brought within the income tax bracket and the top
rate of income tax had risen to 5s in the pound (25 per cent), with
supertax unchanged. Purchase taxes on various commodities continued
to climb. And most middle-class tenants were in accommodation without

the benefit of rent control from 1915, as we shall see shortly. In all, Mrs Alec-Tweedie probably spoke for many when she said, 'The educated middle class, the thrifty backbone, the brains of the country, has been almost taxed out of existence by the war.'[14]

It seems likely that for many middle-class Londoners, most especially those in the professions whose earnings had dropped away and who had not found any lucrative employment elsewhere, real incomes fell by around a third and living standards fell accordingly. A Professional Classes War Relief Council had been formed in October 1914 when the effects of wartime dislocation for the middle classes became apparent. In contrast to the great war relief committees for the workers, largely redundant by the spring of 1915, the Council continued to make urgent appeals for money until the war's end. It was very much a London-based organisation, its chief cheerleaders being the Lord Mayor and City Corporation, and it worked closely with established benevolent funds and the professional associations to coordinate relief in necessitous cases. It offered help with school fees, clothing grants, maternity aid, assistance in finding work and retraining opportunities, ran its own private nursing home, distributed clothing, organised concerts for distressed musicians and art exhibitions for painters struggling to sell their work. For many observers this was one remarkable instance of how the world had been turned upside down by the war: 'The rich have become poor. The poor have become rich.'[15]

This unprecedented decline in inequality – both celebrated and deplored as it was – had an impact beyond the narrowing in the gap of feeding, clothing and household comforts. It had some tangible effects on health and life chances too. It was one more of the ironies of war, arising from this central paradox of 'the poor becoming rich', that amidst so much premature death others might expect to live longer.

The gains in life expectancy, though, were uneven and subject to many fluctuations, inevitably so given the unpredictable movement of infections from one year to another over such a short period. Infant mortality was one accepted indicator of the well-being of the poor. But in the short term, infant deaths could be affected by the weather, especially extremes of heat or cold; and by the fluctuating virulence of epidemic diseases like measles. In addition, during the war years two phenomena in particular moved against an overall fall. These were illegitimacy – illegitimate babies were more likely to die than those born in wedlock – and the closely associated problem of infanticide

and abandonment. We have already seen how the number and proportion of illegitimate births rose in London during the war years, though
not drastically. Even so, the effects on life chances could be huge: in
Kensington in 1917, for instance, mortality among all infants under
twelve months was 130 per thousand, but for illegitimate babies it was
408. There are no statistics, year on year, for infanticide and abandonment, though in 1918 the Commissioner of Police reported sixteen
infants under one year old murdered and twenty-eight abandoned infants
under two, many of whom would have died; on the other hand, that
same year, there were over 800 inquests on children under one year
old in the County of London alone out of 7,600 infant deaths – this
is an especially grey area in the criminal statistics, it seems. Similarly,
cases of abortion brought to the attention of police were unusually
high in 1916 and 1918, but the numbers were tiny and can have borne
no relation to the prevalence of the practice.[16]

With these complexities in mind we can nevertheless see some
implications for infant mortality in London of the dramatic rise in
living standards of the poor. A long-term decline in infant mortality
in London had established itself from around 1898, when about one
in six babies born in the County were dying before their first birthday.
The fall was sharp but uneven, with large annual fluctuations and
spikes in deaths in 1904 and in the hot, dry summer of 1911. During
the war there was another spike in 1915, influenced by a bad measles
epidemic, but the overall trend of the war years was down, with 1916
recording the lowest ratio of infant deaths to live births in London's
history. Overall the infant mortality rate in the five years 1914 to 1918
in the County of London was 103 per thousand live births, whereas
the average for 1909 to 1913 was 108. This did not in itself mark an
astonishing improvement, even though many fewer babies were actually dying in London because of the fall in the birth rate. But these
averages disguise vital local differences. Those boroughs with the highest
infant mortality rates pre-war made by far the greatest gains, while
those with the lowest ratios showed the smallest. So the best improvements were in Finsbury, Shoreditch, Bermondsey, Bethnal Green and
Stepney; those with the lowest gains were Chelsea, Hampstead,
Westminster, Stoke Newington and Woolwich. All the principal
improvements, then, were in working-class boroughs and most of the
smallest in districts with large middle-class populations: Woolwich, as
we shall see in a moment, was subject to exceptional pressures. Once

more there was a levelling up, a coming together of life chances for
new-born infants, between richer and poorer London districts during
the war.[17]

There were two wartime developments that may have made a contribution to this improvement, especially in the poorer boroughs. First, it
seems likely that the decline in drunkenness, impacted upon partly at
least by liquor controls, cut the numbers of babies dying from 'over-
laying', suffocated sharing a bed with their mothers. In London in 1913,
an average of 2.54 babies per thousand live births died in this way
compared to 0.83 in 1919, though the drop was much less sharp for
illegitimate births when measured alone.[18] And second was the greater
attention paid to infant welfare than ever before.

All wars, productive of so much death, provoke anxiety to preserve
the lives of the new emerging generation lest the nation and its fortunes
fail to recover from the slaughter. The First World War was no exception. 'The value of population has never been so appreciated as it is
to-day,' proclaimed the *Daily Telegraph* in a passage quoted with
approval by Islington's Medical Officer of Health in his report for 1916.
There was certainly much to worry a population patriot in London,
where the birth rate had suffered greatly – 110,000 babies born in
London County in 1914 but just 71,000 in 1918, a fall of 36 per cent.
The evident need to protect infant life drew a response from most local
authorities in London, which, with the aid of government grants, began
widely to employ health visitors to support new babies and their mothers
at home. Many also established infant welfare centres for ante- and
post-natal advice and practical assistance. By May 1919 there were
ninety-three health visitors employed by metropolitan borough councils,
though unevenly distributed: Deptford, Hackney and Southwark had
seven each, while Camberwell, Paddington and St Marylebone had none
at all. Many other councils in both London County and the outer ring
provided infant welfare centres for medical treatment and advice, with
dozens established from Acton to Woolwich by the end of the war.
Centres run by voluntary action and funded by subscribers paying for
premises and medical staff were also set up in many places. St
Marylebone, for instance, had numerous voluntary-funded ante-natal
and infant-welfare clinics, providing support for infant feeding, classes
for mothers, day nurseries and a nursery school, one explanation perhaps
for the local council's decision not to employ a health visitor on its
own staff. It was all a revolutionary step forward from pre-war London,

when the Finsbury Milk Depot (1904), the St Pancras School for Mothers (1907) and the North Islington Maternity Centre (1913) had offered pretty much the only infant welfare support in the capital.[19]

Despite these wartime improvements, many elements of pre-war London life proved perniciously resistant to change. Child neglect, ill-treatment and sadism moved to an unfathomable rhythm untouched by improved living standards. We might instance some distressing cases from Hoxton, long known for an element of rough and unforgiving culture in some aspects of family life. Like the 46-year-old soldier's wife sentenced to two months' hard labour in December 1915; though in receipt of 32s 6d a week, little seems to have gone on her six children aged two to twelve, one filthy bed shared by the whole family, the children left to their own devices with 'little or no food' in the house. Or another soldier's wife from a court off Ivy Lane, Hoxton, imprisoned in March 1916 for savagely beating her ten-year-old daughter and neglecting her five younger children, found half-starved, ravenous and cowed. Or a couple from Hackney Wick given hard labour in January 1916 for neglecting their six children aged two to twelve, all filthy and verminous, most suffering from scabies and without adequate clothing. And so on.[20]

Wartime's improved living standards could not eliminate family pathologies like these. And the war itself could be productive of domestic crises and breakdown that added London children to the countless victims of the conflict. The Church of England's Waifs' and Strays' Society found increasing calls on its services to take children into its care during the war. To meet the demand it opened a new London home for 'war cases', the Kitchener Memorial Home at Hillfield Avenue, Hornsey, accommodating forty-eight boys from the spring of 1918.[21] The fortunes of war affected the lives of many of the boys and girls coming into the care of the Society in these years. Like the Hoxton boy, eight years old who, 'Since the father was recalled to his regiment' in late 1914, truanted from school and 'wanders all over London', his mother ('a nice superior women') finding it impossible to cope with him. Or three children from a family in the notoriously rough Lisson Grove area of Marylebone, abandoned by their mother, a munitionette, when their father came home from France and found she 'had been "carrying on" with another man' – 'she appears to have gone wrong since the War'. Or a four-year-old boy from Hoxton whose father was killed in action in March 1916 and who was then neglected by his mother: 'Her Separation Allowance was stopped about Feb: 1st 1916 on account of Misconduct (drinking) & no pension has ever been issued to her.' Or the many others orphaned during the war years: a boy from Bethnal Green, ten years old when his father was killed in action in May 1915, his mother dying from consumption just two years later, his close relations living nearby having too many children of their own to look after him, and his uncles 'mostly serving at the front'; or the five children aged four to thirteen, orphaned in extraordinary circumstances in May 1917, their father dying of pneumonia in France and their mother dying of pneumonia in St Marylebone workhouse infirmary just one week later.[22]

In a number of the Society's cases the ill-health of the mother was largely responsible for a child needing residential care, and here too the war could be a direct factor. A woman from Kentish Town whose first husband was killed on the opening day of the Battle of the Somme remarried shortly after, though her new husband too was called up for the army. She was employed in a factory at Lyme Street, Camden Town, at 'Aircraft work. "covering". 7½d an hour – 36/- in a full week'. By the summer of 1918, however, she was 'Too unwell to work, not very likely to return', and her boy of eleven was taken into the newly opened Kitchener Memorial Home.[23]

Whether this was a case of dope poisoning is not clear, and plainly there are many reasons for being ill. But the very conditions of much of women's labour during the war – close contact with hazardous substances, sometimes intense labour in poor working conditions, long hours forcing tough compromises over family life and childcare – no doubt took their toll on some. This was one conclusion of the Health of Munition Workers Committee in 1915 and one reason why, from that point on, so much attention was paid to improving the working conditions of women in munitions in particular. In 1916 the government factory inspectors were able to report many improvements in working conditions for women in particular, with 'greater cleanliness, better heating, lighting, ventilation and sanitary accommodation, improved first-aid and ambulance arrangements, and the provision of preventive clothing'. An afternoon tea break for women working overtime was found to produce 'very beneficial results' in productivity, helped in those munitions factories run or overseen by the Ministry of Munitions by some 867 canteens established nationwide between November 1915 and November 1918, providing refreshments for something like a million workers. There was also some assistance with childcare in crèches provided close to munitions works. These were run by voluntary organisations and partly funded by the Board of Education: the socialist education reformer Margaret McMillan established some well-known nurseries in this way at Deptford, for instance.[24]

By 1917 there was a widespread consensus that the health of women workers was holding up surprisingly well against the challenges of wartime production. The main reasons were less these improved conditions in the workplace than the general economic conditions brought about by the war. 'There can be little doubt that the high wages, and the better food that the [women] workers have been able to enjoy in consequence, have done much to counteract the strain of long hours', the factory inspectors noted as early as 1915, reporting no marked increase in sickness despite long hours. Barbara Drake reported in 1917 how women in munitions had 'excellent time-keeping and astonishing absence of sickness'. At Woolwich Arsenal, with its higher than average earnings, 'the women are said to have gone up in weight, although working a 65-hour week, including day and night shift'. 'The health of low-paid workers frequently improved after entering munitions work', it was said towards the end of the war, with '"The excitement of doing 'war work'"' adding '"a zest and interest to the work [that] tended to lessen the fatigue experienced" . . .'[25]

There was, though, a health downside to the war that affected women and men alike. Against the trend in London that had set in firmly from around 1865, deaths from pulmonary tuberculosis (TB) rose sharply during the war. There had been periodic spikes against this downward movement, but a sustained rise in the virulence and deadliness of TB had taken place around 1910 and was stubbornly maintained during 1914–18. TB increased the death rate generally in these years for young women aged fifteen to forty-four, and young men too suffered disproportionately compared to older age groups. Other respiratory infections, notably pneumonia, also became more deadly during the war. Both would be overshadowed by another respiratory illness, an influenza epidemic of unexampled malevolence experienced in the autumn and winter of 1918–19 that will be detailed further in its place. Just why this cocktail of respiratory infections, by no means confined to London, should have been so prevalent in the war years has no easy answer. TB, as we have seen, had begun to grow more deadly a few years before 1914; and influenza ravaged populations worldwide, irrespective of their sufferings in the war. Despite the better nutrition of the poorest

Londoners, despite an unequalled improvement in living standards in respect of clothing and domestic comforts, and despite a new growth of welfare provision in the workplace and in infant and maternal care, London's wartime public health could offer no resistance to these great respiratory scourges of the age.[26]

Potential resistance was certainly not aided by one important aspect of London life that remained immune to the social and economic gains brought by the war. This was the London housing problem. It had long been one of the drawbacks of metropolitan life for most wage earners. For in general the accommodation they could afford to rent suffered from three great disabilities: it was often in poor repair; amenities like a WC, water supply, even a kitchen sink had usually to be shared with another family and no working-class house could boast a bath, hence the 'stink' so often complained of by their betters; and affordable living space was frequently inadequate for a family's needs. We have statistics only for this last difficulty, but the extent of the problem on the outbreak of war was such that out of a million homes in the County of London, one third (335,000) were of one or two rooms only; those one- or two-room dwellings were home to 939,000 people, or one in five Londoners in the County; and, in dwellings of all sizes, 759,000 lived at a density of two or more persons per room.[27] There was, though, one saving wartime grace: housing for working-class Londoners was generally excluded from the price rises affecting every other component of their family budget.

This question of rent was of vital importance to working-class families, not least the poorest. 'The chief item in every poor budget is rent,' noted Maud Pember Reeves in 1913, and at that time London rents roughly accounted for one-third of working-class incomes in the capital. It was thought that in the three years or so before the war there had been little or no rise in working-class rents in London with the exception of the Jewish East End and small areas under pressure from competition from commercial or other users in Seven Dials (Holborn), Hammersmith and Paddington. The rent strikes that had occasionally been a collective weapon of resistance in some poor areas of London since the Great Dock Strike of 1889 seem not to have troubled landlords or tenants in London during the years of industrial strife immediately before the war. Nevertheless, Sylvia Pankhurst in Bow (Poplar) had been working towards a 'no vote, no rent' strike connected to women's suffrage and a projected 'great re-housing of the East End population' in 1913, so the idea of rent strikes had at least been in the air. But for the real thing she had to wait until the autumn of 1914, when:

> in the first weeks of the War, I saw the rent strike break out, not for the vote, but from sheer force of economic pressure. Across a neighbouring street was suspended a strip of calico, roughly lettered: 'Please, landlord, don't be offended, don't come for the rent till the War is ended.'[28]

The price rises of August 1914 and the frequent delays in paying separation allowances to the wives of families of reservists called up or men volunteering in the early weeks combined to dislocate working-class budgets. Savings had to be made somewhere, and a few may have optimistically misconstrued the coverage of the 'moratorium', much talked about, which did not in fact apply to weekly rents. The landlord, unofficial banker to the poor, felt the effects of non-payment of rents quickly enough and occasionally responded with peremptory eviction proceedings, sometimes against the families of men now in the army. Alarmed by the effect this would have on the morale of volunteers, Parliament rushed through the Courts Emergency Powers Act on 31 August. It required all evictions and distraints for rent arrears to be authorised by the county court; judges were able to stay an order indefinitely where non-payment was due to financial difficulties arising from the war. In Shoreditch and perhaps elsewhere, the local trades council mobilised volunteers to fend off bailiffs so that court proceedings could be enforced.[29]

But landlords as well as tenants were under pressure. Dan Rider, a wholesale book dealer whose business collapsed with the declaration of war, noted from September 1914 a rise in prosecutions for rate arrears in London of businessmen unable to pay; and pressures on the living standards of the middle classes fed through in landlords trying to screw more from their tenants. At first rent rises were patchy, moved by individual landlords and house agents in Bethnal Green, Hammersmith, Camberwell and doubtless elsewhere. But by early 1915, a combination of high demand for working-class accommodation and landlords seeking to recoup their own rising living costs from their tenants built up to a citywide pressure. In March the *Estates Gazette* reported that 'Rents are showing a tendency to rise' in London and the larger towns, with the numbers of 'empties' falling rapidly. By the autumn of 1915 it thought that 'the housing question is more urgent than ever'.[30]

It was in October 1915 that the rent strike was adopted as a wide-spread device to defend living standards in working-class districts of Britain's major cities – Birmingham, Glasgow, Dublin – and in some metropolitan districts. In London, Dan Rider and others formed the War Rents League to agitate for legal protection for tenants against rent rises during the war and helped organise individual and collective resistance against landlords raising rents or evicting tenants for arrears. The first rent strike they led was that October in Tooting, Wandsworth, where rents of 7s 6d had been raised to 10s for a single landlord's many tenants; under public pressure he withdrew his demand. Elsewhere in south London, in Bermondsey and working-class districts of Dulwich, landlords were also reported to be raising rents; in Woolwich, landlords had increased the rents of over 3,000 houses according to the borough council, who promptly charged them higher rates. By November there were rent strikes in Poplar among 200 tenants whose rents had been put up just 3d a week; at Leyton and Leytonstone a 'Fight the Huns at Home' agitation began against the '"Unparalleled greed of local landlords"'; and in Edmonton three strikes involving 1,000 tenants were causing trouble in that important munitions-making suburb of north London.[31]

This threat to the war effort of workers disgruntled and perhaps made homeless by landlords who were contributing nothing while potentially driving up the costs of making munitions through the wage packet, was plainly intolerable to government. Civil unrest in Glasgow over the rents issue, with trouble in Birmingham, London and elsewhere, forced government reluctantly to control working-class rents country-wide by the end of 1915.

The Increase of Rent and Mortgage Interest (War Restrictions) Act came into force on 23 December. It applied to all London houses with a rateable value of £35 or less a year. Translated into rents, it brought into control most houses rented up to £1 2s 6d a week (or £58 10s a year), so generally all working-class dwellings and many homes of white-collar lower-middle-class tenants like clerks, shopmen, school-teachers and others. Rents were fixed at their 3 August 1914 level, though increases were permitted to cover any rise in local council rates and a 6 per cent contribution to the cost of structural repairs (but not decorations). In fact, economy in council services and the decline in pauperism meant that rates rose only exceptionally in London. So in effect, and notwithstanding the efforts of many landlords to circumvent the Act, there was a virtual rent freeze for working-class tenants for the duration of the war. This was a vital component in keeping the cost of living down, sustaining the value of real wages in working-class family income; and government and the taxpayer could avoid pressure on the wage costs of making munitions and other elements of the war effort – all at the expense of the rentier class.[32]

One crisis, then, was averted. But the housing problem in London continued to deteriorate in other directions as the war went on. Worst of all was the lack of available accommodation to rent. The ground had been laid by a drastic slowdown in metropolitan house building for some years before the war, beginning with a building slump in 1907 that had never properly recovered. It had been especially marked from 1911 to 1913, with most new working-class accommodation confined to the outer suburbs and available only to the better off among the artisan and foreman class, and things were plainly not helped by the London building lockout affecting many projects from the start of 1914. Then from 4 August many building contracts stopped and some were not resumed, while almost no new sites were started. At a time of unprecedented demand, fuelled by an influx of labour into many districts but most of all by the generally improved living standards and desire for domestic comforts affecting millions of its workers, London entered into an effective cessation of house building that would last for over five years.[33]

The wartime housing shortage in London was felt first and sharpest in the munitions-making districts, especially Woolwich. The lack of homes to rent in Woolwich had been a growing problem for some time. 'Even before the War the number of empty houses was rapidly diminishing,' the Woolwich Medical Officer of Health noted in 1914. Once war was declared 'it is practically impossible now for a working class family to find suitable housing accommodation vacant in Woolwich', and cases of overcrowding were 'frequently reported'. The vast numbers of workmen – men they largely were at this point – drawn into the Arsenal and Dockyard quickly made this shortage a crisis. By February 1915 munitions workers at Woolwich had more than doubled from 13,000 to 28,000 and another 7,000 were due there imminently. 'The population of Woolwich has risen from 117,000 to 140,000' without any 'proportionate increase' in housing. 'Men have to travel some miles to get to their homes . . .'[34]

The Asquith government responded with uncharacteristic urgency to this crisis in what was still the nation's premier munitions factory. On 1 February the Office of Works began to build a government housing scheme for Arsenal workers, the Well Hall Garden Suburb in the nearby district of Eltham. By the beginning of December the scheme was completed, with 1,300 dwellings in all, over 1,000 of them houses and the rest flats. The estate was managed by the LCC from 1917. As numbers of workers at the Arsenal continued to rise, far outstripping available housing, 2,700 'temporary bungalows' or 'huts' were run up in Woolwich, Greenwich and Eltham during 1916, and by 1917 some 4,000 men and women were also housed in government-built hostels. Even so, during 1916 and probably for the rest of the war in Woolwich, 'There is not a small house for a working-class family to be had in the borough, and rooms are also unobtainable.' Women munitions workers frequently could find no more living space than sharing a bed with another, 'sleeping "Box and Cox"', or together when on the same shift.[35]

Outside Woolwich, government housing was provided on a smaller scale in 1915 at Crayford and Erith (500 houses between them) and in 1917 with 425 houses at Hendon for aircraft-manufacturing workers, including Airco. In addition, the Port of London Authority built 204 'cottage residences' on 'garden city lines' at Prince Regent's Lane, Plaistow, in 1916, in part to replace houses lost in the extension of the Albert Dock; and the LCC built a single block of flats on the site of a slum clearance area in Southwark. These were virtually the only new dwellings for working-class Londoners built in the five years of war, most in the outer reaches of east and south-east London and most to satisfy specific needs created by the war itself.[36]

The housing shortage was exacerbated by the many people actively seeking accommodation in London in these years, and not only newcomers attracted to the munitions-making districts. Huge numbers of Londoners were on the move. A restless mobility, like 'fish in a river' Charles Booth had called it, had long characterised working-class life in London. The pressures of war – wishing to be near a new job and avoid uncomfortable long commutes in the darkened streets, family dislocation from bereavement or relationship breakdown, the rising living standards prompting many to take more or better space if they could – injected fresh energy into an already fluid housing market. The impact was felt everywhere. In Bermondsey 'no rooms that are at all fit to live in are empty for more than a few days'; in Poplar 'There are no empties. Serious difficulty is now experienced in finding accommodation', and similar stories were heard in 1916 from around Cable Street in the East End, Lambeth, Shoreditch, Hammersmith and Fulham. Sometimes the tide of these movements was not haphazard but continued a change that had almost certainly begun before the war, as at Stanhope Street, north of the Euston Road, where 'artisan workers are moving further out. The new tenants are much more of the casual, or at least unskilled, labouring class.' Some quantification of this restlessness is available from Croydon, where the borough council recorded 33,000 'removals and changes of residence' complicating the administration of food rationing from February 1918.[37]

Croydon was a mixed-class area and the mobility of the London middle classes became a cause for wonder in these years. Rising costs and falling middle-class real incomes for many and the shortage of help in the home seem to have led to a general movement out of larger houses, with an increased demand for flats. 'Everyone tried to get rid of the responsibility of their own house and plump down somewhere else, preferably in as few rooms as possible,' recalled Caroline Playne. 'Houses could be had for a song, flats were at a premium.' It was, she thought, 'a regular game of musical chairs'. As early as April 1915 the *Estates Gazette* reported that 'Many people are giving up house-keeping altogether and storing their furniture and going into lodgings. The furniture depositories are crowded.' At the same time, the demand for smaller houses 'cannot be met' and rents of 'moderate houses' had risen by £10 a year, or as much as a fifth. This may have been one reason why in 1916 there was said to be no shortage of rooms in North Kensington, with many middle-class families probably taking the opportunity to escape from an area long under pressure from working-class colonisation; Paddington, Clapham and Stoke Newington also reported spare accommodation available, and in Bloomsbury, a year later, the mushrooming of agents' boards offering houses to let testified to how 'the War has done much to shatter the settled appearance of the neighbourhood'.[38]

In outer London the difficulties of travel from the City and West End shopping streets during the dark nights was said to be bringing middle-class residents back to central London districts like Holborn from suburbs like Camberwell, reversing for a moment at least a middle-class decentralisation established in London for generations. This might also have been driven by a search for rent-controlled accommodation coming within the scope of the new law of December 1915. On the other hand, the prosperity of small manufacturers in the East End's rag trade was such that it was causing high demand for houses in more suburban Stoke Newington and the northern parts of Hackney by early 1916. It was a movement that provoked an anti-Semitic reaction among local householders: 'Three rooms and bath room, on one floor, every convenience, rent 10s., no Jews', the last a common caveat in newspaper advertisements throughout the war.[39]

It also seems that air raids from 31 May 1915, and the fear of them even before that, drove some families to move if they could. A preference for houses with formerly unpopular basements and cellars surprised many London house agents as early as January 1915, prospective tenants responding to government advice over air raid precautions. When the real thing was under way, especially with the terrifying raids by aeroplanes from mid-1917, the flight of those who could afford it to the suburbs and beyond led to yet more anti-Semitic criticism of the cowardly aliens, even though this was a movement in which the better-off middle classes widely shared. A 'gentleman' from Harrow, who had rented his house for the past eight years, found himself in April 1918 with a notice to quit '"Because of the great influx of people, including very many aliens, from the air-raid districts, who are offering large bonuses to get in"'. The Times intemperately reported an 'Alien Invasion' at Henley around the same time, though the Home Secretary, Sir George Cave, called such stories 'exaggerated'.[40]

All the pressures tending to mobility undoubtedly put great strain on middle-class Londoners in these years. Most, like the gentleman from Harrow, were without rent protection, a loophole that government only reluctantly plugged after the war when the middle-class housing shortage had become both acute and politically embarrassing. But working-class tenants too experienced during the course of the war the fact that the rent-control framework of the 1915 Act was itself hardly watertight. Landlords could seek possession for use by their own families, for instance. This was a reason frequently fabricated, landlords perhaps moving in for a time when the 'controlled' tenant had gone and then reletting at a new and higher rent. Houses could also be sold to new owners who had the right to set the rent afresh and seek a new tenant if it wasn't forthcoming from the old. Landlords sought to exploit other loopholes with varying degrees of success. Evictions in some munitions areas, mainly outside London though with some in Woolwich, Southall and Enfield, were so troublesome that a new regulation under

DORA was enacted to prevent them in scheduled areas: Dartford and Erith were protected in this way from March 1918.[41]

The London housing market came under further pressure in a number of ways. The calls of rising taxation and living costs, restrictions on income from rent control and a reduced demand for whole houses in middle-class areas led to some ground landlords disposing of their London estates, despite the generally unfavourable market conditions for doing so. Sir Nevill Gunter's estate in South Kensington and Chelsea, 1,340 houses with rentals from £40 to £300 a year, eighteen shops, nineteen mansion blocks, three pubs and 150 private stables, came on the market in March 1917; its rack rents were estimated at a princely £176,000 a year. Later in 1917 Lord Alington's huge Hoxton estate came under the hammer; it was said to fill 130 acres, with street frontages totalling a staggering thirteen miles, some 2,500 properties with rack rents amounting to £146,000 a year. And early in 1918 Lord Ashcombe's much smaller 'Cubitt Estate' on and around the Caledonian Road in west Islington was also sold off. Doubtless there were others. All these properties were broken up into many lots under different ownership, each new proprietor seeking to screw profit in one way or another from the investment.[42]

One way of bolstering profits in an era of controlled rents was to save money on repairs. It had never been easier to do so. Borough sanitary inspectors were depleted by enlistment and conscription and frequently not replaced; building labour was scarce so that all repairs, even when ordered, were delayed; and materials proved prohibitively expensive and provided a ready excuse for neglect. Everywhere felt the effects, as at Croydon, for instance, where a 'certain drab character gradually descended . . . shop-fronts became dirty, houses almost dilapidated looking, paint was lacking'.[43]

Everything was made worse by the shortage. Unfit houses closed before the war were reoccupied illegally and sometimes with their windows still boarded up – we might remember poor Rose Johnson, afraid of the dark and found wandering in Hoxton in September 1917, for instance. And London's largest slum area, the Tabard Street district of Southwark, condemned in 1912, had demolition delayed, many houses there continuing in the occupation of their pre-war tenants or relet to new ones, takers always to be found in the circumstances of wartime London. There was a public scandal over this 'London Plague Spot' – 'hovels – not fit for a dog or a donkey' – when nine-year-old

Albert Martin died from sickness 'in a tiny single room', 8 foot by 8 foot and ill-ventilated, which he shared with his mother and three siblings. Similar problems occurred in the Brady Street area of Bethnal Green, condemned in September 1914 but not cleared till two years and more after the war.[44]

In general, then, the shortage was such that whatever housing was left standing had a continuing use for the poorest London tenants. Their plight was hardly eased by continuing demolitions and conversions for industrial users, now so much more profitable than residential accommodation, with businessmen able to afford the remaining available building resources in London. This had been a prominent feature of London life long before 1914 and the war held it back without stifling it altogether. It was a very noticeable trend in Soho in 1916, for instance, and a survey of Stanhope Street, Euston Road, around the same time found families squeezed out by houses turning into factories and workshops for the local woodworking trades. Central London lost a net 4,100 rooms for working-class accommodation in this way during the war years.[45]

With demolitions and conversions for commercial users, and with the drastic decline of new building in London, net additions to the stock of rooms for working-class accommodation slowed right down: in 1904–8 over 200,000 rooms were added in the County and main urban areas, or 40,000 a year; in 1909–13 this fell to under 60,000 or 12,000 a year; in 1914–18 it fell again to fewer than 25,000, or 5,000 a year. That had to be set against a population thought to be rising from the influx into London of munitions workers and others. The figures for 1918 were by far the worst of all. That year there was a net loss of working-class rooms across the whole of Greater London, rural districts as well as urban.[46] It all meant one more giant problem stacking up for what most Londoners felt must surely – at last – be the final year of this dreadful war.

THE NEWS IS *NOT* GOOD! 1918

THE fourth New Year of the war slipped in as silently and joylessly as the third, so much so that it was 'said to be the quietest of this generation'. The north-easterly wind that had been blowing for a fortnight turned icy overnight and brought snow on New Year's morning. Dark cloud lowered all day and only those forced to face the treacherous pavements ventured out. 'Smaller crowds than have been seen for years' attended the sales that began on New Year's Eve, though the ready money in the purses of those who did was widely remarked upon. 'In the mantle and costume departments of West-end houses mothers were seen buying fur-collared coats for daughters on war work', with 'Household linen and hardware' in 'brisk demand'. 'Furniture bargains brought men and women to seek them, and pianos at sale prices were quickly snapped up.'[1]

One source of misery was, though, gratefully absent. The cold was not made sharper this year by any coal shortage, the London rationing arrangements put in place by the Coal Controller at the end of the previous year securing supplies without the need to queue for them. But queues were only too apparent for many articles of food, the shortages now becoming not just inconvenient but painful. All classes suffered, and for the middle classes the meat shortage hit hardest. It developed, according to William Beveridge, 'with catastrophic suddenness at the New Year'. Few cattle were reaching markets and by 4 January London butchers 'were themselves forming queues 500 long at Smithfield'. Shortages drove butchers to close their shops – Georgina Lee in Kensington found her butcher's shut for three days in early January and for another four a couple of weeks later: she, like many wealthy Londoners, relied on supplies of game birds and rabbits sent in from the country by relatives or friends. Everyone went short – Michael MacDonagh was deprived of his Sunday joint for the first time in thirty years of married life and was eating gammon left over from Christmas as late as 13 January. Christopher Addison, now Minister for Reconstruction, was having to make a joint last a week: 'Its final appearance was on Sunday as a beef-steak pudding.' Stories circulated among polite folk of the King dining on tinned salmon at 8d a pound. And shortages were such that the Reform Club and others banned members from bringing guests to lunch – of all the wartime restrictions this proved the most contentious and bitterly fought dispute in clubland, although the Reform's General Committee held the line through all the difficult months to come.[2]

But it was the queues, especially in working-class districts, that gave most cause for concern. Queues for meat but also tea and margarine – butter no longer an option – reached enormous lengths. The lines shuffled along to a rhythm of their own: shortest on Monday, much longer on Tuesday, shorter on Wednesday and Thursday, long and lengthening through Friday and of inordinate size on Saturday. The Metropolitan Police estimated that on most Saturdays from late January to late February more than 500,000 Londoners were on the streets queuing for food at shops throughout the capital. The queues entered so deeply into the Londoners' mindset that people would queue even when not short of a commodity, merely worried that it would not be there when they ran out.[3]

Some queues proved disorderly, especially when shortages of margarine left poor families with the prospect of having only dry bread to eat. There was some trouble everywhere in large cities across England and Wales, and in London disturbances were reported from Tottenham and Tooting in mid-January. The fear of disorder proved worse than the reality, Virginia Woolf hearing of 'food riots & strikes at Woolwich, & the guards have notice to march there at any moment, & fire on the people, which their own Woolwich regiments would refuse to do'. Viscount Sandhurst, the Lord Chamberlain, always worried about the threat of insurrection by untrustworthy workers, convinced himself that 'The discontent is certain to become extreme.' Reuters thought so too, their Press Bureau urging caution when reporting any cases of disorder for fear of leading to more 'food riots'.[4]

Compulsory rationing of those foods in short supply, urged by many for months before and even longer, was now generally seen as the solution. But just how to organise rationing was an immense administrative challenge. It required, in London alone, some 1.6 million households to register with named shops for specific commodities and to apply for and be given a ration card with sufficient detachable coupons for family members to hand over with their purchases. The cards had to be printed and distributed, detailed instructions had to be written and published, the rations per head for over 7.25 million souls had to be stipulated according to the best available scientific knowledge of the day. Much of this work had begun to be planned the previous autumn. Sugar was the first item to be rationed, from 1 January. When Robert Graves was married later that month at St James's, Piccadilly, he found his three-tier wedding cake was adorned with what looked like elaborate icing but proved to be a plaster cast: when lifted off 'a sigh of disappointment rose from the guests'.[5]

Some local rationing schemes for butter and margarine were then trialled in a few London districts through January and building on these a London and Home Counties Rationing Scheme was finally implemented from 25 February. The scheme applied to butter, margarine, uncooked butcher's meat, bacon and ham. It proved an astonishing success. Almost overnight the queues began dramatically to disappear and had virtually gone for all rationed commodities by around 11 March, though smaller numbers continued to queue for cheese, jam and syrup until about the end of April. By then the London scheme was being rolled out nationwide. It had proved a political success too: without rationing, thought William Sandhurst, 'no one (of the mass) would have been persuaded that the rich did not get the best of it, share and share alike being the country's motto'. On the other hand, some London tradesmen found it difficult (or perhaps inconvenient) to keep in step with the new regulations: so many were prosecuted for rationing infringements at Lambeth police court at the end of February that, the *South London Press* wryly noted, they formed their own queue.[6]

One great problem facing the Londoners this winter, then, had receded by mid-March, but no one could be sure that another terrible worry would as quickly disappear. Air raids had continued to plague the winter nights in the New Year much as they had before Christmas. The first, on the night of Monday 28 January, would prove the most destructive of 1918. That night was unusually clear, cloud having covered London for much of the New Year so far, and fearing a resumption of raids a crowd of potential shelterers from the Jewish and Gentile East End had gathered round the locked gates of Bishopsgate Goods Depot in Shoreditch. This had been used as a shelter in the past, but so much damage had been done to goods stored there, and so much filth left behind, that the railway company would only open the gates once a formal 'take cover' alert had been given by police. Three Gothas now neared London from the east. Their approach was apparently signalled nearby with the sounding of maroons or rockets. Unprepared for this sudden noise, maroons at night-time not yet being part of any official policy, the crowd took this to be the first sound of exploding bombs. In a moment, hundreds of people laden with bedding and other household equipment, supplemented by a queue of people across the road waiting for the Olympia Music Hall to open, rushed the station gates. The main gates were found locked, but one side gate was open for a staff entrance and the crowd tried to surge through it. In the melee someone fell and in the crush that immediately followed fourteen died from suffocation and many more were injured. The dead included four members of the Bodie family, among them a baby girl of eighteen months.[7]

This was a disastrous start to a night that saw a total of sixty-five deaths and 159 people injured. From around 8.45 p.m. the Gothas dropped bombs on Poplar and Whitechapel in the east, on the City, on Vauxhall on the South Bank, on Bloomsbury, King's Cross and Camden Town in the north, and St John's Wood near Edgware Road in the west. Around 10 o'clock the anti-aircraft guns stopped firing and for two hours and more came a lull. No 'all clear' sounded but even so many braved the darkened streets and made their way homewards. But in the interval a single Giant had crossed the north Essex coast and just after midnight approached London from the north, fending off fighter attacks and bringing down one British machine. It dropped bombs on Bethnal Green, then looped over the river, turning north close to Waterloo Bridge, where it loosed bombs from the Embankment to Covent Garden before turning eastwards home.

One of the Giant's 300-kilo bombs fell at the rear of Odhams Printing Press at 85–94 Long Acre. With concrete floors 10 inches thick, the building was considered immensely strong and so designated a public air raid shelter. The Rector of St Paul's, Covent Garden, the Reverend Edward Mosse, was busy as always during raids shepherding people into Odhams to join the 600 or so sheltering there as the bomb struck, around 12.20 on the Tuesday morning. It fell in narrow Wilson Street to the rear and penetrated the pavement lights of Odhams' works, exploding in the cellars, severing the gas main and setting fire to the building. Not long after that the rear wall of 92 Long Acre collapsed and with it floors carrying giant reels of newsprint ready for the press, which in turn fuelled the flames. Amid dreadful scenes thirty-eight people died (nine men – including five of Odhams' staff – nineteen women and ten children) and eighty-five were injured: some bodies were never recovered. Others died in Wilson Street, including the Reverend Mosse. This was the worst disaster caused by a single bomb in Britain during the war. Rumours hardened to myths in trying to grasp the terror of it all: 'the poor people were not only burned but *drowned*, through the water-main bursting; to add to all the horrors, *the printers' ink poured over the people, turning them quite black!*' Yet, serendipitously, some benefit flowed from the tragedy. A local boy, his father already dead, lost his mother in the disaster and was taken in by a neighbour who vowed to raise him as her own son. This came out at the mother's inquest and 'money simply poured in' to the Coroner's office to pay for his 'keep and clothe the boy, to see that he got holidays and Xmas and birthday presents, and finally he was installed in the post-office service' like his father. And in a nearby hotel the embarrassments of Robert and Nancy Graves's wedding night, two timorous upper-middle-class virgins, 'were somewhat eased' by the air raid's drama distracting all around them.[8]

There were then two raids on consecutive nights over the weekend of 16–17 February, each by a single Giant. The first killed twelve and injured six in Woolwich and Chelsea, where the first 1,000-kilo bomb dropped on London destroyed part of Wren's Military Hospital, and the second killed twenty-one and injured thirty-two. This Sunday air raid again involved a major disaster: the Giant dropped five high-explosive bombs on St Pancras Station in an unprecedentedly precise bombing cluster, badly damaging Sir George Gilbert Scott's Midland Hotel in particular. Twenty people were killed and twenty-two injured, most in the hotel and in the station's first-class waiting room.[9]

There was then relief for two weeks or so until Thursday 7 March, a night when the aurora borealis was unusually visible from darkened London. Three Giants approached from the north, mainly bombing north-west London, narrowly missing Lord's Cricket Ground, and dropping a single bomb near Clapham Common. In all, twenty-two were killed and twenty-nine injured. They included casualties in a major tragedy at Warrington Crescent, Maida Vale, where a 1,000-kilo bomb completely destroyed five houses and damaged another 135 or so, many seriously, over a wide area. Twelve were killed in Warrington Crescent and twenty-three injured. Among the dead was Lena Ford, who wrote the lyrics for Ivor Novello's 1914 hit song 'Keep the Home Fires Burning'; in the rubble of her home was found 'a short list of other songs, and the last written by Mrs Ford was called, "For Me – Remembrance!"' The devastation drew thousands of sightseers over the next few days, among them the King and Queen on the following Saturday.[10]

For the next two months London was undisturbed by raids. Understandably reassured that normal life might in part be resumed, over the pleasant sunny Whitsun Bank Holiday weekend of 18–20 May many middle-class Londoners took the opportunity to get away from town. For some it no doubt proved a lucky escape. Late on the Sunday night the largest bombing force yet to be assembled against London at night approached from the south-east, some nineteen aircraft, Gothas with a single Giant. They bombed at random over a wide area. Some seventy-two bombs fell from Beckenham to Tottenham and from Kilburn to Ilford, killing thirty-nine and injuring 128. There were major tragedies at Packington Street, Islington, where two eight-roomed multi-occupied houses were hit, killing eight people, and eighteen died when a dairy and adjoining bakery were destroyed in Lower Sydenham Road, Lewisham. Some six Gothas were lost, including three brought down by fighters over east London and Essex and two shot down by anti-aircraft fire as they were crossing the coast.[11]

Though no one realised this at the time, the German raiders would never again visit London, in this war at least. Between May 1915 and May 1918, Zeppelins and bombing planes had killed 668 persons in the Metropolitan Police District and injured 1,938 more. They caused damage to property to the value of over £2 million. The morale of Londoners was never destroyed and the capacity of the great city to wage war was affected not at all. But the nerves of many were shaken, their patience was wearied and their tempers frayed by a bombardment that, though in itself sporadic, had been an ever-present anxiety since the first winter of the war.[12]

The raids had also exposed some fatal weaknesses in the competence of London's governors, whether politician or bureaucrat or professional. At almost every turn in London's response to the air war the authorities were hidebound by a mistrust of the loyalty, goodwill and common sense of the Londoner that had much of class fear and contempt about it. Few things demonstrate this better than the egregious reluctance to issue public air raid warnings lest the Londoners should panic, riot or use them as an excuse to bunk off war work. Yet many Londoners had agitated for adequate warnings from the beginning, some had taken matters into their own hands through night patrols, and a few of their representatives had carried the argument into the House of Commons. The reluctance to respond, the painful process by which warnings of any sort were dragged out of the authorities, the loss of life that might, shamefully, have been mitigated by public warnings, were some of the bleakest tales of official incompetence exposed by the war on London's home front. The official line was adhered to until almost the very end of the bombing. In the aftermath of the tragedies at Bishopsgate Goods Depot and Odhams Printing Press on 28 January, the disaster at St Pancras on 17 February and the devastation in Maida Vale on 7 March, the Home Secretary at last announced that he and the Commissioner of Police had revised their former view and that now maroons would be fired at all hours of the day and night when a raid was impending. These new arrangements were eventually in place for the twenty-sixth and final air raid on London two months later.[13]

There were also confusion and a lack of coordination and planning over air raid shelters. No one could have legislated against the Long Acre tragedy – buildings were inspected by an Advisory Committee of architects on behalf of the police, who permitted only strong structures to be used as public shelters, and experience in the next war showed that no London building was immune to damage from high-explosive bombs. But in and around the tubes there was daily chaos, whether or not a raid was in progress. On 20 March William Sandhurst arrived at Euston Station from Tring around 11 p.m. to find the main concourse full of women and children clutching their most valued household possessions, some asleep on benches, 'some in great spirits, laughing away' and enjoying the companionship of sharing their predicament even with strangers. They were there to be close to the tube at Euston Square in the event of a raid. During the raids themselves the crush got very difficult for all concerned. Michael MacDonagh was at the Elephant and Castle tube station on the night of 28 January to find that a 'mass of humanity . . . packed and blocked the platforms, passages and staircases'. 'Whole families were there – mothers with babies and kiddies wrapped in blankets, sitting and lying everywhere, many of them happily asleep. Not a trace of fear did I notice,' faith in the depth of the tube, once there, overcoming all anxiety. Many travelled on the underground trains until it was plain the 'all clear' had sounded. But in the passages the crush was such that MacDonagh could not reach the City and South London line from the Bakerloo platform and had to leave the station and risk a long walk home to Clapham instead.[14]

It is unsurprising that during the weeks of intermittent raids from late January, all to the terrifying music of the 'Gotha hum' – 'quite unlike any other machine noise', William Sandhurst thought – those who could manage it sought to flee London. The greatest evacuation panic seems to have taken place in March, and again all classes were affected: on the 9th Georgina Lee recorded 'an exodus of children and servants from London', including some of her own servants and her young son, dispatched to his aunt near Bristol; Frederick Robinson noted on the 14th how Londoners were leaving for the country, with a hotel in nearby Weybridge having a waiting list of sixty bookings; and William Sandhurst found 'great crowds at Victoria Station' towards the end of the month, 'a rumour having got abroad among poor people that the Germans were going to blow up London'. On the other hand, and as if the raids were not threat enough, the prospect of looting during a raid and after added to the terrors facing the Londoners and must have deterred many poor people from leaving London even if they could: twenty-three cases of larceny from shops and houses were recorded by police on the two nights of the February raids, with many others doubtless going unreported.[15]

By the time Sandhurst encountered the crowds at Victoria it had become clear to government and the General Staff that further air raids on London were unlikely, at least at present. The Germans now needed every aeroplane at their disposal on the Western Front and for an all-out bombing assault on Paris. For on 21 March 1918 came Ludendorff's great offensive, the 'Kaiser's Battle', along a 200-mile front from the English Channel to beyond Reims. The brunt was borne by the British and was not borne well. On the first day Haig's forces lost 38,500 men, an extraordinary 21,000 of them taken prisoner as the Germans overran defensive positions in place since the first gruelling Somme battle of the summer and autumn of two years before. In places the British were pushed back 4½ miles, conceding nearly 100 square miles of territory, wiping out in one or two days the blood-soaked gains of the whole of

1916. The battle raged over the next few weeks. In places the Allied front collapsed entirely and part of the British Army was in rapid and sometimes disorderly retreat until help came from the less pressed French to the south-east.[16]

By 28 March the German forces had been fought to a standstill on much of the front without making the decisive strategic and diplomatic breakthrough to Paris they sought. The British, though, had lost 160,000 men in a week, 90,000 of them now prisoners of war. And for two more ferocious weeks the fight against the British continued in the German effort to capture the important railway nexus of Amiens, launched in a violent assault on 4 April. For a week and more the exhausted British Army came close to defeat. On 11 April Field Marshal Sir Douglas Haig issued his famous Order of the Day to the beleaguered troops holding the Amiens salient. It was printed in the London papers on 13 April and concluded:

> There is no other course open to us but to fight it out. Every position must be held to the last man: there must be no retirement. With our backs to the wall, and believing in the justice of our cause, each one of us must fight on to the end.
>
> The safety of our homes and the freedom of mankind depend alike upon the conduct of each one of us at this critical moment.

The impact of this astonishing crisis on the Londoners was immense. Once more the guns could be heard and felt from France, 'a curious atmospheric sensation – a kind of pulsation in regular beats'.[17] But it was the fact of the British retreat, and the wonder, after three and a half years of relentless total struggle in the greatest war mankind had ever known, that the Germans could still manage to mount this devastating and potentially conclusive offensive, that racked Londoners to the backbone. The war appeared to be hanging in the balance. Every single sacrifice endured by millions would possibly be set at naught. And throughout those months of March and April the casualty figures seemed to rise and rise: 317,000 men killed, wounded or captured by the advancing German forces in just two months.

The news first sank home on 'Black Saturday' and 'Black Sunday', 23 and 24 March. All were shaken. '"I fear it means disaster,"' David Lloyd George confided to a friend that weekend. Beyond Whitehall anxiety spread to every corner of the capital. 'Great German Offensive raging,' Caroline Playne wrote in her diary on the Sunday:

> Tremendous oppression felt[.] Some papers reported that London took
> the great crisis very fearlessly[.] In reality people looked frightfully
> strained, especially women. Several war supporting people told me that
> you could not trust what the papers said[.] In Williams's shop [this entry
> dated 30 March], I asked for 'Evening paper['] & lady who had bought
> hers, said excitedly: 'The news is NOT good!'[18]

Across London there were 'signs of deep anxiety', according to a
'Clubman' in the *Pall Mall Gazette* on Monday 25 March. 'Men and
women who had never met before formed groups and eagerly discussed'
the situation in France, churches were fuller than usual, people gathered
yet again to see the ambulances dispatched from Charing Cross Station,
the crowds made up of every complexion of Londoner, 'Generals and
privates, flower-sellers, chorus-girls, and gorgeously fur-clad women'. A
day later, 'in trams and omnibuses men & women alike almost all look
either terribly sad or very distracted'. Everyone held his breath. At the
meeting of the LCC in Spring Gardens on the 26th the Chairman
announced he could not open proceedings '"without some reference to
the momentous struggle – taking place almost within sound of these
walls – on which the fate of the world seems to depend"'. As the
weather turned wintry again after a spring-filled weekend, 'The rain
dripped down like the blood of a slaughtered nation and the fog closed
in thick with the possibility of England's ruin and the ruin of humanity
in an endless war': Josephine, the heroine of Romer Wilson's *If All
These Young Men*, 'was overcome with a desire to weep, a wish which
in those days frequently visited both men and women'.[19]

Anxiety, even panic, worked through into public policy. The over-
riding objective of government was now to recruit ever more men for
the army bleeding on the Somme and to keep war supplies at maximum
output. Winston Churchill, Minister of Munitions since the previous
July, appealed to munitions workers to forgo their Easter Bank Holiday;
they readily complied, markedly muting the traditional fun of Hampstead
Heath on the Monday. Exemption certificates were rapidly withdrawn
from young men in some protected employments; on 18 April conscription was extended to Ireland and the upper limit rose to include all
men aged fifty-one or under; dealing in horses for town use was banned
so that every available horse might be requisitioned for the front; and

comb-out raids began again, one on an auction at the Horse Repository in New Kent Road serving both purposes and ending in fifty arrests, many Irish horse traders among them. Meanwhile recruitment of the older men got under way. Georgina Lee's husband, nearly forty-six and in 'delicate health', attended for a two-minute medical examination and to her distress was passed grade 2 and fit to fight: 'It is a mistake. He would never stand the physical labour of a Tommy in the ranks.' And John Galsworthy, fifty years and 343 days old, was examined and, to his relief, was 'totally rejected on score of sight. Must say this Man Power Bill was a case of panic legislation if ever there was one.'[20]

Money was in short supply as well as men. The New Year had opened with a savings drive, rung in by a printed plea from Lloyd George, with a new £5 War Bond issued to attract working-class savers. Even before the great German push the war savings campaign had begun to make a striking impact on London's streets, with the London Tank Week at the beginning of March bringing a tank for a day to many London districts, pressing for money to build – more tanks: it was an extraordinary success, with some £43 million invested in bonds and savings certificates in London, £24.7 million from the City alone. Efforts redoubled from the spring. The success of the tanks brought further savings spectaculars into London's open spaces: a Garden Fête in Trafalgar Square with bands, the fountains playing once more and 'gay little gardens and rockeries'; giant guns were wheeled out to startle the citizens, one on some 'waste ground' opposite Hackney Town Hall against 'a large pictorial representation of a ruined French village . . . as realistic as could be'; and another French village, mocked up in brick and timber in Trafalgar Square, proved a popular draw in October.[21]

The German offensive that began on 21 March and seemed to hold the fate of the war by a thread till the end of April created anxiety on other fronts in London too. In the reckless clamour for men, the fate of the nation depending on the efforts of every single person, pacifism and anti-war propaganda became even less tolerable to the authorities and the diehards. Peace meetings were banned, like one planned in Hyde Park for 14 July to coincide with Bastille Day, and so even were traditional May Day celebrations in north London on the grounds they risked '"grave disorder"', though one was later permitted in Finsbury Park. The suppression of pacifist organisations continued, with the destruction of books and papers seized from the Christian Peace Crusade Movement, 39 Doughty Street, considered to 'interfere with the recruiting and discipline of the Army'. Caroline Playne noted around this time a hardening in 'the general loathing felt for Conscientious Objectors', and Arnold Lupton, a former MP and seventy-one years old, was given six months' imprisonment for having in his Victoria Street flat around a hundred copies of a peace pamphlet.[22]

For the die-hards this was one more excuse to spy enemies everywhere. Fighting parsons, like the Reverend Gough at Holy Trinity, Brompton, decried 'the insidious pacifists in our midst' who advocated a negotiated peace without victory, which '"would prove the futility of Righteousness and the immunity of Sin"'.[23] And that spring, just as 'Intern Them All' began to crank up to a final peak of manic ferocity against enemy aliens, an extraordinary drama unfolded around one of the most eccentric die-hards of them all.

On 16 February, Noel Pemberton Billing's paper, the aptly named *Vigilante*, published an outspoken and prurient attack on Maud Allan, an American exotic dancer whose return to the London stage had been announced by the impresario J. T. Grein, naturalised but of Dutch-Jewish descent and long a presence in London's theatreland. The attack, head-lined 'The Cult of the Clitoris' – a word not then known to many – hinted strongly that Allan was a lesbian and, more importantly, that she was one of a society coterie of sexual perverts susceptible to black-mail by German agents and so actually or potentially disloyal to the war effort. Very unwisely, Allan and Grein chose to sue Billing for libel in a trial that opened at the Old Bailey at the end of May.

Billing conducted his own defence, to the frustration of the claimants' counsel and Mr Justice Darling, the trial judge, but to the amusement and admiration of a packed courtroom. Much of the evidence – or rather, the main allegation – adduced by Billing turned on the existence of 'The Black Book', said to be in the possession of a German prince, containing the names of the 'First 47,000' British men and women 'with records of their alleged moral and sexual weaknesses'. Among the names listed were said to be those of Herbert Asquith, Lord Haldane – and Mr Justice Darling. 'Nothing is talked about these days but the "Black Book",' recorded Michael MacDonagh in his diary. 'We are hilariously asking each other, "Well, is your name in the "Black Book"?' It was eloquent testimony to the credulity and paranoia of a London jury after nearly four years of rumour, dashed hopes and incompetence by those in power at every level that this nonsense was actually believed. Billing was acquitted amid scenes of jubilation in the courtroom and among a thousand or so of his supporters waiting outside. And the puritanical Darling thought it appropriate after the verdict had been given to expatiate on the dangers of immorality and public nudity on the stage – 'worse than nothing are some of the things they wear'. Reflecting on the outcome of this bizarre trial that had held the newspaper-reading public in thrall for some days, Basil Thomson, Assistant Commissioner in charge of the CID at Scotland Yard, wrote on the day of the acquittal that 'every one concerned appeared to have been insane or to have behaved as if he were', and perhaps that was a faithful portrait of much of the public mood in London as it still reeled under the shocks of March and April 1918.[24]

More shocks were to come, all now home-grown even as the agonies of the Western Front continued to rage back and forth. Cynicism over inequalities of sacrifice was fuelled that summer by scandals attaching to the bubble-like rise in share values for some firms involved in munitions contracts, a few people at least plainly doing very well out of the war, and what seemed like abuse of the honours system with the names of those receiving the newly created award of OBE filling sixty quarto pages of the *London Gazette*.[25]

At the same time, strikes broke out in an echo of the industrial unrest of the previous year. In August London's buses and trams were halted for some days by a strike of women workers for equal pay with men doing the same work, the men having been given a war bonus but not the women; the dispute was settled by arbitration and the women's demand was quickly conceded. In September, worrying indeed for the war effort, a railway strike spread to the GWR and closed Paddington Station for a time; worries over the temper and loyalty of the workers in the East End once more induced the authorities to move a company of Scots Guards to Stratford in order to snuff out any trouble should it start. But most disturbing of all for the Londoners was a strike by Metropolitan Police officers on 30–31 August. It seemed to indicate that the very fabric of civil society in the capital had been shaken, even ruptured. Indeed, Lloyd George told a confidant he had been 'really face to face with a revolution'.[26]

The police officers' grievances had been brewing for some time. The oldest was over recognition of the National Union of Police and Prison Officers as a negotiating body for the men. Sir Edward Henry had outlawed it since before the war and in 1916 some officers were dismissed when it was discovered that they were members. The immediate linked cause was pay – linked because the men argued that if they had had a union then their pay would never have dragged so far behind the cost of living, as indeed it had. There was a third but subsidiary grievance over the inadequate pensions given to the widows of men dying in service. This last complaint had Henry's sympathy and he was pressing the Home Office to take action that August. But the first claim for trade union recognition was anathema to him as entirely inappropriate in a force under something close to military discipline; and the second – increased wages – he shelved, worried it would get in the way of a rise in pensions. This last was a fatal error: had the demand for improved pay been heeded it is inconceivable that a strike over union recognition alone could ever have been mounted.

The immediate spark was the dismissal on 25 August of a PC stationed at Hammersmith who had declared himself to be a union member. Two days later the union presented the Commissioner with an 'ultimatum' for an increased war bonus, union recognition and the reinstatement of the Hammersmith PC. They demanded an answer – echoes of 1914 here – by midnight on 29 August. No answer came.

The strike began just after midnight on Friday the 30th. Union membership had grown steadily since 25 August and increased apace on the day before the strike. Night-duty men deserted their beats and reported to police stations across the capital to announce they were on strike. Senior officers had grossly underestimated both the men's bitterness and the new-found strength of the union. Police stations next morning were frequently surrounded by cheering strikers and found themselves with just one or two PCs to deploy. Some areas, like the Tower Bridge police station's district in Southwark, had not a single officer to put on the streets. When the *Star*, a popular London evening paper, sent a reporter into the West End he came across just one policeman. At the chief magistrate's Bow Street police court the daily Black Maria failed to arrive from Brixton Prison. Later in the day, City of London police officers joined their Metropolitan colleagues on strike. By midday it was said that 12,000 men were out, with a shift yet to report for duty. Among the speakers that afternoon at a mass meeting of strikers on Tower Hill were representatives of the London Trades Council – and Noel Pemberton Billing, MP, 'received with prolonged cheering and the singing of "For he's a jolly good fellow"'. The authorities reacted too: soldiers in 'the tin hats of active service' and bearing rifles guarded government offices where policemen had formerly stood.[27]

For the whole of 30 and much of 31 August the police were largely absent from London's streets, except when marching and demonstrating in civilian clothes in their own cause. There were noisy and ill-tempered protests in Downing Street around the Prime Minister's front door and outside Scotland Yard, where it was said that special constables reporting for duty were kicked and abused; there were also violent scenes involving strikers at Paddington Green police station and elsewhere. Awareness that their city was without police dawned slowly on the Londoners. Cynthia Asquith, cycling to the Adelphi on the Saturday for her first morning's work as J. M. Barrie's secretary, 'didn't feel the lack of policemen (they were all out on strike) and I didn't know how to take advantage of their absence, which seemed unimaginative'. Some others were more worldly. The *South London Press* reported that there were some seventy burglaries during the strike and there was an isolated case or two of looting. But in general the Londoners behaved with exemplary self-control.[28]

After a meeting of strikers' representatives with the Prime Minister, convened at his urgent request on the Saturday afternoon, the men were quickly granted their pay rise and promised a negotiating machinery which in the event fell short of union recognition. There was a return to work during the evening of 31 August, after London had been largely without a police force for some forty-four hours. Sir Edward Henry shouldered the blame and was forced to resign at the behest of Lloyd George, who reasonably thought that Henry had handled the men's demands incompetently. He was replaced by Lieutenant-General Sir Nevil Macready, a senior Staff Officer at the War Office and considered an unflappably safe pair of hands. Sir George Cave and the Home Office slid away from the crisis with little opprobrium coming their way for a dispute they should have foreseen and forestalled. But the Metropolitan Police lost credit among patriots of every class, and the faith of some middle-class Londoners was badly shaken: the strike 'takes away my respect for the police,' wrote Viscount Sandhurst, 'by which I've always sworn'.[29]

The absence of police on the last days of August had imparted 'a strange and rather exciting aspect' to traffic management in central London. Many would have thought the streets already exciting enough. The queuing habit had not yet finally established itself at the bus and tram stops, though noted as an emerging virtue in Stoke Newington High Street in March, for instance, and soon generally adopted by the

LCC and other tramway authorities. But the dangers of crowds milling for buses 'at certain termini and stopping places in London' were still complained about in the House of Commons the August of the police strike, with calls for a ticket-based queuing system like that of Paris dismissed as impracticable by the Home Office. 'So difficult was it to get a bus by the end of the war and directly after, that I never . . . felt easy about trying to catch a bus at rush hours,' recalled Beatrice Brown, then seventeen years old and living in Swiss Cottage. 'In the end we were made to queue up at the bus stops', but that was a very late wartime development. And street accidents, peaking in 1915 and then declining in numbers as buses, cars and private commercial motors became less common on the streets, still caused over 600 deaths in 1918 and 15,000 injuries. Michael MacDonagh's diary was silent for the whole of September after he was knocked down early one evening by a bus that mounted the pavement in Clapham, killing two women pedestrians and causing severe injuries to others.[30]

These shocks and difficulties, though, have to be put in the context of a rapidly improving feeling about the war that was everywhere noticeable in London from May 1918. The fine weather undoubtedly helped. Caroline Playne, that nervously alert observer of the Londoner's shifting moods, watched at the Bank Holiday as the 'clothes of ordinary crowds were fresher and gayer'. 'The Saturday crowd of pleasure seekers in London seemed as gay & as numerous as in pre-war days,' she noted at the time. An important element in this undoubtedly was the great relief felt after the shocking war news of March and April. Londoners had stared what looked like defeat in the face. When it did not come the relief felt like salvation. They 'threw off depression & became more cheerful than at any other time in the war,' Playne wrote later.[31]

One of the spirit-lifting attractions in May was a great procession of American troops watched by hundreds of thousands of Londoners wearing or waving the 'Stars and Stripes'. Indeed, London seemed filled with Australians and New Zealanders, Canadians and Americans for the rest of the year. Between May and November 114,000 American troops landed in the Port of London on ninety-five ships, and most stayed some time in the capital before embarking for France. On 4 July they celebrated Independence Day with a baseball match at Chelsea Football Club's ground at Stamford Bridge, and in central London 'Drags full of American soldiers driving through the town on pleasure bent have been widely cheered all day . . . They look such smart, business-like fellows too!' Georgina Lee thought. St James's Square was even colonised by the all-conquering Americans, a huge wooden series of buildings like the spokes of a wheel radiating from the statue of King William III comprising the Washington Inn, a hostel for US army officers that remained in the square until 1921.[32]

Less obtrusive but no less welcome were thousands of ANZAC troops visiting London on leave. Like Private Robert Maddison, back from the Italian front, who reached London happily on 28 March with the German offensive still at full throttle. He was shown round some of the London sights by a contact, perhaps organised by ANZAC head-quarters, living at Honor Oak Park. It was all staggering to him – St Paul's was 'an eye opener', at the Houses of Parliament 'everything was beautiful it opens one eyes', and so too Westminster Abbey, 'where all the people are buried you can go back 1000 years back'; on the other hand, Hampstead Heath could 'not [be] compared to some places in Sydney', but he was impressed by 'rotton row' in the Park, 'where all the love making goes on and you see nothing else but Style there', and by 'the underground Railway which is called the tube', another 'eye opener'.[33]

No doubt these exotic strangers added much to the joys of London life as the clouds continued to lift across the summer and autumn of 1918. Life had rarely been more zestful among the wealthy young of the West End, and especially young women for whom the hitherto unsavoury term 'flapper' was gaining wide and respectable currency this year. It had indeed been a good year for women. From early in 1917 it looked clear that some at least would get the vote they had demanded for so long and at so much cost. But progress during that difficult year had been grindingly slow. A Speaker's Conference had recommended some sort of enfranchisement in January 1917 without determining an age limit or other conditions; a Bill was introduced to the House of Commons in May but it had a troubled progress through the Lords, not over women getting the vote but over a proposal to introduce proportional representation. That element was eventually dropped, but the Bill still hung in suspense at the end of the parlia-mentary session in February 1918. To the relief and delight of all suffragists the royal assent was given on 6 February, enfranchising married women and women registered as separate householders, provided that they were aged thirty and above. 'Our joy was too over-whelming to find utterance,' recalled H. W. Nevinson, a tireless male campaigner for the women's vote, who read the news as it was tapped out letter by letter over the wire at the National Liberal Club and who was given a dinner in honour of his contribution at the Grafton Galleries at the end of April. That month admiring crowds watched women of the Land Army march through central London to a meeting in Hyde Park, accompanied by hay wagons and carrying 'rakes, forks, spades and saws'; one had a champion egg-laying duck in her arms. And at the end of June 3,000 young women munitions workers marched to great applause to congratulate the King and Queen on their silver wedding anniversary.[34]

It was young women too who seemed to lead a riot of pleasure in the West End. They were enthusiastically egged on by society men like the Prince of Wales and his entourage – 'a dapper little fellow – too small – but really a pretty face,' thought Cynthia Asquith, who disliked the 'teasing catastrophic music thrummed out by leering Negroes' at a dance the Prince attended in March. But jazz was becoming the music of the hour for London's society smart set and others on its fringes, made especially fashionable by the American forces in London, a jazz band and quartet of minstrels from the USS *Nevada* were a hit in London in early August, for instance. Parties at West End houses, excursions to the theatre or the opera, dinner dances at the Ritz and other smart hotels or at any one of a burgeoning number of nightclubs, all revived London's pleasures to pre-war levels and beyond, despite a 'curfew' from 2 April bringing forward restaurant and other closing times – all food to be served by 9.30, all premises to go dark by 10 p.m. – with theatres forced to have all lights out by 10.30. London's pleasures began and finished earlier than ever before but were relished nonetheless. And we have already seen, in the ready access to cocaine and opium in these months, how much risk the well off and their hangers-on would take to enjoy themselves in ever more frantic ways. '[A]ny one who lived in London during those feverish months' after the March offensive, wrote Stephen McKenna a couple of years later, 'had forced upon his notice a spectacle of debauchery which would have swelled the record of scandal if it had been made public but which is mercifully forgotten because it was incredible.'[35]

One unexpected development ran in parallel with the deaths and injuries still daily accumulating in enormous numbers on the battlefields – there were nearly 360,000 British casualties combined in August, September and October, for instance. This was influenza, given the comforting appellation 'Spanish' to denote it was an imported and not a home-grown disease. Flu, like other respiratory diseases, had dogged the war years, killing just over 1,000 Londoners in 1915 and just under in 1916. But in 1918–19 it swept every corner of the globe as one of the greatest and most devastating pandemics ever recorded. There were three epidemics in London during those years. It first appeared in late June and the first half of July 1918; at that point it was generally mild and rarely fatal. Over a three-week spell 697 Londoners died, the bulk of them in the prime of life, aged twenty to fifty-five. Flu affected all classes: Cynthia Asquith and a friend or two went down with it, for example, and it caused queues at surgeries and pharmacies and the closure of some LCC schools.[36]

Those thousands who caught it at this point could count themselves lucky as they were then immune to the much more ferocious strain that showed itself in mid-October and lasted nearly till Christmas. This pernicious and terrifying epidemic, now accompanied by 'a most deadly species of septic pneumonia', killed more than 1,000 Londoners a week over a ten-week period that saw 11,471 die in all. The worst weeks followed each other at the end of October and beginning of November, when 5,000 died in a fortnight. The age range from twenty-five to forty-five was hit especially hard, with no person immune through fitness – Airco's test pilot, Captain Benfield Hucks, thirty-four, died of flu in early November, for instance. The sickness struck whole families, with everyone bedridden, dependent on the kindness of neighbours for subsistence, doctors given latchkeys so they might call in when no one could get up to answer the door. The numbers and mortality were such that at the London Hospital cases were only admitted *in extremis* – of 140 taken in during this outbreak ninety-six died. Bus and tram services were hit by staff shortages, shop assistants were laid low in their hundreds, school classes were without teachers, sick firemen left emergency crews depleted, half the nurses at Guy's Hospital were on the sick list. The queue of victims awaiting burial in parts of south London, made more difficult by labour shortages and a trade union work to rule, put undertakers and public mortuaries under severe strain through the numbers of corpses on their hands. This, though, would prove the worst outbreak by far. When flu returned in its third and final epidemic from early February 1919 to the end of March it killed 3,121 Londoners in seven weeks. It never again attained the virulence of the outbreak of autumn 1918.[37]

Influenza cast a pall over that autumn, despite what was increasingly becoming clear to everyone in London: that the war was at last being won. At the end of September that indefatigable City diarist Frederick Robinson – his war diary now 3,333 pages long – noted that he and those around him were sanguine that the war really would be over by Christmas. Political shifts in Germany led on 4 October to the new German socialist government proposing an armistice to President Wilson. Most significant of all, on 12 October Germany declared it would withdraw unconditionally from all occupied territory, including land in Belgium overrun in August 1914 for which Britain had gone to war in the first place. The news was received with great joy in London on Sunday 13 October. 'All faces glad in London,' noted Colonel Repington in his diary that day, 'and people feel that it is the beginning of the end.' There was said to be 'spontaneous cheering' in cinemas and theatres and in the streets. 'A gloriously fine day,' recorded Caroline Playne. 'Relief is felt generally, people look brighter but the thing is not yet quite believed or accepted.' They were right to be sceptical, for next day Hallie Miles was woken by newsboys crying, '"The War Over! The War Over!"' Something like it was indeed approaching, though. 'Peace is almost in sight,' wrote Michael MacDonagh, still recovering from his road accident, a few days later.[38]

By the beginning of November, as news of the slow unravelling of the apparently indomitable German war machine arrived each morning and evening in the papers, it was clear to all that peace was nearly at hand, even imminent. On 4 November London's traffic was brought to a halt as the first of around 400 captured German guns arrived in the capital from France, some to form part of the Lord Mayor's Procession on the 9th, then joining the rest to make an exultant triple avenue along the Mall from Buckingham Palace to Admiralty Arch. On the night of 9 November at the Lord Mayor's Dinner at Guildhall, David Lloyd George confirmed the news that, in rumour form, had set 'All London . . . already throbbing' throughout the day: the Kaiser had abdicated. Surely now, at last, peace was only days, even hours, away.[39]

I3

THE MOST WONDERFUL DAY
IN ALL OUR LIVES

JUST before 11 o'clock on the morning of 11 November 1918, Winston Churchill stood at his office window in Northumberland Avenue looking towards Trafalgar Square. He was recalling the moments in the Admiralty over four years before when he waited for 11 o'clock at night to signal that war with Germany had begun. Suddenly two maroons exploded as if to warn of an air raid.

I looked again at the broad street beneath me. It was deserted. From the portals of one of the large hotels absorbed by Government Departments darted the slight figure of a girl clerk, distractedly gesticulating . . . then from all sides men and women came scurrying into the street. Streams of people poured out of all the buildings. The bells of London began to clash. Northumberland Avenue was now crowded with people in hundreds, nay, thousands, rushing hither and thither in a frantic manner, shouting and screaming with joy. I could see that Trafalgar Square was already swarming. Around me in our very headquarters, in the Hotel Metropole, disorder had broken out. Doors banged. Feet clattered down corridors. Everyone rose from the desk and cast aside pen and paper. All bounds were broken. The tumult grew. It grew like a gale, but from all sides simultaneously. The street was now a seething mass of humanity. Flags appeared as if by magic. Streams of men and women flowed from the Embankment. They mingled with torrents pouring down the Strand on their way to acclaim the King . . . [T]he strict, war-straitened, regulated streets of London had become a pandemonium.[1]

At the Air Ministry in the former Hotel Cecil, John Hammerton and other newspaper editors were at a meeting with the Chief of the Air Staff when they were suddenly disturbed by 'an all pervading brouhaha: bells ringing, guns firing, engines whistling, motor horns hooting, amid a tremendous babel of human voices such as ear had never heard'. From the Air Ministry and all over Whitehall, paper, the main weapon with which so much of the war had been waged in London, fluttered to the crowded streets below as a million forms and sheets of office stationery, even toilet paper, were torn to pieces and thrown from every office window. Nearby, seventeen-year-old Edith Summerskill was at King's College when her physics class was told that the Armistice had been signed – 'We leapt from our seats and yelling with excitement and relief poured into the Strand.'[2]

In the City, as across London, the maroons had also sounded at 11 a.m. They were quickly followed by anti-aircraft fire, which made many think it was a surprise air raid, and then the all clear, sounded by buglers but almost drowned by the ringing of hundreds of church bells, largely silent for more than four years, and by ships' sirens on the river. In an instant 'men and women poured into the streets by tens of thousands'. Many made for the Mansion House, in front of which there was soon 'a solid mass of shouting, singing humanity, a-flicker with waving flags and handkerchiefs; in windows, on housetops, even on lamp-posts, there was not room for another soul'. Among them was Cecil Hewitt, another seventeen-year-old and a clerk at a Cannon Street clothing warehouse; he tried to join in the thousands singing the Old Hundredth, astonished that everyone seemed to know the words, but his throat was dry and paralysed with emotion.[3]

Near Victoria Station Lucy Masterman watched from her window as 'The girls of a small factory in our street poured out in a stream. Some enterprising soul had printed a number of posters with the Union Jack. These they folded into cocked hats, put them on and proceeded to dance Roger de Coverley up and down the street to the rhythm of their own handclaps.' There would be dancing everywhere. Ernest Thurtle, invalided from the army with a throat wound and working for the Ministry of Munitions on gas mask production, walked past a pub near Euston Station and came across 'about a dozen women who had joined hands and were dancing round in a ring. Seeing me in uniform, one of them grabbed my arm and pulled me into the circle.' 'At the corner of Chancery Lane,' observed Caroline Playne, 'a stout policeman on point duty was surrounded by girls all clamouring to dance with him. The London bobby rose to the occasion – without a word he took one after another for a turn on the narrow pavement as they stood, whilst his countenance remained absolutely impassive.' 'This is the most wonderful day in all our lives,' recorded Hallie Miles in her diary. 'Perfect strangers smiled to each other and said, "Isn't it glorious?" and some even *kissed* each other in the street!'4

Every vehicle was commandeered for jubilation. Buses ran wildly off their routes, carrying no one inside but with their upper decks filled to toppling with cheering flag-waving horn-blowing passengers. Taxi cabs balanced a dozen on their roofs, while others perched on the running boards. Hundreds of flag sellers with trays of Union Jacks on sticks 'appeared from nowhere' and sold their stock in minutes. Most of all it seemed that the great object of everyone was to make a noise and no method seemed too eccentric. Michael MacDonagh witnessed 'a colonel in uniform squatted on the top of a motor-car sounding a dinner-gong and a parson marching at the head of a group of his parishioners singing lustily with a Union Jack stuck in the top of his silk hat'. Georgina Lee walked from Brompton to Hyde Park through 'a pandemonium of cheering and shouting, lorries full of soldiers and munitioneers waving flags and letting off crackers'. In every London district the same 'great multitudes' experienced in that single moment the 'restoration of joyousness in the twinkling of an eye', many heading for their local town halls as the natural centre of civic ceremony: the green outside Southwark Town Hall was converted into a 'dancing lawn' for the rest of the day.5

London was where everyone wanted to be. Duff Cooper, on leave from the army and staying with friends in Norfolk, caught the first available train to Liverpool Street. Others made a dash from the Home Counties by motor if they could lay their hands on petrol. And many of those in the inner suburbs moved by tube, or by bus as far as they could and then on foot, towards the centre, to Downing Street, to Parliament Square and to Buckingham Palace, where the tide flowed fullest. That afternoon and evening the King and Queen and other members of the royal family appeared on the balcony to exultant cheers from the great crowd below. Chartres Biron, a London magistrate, was among them with his young niece. A military band played '"Tipperary" and other English and American war songs; then the bandmaster stopped and after a pause moved his baton and played "Home Sweet Home". There must have been tens of thousands of people, men, women and children. With one accord all burst into tears, we were taken off our guard.'[6]

By dusk it had begun to rain and a steady downpour, later turning to drizzle, set in for the night. It didn't dampen spirits. Bonfires were lit in celebration across London for the first time since before the war, more and larger than on any Guy Fawkes Night. Searchlights played at random over the city. Theatres and restaurants lit all their lights, dazzling those in the West End long used to darkness: some, like the Trocadero, near Piccadilly Circus, put up strings of temporary lights to make the most of the moment. The early-closing order was lifted for restaurants and clubs, theatres and music halls. Every eating house in central London had been full since the last maroons had sounded: A. C. Armstrong, a magazine publisher in the City, at last found it 'possible to squeeze into the Holborn Restaurant' at 10 o'clock at night, 'where dozens of excited citizens of mature age were found standing on the tables calling for cheers from a milling mob of delirious celebrators'. There was much taunting of 'Kaiser Bill' but little jingoism, hatred temporarily suspended. There was some drunkenness, though not a great deal by all accounts, as the pubs were kept to DORA's hours, but doubtless some licence was given and taken. 'Whilst one lived that had seen it the question would be asked: What did you do on Armistice Night?' In general, though, the good humour and restrained boisterousness of the crowds were most generally remarked upon, with little complaint of disorder or riot.[7]

The celebrations went on for something like a week. The King and Queen, who had undertaken an impromptu drive through the West End into the City on Armistice Day, retraced their route more formally on Tuesday in a procession to St Paul's for a thanksgiving service. That night great bonfires were lit again in London, most memorably in Piccadilly Circus and Trafalgar Square, where the plinth of Nelson's Column was damaged by fireworks and revelry. The flames were fed by advertising hoardings and whatever came to hand. Australian soldiers, always notable in descriptions of the celebrations, were said to have 'calmly cut the hosepipes' if firemen tried to intervene too early. 'Pickpockets have had a record week,' recorded Ferdinand Tuohy, 'second only to the hawkers and street vendors selling the flags and favours of all nations and picture postcards of the Kaiser behind prison bars.' And among the songs which kept breaking out whenever a crowd gathered – 'Tipperary', 'Take Me Back to Blighty', 'Over There' – it was in this week that 'Land of Hope and Glory' 'has come to be recognised as Britain's second National Anthem'.[8]

Yet tears, as in the crowds moved by 'Home Sweet Home' outside Buckingham Palace, were never far away. On Tuesday a memorable procession of blinded soldiers, arms linked and accompanied by a few nurses, walked through Regent Street; passers-by, unable to cheer the marching men, had to turn away from the pity of it all.[9] And across London countless moments might have been recorded like these:

> Florence Younghusband was on the top of a bus when the guns were fired. In front of her were two soldiers one with his face horribly scarred. He looked straight ahead and remained stonily silent; the other just bowed his head in his hand and burst out crying. The omnibus conductress dropped into the seat by Florence, leant her head on her shoulder and cried too. 'I lost my man two months ago, I can't be happy today', she murmured.[10]

In just over four years the war had become such a pervasive element of life in London that for many it seemed impossible to imagine what might come after. For some the end of the war was itself an alarming prospect, like the waitress in Mary Ward's *Harvest* earning 7s or 8s a day, 'And now the war's goin' to stop. Do you think I want it to stop? I don't think. Me and my sister'll be starvin' again.' This fear of the future shaded the Armistice: 'no citizen knows what is going to happen to himself or his children, or to his own social circle, or to the state or the Empire,' thought Beatrice Webb in Grosvenor Road, Westminster, a week before the final maroons of the war sounded.[11] And although Armistice Day, or Armistice Week we might call it, pushed these feelings to the back of most minds they undoubtedly revived in the run-up to 1919. What sort of London would the 7 million face as a new post-war era began slowly to assert itself?

First, of course, it was a post-war era that had to live with the dreadful consequences of the war in men killed and wounded, the enduring pain of bereavement and the legacy of remembrance, symbolised so powerfully in the capital through Edwin Lutyens's monumental Cenotaph, unveiled on 11 November 1920, and the Tomb of the Unknown Soldier, interred in Westminster Abbey on the same day. The British lost some 745,000 men killed out of the 6.2 million who enlisted, or 12 per cent; a further 1.7 million were wounded (27 per cent), with

1.2 million disabled officers and men still receiving pensions in 1921. Just how many of these were Londoners is unknown. It is likely, given the enthusiasm with which London men enlisted voluntarily in the early months of the war, that something above the capital's share of the nation's men of military age would have suffered, say some 100,000 men killed and around 230,000 wounded; these, together with the casualties from air raids, were the direct costs in flesh and blood of the First World War in London.[12]

Second, some things had to be undone to restore the city to a semblance of normal life. Demobilisation of 2.6 million men from the army at the rate of 10,000 and more a day proceeded through 1918 and for the first six months of 1919. Some at least of London's employers, like Sainsbury's, honoured as best they could their promise to take men back who had volunteered for service, often at the expense of female assistants. Over the same period 90 per cent of the nation's women munitions workers were discharged from their employment, many unwillingly.

For men and women returning to the labour market, employment in London remained buoyant until a slump in engineering brought something approaching large-scale unemployment back to the capital, as to many other industrial areas of the country, from February to August 1921. This time, though, the effects on men and women out of work were mitigated by improvements in unemployment insurance and in the new-found readiness of London poor-law authorities to give relief to the unemployed outside the workhouse. These were both new departures made inevitable by the shared experience of war: there would be no return to the harsh regime of incarceration and dependence on charity that had been the lot of the pauper before 1914. Those many women who did not return to the labour market, especially married women, came home to a life of unpaid domestic labour. Those going back to paid domestic service or entering it for the first time found wages and conditions radically improved since before the war: no domestic servant would any longer contemplate a working life under the old system as a 'slavey' or something little better; and the numbers of domestic servants in any event never matched those of pre-war London. Indeed, many girls and young women found work in entirely new jobs in the expanding manufacturing industries of post-war London and in the ever-increasing demand for shop and office work.[13]

So, even when things got back to 'normal', everything had changed. When, at the end of the 1920s, social scientists at the London School of Economics came to update Charles Booth's poverty investigations of forty years before they found that

Across every path of gradual progress the Great War of 1914–18 cut a deep gash which has not yet closed up. The reader of the present volume will again and again be confronted with the fact that the most fruitful comparison is not so much between now and forty years ago as between post-war and pre-war conditions – so much greater and more striking have sometimes been the sudden changes wrought in the conditions of London Life and Labour by the great catastrophe, than by the slighter and more gradual movements of the whole of the preceding generation.[14]

To a very large extent what was true for London was true for the nation as a whole. So, for instance, though with significant local variations, London and the nation were both affected by the political shifts that the war hastened in the rise of the Labour Party and the increasing importance of trade unions in the economic and political life of the nation; in the enfranchisement of women and their enhanced involvement in political life; in the increasing penetration of the state, by both local and central government, in the daily life of ordinary citizens, especially in the provision of services to protect health and welfare and to build modern housing accommodation for working-class families; in the continuing restrictions on access to alcohol that seem to have impacted so much on levels of public drunkenness; and in the growth of office work that increased the proportion of the salaried classes in both bureaucracy and management. And the nation and the Londoners had to live with the long-term psychological and social effects of a reduced marriage rate, and of bereavement and the memory of war, constantly reinvented in the public psyche through poetry, fiction, the cinema and memoir.

But among these consequences of the war that London shared with the nation there were some important specific effects that altered the course of metropolitan history for a generation and more to come. In general they built on tendencies that were discernible before the war; though this is not true in all cases, it is probable that most of these elements might have emerged at some time or another. The war, though, quickened these tendencies and forced through in the course of the following two decades changes that appeared as a social revolution in London for those who lived there then.

One was a westward shift in the economic balance of power within London. Until 1914 London's industrial might had tended to look eastward for expansion along the River Thames and around the Port of London, and to a lesser extent to the north-east along the River Lea. But much armaments manufacture in London during the war planted itself in the west, exploiting underused road and rail connections rather than river traffic, and building on the new industries – especially motor and to a lesser extent aeroplane manufacture – that had begun to settle in west London even before 1914. Entirely new industrial areas had grown up during the war almost overnight in Park Royal, Perivale and Greenford, straddling the borders of Wembley and Acton; already emerging industrial areas at Southall, Norwood and Hayes were greatly extended; and Hendon, Colindale, Northolt and Hounslow saw the expansion of aeroplane manufacture and an extraordinary multiplication of aerodromes during the war.

These wartime developments, even when decommissioned for government and military uses, were quickly resurrected for peacetime functions. So redundant but well-built Ministry of Munitions factories, all connected to good transport links, were sold off to manufacturing and distribution companies from 1920. And the numerous aerodromes of west Middlesex, like those at Hendon, Northolt and the 'London terminal aerodrome at Hounslow', close to what became in the 1940s London Airport at Heathrow, were relinquished by the Air Ministry for civil aviation within six months or so of the Armistice. The historic connection between west London and air travel, which later had such a stunning impact on the economic fortunes of the capital, had its foundations laid during these years of the First World War.[15]

This western shift of the economic energy of the metropolis, with its new mass-production manufactures in domestic commodities based on electrical engineering and motor-component manufacture in particular and largely reliant on large numbers of women workers, had an enormous influence on the remarkable prosperity of London in the interwar period, including the years of the Great Depression. It was also a key driver in the extraordinary suburban growth of London in the 1920s and 1930s; suburban housing development affected every quadrant of the metropolis but once more it was most dynamic in west Middlesex. All these seeds too were planted and nurtured in London between 1914 and 1918.[16]

Second, and in part related to this powerful push that the war gave London's manufacturing economy, the economic gains won by working-class Londoners from 1914 to 1918 were never reversed. The war largely wiped away the absolute poverty that Charles Booth uncovered in the 1880s and 1890s and which had continued to blight the lives of millions of Londoners right up to the end of 1914: 'the reduction of the proportion of persons in poverty in the forty years is enormous, whichever figures we take,' the *New Survey* concluded, with one measure in east London showing that family poverty of 38 per cent around 1890 had fallen to 6 per cent by 1930. The war was the watershed here and it washed away for ever the scourge of mass poverty that had made the East End of London a byword throughout the world for degradation before 1914.[17]

We might mention here two further specific consequences of the war for London. One was the decline in its foreign-born population, reversing a trend towards the making of a cosmopolitan metropolis that had begun to establish itself powerfully since the 1880s. The fall of some 16 per cent in persons born abroad but living in London by 1921 compared to 1911 was largely made up of the drastic reduction in the numbers of Germans and Austrians living in London, perpetuated by anti-alien immigration restrictions that tightened after the war. Even the French and the Italians did not quite return in the numbers they had reached before 1914. London had suddenly become more insular and remained so for another generation, until a new cosmopolitan revolution began rapidly to assert itself from the late 1940s.[18]

Another consequence arose from the bitter experience of the air war against London. As war once more began to look a probability from the mid-1930s, with attention shifting to rearmament and the defence of the realm, two conflicting preoccupations with London emerged. On the one hand, there was a determination not to repeat the confusion and incompetence that compromised the safety of Londoners during the Great War. So the planning of air raid precautions in respect of warnings, shelters, welfare provision and evacuation, all so woefully lacking for the first war, were put meticulously in place for a second. But on the other hand, there grew a conviction that no amount of planning could in reality protect this enormous city and its people from the bomber. The vulnerability of London to aerial bombardment was one element in the emerging consensus among planners and politicians in the 1930s that the capital was far too big and needed to lose both industry and people to protect not just itself but the nation as a whole. Decentralisation policies of the 1930s and 1940s had their roots in these arguments, and they in turn were fuelled by London's wartime experiences between 1914 and 1918.

A hundred years on, then, and London has never forgotten the agony and sacrifice of what, for Great Britain at least, remains the Great War. Its effects on London, though, were not confined to remembrance celebrations, however moving, on and around every 11 November. For the First World War changed London and the Londoner for the rest of the twentieth century – and beyond.

ACKNOWLEDGEMENTS

I'VE had much support from many individuals and institutions during the writing of this book. Louise Raw gave me valued help at the outset in researching women's lives and has been a tireless source of encouragement since. Ann Stephenson has been an enterprising and inexhaustible research assistant for many other elements of the project. And Julia Wynn ably assisted with picture research. Several people have read and commented helpfully on various chapters of the book in draft, and I am grateful to Sally Alexander (as always), and to Jan Rüger, my colleague from Birkbeck.

I am also grateful to the librarians and archivists at the following London institutions: the British Library, the British Library Newspaper Library, the London Library, Senate House Library (especially Special Collections), the Reform Club (especially Simon Blundell), the Imperial War Museum, London Metropolitan Archives, the Museum of London Docklands, the London Transport Museum (especially Sam Mullins), the Royal London Hospital Archives, the Women's Library, the Mary Ward Centre at Queen's Square, the Children's Society Records and Archive Centre (especially Gabrielle St John-McAlister), the National Archives at Kew, the Bishopsgate Institute (especially Stefan Dickers, and Emma and David Robinson for help with the Wensley Family Archive), and to the archives and local history libraries of the London Boroughs of Brent, Ealing, Hackney, Southwark and Wandsworth. I would also like to acknowledge the assistance of the Australian War Memorial in Canberra for help in accessing diaries of ANZAC soldiers who spent part of their war in London.

I am grateful to the following for granting permission to cite copyright material: text from volumes 1 and 3 of *The World Crisis* is reproduced with permission of Curtis Brown, London, on behalf of the Estate of Sir Winston Churchill, copyright Winston S. Churchill; thanks to David Paul Publishing for allowing me to use extracts from Esther Kreitman's novel *Diamonds*; text from *Mr Britling Sees It Through* is reproduced by permission of United Agents on behalf of the Literary Executors of the Estate of H. G. Wells; excerpts from David Lloyd George's *War Memoirs* are reproduced by permission of the Beaverbrook Foundation; excerpts from Vera Brittain's *Testament of Youth* are printed with the permission of The Orion Publishing Group, copyright the Estate of Vera Britain; Mrs Lavinia Anson kindly gave me permission to cite the unpublished diaries of her aunt, Winifred Tower. Efforts have been made to trace the copyright holders of all the published works cited here that are not known to be in the public domain, but in a number of cases without success. Any outstanding permissions will be gratefully acknowledged in future editions. For holdings of diaries at the Imperial War Museum, I have made every effort to contact copyright holders through the Museum, but in the cases of Captain HC Meysey-Thompson, Mrs L. Peile and the anonymous lady diarist from Kensington (Miscellaneous 522) they are unknown. Should any copyright holder contact me I shall be pleased to acknowledge my debt in later editions.

In bringing this book to a close I have received boundless support from my publishers, Stuart Williams, Jörg Hensgen and Katherine Ailes, from Lesley Levene for her excellent copy-editing, and from my agent Maggie Hanbury, who has been a tireless help to me over three decades, and her assistant Harriet Poland. Finally my warmest thanks go to Rosie Cooper, who has had to endure the ups and downs of an author's life over what is now too many years to mention.

ILLUSTRATIONS

Scene at Buckingham Palace © Imperial War Museums (Q65496)

James Keir Hardie © Illustrated London News Ltd/Mary Evans

Recruits at the Whitehall Recruiting Office © Imperial War Museums (Q42033)

B-type bus © TfL from the London Transport Museum

Victoria Station © Imperial War Museums (Q30511)

Belgian soldier's funeral. Reproduced courtesy of the Royal London Hospital Archives

Sleeping quarters in the Great Hall at Alexandra Palace © Imperial War Museums (Q64157)

Chrisp Street anti-German Lusitania riots © Mary Evans/Pharcide

WE ARE RUSSIANS sign chalked on shop in east end of London. Photo from Topical Press Agency/Getty Images

Zeppelin, from *Zeppelins Over England* by Treusch von Buttlar Brandenfels, translated by Huntley Paterson (George G. Harrap & Co. Ltd., London, 1931)

Gotha bomber, from *The German Air Raids on Great Britain, 1914–1918* by Captain James Morris (Sampson Low, Marston & Co., Ltd, 1925)

Air Raid Damage in the UK © Imperial War Museums (HO122a)

Bomb damage to property at Terb Road © Imperial War Museums (Q94737)

A tortoise at London zoo with an advert for more shells on its shell © Illustrated London News Ltd/Mary Evans

A woman dressed as 'Belgium' © Illustrated London News Ltd/Mary Evans

School of Building © London Metropolitan Archives, City of London ('*Collage*' *image database: 180228*)

A factory manufacturing petrol tins. Source: A. and I. M. McCulloch

Women munitions workers' football team © Imperial War Museums (HU70114)

Women bus conductors © TfL from the London Transport Museum

Outside Charing X Station © Imperial War Museums (art.IWM ART 2759)

Turner Ward London Hospital. Reproduced courtesy of the Royal London Hospital Archives

Convalescent soldiers arrive at the Palace Theatre © Imperial War Museums (Q96368)

Service at a street shrine © Imperial War Museums (HU58985)

St Augustine's Hall, Victoria Park © London Metropolitan Archives, City of London ('Collage' image database: 203269)

Page from Tatler magazine © Victoria and Albert Museum, London

Damage caused by the Silvertown explosion © Museum of London

Temporary hutments. Reproduced courtesy of the Greenwich Cultural Heritage Centre

Boys queueing for coal © Imperial War Museums (Q96383)

Armistice Day celebrations in Trafalgar Square. Photo from Popperfoto/ Getty Images

NOTES

Preface: London and the First World War

1. Hallie Eustace Miles, *Untold Tales of War-Time London*, 1930, p. 11.

1: An Immense Sense of Waiting

1. *The Times*, Saturday 2 May 1914.
2. *The Times*, Friday 5 June 1914. Mrs Hewlett was married to the novelist Maurice Hewlett: see *ODNB*, 'Maurice Hewlett', and www.gracesguide.co.uk/ Hilda_B_Hewlett [19 December 2012].
3. Registrar-General of Births, Deaths, and Marriages in England, *Annual Summary of Marriages, Births, and Deaths in England and Wales and in London . . . 1912*, 1913, pp. 6–9, 57.
4. London County Council, *London Statistics. 1912–13 . . . Vol. XXIII*, 1914, pp. 46–9, 56–7.
5. Ibid., pp. 79–81.
6. See Jerry White, *London in the Nineteenth Century: A Human Awful Wonder of God*, 2007, pp. 145–6, and *London in the Twentieth Century: A City and Its People*, 2001, pp. 103–4; Panikos Panayi (ed.), *Germans in London since 1500*, 1996, passim.
7. On the relative stability of the condition of workers in London from 1900 to 1914 see Sir Hubert Llewellyn Smith (ed.), *The New Survey of London Life and Labour. Vol. I, Forty Years of Change*, 1930, Chs. III, IV, X; and Arthur L. Bowley, *Prices and Wages in the United Kingdom, 1914–1920*, Oxford, 1921, p. 87. For the numbers of millionaires see W. D. Rubinstein, *Men of Property: The Very Wealthy in Britain since the Industrial Revolution*, 1981, pp. 102–7.
8. Stephen McKenna, *While I Remember*, 1921, p. 79.
9. See, for instance, the Court Circular columns of *The Times*, 9 and 11 May 1914.
10. Osbert Sitwell cited in Peter Thorold, *The London Rich: The Creation of a Great City, from 1666 to the Present*, 1999, p. 315.

11. D. Nichols Pigache, *Café Royal Days*, 1934, pp. 187–8.

12. Charles Booth, *Life and Labour of the People in London. Series I, Poverty, Vol. I, East, Central and South London*, 1892, pp. 131ff; Booth's findings are helpfully summarised in Sir Hubert Llewellyn Smith (ed.), *The New Survey of London Life and Labour. Vol. VI, Social Survey II, Western Area*, 1934, p. 88.

13. Maud Pember Reeves, *Round About a Pound a Week*, 1913, passim. The book was not reviewed in *The Times* and was panned for its statist socialist remedies by Helen Bosanquet in the *Economic Journal* of March 1914, pp. 109–12.

14. See, for instance, Anon., *Sweated Industries, Being a Handbook of the 'Daily News' Exhibition*, 1906, and James A. Schmiechen, *Sweated Industries and Sweated Labour: The London Clothing Trades 1860–1914*, 1984, passim.

15. For London's industrial structure in these years see Michael Ball and David Sunderland, *An Economic History of London, 1800–1914*, 2001, Ch. 4, and for detailed figures of employment for persons living in the County of London see Census of England and Wales 1911, *Occupations and Industries Pt. II*, Cd. 7019, pp. 293–6.

16. London County Council, *London Statistics. 1912–13*, pp. 64–5.

17. Booth, *Life and Labour, Poverty, Vol. I*, p. 131.

18. Alexander Paterson, *Across the Bridges – or Life by the South London River-Side*, 1911, p. 152.

19. Chris Massie, *The Confessions of a Vagabond*, 1931, pp. 126–7.

20. London County Council, *London Statistics. 1911–12 . . . Vol. XXII*, 1912, pp. 241–2; London County Council, *London Statistics. 1913–14 . . . Vol. XXIV*, p. 292.

21. See Richard Mudie-Smith (ed.), *The Religious Life of London*, 1904, especially pp. 15ff; H. Wilson Harris and Margaret Bryant, *The Churches and London (An Outline Survey of Religious Work in the Metropolitan Area)*, 1914, especially pp. 32 and 41–2; Hugh McLeod, *Class and Religion in the Late Victorian City*, 1974.

22. Paterson, *Across the Bridges*, p. 153.

23. London County Council, *London Statistics. 1912–13*, pp. 296–7.

24. David Lloyd George, *War Memoirs*, 2 vols, new edition, 1938, Vol. II, pp. 1141–2.

25. Raymond Postgate, *The Builders' History*, 1923, pp. 414–23; Survey of London, *County Hall (Monograph 17)*, 1991, pp. 53–4.

26. *The Times*, 28 and 29 May 1914.

27. *The Times*, 29 and 30 July 1914.

28. *The Times*, 1 May and 29 July 1914.

29. *The Times*, 19 May 1914; the strike ended on 28 May (see *The Times* of that date) with advance payment of the Trade Board minimum wage and limited union recognition of the carmen's union.

30. *The Times*, 28 May 1914.

31. *The Times*, 4, 7–8, 10–11 July 1914.

32. *The Times*, 1–11 July, 31 July and 1 August 1914.

33. Albert Marrin, *The Last Crusade: The Church of England in the First World War*, Durham, North Carolina, 1974, pp. 54–5.

34. See, for example, *The Times*, 13, 22, 23, 25, 27 May, 4, 5, 8, 9, 13, 15 and 16 June 1914; for lively recollections of some of these events see E. Sylvia Pankhurst, *The Suffragette Movement: An Intimate Account of Persons and Ideals*, 1931, pp. 544ff.

35. *The Times*, 25 May, 8 and 15 June 1914.
36. *The Times*, 25 May 1914.
37. *The Times*, 26 June 1914.
38. *The Times*, 1–2 June 1914.
39. *The Times*, 13 July 1914.
40. Ferdinand Tuohy, *The Crater of Mars*, 1929, p. 1.
41. *The Times*, 17 July 1914. For an excellent review of domestic events this July in London and beyond see Geoffrey Marcus, *Before the Lamps Went Out*, 1965, pp. 212–24.
42. *The Times*, 11 July 1914.
43. *The Times*, 6 July 1914; there was an extensive and enthusiastic report in the *South London Press (SLP)*, 10 July 1914.
44. Winston S. Churchill, *The World Crisis, Vol. I, 1911–1914*, 1923, pp. 151–2.
45. 'Diary of a London Lady (Anonymous)', MISC 29/522 (IWM), 23–29 July 1914. For the small disruption to continental travel plans at this time see *The Times*, Friday 31 July 1914.
46. See, for example, W. R. Inge, *Diary of a Dean: St Paul's 1911–1934*, 1949, p. 29; McKenna, *While I Remember*, p. 139; F. W. Pethick-Lawrence, *Fate Has Been Kind*, 1942, p. 107; Caroline E. Playne, *Society at War, 1914–1916*, 1931, p. 28; Ernest Thurtle, *Time's Winged Chariot: Memories and Comments*, 1945, p. 44.
47. See Christopher Clark, *The Sleepwalkers: How Europe Went to War in 1914*, 2012, pp. 492–4.
48. For the LCC's holiday see London County Council, *The Council and the War*, 1920, p. 1. Edward Ezard, *Battersea Boy*, 1979, pp. 149–50. Anon., *Thomas Hancock Nunn: The Life of a Social Reformer. Written by His Friends for His Friends*, 1942, pp. 133–4. Gavin Roynon (ed.), *Home Fires Burning: The Great War Diaries of Georgina Lee*, Stroud, 2006, pp. 2–3. For the besieged railway stations see McKenna, *While I Remember*, p. 139. The rail and steamboat plans are in *The Times*, 31 July 1914.
49. Lloyd George, *War Memoirs*, Vol. I, pp. 61–2; Marcus, *Before the Lamps Went Out*, pp. 244–8; David Kynaston, *The City of London. Vol. II, Golden Years 1890–1914*, 1995, pp. 600ff, who cites the banker Smith St Aubyn.
50. 'Diary of a London Lady (Anonymous)', Thursday 30 July 1914. Sainsbury Archive, WAR/1/1, Letter to Managers, 31 July 1914. *The Times*, 1 August 1914.
51. On the rise in prices see Simon Litman, *Prices and Price Control in Great Britain and the United States during the World War*, New York, 1920, p. 24. On diaries see Hallie Eustace Miles, *Untold Tales of War-Time London*, 1930, p. 13, 1 August 1914.
52. Frederick Willis, *London General*, 1953, pp. 190–91.
53. Arthur Foley Winnington-Ingram, *Fifty Years' Work in London (1889–1939)*, 1940, p. 108.
54. Tuohy, *Crater of Mars*, pp. 2–3.
55. *The Times*, Monday 3 August 1914.
56. On the Neutrality League's preparations from 30 July see Stephen Hobhouse, *Forty Years and an Epilogue: An Autobiography (1881–1951)*, 1951, p. 141. For flooding by leaflets see Henry Fuller Morriss, *Bermondsey's 'Bit' in the Greatest War*, 1923, pp. 2–3. For the Trafalgar Square demonstration see R. M. Fox, *Smoky Crusade*, 1937, pp. 189–90; *The Times*, Monday 3 August 1914;

see also Fenner Brockway, *Inside the Left: Thirty Years of Platform, Press, Prison and Parliament*, 1942, p. 43; Norman and Jeanne MacKenzie (eds), *The Diary of Beatrice Webb. Vol. 3, 1905–1924: 'The Power to Alter Things'*, 1984, p. 212; Ken Weller, *'Don't be a Soldier!' The Radical Anti-War Movement in North London 1914–1918*, 1985, Ch. 6.

57. *The Times*, Monday 3 August 1914; *Manchester Guardian*, 5 August 1914; Marcus, *Before the Lamps Went Out*, pp. 256–7.

58. Fox, *Smoky Crusade*, p. 190.

59. Catriona Pennell, *A Kingdom United. Popular Responses to the Outbreak of the First World War in Britain and Ireland*, Oxford, 2012, p. 31.

60. Anon., *A Soldier's Diary of the Great War*, 1929, p. 3. MacKenzie and MacKenzie (eds), *Diary of Beatrice Webb. Vol. 3*, p. 212. See also Adrian Gregory, *The Last Great War: British Society and the First World War*, Cambridge, 2008, p. 24; Michael S Neiberg, *Dance of the Furies: Europe and the Outbreak of World War I*, Cambridge, Mass., 2011, p. 143; Pennell, *Kingdom United*, p. 4; C. à Court Repington, *The First World War, 1914–1918: Personal Experiences of Lieut.-Col. C. à Court Repington*, 2 vols, 1921, Vol. I, p. 18; Henry Wickham Steed, *Through Thirty Years, 1892–1922: A Personal Narrative*, 2 vols, 1924, Vol. II, pp. 36–7.

61. MacKenzie and MacKenzie (eds), *Diary of Beatrice Webb. Vol. 3*, p. 212. John Middleton Murry, *Between Two Worlds: An Autobiography*, 1935, pp. 295–6. Philip Gibbs, *The Soul of War*, 1915, p. 3. Beatrice Curtis Brown, *Southwards from Swiss Cottage*, 1947, pp. 28–9. Mary Agnes Hamilton, *Dead Yesterday*, 1916, pp. 202–3, 212. For Buckingham Palace see Celia Lee, *Jean, Lady Hamilton 1861–1941: A Soldier's Wife (Wife of General Sir Ian Hamilton). A Biography from Her Diaries*, 2001, p. 109. *Neutrality League Announcement No. 2*, circulated 3 August 1914, in Playne MSS Collection, Senate House Library, MS1112, folder 9. For the short shrift see Hamilton, *Dead Yesterday*, pp. 215–17; Hobhouse, *Forty Years and an Epilogue*, p. 152.

62. Pethick-Lawrence, *Fate Has Been Kind*, p. 110. Frederick Arthur Robinson, 'MS Diary 1914–1918', 11335 P. 401–402 (IWM), 2 August 1914. Anon., *Thomas Hancock Nunn*, pp. 133–4. McKenna, *While I Remember*, p. 141 (see also *The Times*, 4 August 1914). Ford Madox Ford, *Some Do Not . . .*, 1924 (Everyman edn, 1992), p. 204.

63. Alfred James Hurley, *Days That are Gone: Milestones I have Passed in South-West London*, 1947, p. 53. Murry, *Between Two Worlds*, pp. 295–6. *The Times*, 4 August 1914.

64. Edward Grey, Viscount of Falloden, *Twenty-Five Years, 1892–1916*, 2 vols, 1925, Vol. II, p. 20.

65. Brown, *Southwards from Swiss Cottage*, p. 29. For the straw hats see Michael MacDonagh, *In London during the Great War: The Diary of a Journalist*, 1935, pp. 7–10.

66. Pethick-Lawrence, *Fate Has Been Kind*, pp. 110–11. Neiberg, *Dance of the Furies*, p. 6, shows how this was the view in every belligerent country in Europe during these days of July and August 1914.

67. *The Times*, Wednesday 5 August 1914.

68. *The Times*, Wednesday 5 August 1914.

69. C. H. Rolph, *London Particulars*, Oxford, 1980, p. 128.

70. J. B. Booth, *The Days We Knew*, 1943, p. 2.

2: *An Altogether New London: 1914*

1. Ernest Thurtle, *Time's Winged Chariot: Memories and Comments*, 1945, pp. 44–5.
2. Caroline E. Playne, *Society at War, 1914–1916*, 1931, p. 29.
3. 'Diary of a London Lady (Anonymous)', MISC 29/522 (IWM), Wednesday 5 August 1914; Georgina Lee, another Kensington diarist writing on the same day, also used the same expression 'lost their heads': Gavin Roynon (ed.), *Home Fires Burning: The Great War Diaries of Georgina Lee*, Stroud, 2006, p. 6.
4. Michael MacDonagh, *In London during the Great War: The Diary of a Journalist*, 1935, pp. 12–13.
5. 'Diary of a London Lady (Anonymous)', Wednesday 5 August 1914.
6. MacDonagh, *In London during the Great War*, p. 14, Saturday 8 August 1914. *SLP*, 7 August 1914. 'Diary of a London Lady (Anonymous)', Wednesday 5 August 1914.
7. Simon Litman, *Prices and Price Control in Great Britain and the United States during the World War*, New York, 1920, p. 24.
8. Frederick Arthur Robinson, 'MS Diary 1914–1918', 11335 P. 401–402 (IWM), 7 August 1914. He was right about the notes: they were soon replaced by Bank of England notes and withdrawn. See also David Lloyd George, *War Memoirs*, 2 vols, new edn, 1938, Vol. I, pp. 65–8; David Kynaston, *The City of London. Vol. III, Illusions of Gold 1914–1945*, 1999, Ch.1.
9. Sainsbury Archive, Museum of London Docklands, WAR/1/774, Letter to Managers, 6 August 1914.
10. 'Britain's Motto. "Business as Usual". Not least at Marshall & Snellgrove': advert in *The Times*, 17 August 1914.
11. *The Times*, 15 and 17 August 1914; E. Sylvia Pankhurst, *The Suffragette Movement: An Intimate Account of Persons and Ideals*, 1931, p. 591; Martha Vicinus, *Independent Women: Work and Community for Single Women 1850–1920*, 1985, pp. 279–81.
12. See Martin Pugh, *Speak for Britain! A New History of the Labour Party*, 2010, pp. 104–6; Raymond Postgate, *The Builders' History*, 1923, p. 423; and *The Times*, 15 August 1914.
13. R. M. Fox, *Smoky Crusade*, 1937 p. 192; Ken Weller, *'Don't be a Soldier!' The Radical Anti-War Movement in North London 1914–1918*, 1985, pp. 37–9; Raymond Postgate, *The Life of George Lansbury*, 1951, p. 152.
14. *Hackney and Kingsland Gazette* (*HKG*), Wednesday 7 October 1914.
15. For the general absence of dissent against the war at this time see Brock Millman, *Managing Domestic Dissent in First World War Britain*, 2000, pp. 37ff.
16. For Walworth and others see *SLP*, Friday 14 August 1914, the 'clear conscience' coming from Rotherhithe. St Matthew's is in Jeffrey Cox, *The English Churches in a Secular Society. Lambeth 1870–1930*, Oxford, 1982, p. 246. More generally see Albert Marrin, *The Last Crusade: The Church of England in the First World War*, Durham, North Carolina, 1974, pp. 68–81.
17. *SLP*, Friday 18 September 1914; see also 9 October and 6 November 1914; Henry Fuller Morriss, *Bermondsey's 'Bit' in the Greatest War*, 1923, p. 4; Fenner Brockway, *Bermondsey Story: The Life of Alfred Salter*, 1949, pp. 60–61.
18. The bread riots are in 'Diary of a London Lady (Anonymous)', Sunday 2 August 1914. Roynon (ed.), *Home Fires Burning*, p. 5. The (Hoxton) clergyman was

Robert R. Hyde, *Industry was My Parish*, 1968, p. 53. Norman and Jeanne MacKenzie (eds), *The Diary of Beatrice Webb. Vol. 3, 1905-1924: 'The Power to Alter Things'*, 1984, p. 214. The 'new democracy' is in John F. Macdonald, *Two Towns – One City: Paris – London*, 1917, pp. 105–6, writing about 1914.

19. For officers and buses see Paul Fussell, *The Great War and Modern Memory*, 1975, illustrated edn, 2000, p. 97. A. Hamilton Gibbs, *Gun Fodder: The Diary of Four Years of War*, Boston, Mass., 1919, pp. 5–7.

20. Ibid., p. 5. The cheering crowds are in *SLP*, 7 August 1914, and the staring ones in Anon., *A Soldier's Diary of the Great War*, 1929. Rudolf Rocker, *The London Years*, 1956, p. 241.

21. For the first posters see Richard Morris, *The Man Who Ran London during the Great War: The Diaries and Letters of Lieutenant General Sir Francis Lloyd GCVO, KCB, DSO (1853-1926)*, Barnsley, 2009, pp. 78–9. H. Keatley Moore and W. C. Berwick Sayers (eds), *Croydon and the Great War: The Official History of the War Work of the Borough and Its Citizens from 1914 to 1919. Together with the Croydon Roll of Honour*, 1920, pp. 19–20. Arthur Newton, *Years of Change: Autobiography of a Hackney Shoemaker*, 1974, p. 48. Morriss, *Bermondsey's 'Bit' in the Greatest War*, Ch.2. Edward Ezard, *Battersea Boy*, 1979, p. 150. Anon., *A Record of the Honoured Men of Wimbledon & Merton Who Fell in the Great War 1914-18, with Notes of Local Activities during the Same Period*, 1921, pp. 77–8.

22. H. C. Meysey-Thompson, 'Diary 1914-1918', 92/19/1 (IWM), pp. 1–3, 5–10 August 1914. He became a Captain in the King's Rifle Corps.

23. Samantha L. Bird, *Stepney: Profile of a London Borough from the Outbreak of the First World War to the Festival of Britain, 1914-1951*, Newcastle upon Tyne, 2011, p. 15. Richard Church, *The Golden Sovereign: A Conclusion to 'Over the Bridge'*, 1957, pp. 218–20. Thurtle, *Time's Winged Chariot*, pp. 45–7. Bermondsey Metropolitan Borough Council, Council Minutes, 14 August 1914; Reform Club, General Committee Minutes 1908–19, p. 339, 13 August 1914, p. 342, 3 September 1914.

24. On class differences in recruitment see Jay M. Winter, *The Great War and the British People*, 1986, pp. 36 and 63. On regional differences see Catriona Pennell, *A Kingdom United: Popular Responses to the Outbreak of the First World War in Britain and Ireland*, Oxford, 2012, p. 149 (recruitment in London was not as high as in some other areas); see also Adrian Gregory, *The Last Great War: British Society and the First World War*, Cambridge, 2008, p. 81, and David Silbey, *The British Working Class and Enthusiasm for War, 1914–1916*, 2005, Ch.3.

25. Viscount [William] Sandhurst, *From Day to Day: 1914-1915*, 1928, p. 31, 1 September 1914.

26. Pennell, *A Kingdom United*, p. 145 (recruitment from 30 August) and pp. 60–61 (posters and songs). Hallie Eustace Miles, *Untold Tales of War-Time London*, 1930, p. 22, 31 October–4 December 1914; for the Eustace Miles Restaurant see Col. Nathaniel Newnham-Davis, *The Gourmet's Guide to London*, 1914, Ch. XII. For the City banner see Ruth Slate, *Dear Girl: The Diaries and Letters of Two Working Women (1897-1917)*, edited by Tierl Thompson, 1987, p. 250, 9 October 1914. For the Lord Mayor's Show see Robinson, 'MS Diary', 9 November 1914, and MacDonagh, *In London during the Great War*, p. 37 and p. 43 for the funeral and aftermath.

27. Norman Flower (ed.), *The Journals of Arnold Bennett*, 3 vols, 1932–3, Vol.II, p. 108. Robinson, 'MS Diary', 10 November 1914.

28. N. B. Dearle, *An Economic Chronicle of the Great War for Great Britain and Ireland*, 1929, p. 3.

29. *HKG*, Friday 14 August 1914. E. Sylvia Pankhurst, *The Home Front: A Mirror to Life in England during the World War*, 1932, pp. 21ff. For SSFA figures London-wide see *The Times*, Sunday 22 November 1914. Stephen 'Johnny' Hicks, *Sparring for Luck*, 1982, pp. 13–14.

30. Miles, *Untold Tales*, p. 14, 5 August–26 September 1914.

31. H. G. Wells, *Mr Britling Sees It Through*, 1916, p. 230.

32. Winifred L. B. Tower, 'Journal, 26 July to October 1914, and Some Diary Notes, October 1914 to February 1916', P. 476 (IWM), 'Diary Notes', p. 18.

33. For buses see T. C. Barker and Michael Robbins, *A History of London Transport: Passenger Travel and the Development of the Metropolis. Volume II, The Twentieth Century to 1970*, 1974, pp. 192–4. For taxis see *Report of the Commissioner of Police of the Metropolis for the Year 1914*, Cd. 8188, 1916, p. 9. For demand see R. D. Blumenfeld, *All in a Lifetime*, 1931, pp. 6–7, 22 August 1914. *The Journals of Arnold Bennett*, Vol. II, p. 108.

34. For Hyde Park see 'Diary of a London Lady (Anonymous)', Wednesday 5 August 1914; for Green Park see Sandhurst, *From Day to Day: 1914–1915*, p. 21, 21 August 1914. C. H. Rolph, *London Particulars*, Oxford, 1980, p. 129. Meysey-Thompson, 'Diary', p. 4, 12 August 1914. Alfred Stokes, *East Ham: From Village to County Borough*, 3rd edn, 1933, p. 173.

35. Tower, 'Journal, Diary Notes', p. 18.

36. Joseph G. Broodbank, *History of the Port of London*, 2 vols, 1921, Vol. II, pp. 469–70.

37. For the Foreign Office see G. A. R. Riddell, *Lord Riddell's War Diary 1914–1918*, 1933, p. 13. For the lake see MacDonagh, *In London during the Great War*, pp. 59–60. For Londoners on the lookout see Macdonald, *Two Towns – One City*, p. 121. For the Admiralty's fear of raids see Winston S. Churchill, *The World Crisis, Vol. I, 1911–1914*, 1923, pp. 251, 253. Mary Coules, 'First World War Papers. Journal *c*.June 1914–Nov. 1915', 97/25/1, Journal, n.p., probably early September 1914. 'Daddy' was the news editor of Reuters, 24 Old Jewry.

38. *HKG*, 7 October 1914, for instance, warned that Zeppelin raids were thought to be imminent. Miles, *Untold Tales*, pp. 29–30, 29–30 October 1914. Reform Club Minutes, p. 346, 8 October 1914.

39. Tower, 'Journal, Diary Notes', p. 18.

40. *The Times*, Friday 11 September, Thursday 17 September, Tuesday 6 October 1914. See also the excellent Neil Hanson, *First Blitz: The Secret German Plan to Raze London to the Ground in 1918*, 2008, pp. 33–4.

41. *The Journals of Arnold Bennett*, Vol. II, p. 109, 4 November 1914. D. S. Higgins (ed.), *The Private Diaries of Sir H. Rider Haggard*, 1980, p. 9, 4 October 1914, after a week in London. Wells, *Mr Britling Sees It Through*, p. 234. John Galsworthy, *Saint's Progress*, 1919, p. 181.

42. Higgins (ed.), *The Private Diaries of Sir H. Rider Haggard*, p. 9. *HKG*, Friday 16 October 1914.

43. *Parliamentary Debates, Fifth Series, Vol. LXVIII, House of Commons, 1st Vol. of Session 1914–15*, cols. 339–40, 7 November; 933–4, 24 November;

1099–1100, 25 November; 1325–6, 26 November 1914. The figures are for the City and Metropolitan Police District.

44. 'Diary of a London Lady (Anonymous)', Friday 14 August 1914. Blumenfeld, *All in a Lifetime*, pp. 9–10, 29 August; see also Mrs C. S. Peel, *How We Lived Then: 1914–1918: A Sketch of Social and Domestic Life in England During the War*, 1929, p. 28.

45. For Guy's see H. C. Cameron, *Mr Guy's Hospital 1726–1948*, 1954, pp. 323–4. For the London and its first arrivals of wounded see Sydney Viscount Knutsford Holland, *In Black and White*, 1926, pp. 274–6; A. E. Clark-Kennedy, *The London: A Study in the Voluntary Hospital System. Vol. 2, The Second Hundred Years 1840–1948*, 1963, p. 125. For the officers see MacDonagh, *In London during the Great War*, p. 19, 30 August 1914.

46. Sandhurst, *From Day to Day: 1914–1915*, p. 78, 22 October 1914; for military hospitals in London and elsewhere in the UK see Sir W. G. Macpherson, *Medical Services: General History Vol. I, Medical Services in the United Kingdom etc.*, 1921. For the London Ambulance Column see Emily Mayhew, *Wounded: From Battlefield to Blighty, 1914–1918*.

47. F. Scott Fitzgerald, *Tender is the Night*, 1934, Bk I, Ch. XIII. On the London railway stations see Adrian Gregory, 'Railway Stations: Gateways and Termini', in Jay Winter and Jean-Louis Robert (eds), *Capital Cities at War: Paris, London, Berlin 1914–1919. Vol. 2, A Cultural History*, Cambridge, 2007, pp. 23, 34–6, 44–6.

48. Miles, *Untold Tales*, p. 18, 26 September–28 October 1914.

49. Blumenfeld, *All in a Lifetime*, pp. 13–14, 29 September 1914; MacDonagh, *In London during the Great War*, p. 32.

50. W. N. P. Barbellion, *The Journal of a Disappointed Man*, 1919, p. 141, c.15 October 1914.

51. Moore and Sayers (eds), *Croydon and the Great War*, p. 23.

52. *The Times*, Monday 14 December 1914.

53. Reform Club Minutes, pp. 338–9, 13 August 1914; Reform Club Letter Books 1913–14, pp. 758–9, 857, 933–4, 956–7; 1914–15, pp. 57–8.

54. *The Journals of Arnold Bennett*, Vol. II, p. 107, 25 October and 104, 14 September 1914. *The Times*, Monday 14 December 1914.

55. *The Times*, 21 and 26 December 1914.

56. *The Times*, 28 December 1914.

57. *The Times*, 28 December 1914.

58. Rt Hon. Christopher Addison, *Four and a Half Years: A Personal Diary from June 1914 to January 1919*, 2 vols, 1934, Vol. I, p. 49, Saturday 5 December 1914. MacDonagh, *In London during the Great War*, p. 45, Christmas Day 1914.

59. London Hospital, House Committee Minutes, 16 November and 7 December 1914; Roynon (ed.), *Home Fires Burning*, p. 71, 23 December 1914.

60. Robinson, 'MS Diary', 25 December 1914.

61. *HKG*, Monday 28 December 1914.

62. MacKenzie and MacKenzie(eds), *Diary of Beatrice Webb. Vol. 3*, p. 220, 3 November 1914.

3: A War for Purity

1. *The Times*, 10 August 1914.
2. *The Times*, 16 August 1914.
3. H. Wilson Harris and Margaret Bryant, *The Churches and London (An Outline Survey of Religious Work in the Metropolitan Area)*, 1914, pp. 1–42, 244–50.
4. *The Times*, 31 May 1911 and 21 November 1911; see also Edward J. Bristow, *Vice and Vigilance: Purity Movements in Britain since 1700*, Dublin, 1977, pp. 144–5.
5. E. Sylvia Pankhurst, *The Suffragette Movement: An Intimate Account of Persons and Ideals*, 1931, pp. 521–3.
6. John Grigg, *The Young Lloyd George*, 1973, pp. 99–100, 132–4; John Grigg, *Lloyd George: The People's Champion 1902–1911*, 1978, p. 71.
7. Harris and Bryant, *The Churches and London*, pp. 238–9.
8. J. R. Watson, 'Soldiers and Saints: The Fighting Man and the Christian Life', in Andrew Bradstock, Sean Gill, Anne Hogan and Sue Morgan (eds), *Masculinity and Spirituality in Victorian Culture*, Basingstoke, 2000, pp. 10–26.
9. 'Lord Kitchener's Counsel' to the BEF cited in *The Times*, 19 August 1914. See also Adam Hochschild, *To End All Wars: How the First World War Divided Britain*, 2011, p. 103.
10. *The Times*, 16 November 1914.
11. Hochschild, *To End All Wars*, pp. 179–80, 211.
12. Stephen McKenna, *While I Remember*, 1921, pp. 84–5. See also Arthur Marwick, *The Deluge: British Society and the First World War*, 2nd edn, 2006, p. 90; Adrian Gregory, *The Last Great War: British Society and the First World War*, Cambridge, 2008, pp. 160–61.
13. *The Times*, 3 October 1914.
14. The survey is cited in a *Times* editorial, 17 October 1914. The pub counts are in *HKG*, 30 October 1914, and so is an instance of a magistrate (Chartres Biron) jumping on the bandwagon. For the temperance organisations see *SLP*, 13 November 1914, and *HKG*, 6 November 1914. Bermondsey Metropolitan Borough Council, Council Minutes, Vol. 15, 20 October 1914, reported in *SLP*, 23 October 1914. D. S. Higgins (ed.), *The Private Diaries of Sir H. Rider Haggard*, 1980, p. 10, 17 October 1914.
15. *SLP*, 23 October 1914.
16. Higgins (ed.), *The Private Diaries of Sir H. Rider Haggard*, pp. 22–3, 16 February 1915. Children Act 1908, 8 Edw. 7, c67, sec. 120. Despard's letter is in *The Times*, 8 October 1914; for her relationship with her brother see Hochschild, *To End All Wars*, pp. 14–15. *Charity Organisation Review* (COR), Vol. XXXVI, No. 215, p. 301, November 1914. Helen Fraser, *Women and War Work*, New York, 1918, p. 75.
17. For drink restrictions see Henry Carter, *The Control of the Drink Trade in Britain: A Contribution to National Efficiency during the Great War 1915–1918*, 2nd edn, 1919, pp. 35–7; Arthur Shadwell, *Drink in 1914–1922: A Lesson in Control*, 1923, p. 4. For the pub owners' agreement see *SLP*, 6 November 1914. These early reductions in pub opening hours were brought about not by DORA but by the Temporary Restrictions Act 1914.
18. See the article by The Countess Ferrers, Vice-President of the North-East London District of the SSFA in *COR*, Vol. XXXVIII, No. 223, pp. 9–10, July 1915.

Paddington Board of Guardians circulated to other London boards a resolution opposing aid to unmarried dependants (Wandsworth Board of Guardians, Minutes of the Board, 7 January 1915). See also E. Sylvia Pankhurst, *The Home Front: A Mirror to Life in England during the World War*, 1932, pp. 107–8; Arthur Marwick, *The Deluge*, pp. 82–3.

19. Pankhurst, *The Home Front*, pp. 99–100; that there was an 'outcry' see, for example, the letter of protest from the Women's Local Government Society in *SLP*, 18 December 1914. For the Home Office see *HC Debates*, 1914–15, Vol. LXVIII, cols. 1143–4, 25 November 1914. On the complaints to the women police see Fraser, *Women and War Work*, pp. 74–5.

20. *The Times*, 13 October 1914 (YWCA); 19 September 1914 (formation of war babies' and Mothers' League, then at 411 Oxford Street); 23 April 1915 (Women's Imperial Health Association); 6 May 1915 (WSPU); 11 and 18 June 1915 (the Bishop and the Committee). See also Christopher Addison, *Politics from Within, 1911–1918: Including Some Records of a Great National Effort*, 2 vols, 1924, Vol. II, pp. 43–4.

21. Figures for births in the County of London and some surrounding districts are to be found in London County Council, *London Statistics. 1915–20 . . . Vol. XXVI*, 1921, p. 46.

22. David Lloyd George, *War Memoirs*, 2 vols, new edn, 1938, Vol. I, pp. 193–4.

23. *The Times*, 5, 8 and 9 March 1915.

24. *The Times*, 2 April 1915. For the 50,000 letters see Mrs C. S. Peel, *How We Lived Then: 1914–1918: A Sketch of Social and Domestic Life in England during the War*, 1929, p. 64.

25. For the King and the Cabinet see John Grigg, *Lloyd George: From Peace to War 1912–1916*, 1985, pp. 230–33; for Rosebery see Viscount [William] Sandhurst, *From Day to Day: 1914–1915*, 1928, p. 175, 16 April 1915; R. D. Blumenfeld, *All in a Lifetime*, 1931, p. 23. See also Gregory, *The Last Great War*, pp. 95ff.

26. Edith Marjorie Bunbury, 'Diary of the European War Sept. 1914–Nov. 1915', A/FH/F15/001/002 (LMA), n.p., 18 and 30 March, 7 April 1915.

27. Addison, *Politics from Within*, Vol. II, pp. 46–7.

28. See Alexander Pulling (ed.), *Defence of the Realm Acts and Regulations Passed and Made to July 31st, 1915*, 1915, pp. 47–58; *HC Debates*, 1914–15, Vol. LXXIV, cols. 829–30, 29 September 1915; Carter, *The Control of the Drink Trade in Britain*, pp. 141 and (for Enfield Lock) 173–5.

29. *HKG*, 22 November 1915.

30. Reform Club Letter Book 1915–16, pp. 130–31, 4 December 1915, to Col. A.M Murray (late RA), CB, MVO.

31. See, for example, Reform Club, General Committee Minutes 1908–1919, p. 372, 14 April 1915.

32. For early protest meetings and the League of the Man in the Street see *HKG*, 15 January and 28 April 1915; see also, for the League and *John Bull*, Gregory, *The Last Great War*, pp. 109–10. For Thorne's claim see *HC Debates*, 1916, Vol. LXXX, col. 405, 21 February 1916. For the no-beer pub see John Gray, *Gin and Bitters*, 1938, p. 110; his father was a publican in Finchley; beer would, though, be kept back for 'a favoured few', including the local police.

33. Commission of Enquiry into Industrial Unrest. No. 5 Division. *Report of the Commissioners for the London and South-Eastern Area*, Cd. 8666, 1917, pp. 4, 8.

34. Arthur Gleason, *Inside the British Isles*, 1917, p. 22.

35. Arthur Foley Winnington-Ingram, *The Potter and the Clay*, 1917, p. 47.

36. Shadwell, *Drink in 1914–1922*, App. VI.

37. *HKG*, 7 and 28 September 1914; *The Times*, 8 September 1914.

38. Michael MacDonagh, *In London during the Great War: The Diary of a Journalist*, 1935, p. 44, 16 December 1914.

39. For Hedderwick, always keen to get his name in the papers, see *HKG*, 18 November 1914. For puritans in the Commons see *HC Debates*, 1914–15, Vol. LXVIII, cols. 762–3, 23 November, and 1305, 26 November 1914. For pressure from the London press see, for instance, the editorial in the *SLP*, 4 December 1914. For Charrington see *ODNB*; and (before the war) Guy Thorne, *The Great Acceptance: The Life Story of F. N. Charrington*, 1912, passim.

40. See Jan Rüger, 'Entertainments', in Jay Winter and Jean-Louis Robert (eds), *Capital Cities at War: Paris, London, Berlin 1914–1919. Vol. 2, A Cultural History*, Cambridge, 2007, pp. 109–15.

41. *The Times*, 25 January 1915.

42. Sandhurst, *From Day to Day: 1914–1915*, p. 189, 5 May 1915 (for the meeting with the Bishop), pp. 218–19, 26 May 1915 (at the Empire).

43. Ibid., p. 320, 3–6 November 1915.

44. Viscount [William] Sandhurst, *From Day to Day: 1916–1921*, 1929, p. 34, 19–20 March 1916.

45. Ibid., pp. 115–16, 9–13 November 1916.

46. For Smith-Dorrien's campaign see *The Times*, 9 October 1916. MEPO 2/1691, 'Indecency in Cinemas': Commissioner's letter to Marchant, 8 December 1916; 'List of 19 Cinemas' visited by Miss Fraser, probably early 1916.

47. For the children's attendants see MEPO 2/1691, letter from Clerk of the LCC, 6 May 1916, and letter from Commissioner to Home Secretary , 28 July 1916; for posters see *The Times*, 9 and 10 November 1916. *HC Debates*, 1916, Vol. LXXXVII, col. 582, 14 November 1916.

48. The attendance figures are in Rüger, 'Entertainments', in Winter and Robert (eds), *Capital Cities at War. Vol. 2*, p. 108. MacDonagh, *In London during the Great War*, p. 44, 16 December 1914. For Dean Inge see *The Times*, 19 February 1916; for Billing see *ODNB*.

49. Mrs Ethel Alec-Tweedie, *Women and Soldiers*, 1918, pp. 56ff, 90–92.

50. See *The Times*, 24 and 26 January, 14 February 1916.

51. For the row about women preachers see *The Times*, 9 and 17 August, 13 September 1916; and 26 September for the Bishop's statement.

52. *The Times*, 16 October 1916. For the Mission generally see Alan Wilkinson, *The Church of England and the First World War*, 1978, pp. 72–8.

53. See Caroline E. Playne, *Britain Holds On, 1917, 1918*, 1933, p. 121; *The Times*, 29 August, 3 and 17 September 1917.

54. Arthur Foley Winnington-Ingram, *Fifty Years' Work in London (1889–1939)*, 1940, pp. 126ff.

55. Cited in Gregory, *The Last Great War*, p. 168.

56. *The Times*, 10 August 1914.

4: The All-Invading Alien

1. George Cross, *Suffolk Punch: A Business Man's Autobiography*, 1939, pp. 217, 274. Ferdinand Tuohy, *The Crater of Mars*, 1929, p. 3. For the musicians see John Lucas, *Thomas Beecham: An Obsession with Music*, 2008, p. 118. Gordon D. Hodge, *56 Years in the London Sugar Market*, 1960, pp. 22–3.

2. The UK figures are given in *HC Debates*, 1914, Vol. LXVI, cols. 564–5, 9 September 1914. The number of Germans and Austro-Hungarians registered in the Metropolitan Police District in December 1917 totalled 39,401; it is likely that many hundreds more will have been deported since the outbreak of war. See *Report of the Commissioner of Police of the Metropolis for the Years 1918 and 1919*, Cd. 543, 1920, Part II, p. 22. For a detailed review of the Act and its operation see Panikos Panayi, *The Enemy in Our Midst: Germans in Britain during the First World War*, New York, 1991, pp. 46–51.

3. *HKG*, 7 August 1914; *SLP*, 7 August 1914.

4. 'Diary of a London Lady (Anonymous)', MISC 29/522 (IWM), 7, 19 and 30 August 1914.

5. Harold Brust, *In Plain Clothes: Further Memoirs of a Political Police Officer*, 1937, p. 86. For the 9,000 see Catriona Pennell, *A Kingdom United: Popular Responses to the Outbreak of the First World War in Britain and Ireland*, Oxford, 2012, p. 106. Basil Thomson, *Queer People*, 1922, p. 38. H. L. Cancellor, *The Life of a London Beak*, 1930, pp. 30–31.

6. See generally Thomas Boghardt, *Spies of the Kaiser: German Covert Operations in Great Britain during the First World War Era*, Basingstoke, 2004, pp. 105ff. The observer was Walter Hambrook, *Hambrook of the Yard*, 1937, pp. 133ff. For the women see Herbert T. Fitch, *Traitors Within: The Adventures of Detective Inspector Herbert T. Fitch*, 1933, pp. 132–9.

7. *HC Debates*, 1914, Vol. LXVI, col. 267. For Olympia see Basil Thomson, *The Scene Changes*, 1939, p. 235. For the vans see Brust, *In Plain Clothes*, pp. 87–8. See generally Panikos Panayi, 'An Intolerant Act by an Intolerant Society: The Internment of Germans in Britain during the First World War', in David Cesarani and Tony Kushner (eds), *The Internment of Aliens in Twentieth Century Britain*, 1993, pp. 53–75. Arrests had preceded the large round-up that proceeded from 28 August.

8. For Prince Louis see Winston S. Churchill, *The World Crisis, Vol. II, 1915*, 1923, Folio Society edn, 2007, pp. 322–3. For Robert Kay and others see David Kynaston, *The City of London. Vol. III, Illusions of Gold 1914–1945*, 1999, pp. 27–8. J. D. Scott, *Siemens Brothers 1858–1958: An Essay in the History of Industry*, 1958, p. 82. London Hospital, House Committee Minutes, 4 October 1915. *HC Debates*, 1914, Vol. LXVIII, col. 1299, 26 November 1914.

9. Reform Club, General Committee Minutes 1908–1919, p. 342, 3 September 1914. Sainsbury Archive, EMP/10/3, memories of George Ridgway of Cricklewood. Henry Fuller Morriss, *Bermondsey's 'Bit' in the Greatest War*, 1923, p. 5. J. A. R. Pimlott, *Toynbee Hall: Fifty Years of Social Progress 1884– 1934*, 1935, p. 190. For the King of Belgium see *SLP*, 5 February 1915. Street name changes required the borough council to lobby the LCC; it did not happen overnight.

10. *HKG*, 14 September 1914; *The Times*, 26 September and 26 October 1914.

11. See Panikos Panayi, 'Anti-German Riots in Britain during the First World War',

in Panikos Panayi (ed.), *Racial Violence in Britain in the Nineteenth and Twentieth Centuries*, 1996, pp. 64–91, especially pp. 68–70; *SLP*, 23 October 1914.

12. *SLP*, 23 October 1914.
13. For the work of the London Society for Women's Suffrage see Helen Fraser, *Women and War Work*, New York, 1918, p. 13; Ray Strachey, *Women's Suffrage and Women's Service: The History of the London and National Society for Women's Service*, 1927, pp. 25–6; Mary S. Allen, *Lady in Blue*, 1936, p. 27.
14. For Dulwich see *SLP*, 4 September 1914; *HKG*, 9 September 1914; Morriss, *Bermondsey's 'Bit' in the Greatest War*, pp. 210–12, and Bermondsey Metropolitan Borough Council, Council Minutes, Vol. 15, 3 November 1914. London Hospital Minutes, 19 October 1914. For Bart's see Viscount [William] Sandhurst, *From Day to Day: 1914–1915*, 1928, p. 74. For the hospitals generally see Sir W. G. Macpherson, *Medical Services: General History Vol. I, Medical Services in the United Kingdom etc.*, 1921, pp. 108–9: there was only one other Belgian hospital outside London, in Folkestone. The numbers of Belgians in the country are in *HC Debates*, 1914–15, Vol. LXXI, col. 818, 29 April 1915.
15. Hallie Eustace Miles, *Untold Tales of War-Time London*, 1930, pp. 60–63, 27 June 1915.
16. Mary Coules, 'First World War Papers. Journal *c.*June 1914–Nov. 1915', 97/25/1, n.p., silences in original. Rose Macaulay, *Non-Combatants and Others*, 1916, pp. 49–50. Playne MSS Collection, Senate House Library, MS1112, Folder 126, Diary 1918, 26 March 1918.
17. *HKG*, 23 October 1914.
18. *HKG*, 10 May 1915.
19. *The Times*, Thursday 13 May 1915. See also W. T. Reay, *The Specials – How They Served London: The Story of the Metropolitan Special Constabulary*, 1920, pp. 159–65; for numbers of arrests etc. see *HC Debates*, 1914–15, Vol. LXXI, col. 1970, 17 May 1915. For an excellent full account see Panayi (ed.), *Racial Violence in Britain*, pp. 64–91. See also Howard Bloch and Graham Hill (eds), *Germans in London: No. 1 East Ham and West Ham Documentary Sources 1865–1919*, 2000.
20. *SLP*, 21 May 1915; *HKG*, 14 May 1915. Cancellor, *The Life of a London Beak*, pp. 43–5.
21. Joseph Williamson, *Father Joe: The Autobiography of Joseph Williamson of Poplar and Stepney*, 1963, pp. 22–3; the south London case is in Mrs C. S. Peel, *How We Lived Then: 1914–1918: A Sketch of Social and Domestic Life in England during the War*, 1929, pp. 37–8. Norman Flower (ed.), *The Journals of Arnold Bennett*, 3 vols, 1932–3, Vol. II, p. 132, 17 and 19 May 1915. For Hun-coddlers see Stephen Hobhouse, *Forty Years and an Epilogue: An Autobiography (1881–1951)*, 1951, p. 145 – Hobhouse was the FEC's chairman. Friends' Emergency Committee, *Report for the Half-Year Ending June 30th, 1915*, 1915, pp. 4–5, 7–8.
22. For the LSE march see Michael MacDonagh, *In London during the Great War: The Diary of a Journalist*, 1935, pp. 61–2, 11 May 1915. *HC Debates*, 1914–15, Vol. LXXI, col. 1618, 11 May 1915; cols. 1841ff, 13 May 1915.
23. *HC Debates*, 1914–15, Vol. LXXII, cols. 359–60; Vol. LXXIII, col. 17; Vol. LXXIV, cols. 7–8, 1468. See generally Panayi, 'An Intolerant Act', in Cesarani and Kushner (eds), *The Internment of Aliens in Twentieth Century Britain*, pp. 58ff.

24. For Rocker and the East End Jewish background see William J. Fishman, *East End Jewish Radicals 1875–1914*, 1975, Ch. 9.

25. Rudolf Rocker, *The London Years*, 1956, p. 249; Fermin Rocker, *The East End Years: A Stepney Childhood*, 1998, p. 125.

26. Brust, *In Plain Clothes*, p. 88.

27. Rocker, *The London Years*, pp. 252–8.

28. Ibid., pp. 328–9.

29. MEPO 2/1633.

30. Churchill, *World Crisis, Vol. II*, p. 38.

31. Thomas Burke, *Out and About: A Note-Book of London in War-Time*, 1919, pp. 26–7, written in 1917. Schonk is an offensive name for a Jew, according to the *Oxford English Dictionary*, which gives its first written appearance as 1938.

32. Burke, *Out and About*, p. 52; MEPO 2/1714, Report of Sub-Divisional Inspector, Tottenham Court Road Police Station, 6 November 1916.

33. Burke, *Out and About*, p. 52. The numbers of Chinese sailors in 1915 are in *HC Debates*, 1916, Vol. LXXXIV, col. 1683, 26 July 1916.

34. *The Times*, 11 September 1916. Edward Tupper, *Seamen's Torch: The Life Story of Captain Edward Tupper, National Union of Seamen*, 1938, pp. 125–7, 164–6. The Pennyfields population is in Survey of London, *Vols XLIII–IV, Poplar, Blackwall and the Isle of Dogs. The Parish of All Saints*, 1994, p. 113. For a wartime picture of Chinatown in 1917 that makes no large claims for expansion see Thomas Burke in the *Evening News*, 24 October 1917, and Burke, *Out and About*, pp. 35–48.

35. London Hospital Minutes, 12 and 27 February 1917 and 16 September 1918; an earlier attempt to recruit 'Chinese gentlemen' to the medical staff met with a refusal to work with 'coloured doctors' on the part of other medics. For Bethnal Green see *HKG*, 19 January 1917. For the Air Ministry see *HC Debates*, 1918, Vol. 106, col. 1405, 4 June 1918.

36. *COR*, Vol. XLII, No. 251, November 1917, pp. 180–93, W. G. Martley, 'Seamen Ashore in the Port of London'. For Cable Street, see Michael Banton, *The Coloured Quarter: Negro Immigrants in an English City*, 1955, pp. 31ff; Peter Fryer, *Staying Power: The History of Black People in Britain*, 1984, pp. 295–6. *The Times*, 3 July 1917.

37. For the Unionist clubs see *HKG*, 21 January 1916. For the LCC see *HC Debates*, 1916, Vol. LXXXI, cols. 1472–3, 1774–5, 10 and 12 April 1916. Bermondsey Council Minutes, 4 July 1916. In the House of Commons see for one instance among many *HC Debates*, 1916, Vol. LXXXIV, cols. 1354–5, 24 July 1916. For the LSE see Kynaston, *City of London. Vol. III*, p. 29, March 1917. For the Unseen Hand, very commonly referred to, see Frederick Arthur Robinson, 'MS Diary 1914–1918', 11335 P. 401–402 (IWM), 7 and 14 June, 27 October 1916. For suicides see *SLP*, 14 July 1916; *The Times*, 8 September 1916.

38. *HC Debates*, 1916, Vol. LXXXIII, cols. 731–2, 27 June 1916.

39. For the Russian background to migration see Fishman, *East End Jewish Radicals*, Ch. 1; for the war and the Jews in the East End generally see the excellent Julia Bush, *Behind the Lines: East London Labour 1914–1919*, 1984, Ch. 6.

40. See ibid., pp. 171ff.

41. For the British government's objectives see *HC Debates*, 1916, Vol. LXXXIV,

cols. 178–9, 11 July 1916; Vol. LXXXVIII, cols. 305–6, 29 November 1916. For the FJPC see *HC Debates*, 1916, Vol. LXXXVII, cols. 1187–8, 21 November 1916; Bush, *Behind the Lines*, pp. 174ff.

42. *The Times*, 21 May 1917; *HC Debates*, 1917, Vol. XCIII, cols. 2266, 23 May, and 2639–41, 25 May 1917; Vol. XCIV, cols. 582–3, 11 June 1917.

43. *The Times*, 25 July 1917. On the raid see *HC Debates*, 1917, Vol. XCVI, cols. 2096–7, 1 August 1917; Thomson, *The Scene Changes*, p. 351; Bush, *Behind the Lines*, p. 181.

44. Cancellor, *The Life of a London Beak*, pp. 69–75.

45. *HKG*, 18 April 1917.

46. *HKG*, 3 October 1917. Mrs Ethel Alec-Tweedie, *Women and Soldiers*, 1918, p. 112.

47. For Commercial Road see *The Times*, 9 August 1917. For Jews in the army see the letter from Henry Goodman about the Hackney Reserve Battalion of the 10th Territorials in *HKG*, 12 October 1914. For Bethnal Green see *The Times*, 25 September 1917; Bush, *Behind the Lines*, pp. 181–2; for the closest pre-war comparison see Bernard Gainer, *The Alien Invasion: The Origins of the Aliens Act of 1905*, 1972, p. 58 – Cornwall Street, St George's-in-the-East, November 1901.

48. J. B. Booth, *Miss 'Billie' Tuchaud: Her Life and Letters*, 1918, pp. 180–82.

49. *The Times*, 13, 15 and 29 July, and 14 August 1918; MacDonagh, *In London during the Great War*, pp. 309–10, 24 August 1918.

50. The cases are taken from a lengthy list in *The Times*, 4 September 1918; for repatriation see *The Times*, 15 October 1918; *HC Debates*, 1918, Vol. 108, cols. 263–4 and 330, 17 October 1918.

51. *HC Debates*, 1918, Vol. 108, col. 545ff, 11 July 1918; see also, for example, Viscount [William] Sandhurst, *From Day to Day: 1916–1921*, 1929, pp. 263–4, 12–24 August 1918.

52. Wandsworth Board of Guardians, Minutes of the Board, 30 January 1919.

53. H. V. Marrot, *The Life and Letters of John Galsworthy*, 1935, pp. 419–20, 441, 445–6, 483, 581.

54. Sir Hubert Llewellyn Smith (ed.), *The New Survey of London Life and Labour. Vol. I, Forty Years of Change*, 1930, p. 82.

55. London Hospital Minutes, 23 November and 2 December 1914. Bermondsey Metropolitan Borough Council, Public Health Committee Minutes, 1913–15, 15 September and 24 November 1914, 26 January 1915; Council Minutes, Vol. 16, 21 December 1915. For Mill Hill see *HC Debates*, 1916, Vol. LXXXI, col. 766, 29 March 1916. For Fairfax see *History of the Ministry of Munitions. Vol. VIII, Control of Industrial Capacity and Equipment, Part II*, pp. 214–15.

5: Work, Work, Work

1. *Acton Gazette*, 7 August 1914.

2. *Daily News*, 25 August 1914.

3. David Kynaston, *The City of London. Vol. III, Illusions of Gold 1914–1945*, 1999, pp. 10–13, 22–3, 38; R. C. Michie (ed.), *The Development of London as a Financial Centre*, 4 vols, 2000, Vol. 3, pp. vii–ix.

4. C. Sheridan Jones, *London in War-Time*, 1917, p. 47, for the journal closures, and for the pruning, Arthur C. Armstrong, *Bouverie Street to Bowling Green Lane: Fifty-Five Years of Specialized Publishing*, 1946, p. 116. J. A. Hammerton, *Books and Myself: Memoirs of an Editor*, 1944, p. 256. Susan Lowndes (ed.), *Diaries and Letters of Marie Belloc Lowndes 1911–1947*, 1971, p. 49, 25 January 1915. For the compositors see *HC Debates*, 1914–15, Vol. LXXII, cols. 1920–21, 1 July 1915. J. M. Dent, *The Memoirs of J. M. Dent 1849–1926, with Some Additions by Hugh R. Dent*, 1928, p. 211, letter to an American friend, 29 December 1916. Jane Ridley, *Edwin Lutyens: His Life, His Wife, His Work*, 2002, p. 211; the *Post Office Directory* for 1915 shows some fourteen houses in Queen Anne's Gate filled with architects', civil engineers' and contractors' offices.

5. For Wardour Street and around see *Estates Gazette (EG)*, 12 June 1915, p. 744, and 2 March 1918, p. 203. For the City see Kynaston, *The City of London. Vol. III*, pp. 22–3; for byrites, a paint pigment formerly a German monopoly, see F. J. Ryland, *Specks on the Dusty Road*, Birmingham, 1937, pp. 126, 131ff.

6. For sweating see E. Sylvia Pankhurst, *The Home Front: A Mirror to Life in England during the World War*, 1932, pp. 51–2; *Annual Report of the Chief Inspector of Factories and Workshops for the Year 1914*, Cd. 8051, 1915, pp. 32, 42. For Shoreditch see Christopher Addison, *Four and a Half Years: A Personal Diary from June 1914 to January 1919*, 2 vols, 1934, Vol. I, p. 41; Addison was the Liberal MP for Hoxton. For the unemployment among women see Gail Braybon, *Women Workers in the First World War*, 1981, p. 44. For little abnormal distress see *COR*, Vol. XXXVI, No. 213, September 1914, p. 191.

7. For the trouser makers see Jerry White, *Rothschild Buildings: Life in an East-End Tenement Block, 1887–1920*, 1980, pp. 212ff. For the shirt maker, theatrical costumier and furrier see *Report of Chief Inspector of Factories for 1914*, pp. 42 and 34. For Dalston see 'A People's Autobiography of Hackney', *Working Lives. Vol. 1 (1905–45)*, 1976, pp. 8–12, Emily Bishop, b. 1899.

8. For changes to machinery and processes see Adam W. Kirkaldy (ed.), *Industry and Finance (Supplementary Volume), Being the Results of Inquiries Arranged by the Section of Economic Science and Statistics of the British Association during the Years 1918 and 1919*, 1920, pp. 74–5. For demand for workshop space see *EG*, 2 January 1915, p. 18, and 1 January 1916, p. 11. The adverts are in *HKG*, 14 November 1917. Esther Kreitman, *Diamonds*, 1944, 1st English edn, 2010, p. 230.

9. Islington Metropolitan Council *Annual Report on the Health & Sanitary Condition of the Metropolitan Borough of Islington*, 59th Annual Report, 1914, pp. 199–200; Henry Fuller Morriss, *Bermondsey's 'Bit' in the Greatest War*, 1923, pp. 34–8, 70–96, 193–200.

10. For the boom see *EG*, 6 January 1917. For the snow see *SLP*, 29 January 1915; *HKG*, 27 January 1915; *The Times*, 23 January 1915, cited in *COR*, Vol. XXXVII, No. 218, February 1915, p. 58.

11. Michael MacDonagh, *In London during the Great War: The Diary of a Journalist*, 1935, pp. 53–4, 14 January 1915.

12. The numbers of dock labourers are in London County Council, *London Statistics. 1914–15 . . . Vol. XXV*, 1916, p. 392. For dockers young and old see H. L. Cancellor, *The Life of a London Beak*, 1930, pp. 52–3. For the Port

generally see Joseph G. Broodbank, *History of the Port of London*, 2 vols, 1921, Vol. II, pp. 459–84.

13. London County Council, *London Statistics. 1915–20 . . . Vol. XXVI*, 1921, pp. 76, 153, 217; London County Council, *London Statistics. 1914–15*, p. 248; *Report of the Commissioners of Prisons and the Directors of Convict Prisons, with Appendices (For the Year ended 31st March, 1919)*, Cd. 374, 1919, p. 5.

14. Bermondsey Metropolitan Borough Council, Public Health Committee Minutes, 25 May 1915. For the builder see C. à Court Repington, *The First World War, 1914–1918: Personal Experiences of Lieut.-Col. C. à Court Repington*, 2 vols, 1921, Vol. II, p. 5, 24 July 1917. Gavin Roynon (ed.), *Home Fires Burning: The Great War Diaries of Georgina Lee*, Stroud, 2006, pp. 210–11, 26 March 1917. For the funerals see *SLP*, 29 December 1916, 5 January 1917. Elspet Fraser-Stephen, *Two Centuries in the London Coal Trade: The Story of Charringtons*, 1952, pp. 116–17. For the milkman see *HKG*, 20 October 1915. Jim Golland (ed.), *When I was a Child: Memories of Childhood in Pinner, Middlesex*, 1984, p. 12.

15. Sainsbury Archive, WAR/1/870, Letters to Managers, 7 and 11 September 1914; Bridget Williams, *The Best Butter in the World: A History of Sainsbury's*, 1994, p. 65. *Daily Mail*, 8 September 1914. For the Army and Navy and elsewhere see Sir Henry Lucy, *The Diary of a Journalist: Fresh Extracts. Vol. III*, 1923, p. 206, 29 May 1915.

16. For the railways see *SLP*, 11 June 1915; *The Times*, 7 June 1915. London County Council, *The Council and the War*, 1920, p. 35: by the end of the war there were 1,716 women tram conductors. For the LGOC see T. C. Barker and Michael Robbins, *A History of London Transport: Passenger Travel and the Development of the Metropolis. Volume II, The Twentieth Century to 1970*, 1974, pp. 197–8. For the clippie's celebrity status see, for example, Sheila Benson, *This is the End*, 1917, p. 113; Gilbert Stone (ed.), *Women War Workers*, 1917, pp. 109ff.

17. For the De Vere see George Cross, *Suffolk Punch: A Business Man's Autobiography*, 1939, p. 279. MacDonagh, *In London during the Great War*, p. 55, 18 March 1915. Reform Club Letter Book 1913–1914, p. 815, 29 September, and p. 949, 10 or 11 November 1914; 1914–15, p. 505, 22 April, and p. 558, 4 May 1915.

18. *SLP*, 10 and 17 September 1915; 31 August 1917. For the sugar boilers see Antony Hugill, *Sugar and All That . . . A History of Tate & Lyle*, 1978, p. 68.

19. For the taxi drivers see *HC Debates*, 1914–15, Vol. LXX, cols. 550–51, 1 March 1915; 1917, Vol. XC, col. 1158, 20 February 1917. London Hospital, House Committee Minutes, 31 May 1915, 7 February, 29 May and 11 December 1916; 10 June 1918.

20. For the march see MacDonagh, *In London during the Great War*, pp. 71–2, 17 July 1915; *The Times*, 19 July 1915; David Lloyd George, *War Memoirs*, 2 vols, new edn, 1938, Vol. I, pp. 174–5 (he gets the date wrong). For the significance of this event in the suffrage campaign see Angela K. Smith, *Suffrage Discourse in Britain during the First World War*, Aldershot, 2005, pp. 71–6. For the numbers employed see *History of the Ministry of Munitions*, 12 vols, 1919–22, Vol. IV, Part IV, p. 146.

21. For wages at Woolwich see Barbara Drake, *Women in the Engineering Trades*, 1917, p. 51n. *HKG*, 2 July 1917. For the status of munitionettes generally see

Angela Woollacott, *On Her Their Lives Depend: Munitions Workers in the Great War*, Berkeley, California, 1994, pp. 1ff.

22. The survey is in Kirkaldy (ed.), *Industry and Finance*, p. 28. For domestic servants and munitions see Drake, *Women in the Engineering Trades*, pp. 41–2; Braybon, *Women Workers in the First World War*, p. 49. For the LGOC see Barker and Robbins, *A History of London Transport*, p. 198. For Alice Kedge see Joyce Marlow (ed.), *Women and the Great War*, 1999, p. 85. For the lady see Lucy, *The Diary of a Journalist*, p. 219, 26 September 1915. Viscount [William] Sandhurst, *From Day to Day: 1916–1921*, 1929, p. 237, 11–17 March 1918. Anne Olivier Bell (ed.), *The Diary of Virginia Woolf. Vol. I, 1915–1919*, 1977, p. 63, 19 October 1917; see also Alison Light, *Mrs Woolf and the Servants*, 2007, pp. 136ff. Mrs Ethel Alec-Tweedie, *Women and Soldiers*, 1918, pp. 41–2. See also Janet S. K. Watson, 'Khaki Girls, VADs, and Tommy's Sisters: Gender and Class in First World War Britain', *International History Review*, Vol. 19, No. 1, February 1997, pp. 32–51, 50–51.

23. For Woolwich see Survey of London, *Vol. 48, Woolwich*, 2012, p. 176. *Munitions*, Vol. VIII, Part II, pp. 33–4, 38; Vol. XI, Part IV, pp. 1–2. For aircraft pre-war see J. E. Martin, *Greater London: An Industrial Geography*, 1966, p. 43.

24. *Munitions*, Vol. VIII, Part II, pp. 16, 34, 38; Vol. XI, Part V, p. 19.

25. For Lloyd George see Samantha L. Bird, *Stepney: Profile of a London Borough from the Outbreak of the First World War to the Festival of Britain, 1914–1951*, Newcastle upon Tyne, 2011, pp. 36–7; *Munitions*, Vol. II, Part II, pp. 123–4. Cross, *Suffolk Punch*, pp. 283–4. For Glover's see Tottenham History Workshop, *How Things Were: Growing up in Tottenham, 1890–1920*, 1982, p. 69. For Klinger and gas masks generally see *Munitions*, Vol. XI, Part II, pp. 68–81, 103–4. W. F. Watson, *Machines and Men: An Autobiography of an Itinerant Mechanic*, 1935, pp. 146–51. Adam Gowans Whyte, *Forty Years of Electrical Progress: The Story of G.E.C.*, 1930, p. 86. A list of munitions makers' former trades is in Bird, *Stepney*, p. 37.

26. London County Council, *The Council and the War*, 1920, pp. 32–4; H. Keatley Moore and W. C. Berwick Sayers (eds), *Croydon and the Great War: The Official History of the War Work of the Borough and Its Citizens from 1914 to 1919. Together with the Croydon Roll of Honour*, 1920, p. 133. Broodbank, *History of the Port of London*, Vol. II, p. 470.

27. J. D. Scott, *Siemens Brothers 1858–1958: An Essay in the History of Industry*, 1958, pp. 228–30. *Munitions*, Vol. VIII, Part I, pp. 35, 44, 46, 52–3, 55; Part II, pp. 139–40, 158, 174–5, 184.

28. For Park Royal, also often known as Perivale, see Grange Museum of Community History and Brent Archive, *Places in Brent: Twyford and Park Royal*, c.2001, pp. 6–8; G. W. R. Gray, *The Rise and Decline of the Park Royal Industrial Estate*, Oxford Polytechnic, Department of Town Planning, MSc Project, 1980, passim; Philip Grant, 'Brent's Women at War and at Peace, 1914–1919', 2010, www. brent.gov.uk/archives, pp. 2–3; Arnold Charles Lee, *As I Recall: The Memoirs of Arnold Charles Lee*, 2010, p. 7. For Park Royal and west London generally see Martin, *Greater London*, pp. 30–31, 40; *Munitions*, Vol. VIII, Part II, pp. 166–7, 173–4, 183–4.

29. Charles Wilson and William Reader, *Men and Machines. A History of D. Napier & Son, Engineers, Ltd 1858–1958*, 1958, pp. 101–10; Alan Vessey, *Napier Powered*, Stroud, 1997, pp. 30ff. For the west London aircraft industry see

Geoffrey Hewlett, *Aviation in and around Brent during the First World War*, 1984, passim. For Waddon see *Munitions*, Vol. VIII, Part II, pp. 204–5.

30. James Royce, *I Stand Nude*, 1937, p. 191.

31. Rose Neighbour (as told to Muriel Burgess), *All of Me: The True Story of a London Rose*, 1979, pp. 7–8; both husbands were away in the army, it seems. Edith Hall, *Canary Girls and Stockpots*, Luton, 1977, pp. 8–11. Naomi Loughnan is in Stone (ed.), *Women War Workers*, pp. 36–45. Sylvia Townsend Warner, *With the Hunted: Selected Writings*, Norwich, 2012, pp. 23–9, 'The Night Shift', *Blackwood's Magazine*, February 1916. See also the excellent oral history of women at Woolwich Arsenal in Deborah Thom, *Nice Girls and Rude Girls: Women Workers in World War I*, 1998, Ch. 7.

32. *The Aircraft Rag. The Magazine of the Employees of the Aircraft Manufacturing Co. Ltd*, Vol. I, No. I, May 1917, pp. 3, 10; Vol. I, No. 2, June 1917, p. 43; Vol. I, No. 4, August 1917, pp. 83ff; Vol. I, No. 6, November 1917, pp. 212, 222; Vol. 2, No. 2, May 1918, pp. 197–8; Vol. I, No. 9, January 1918, p. 21 (the optimist).

33. *HC Debates*, 1914–15, Vol. LXX, cols. 1557–8, 11 March 1915; 1916, Vol. LXXXI, cols. 1489–90, 10 April 1916; *Report of Chief Inspector of Factories for 1917*, p. 18.

34. *Report of Chief Inspector of Factories for 1917*, pp. 21ff; Thom, *Nice Girls and Rude Girls*, Ch. 6; Lloyd George, *War Memoirs*, Vol. I, pp. 352–3.

35. For smoking see three offences reported in *SLP*, 23 March and 29 June 1917. For Camberwell see *SLP*, 8 and 15 September 1916; *The Times*, 13 September 1916. Lloyd George, *War Memoirs*, Vol. I, pp. 353–4.

36. For Napier's see *HC Debates*, 1916, Vol. LXXXII, cols. 17–18, 3 May 1916; Vol. LXXXI, cols. 739–40, 29 March 1916.

37. For Rose see *HKG*, 14 September 1917.

38. Bermondsey MBC, Council Minutes, 7 March 1916, 16 April 1917. Wandsworth Board of Guardians, Minutes of the Board, 28 October 1915. For the Bank of England in 1915 see Lucy, *Diary of a Journalist*, p. 206, 29 May 1915; for banking generally see Kynaston, *The City of London. Vol. III*, p. 25; see also Stone (ed.), *Women War Workers*, Ch. IV, Marie W. Seers, 'Banking'. The balance between commerce and manufacturing is in Jay M. Winter, *The Great War and the British People*, 1986, p. 46.

39. MacDonagh, *In London during the Great War*, p. 119, 7 August 1916. Kreitman, *Diamonds*, pp. 226–7.

40. Alec-Tweedie, *Women and Soldiers*, pp. 3–4.

41. For propaganda see Lucy Masterman, *C. F. G. Masterman: A Biography*, 1939, Ch. 11. *The London Censorship 1914–1919. By Members of the Staff Past and Present*, n.d. [1919], p. 7. For male staff at the Ministry of Munitions see Harold Bellman, *Cornish Cockney: Reminiscences and Reflections*, 1947, p. 59. *Munitions*, Vol. II, Part II, pp. 249–59.

42. *HC Debates*, 1917, Vol. XC, col. 1476, 22 February 1917; 1918, Vol. 107, cols. 1401–2, 1 July 1918. Rose E. Squire, *Thirty Years in the Public Service: An Industrial Retrospect*, 1927, p. 180. Norman Flower (ed.), *The Journals of Arnold Bennett*, 3 vols, 1932–3, Vol. II, pp. 228–9, 28 April 1918. For the Lord Mayor's Show see MacDonagh, *In London during the Great War*, p. 146, 9 November 1916.

43. Wensley Family Archive (*c.*1890–1950): Correspondence, File 1/4, f. 88, Alice Stockwell to Edie Wensley, 17 May 1916.

44. Wensley Family Archive, File 1/6, f. 139, Freda Creighton (25 Sidney Avenue, Bowes Park) to Edie, 11 April 1917.
45. Wensley Family Archive, File 1/7, f. 153, Bobbie Kaine (168 Brompton Road, London, SW3) to Edie, 11 June 1917. 'They Didn't Believe Me', by Jerome Kern with lyrics by Herbert Reynolds, was the popular hit of Christmas 1915.
46. Wensley Family Archive, File 1/6, f. 148, Daisy Parsons to Edie, 21 May 1917, and File 1/9, f. 216, 19 June 1918.

6: *Zeppelin Nights: 1915*

1. D. S. Higgins (ed.), *The Private Diaries of Sir H. Rider Haggard*, 1980, p. 21, 1 January 1915.
2. Anne Olivier Bell (ed.), *The Diary of Virginia Woolf. Vol. I, 1915–1919*, 1977, p. 4, 1 January 1915. See also *The Times*, 1 January 1915, which also reports on the weather and its effects.
3. Vera Brittain, *Testament of Youth: An Autobiographical Study of the Years 1900–1925*, 1933, pp. 118–19.
4. For the bets see Frederick Arthur Robinson, 'MS Diary 1914–1918', 11335 P. 401–402, 10 February, and for people getting used to the war 14 January 1915. Michael MacDonagh, *In London during the Great War: The Diary of a Journalist*, 1935, p. 51, 3 January 1915. Norman Flower (ed.), *The Journals of Arnold Bennett*, 3 vols, 1932–3, Vol. II, pp. 122, 130, 16 January and 12 May 1915.
5. John Middleton Murry, *Between Two Worlds: An Autobiography*, 1935, pp. 343–4.
6. London Ambulance Service (LAS) records, PH/LAS/1/2. *EG*, 6 March 1915, p. 302. *HC Debates*, 1914–15, Vol. LXXV, col. 191, 27 October 1915.
7. See Eric R. Watson (ed.), *Trial of George Joseph Smith*, 1922, passim and p. 48 for women in the courtroom; Arthur Fowler Neil, *Forty Years of Man-Hunting*, 1932, Ch. II.
8. Watson (ed.), *Trial of George Joseph Smith*, p. vii.
9. R. D. Blumenfeld, *All in a Lifetime*, 1931, pp. 20–21, 9 March, and p. 27, 20 August 1915. *The Times*, 1 September 1915, 'Vanished Street Musicians'.
10. The minister was Christopher Addison, *Four and a Half Years: A Personal Diary from June 1914 to January 1919*, 2 vols, 1934, Vol. I, p. 55, 15 January 1915. Lady Cynthia Asquith, *Diaries 1915–1918*, 1968, p. 8, 16 April 1915: she 'finally ran down skirt'. Simon Litman, *Prices and Price Control in Great Britain and the United States during the World War*, New York, 1920, pp. 24–5 (food), 34–5 (coal). Reform Club Letter Books 1915–1916, p. 158, 14 December and pp. 176–7, 17 December 1915.
11. On refuse see Bermondsey Metropolitan Borough Council, Council Minutes, 2 March 1915. For snow clearing see *HKG*, 3 December 1915. London Hospital, House Committee Minutes, 17 May 1915. For the LCC see A. G. Gardiner, *John Benn and the Progressive Movement*, 1925, p. 402; Bernard Donoughue and G. W. Jones, *Herbert Morrison: Portrait of a Politician*, 1973, p. 39. For Westminster see *Daily News*, 13 December 1915, letter from S. K. Ratcliffe. *HKG*, 15, 17, 19 November 1915. For Kew see *HC Debates*, 1914–15, Vol. LXXVII, col. 12, 20 December 1915.

12. *HKG*, 12 March 1915, for a charge of crying false news. The forgers are in Basil Thomson, *Queer People*, 1922, Ch. VI.

13. See, for example, the 'Editorial Notes' in COR, Vol. XXXVII, No. 220, April 1915, pp. 169–70.

14. For the trams see *The Times*, 17, 20, 25, 31 May and 2 June 1915. For the police see HC *Debates*, 1914–15, Vol. LXX, col. 979, 4 March 1915.

15. For Neuve Chapelle see Trevor Wilson, *The Myriad Faces of War: Britain and the Great War, 1914–1918*, Cambridge, 1986, pp. 122–5. For the monthly casualties see Winston S. Churchill, *The World Crisis. Vol. III, 1916–1918*, 1927, Folio Society edn, 2007, Appendix A. The 'orgy of political intrigue' is in Stephen McKenna, *While I Remember*, 1921, p. 178.

16. For Aubers and Festubert see London County Council, *Record of Service in the Great War 1914–18 by Members of the Council's Staff*, 1922, pp. 23–5; Adrian Gregory, *The Last Great War: British Society and the First World War*, Cambridge, 2008, p. 123. For Loos see Wilson, *The Myriad Faces of War*, pp. 258–9.

17. Philip Gibbs, *Realities of War*, 1920, pp. 139–40.

18. Asquith, *Diaries 1915–1918*, p. 17, 8 May 1915. Mary Coules, 'First World War Papers. Journal c.June 1914–Nov. 1915', 97/25/1, 'Journal', n.p. Gavin Roynon (ed.), *Home Fires Burning: The Great War Diaries of Georgina Lee*, Stroud, 2006, pp. 88, 100, 101, 107, 141. Edith Marjorie Bunbury, 'Diary of the European War Sept. 1914–Nov. 1915', A/FH/F15/001/002, 3 and 14 July, 2 and 12 September 1915. John Julius Norwich (ed.), *The Duff Cooper Diaries 1915–1951*, 2005, pp. 17ff, 1 October 1915 and following; see also Asquith, *Diaries 1915–1918*, pp. 90–91, 19 October 1915.

19. Frederick Brittain, 'World War I Diaries. The Military Hospital Chelsea, Dec. 1914 to Aug. 1915; Aboard the Hospital Ship Egypt, Aug. 1915 to April 1919', 99/51/1 (IWM), p. 7, 15 March, and p. 8, 16 May and 11 June 1915. London Hospital Minutes, 17 May 1915.

20. Captn. Ralph Ingram Moore, 'Diary 1915–16', PR 88/206 (AWM), 30 October 1915 and following.

21. For the schools see H. J. Bennett, *I was a Walworth Boy*, 1980, p. 43; *HKG*, 24 February 1915. On the town halls see (for Bethnal Green) *HKG*, 19 February 1915; Bermondsey Council Minutes, 6 July 1915. Cavell's statue, by George Frampton, was unveiled on 17 March 1920; her body was returned to England and buried at Norwich Cathedral in May 1919. London Hospital Minutes, 18 October and 1 November 1915. Asquith, *Diaries 1915–1918*, p. 94, 29 October 1915.

22. Sir Henry Lucy, *The Diary of a Journalist: Fresh Extracts. Vol. III*, 1923, pp. 217–18, 24 September 1915.

23. Lucy Masterman, *C. F. G. Masterman: A Biography*, 1939, p. 305.

24. Winston S. Churchill, *The World Crisis. Vol. II, 1915*, 1923, Folio Society edn, 2007, pp. 37–8. For the Chelmsford rumour see *HKG*, 8 January 1915. London Hospital Minutes, 11 January 1915. Susan Lowndes (ed.), *Diaries and Letters of Marie Belloc Lowndes 1911–1947*, 1971, p. 47. For the East Anglian raids see Joseph Morris, *The German Air Raids on Great Britain 1914–1918*, 1925, pp. 17–18. Hallie Eustace Miles, *Untold Tales of War-Time London*, 1930, pp. 31–2, 26 January 1915. *HKG*, 22 January 1915.

25. Asquith, *Diaries 1915–1918*, p. 13, 28 April 1915. Miles, *Untold Tales of War-Time London*, p. 34, 26 January–22 February 1915.

26. For the Estuary Raids see Morris, *The German Air Raids on Great Britain 1914–1918*, pp. 25–8. *HKG*, 26 May 1915.

27. The best account of the raid is in Frank Morison, *War on Great Cities: A Study of the Facts*, 1937, pp. 37ff; see also Morris, *The German Air Raids on Great Britain 1914–1918*, pp. 30ff. The music hall is in MEPO 2/1650, report from H Division, 1 June 1915. Sylvia E. Pankhurst, *The Home Front: A Mirror to Life in England during the World War*, 1932, pp. 192–4.

28. Morison, *War on Great Cities*, pp. 57–67; LAS, Call Log Book, 7–8 September 1915. See also Douglas H. Robinson, *The Zeppelin in Combat: A History of the German Naval Airship Division, 1912–1918*, 1962, pp. 103ff.

29. Miles, *Untold Tales of War-Time London*, pp. 69ff. Morison, *War on Great Cities*, pp. 68–82; for the clock at the Dolphin see the photo opp. p. 74. For Asquith see Mark Pottle (ed.), *Champion Redoubtable: The Diaries and Letters of Violet Bonham Carter 1914–1945*, 1998, p. 78, 16 September 1915.

30. Coules, 'Journal', n.p. Robinson, 'Diary', 10 September 1915. Flower (ed.), *The Journals of Arnold Bennett*, Vol. II, pp. 143–4, 11 September 1915. Viscount [William] Sandhurst, *From Day to Day: 1914–1915*, 1928, pp. 292–3, 11–12 September 1915.

31. Morison, *War on Great Cities*, pp. 87ff. Mrs Desmond 'Rita' Humphreys, *Recollections of a Literary Life*, 1936, pp. 236–7, was at Wyndham's Theatre that night. Rose Macaulay, *Non-Combatants and Others*, 1916, p. 64. Sandhurst, *From Day to Day: 1914–1915*, pp. 308–9, 13 October 1915. The cigarette ends are in Pankhurst, *The Home Front*, p. 192; for the street lamps, 200–300 smashed in Shoreditch in September, see *HKG*, 6 October 1915.

32. *HKG*, 2 June 1915. Violet Hunt and Ford Madox Hueffer, *Zeppelin Nights: A London Entertainment*, 1916, pp. 1–2.

33. A. Rawlinson, *In Defence of London, 1915–1918*, 1923, p. 50.

34. For the numbers of guns see ibid., p. 55. For the Lord Mayor's Show see MacDonagh, *In London during the Great War*, p. 88, 10 November 1915. Henry Fuller Morriss, *Bermondsey's 'Bit' in the Greatest War*, 1923, p. 47.

35. Miles, *Untold Tales of War-Time London*, p. 74, 6 October 1915.

36. For Bart's see Sandhurst, *From Day to Day: 1914–1915*, p. 312, 20–22 October 1915. *HC Debates*, 1914–15, Vol. LXXIV, col. 2120, 21 October 1915; Vol. LXXV, cols. 336–40, 28 October 1915.

37. Miles, *Untold Tales of War-Time London*, p. 74, 2–5 October 1915, 'They say that London has not been so dark since the days of George the First . . .' *HKG*, 2, 5, 7 July, 15 September, 18, 20, 22, 25 October 1915. Morris, *The German Air Raids on Great Britain 1914–1918*, Ch. VI.

38. For Kitchener's request see Bermondsey Council Minutes, 4 May 1915. For Shoreditch see *HKG*, 16 June 1915. *Hampstead and Highgate Express*, 31 July 1915; see also Caroline E. Playne, *Society at War, 1914–1916*, 1931, p. 295.

39. *The Times*, 4 October 1915; MacDonagh, *In London during the Great War*, pp. 78–9, 2 October, and pp. 79–80, 6 October 1915 for the white feathers. *HKG*, 11 October 1915.

40. Sandhurst, *From Day to Day: 1914–1915*, p. 220, 29 May 1915, in the aftermath of the anti-German riots which he thought had 'whetted' the Londoners' 'appetite for loot'. For the moves towards conscription see Wilson, *Myriad Faces of War*, pp. 166–9.

41. Playne, *Society at War, 1914–1916*, p. 274; Brock Millman, *Managing Domestic Dissent in First World War Britain*, 2000, pp. 51–6.

42. Edward Legge, *King Edward, The Kaiser and War*, 1917, pp. 119–20. Miles, *Untold Tales of War-Time London*, p. 49, 25 April–3 May and pp. 40ff, 5 March 1915; see also Roynon (ed.), *Home Fires Burning*, p. 125, 7 August 1915. John Bickersteth (ed.), *The Bickersteth Diaries 1914–1918*, 1995, p. 52.

43. Arthur James Rixon, 'Diaries 1915–16', 99/13/1 (IWM), 19 August 1915; Sergeant-Major Rixon was killed in action, 9 April 1917, Ypres.

44. Celia Lee, *Jean, Lady Hamilton 1861–1941: A Soldier's Wife (Wife of General Sir Ian Hamilton). A Biography from Her Diaries*, 2001, p. 121.

45. Masterman, *C. F. G. Masterman*, p. 305. *The Times*, 20, 22, 27, 28 and 31 December 1915. *SLP*, 31 December 1915.

46. Brittain, *Testament of Youth*, pp. 188, 231–2, 236. Clare was Roland's sister.

7: *Come Home, Come Home, You Million Ghosts*

1. COR, Vol. XL, No. 236, August 1916, pp. 47ff. For the war causes see E. Sylvia Pankhurst, *The Home Front: A Mirror to Life in England during the World War*, 1932, pp. 38–9; Caroline E. Playne, *Society at War, 1914–1916*, 1931, pp. 47ff.

2. H. V. Marrot, *The Life and Letters of John Galsworthy*, 1935, pp. 447–8. Sainsbury Archive, WAR/1/872, Letter to Managers, 18 August 1914. Bermondsey Metropolitan Borough Council, Council Minutes, Vol. 15, 3 November 1914.

3. See *HKG*, 1 May (for St George's Day) and 5 July 1916 (for the truce); Bermondsey Council Minutes, 7 November 1916. The advert is for W. Jelks and Sons, see *The Times*, 24 May 1916, frequently repeated.

4. *The Times*, 13 June (for the women's bureau head) and 20 June 1916 (for Lady Gort et al.). Lady Cynthia Asquith, *Diaries 1915–1918*, 1968, p. 291, 13 April 1917. J. B. Booth, *Miss 'Billie' Tuchaud: Her Life and Letters*, 1918, pp. 97–8.

5. COR, Vol. XXXVII, No. 222, June 1915, p. 284; Cecil Chapman, *The Poor Man's Court of Justice: Twenty-Five Years as a Metropolitan Magistrate*, 1925, pp. 231–3, for the two named frauds; *HKG*, 23 August (for the amputee), 15 and 22 December 1916.

6. C. Sheridan Jones, *London in War-Time*, 1917, pp. 64–5.

7. For the great sale of April 1915 see *EG*, 17 April 1915, pp. 489–93, 1 May 1915, p. 553. Viscount [William] Sandhurst, *From Day to Day: 1916–1921*, 1929, p. 228, 3 February 1918 (Lady Sandhurst was the daughter); for the necklace see *Manchester Guardian*, 24 June 1918. *The Times*, 13 July 1916.

8. For Mrs Sassoon see Lady Cynthia Colville, *Crowded Life*, 1963, pp. 90–91. Marrot, *The Life and Letters of John Galsworthy*, pp. 423–5, September to November 1916. For Lamington see C. à Court Repington, *The First World War, 1914–1918: Personal Experiences of Lieut.-Col. C. à Court Repington*, 2 vols, 1921, Vol. II, p. 165, 2 January 1918.

9. Jeffrey S. Reznick, *Healing the Nation: Soldiers and the Culture of Caregiving in Britain during the First World War*, Manchester, 2004, pp. 54–6, for the nurse ratios, and pp. 55–6 for Mrs Guest's. Robert Graves, *Goodbye to All That*, 1929 (Penguin edn, 1986), p. 187.

10. Repington, *The First World War, 1914–1918*, Vol. I, p. 428, 10 January 1917.

11. Arthur Roland Pelly, 'MS Diary 1915', 91/15/1 (IWM), 12–13 August; 15 September; 5, 7 October; 12, 25, 26 November; 15 December 1915.

12. *The Times*, 3 April 1916, Court Circular.

13. For sacrifice and fun see Caroline E. Playne, *Britain Holds On, 1917, 1918*, 1933, pp. 167–8. Hallie Eustace Miles, *Untold Tales of War-Time London*, 1930, p. 10. The poetry reading was a big occasion: see Susan Lowndes (ed.), *Diaries and Letters of Marie Belloc Lowndes 1911–1947*, 1971, p. 71, 12 April 1916; Asquith, *Diaries 1915–1918*, p. 152, 11 April 1916. London Hospital, House Committee Minutes (London Hospital Archive), 21 June 1915. For the Academy see Gavin Roynon (ed.), *Home Fires Burning: The Great War Diaries of Georgina Lee*, Stroud, 2006, p. 80, 21 January 1915.

14. Asquith, *Diaries 1915–1918*, pp. 133–4, 21 February 1916.

15. For the Alhambra see Repington, *The First World War, 1914–1918*, Vol. I, pp. 68–9, 18 November 1915. Booth, *Miss 'Billie' Tuchaud*, pp. 48–9.

16. Playne, *Society at War, 1914–1916*, p. 36. Roynon (ed.), *Home Fires Burning*, p. 12, 14 August 1914.

17. *HKG*, 26 November 1915; Anon., *A Record of the Honoured Men of Wimbledon & Merton Who Fell in the Great War 1914–18, with Notes of Local Activities during the Same Period*, 1921, pp. 99–100. Roynon (ed.), *Home Fires Burning*, passim.

18. E. Sylvia Pankhurst, *The Home Front: A Mirror to Life in England during the World War*, 1932, p. 207. Asquith, *Diaries 1915–1918*, p. 34, 31 May 1915.

19. Anon., *A Record of the Honoured Men of Wimbledon & Merton . . .*, pp. 63–4.

20. W. T. Reay, *The Specials – How they Served London: The Story of the Metropolitan Special Constabulary*, 1920, pp. 20ff. Lord William Beveridge, *Power and Influence*, 1953, p. 121.

21. Roynon (ed.), *Home Fires Burning*, p. 51, 25 October 1914.

22. Mrs Ethel Alec-Tweedie, *Women and Soldiers*, 1918, p. 54. For station buffets generally see Richard Morris, *The Man Who Ran London during the Great War: The Diaries and Letters of Lieutenant General Sir Francis Lloyd GCVO, KCB, DSO (1853–1926)*, Barnsley, 2009, pp. 87, 114. For Lady Bee see Repington, *The First World War, 1914–1918*, Vol. I, p. 390, 20 November 1916. For Katharine see Asquith, *Diaries 1915–1918*, p. 47, 25 June 1915.

23. Roynon (ed.), *Home Fires Burning*, p. 94, 18 March 1915. London Hospital Minutes, 26 October 1914, Matron's Report of 18 October, pp. 2–5.

24. For the other ranks of VADs see Sir W. G. Macpherson, *Medical Services: General History. Vol. I, Medical Services in the United Kingdom etc.*, 1921, pp. 141–2. Winifred L. B. Tower, 'Journal, 26 July to October 1914, and Some Diary Notes, October 1914 to February 1916', p. 20, probably September 1915. Asquith, *Diaries 1915–1918*, pp. 280–82 and 285, 20–21 and 28 March 1917.

25. Diana Cooper, *The Rainbow Comes and Goes*, 1958, pp. 123, 127–8, 136, 163. Asquith, *Diaries 1915–1918*, p. 223, 5 October 1916.

26. Cooper *The Rainbow Comes and Goes*, p. 166.

27. Enid Bagnold, *A Diary Without Dates*, 1918 (Windmill Library edn, 1933), pp. 41–2.

28. Ibid., p. 56.

29. Vera Brittain, *Testament of Youth: An Autobiographical Study of the Years 1900–1925*, 1933, p. 210.

30. Bagnold, *Diary Without Dates*, pp. 22–4.

31. London Hospital Minutes, 12 November 1917. Pelly, 'MS Diary 1915', 19 October and 31 December 1915.

32. Deborah Thom, *Nice Girls and Rude Girls: Women Workers in World War I*, 1998, pp. 18–19.

33. David John Robinson, 'The Wensley Family at War, Work and Play (1890 to 1950)', unpublished typescript, 2007, Ch. 3.

34. Wensley Family Archive (*c.*1890–1950): Correspondence, File 1/7, f151, Daisy Parsons to Edie Wensley, 8 June 1917; f164, Maud Davis to EW, 19 and 25 August 1917; f159, HW to EW, 1 [?3] August 1917.

35. Robinson, 'The Wensley Family at War, Work and Play (1890 to 1950)', Ch. 4. The Alliance of Honour membership certificate is in File 1/7, f167, 9 October 1917.

36. Robinson, 'The Wensley Family at War, Work and Play (1890 to 1950)', Ch. 4.

37. Wensley Family Archive, File 1/10, f239.

38. Stella Benson, *This is the End*, 1917, p. 97.

39. C. Delisle Burns, *A Short History of Birkbeck College (University of London)*, 1924, pp. 148–9. London County Council, *Record of Service in the Great War 1914–18 by Members of the Council's Staff*, 1922.

40. For Trafalgar Street see *SLP*, 30 July and 17 September 1915; 6, 13, 20 and 27 October 1916. Mark Connelly, *The Great War, Memory and Ritual: Commemoration in the City and East London, 1916–1939*, 2002, p. 26 for the Mawney Estate, Romford, and passim for an excellent overview of the phenomenon. For a similar tribute in a London slum street see Jerry White, *The Worst Street in North London: Campbell Bunk, Islington, Between the Wars*, 1986, pp. 110–11. For the Bishop of London, see, for instance, his dedication of a shrine in De Beauvoir Town, *HKG*, 20 October 1916.
    For Dalston see *HKG*, 20 July 1917 and for watchnight, 3 January 1916. For Roman Catholic churches see, for instance, *Catholic Herald*, 1 January 1916; for Anglican churches see Adrian Gregory and Annette Becker, 'Religious sites and practices' in Jay M. Winter and Jean-Louis Robert (eds), *Capital Cities at War: Vol. 2, A Cultural History, Paris, London, Berlin 1914–1919*, Cambridge, 2007, pp. 383–427; and W. R. Titterton, *London Scenes*, 1920, pp. 128–30, probably written 1917.

41. D. S. Higgins (ed.), *The Private Diaries of Sir H. Rider Haggard*, 1980, p. 44, 24 December 1915. Anon., *Thomas Hancock Nunn: The Life of a Social Reformer. Written by His Friends for His Friends*, 1942, p. 138. Playne MSS Collection, Senate House Library, MS1112, Folder 6, Diary 1916, 26 November 1916.

42. S. C. Williams, *Religious Belief and Popular Culture in Southwark c. 1880–1939*, Oxford, 1999, pp. 100 and 69–70; see also Playne, *Society at War, 1914–1916*, p. 246.

43. J. M. Dent, *The memoirs of J. M. Dent 1849–1926, with Some Additions by Hugh R. Dent*, 1928, p. 217, letter to Miss Vida Scudder, 27 July 1917. Andrew Lycett, *Conan Doyle: The Man Who Created Sherlock Holmes*, 2007, pp. 359, 367–8.

44. For the Bishop see Alan Wilkinson, *The Church of England and the First World War*, 1978, p. 179. W. R. Inge, *Diary of a Dean: St Paul's 1911–1934*, 1949, p. 35, 23 January 1917. Playne, *Society at War, 1914–1916*, p. 243. Asquith, *Diaries 1915–1918*, pp. 171–2, 206, 245–6, 5–6 June, 17 August, 16 December 1916. John Julius Norwich (ed.), *The Duff Cooper Diaries 1915–1951*, 2005, p. 46, 14 January 1917.

45. *Observer*, 31 December 1916; *HKG*, 5 April 1916.

46. Anon., *Thomas Hancock Nunn*, p. 138. Ford Madox Ford, *Some Do Not . . .*, 1924, p. 193. Roynon (ed.), *Home Fires Burning*, p. 103, 2 May 1915. G. S. Street, *At Home in the War*, 1918, p. 17.

8: *In Imminent Fear of an Earthquake: 1916*

1. For the trees see Gavin Roynon (ed.), *Home Fires Burning: The Great War Diaries of Georgina Lee*, Stroud, 2006, pp. 162–3, 1 April 1916; for the 'macintoshes' see Arnold Bennett, *The Pretty Lady: A Novel*, 1918, p. 320.

2. Viscount [William] Sandhurst, *From Day to Day: 1916–1921*, 1929, p. 51, 2–10 May 1916. The Act became operative on 25 May.

3. Richard Church, *The Golden Sovereign: A Conclusion to 'Over the Bridge'*, 1957, p. 221.

4. The estimates are in Adrian Gregory, *The Last Great War: British Society and the First World War*, Cambridge, 2008, p. 101.

5. *HKG*, 1 March 1916; see, for example, *SLP*, 25 February 1916 and subsequent issues. For Hamilton see *HC Debates*, 1916, Vol. LXXXIV, cols. 643–4, 17 July 1916. C. à Court Repington, *The First World War, 1914–1918: Personal Experiences of Lieut.-Col. C. à Court Repington*, 2 vols, 1921, Vol. I, p. 120, 4 February 1916.

6. Walter Southgate, *That's the Way It was: A Working-class Autobiography 1890–1950*, 1982, pp. 118–19. Bernard Donoughue and G. W. Jones, *Herbert Morrison: Portrait of a Politician*, 1973, pp. 40–41; Lord [Herbert] Morrison of Lambeth, *Herbert Morrison: An Autobiography*, 1960, pp. 65–6.

7. Stephen Hobhouse, *Forty Years and an Epilogue: An Autobiography (1881–1951)*, 1951, pp. 155ff. R. M. Fox, *Smoky Crusade*, 1937, pp. 226ff. Fenner Brockway, *Inside the Left: Thirty Years of Platform, Press, Prison and Parliament*, 1942, p. 77; Fenner Brockway, *Bermondsey Story: The Life of Alfred Salter*, 1949, p. 65. For the wider picture see John W. Graham, *Conscription and Conscience: A History 1916–1919*, 1922, Chs. II–III; the excellent David Boulton, *Objection Overruled*, 1967, Chs. 5–8; Ken Weller, *'Don't be a Soldier!' The Radical Anti-War Movement in North London 1914–1918*, 1985, Ch. 9.

8. For Camden see Wal Hannington, *Never on Our Knees*, 1967, pp. 36–7. For Pankhurst see Barbara Winslow, *Sylvia Pankhurst: Sexual Politics and Political Activism*, 1996, pp. 80–81. For Bermondsey see *SLP*, 7 January 1916. For the NLHL see Fox, *Smoky Crusade*, pp. 195–8. For the Brotherhood Church see Weller, *'Don't be a Soldier!'*, Ch. 16.

9. Keith Robbins, *The Abolition of War: The 'Peace Movement' in Britain, 1915–1919*, Cardiff, 1976, pp. 77ff. For the Federal Council see *SLP*, 7 April 1916. Brockway, *Inside the Left*, p. 70.

10. For violence against the NCF, see *HC Debates*, 1916, Vol. LXXXII, cols. 1534–5, 17 May 1916. For Trafalgar Square see E. Sylvia Pankhurst, *The Home Front: A Mirror to Life in England during the World War*, 1932, pp. 304–6; Brock Millman, *Managing Domestic Dissent in First World War Britain*, 2000, pp. 84–6.

11. Hobhouse, *Forty Years and an Epilogue*, pp. 153–4.

12. For Chiswick see *Manchester Guardian*, 15 September 1916; for the Ring see *SLP*, 8 September 1916. For Soho see *HC Debates*, 1916, Vol. LXXXVIII, col. 1454, 20 December 1916. See also Millman, *Managing Dissent*, pp. 78–9. For false papers see *HKG*, 25 September 1916; *SLP*, 6 October 1916.

13. Michael MacDonagh, *In London during the Great War: The Diary of a Journalist*, 1935, pp. 118–19, 7 August 1916. Frederick Arthur Robinson, 'MS Diary 1914–1918', 11335 P. 401–402, 21 June and 31 July 1916. For street watering and schools see *HC Debates*, 1916, Vol. LXXXII, cols. 1793 and 2572–3, 22 May 1916; *HC Debates*, 1916, Vol. LXXXI, cols. 2441–6, 19 April 1916.

14. Christopher Addison, *Four and a Half Years: A Personal Diary from June 1914 to January 1919*, 2 vols, 1934, Vol. I, p. 215. On early closing see 'A Protest' by a 'Dalston Tradesman', *HKG*, 20 October 1916.

15. Edward Legge, *King Edward, The Kaiser and War*, 1917, p. 124, for club spending. Reform Club Letter Book, 1915–16, p. 647, 1 May 1916 for the reduction in accounts for 1915; p. 666, 6 May 1916 for resignations taking effect in May; 1916–17, p. 306, 17 November 1916, for the game. See Sir Henry Lucy, *The Diary of a Journalist: Fresh Extracts. Vol. III*, 1923, pp. 275–6, for clubs commandeered. Numbers of club members (the Reform had 1,400) from Karl Baedeker, *London and Its Environs: Handbook for Travellers*, 1911, p. 61.

16. Lucy, *The Diary of a Journalist*, p. 269, 22 July 1916. For Ciro's see Sandhurst, *From Day to Day: 1916–1921*, pp. 119–20, 21–25 November 1916; *The Times*, 4 September, 1, 24 November, 13, 15, 21, 26 December 1916.

17. Sandhurst, *From Day to Day: 1916–1921*, p. 111, 27 October 1916. *The Times*, Law Reports, 31 January and 6 February 1917.

18. George Bernard Shaw, *Heartbreak House*, 1919, Preface. John Lucas, *Thomas Beecham: An Obsession with Music*, 2008, pp. 131–2; W. N. P. Barbellion, *The Journal of a Disappointed Man*, 1919, pp. 234–5, *c.*5 May 1916. Wensley Family Archive (*c.*1890–1950): Correspondence, Folder 1/5, folio 123, letter to Edie Wensley from Freda Creighton, 23 November 1916.

19. MacDonagh, *In London during the Great War*, pp. 143–4, mid-October 1916; p. 146, 9 November 1916 (Lord Mayor's Show). Capt. Ralph Ingram Moore, 'Diary 1915–16', PR88/206 (AWM), pp. 169–72, 25 April 1916. For the submarine see *HC Debates*, 1916, Vol. LXXXIV, cols. 1195–6, 20 July 1916; Robinson, 'Diary', 21 July 1916.

20. For the Irish club raids see *HC Debates*, 1916, Vol. LXXXII, col. 1809, 22 May; Vol. LXXXIV, cols. 2068–9, 31 July; Vol. LXXXV, cols. 1024–5, 9 August 1916. For the trenches see Richard Morris, *The Man Who Ran London during the Great War: The Diaries and Letters of Lieutenant General Sir Francis Lloyd GCVO, KCB, DSO (1853–1926)*, Barnsley, 2009, p. 99. For Kitchener and the cheers see Norman Flower (ed.), *The Journals of Arnold Bennett*, 3 vols, 1932–3, Vol. II, pp. 165–6, 8 June; Playne MSS Collection, Senate House Library, MS1112, Folder 6, Diary 1916; see generally MacDonagh, *In London during the Great War*, pp. 109–10, 6 June 1916.

21. Sandhurst, *From Day to Day: 1916–1921*, pp. 67–8, 22–3 June 1916; Vera Brittain, *Testament of Youth: An Autobiographical Study of the Years 1900–1925*, 1933, p. 274.

22. Playne MSS, Diary 1916, 1 and 4 July 1916. London Hospital, House Committee Minutes, 10 July 1916. Brittain, *Testament of Youth*, pp. 279–80. Robert Graves, *Goodbye to All That*, 1929 (Penguin edn, 1986), p. 187.

23. Brittain, *Testament of Youth*, pp. 279–80.

24. R. D. Blumenfeld, *All in a Lifetime*, 1931, p. 65, 20 October 1916.

25. F. M. Cutlack (ed.), *War Letters of General Monash*, Sydney, 2nd edn, 1934, p. 141, 16 October 1916. London County Council, *Record of Service in the Great War 1914–18 by Members of the Council's Staff*, 1922, p. 47; Bermondsey Metropolitan Borough Council, Council Minutes, Vol. 16, 17 October 1916. For the whistling see *HC Debates*, 1916, Vol. LXXXV, cols. 1632–3, 15 August 1916. Todd Longstaffe-Gowan, *The London Square: Gardens in the Midst of Town*, 2012, pp. 203–4.

26. Ian F. W. Beckett, *The Making of the First World War*, 2012, Ch. 5; Jan Rüger, 'Entertainments', in Jay Winter and Jean-Louis Robert (eds), *Capital Cities at War: Paris, London, Berlin 1914–1919. Vol. 2, A Cultural History*, Cambridge, 2007, pp. 128–9. For the queues see *The Times*, 5 September 1916. Lady Cynthia Asquith, *Diaries 1915–1918*, 1968, p. 214, 9 September 1916. D. S. Higgins (ed.), *The Private Diaries of Sir H. Rider Haggard*, 1980, p. 84, 27 September 1916; Robinson, 'Diary', 8 September 1916.

27. Hallie Eustace Miles, *Untold Tales of War-Time London*, 1930, pp. 88–9, 1–15 January, pp. 89–90, 1 February 1916. For the raids of January to August 1916 see Joseph Morris, *The German Air Raids on Great Britain 1914–1918*, 1925, pp. 75–120. Blumenfeld, *All in a Lifetime*, p. 50, 11 February 1916. For the scare see Roynon (ed.), *Home Fires Burning*, p. 153, 1 February 1916. For the adverts see Sandhurst, *From Day to Day: 1916–1921*, p. 48, 21–24 April 1916.

28. For the Commissioner's view see ibid., pp. 26–7, 26 February 1916. London Hospital, Minutes, 20 March 1916. For the PO warnings see Robinson, 'Diary', 12 February 1916.

29. *HC Debates*, 1916, Vol. LXXX, col. 81ff, 16 February 1916. For Lloyd-George's view see G. A. R. Riddell, *Lord Riddell's War Diary 1914–1918*, 1933, p. 156, 17 February 1916. For Billing see *ODNB*; for the Liberal view see A. G. Gardiner, *John Benn and the Progressive Movement*, 1925, pp. 438–9, citing a letter from John Williams Benn of 13 March 1916; Billing forced his first adjournment debate on air defences on 5 April 1916: *HC Debates*, 1916, Vol. LXXXI, col. 1299ff.

30. See Morris, *The German Air Raids on Great Britain 1914–1918*, pp. 75, 94–5, 105–9, 119.

31. Cutlack (ed.), *Letters of General Monash*, p. 124, 18 July 1916.

32. Morris, *The German Air Raids on Great Britain 1914–1918*, pp. 120–22; Frank Morison, *War on Great Cities: A Study of the Facts*, 1937, pp. 99–100; Douglas H. Robinson, *The Zeppelin in Combat: A History of the German Naval Airship Division, 1912–1918*, 1962, pp. 167–9.

33. H. V. Marrot, *The Life and Letters of John Galsworthy*, 1935, p. 422, 3 September 1916; Robinson, *The Zeppelin in Combat*, pp. 169–79.

34. Morison, *War on Great Cities*, pp. 102–5; Robinson, *The Zeppelin in Combat*, pp. 1–11, 183–9.

35. MacDonagh, *In London during the Great War*, pp. 134–5; Peterson was mistaken for the captured commander, whose name wrongly appeared on the coffin.

36. Morris, *The German Air Raids on Great Britain 1914–1918*, pp. 145–8; Robinson, *The Zeppelin in Combat*, pp. 193–6. MacDonagh, *In London during*

the Great War, pp. 135–6, 2 October 1916; see also the very similar recollection in Fox, Smoky Crusade, p. 223.

37. Morris, The German Air Raids on Great Britain 1914–1918, pp. 206–7.

38. Roynon (ed.), Home Fires Burning, p. 152. 25 January 1916. Reform Club General Committee Minutes 1908–19, p. 426, 9 March 1916 (cigars); Letter Book, 1915–16, p. 234, 1 January (bread), p. 751, 31 May (rolls); 1916–17, p. 255, 30 October 1916 (soap). HC Debates, 1916, Vol. LXXXII, cols. 910–11, 11 May 1916; Vol. LXXXIII, cols. 19–21, 20 June 1916; Vol. LXXXIV, cols. 650–51, 17 July 1916; for the songbirds see Vol. LXXXI, col. 2314, 19 April 1916. Wandsworth Board of Guardians, Minutes of the Board, 2 March, 20 July, 12 October 1916. Simon Litman, Prices and Price Control in Great Britain and the United States during the World War, New York, 1920, pp. 24–5, 89.

39. HC Debates, 1916, Vol. LXXXV, col. 2505ff, 22 August 1916; Sir William Beveridge, British Food Control, 1928, p. 1.

40. H. Keatley Moore and W. C. Berwick Sayers (eds), Croydon and the Great War: The Official History of the War Work of the Borough and its Citizens from 1914 to 1919. Together with the Croydon Roll of Honour, 1920, pp. 213–14; Anon., A Record of the Honoured Men of Wimbledon & Merton Who Fell in the Great War 1914–18, with Notes of Local Activities during the Same Period, 1921, pp. 53–4. Bermondsey Council Minutes, 19 December 1916. HC Debates, 1916, Vol. LXXXVIII, col. 374, 29 November (church lands), and col. 619, 4 December 1916 (the parks). For Hampstead see Anon., Thomas Hancock Nunn: The Life of a Social Reformer. Written by His Friends for His Friends, 1942, p. 136. MacDonagh, In London during the Great War, p. 164.

41. On the political importance of the food question see Beveridge, British Food Control, Ch. III; David Lloyd George, War Memoirs, 2 vols, new edn, 1938, Vol. I, pp. 576, 755; for a useful overview of the political crisis that December see Trevor Wilson, The Myriad Faces of War: Britain and the Great War, 1914–1918, Cambridge, 1986, pp. 418ff.

42. MacDonagh, In London during the Great War, pp. 156–7, 8 December 1916. Playne MSS, Diary 1916, 9 December 1916.

43. For the delay in appointing a Controller see Addison, Four and a Half Years, Vol. I, pp. 268–9, 4 December 1916.

44. Sandhurst, From Day to Day: 1916–1921, p. 130, 18 December 1916. MacDonagh, In London during the Great War, pp. 161–2, Christmas Day; Playne MSS, Diary 1916, 14, 15, 23, 27 December 1916; The Times, 27 December 1916.

45. Playne MSS, Diary 1916, 31 December 1916.

9: Harlot-Haunted London

1. Report from the Joint Select Committee of the House of Lords and the House of Commons on the Criminal Law Amendment Bill and Sexual Offences Bill [H.L.] together with the Proceedings of the Committee, Minutes of Evidence and Appendices, Cd. 145, 1918, qq867–8; Hon. Trevor Bigham, Assistant Commissioner, Metropolitan Police.

2. *Report from the Joint Select Committee on the Criminal Law Amendment Bill*, qq120–22.
3. *Report from the Joint Select Committee on the Criminal Law Amendment Bill*, q914ff; for Miss MacDougall see Lilian Wyles, *A Woman at Scotland Yard: Reflections on the Struggles and Achievements of Thirty Years in the Metropolitan Police*, 1952, pp. 103ff.
4. *The Times*, 24 February 1917.
5. Norman Flower (ed.), *The Journals of Arnold Bennett*, 3 vols, 1932–3, Vol. II, pp. 156–7, 7 March 1916; 199, 8 June 1917; *grues* in this context meant prostitutes. Arnold Bennett, *The Pretty Lady: A Novel*, 1918, pp. 197–8.
6. *Report of the Commissioner of Police of the Metropolis for the Year 1917*, Cd. 9204, 1918, p. 19; *Report . . . for the Years 1918 and 1919*, Cd. 543, 1920, p. 15; London County Council, *London Statistics. 1915–20 . . . Vol. XXVI*, 1921, pp. 214–15.
7. On the expulsion see *Report from the Joint Select Committee on the Criminal Law Amendment Bill*, q185, Sir Ernley Blackwell.
8. MEPO2/1714, Report of SD Inspector, Tottenham Court Road Police Station, D Division, 6 November 1916.
9. MEPO2/1714, Reports of SD Inspector, Tottenham Court Road Police Station, D Division, 6 November 1916 and 10 March 1917. For press reports see *The Times*, 7 April, 1 May, 10 August, 4 October, 11 December 1917. MEPO2/1691, Memo of Superintendent, E Division, Bow Street Police Station, 29 January 1917.
10. The amateurs are in *Report from the Joint Select Committee on the Criminal Law Amendment Bill*, q186ff, Sir Ernley Blackwell.
11. For King George Hospital in Stamford Street see Jeffrey S. Reznick, *Healing the Nation: Soldiers and the Culture of Caregiving in Britain during the First World War*, Manchester, 2004, Ch. 3. The nickname is in Alan A. Jackson, *London's Termini*, Newton Abbot, 1969, p. 223. For prostitution pre-dating the railway see Jerry White, *London in the Nineteenth Century: A Human Awful Wonder of God*, 2007, pp. 295-7. For gay sex and the Union Jack Club between the wars see Matt Houlbrook, *Queer London: Perils and Pleasures in the Sexual Metropolis, 1918–1957*, Chicago, 2005, pp. 121–2.
12. For police charges at Tower Bridge see, for instance, *SLP*, 26 November 1915. MEPO2/1698, Report of Acting Superintendent Kennington Road Police Station, L Division, 10 February 1916. *The Times*, 22 February 1917.
13. For the larking see *SLP*, 2 March 1917; for Newman, Brown, Taylor and Thatcher see 9 March 1917; for Tate and the girl from Bath see *The Times*, 1 March 1917; and for the Hoxton women see *SLP*, 29 September 1916.
14. For the ins and outs see *SLP*, 23 February 1917, and for Yates, 11 January 1918; for the dentist see *SLP*, 20 April 1917, and for the music hall artistes 22 September 1916 and also (at Russell Grove, a black couple) 8 February 1918; for McGann see *SLP*, 3 August 1917, and Emily, 27 September 1918.
15. MEPO2/1698, correspondence from Sir Francis Lloyd, 31 December 1915, citing *The Times*'s report of the same date, and subsequent Reports from Superintendents on the Drugging Allegations.
16. For F. B. Meyer see *ODNB*.
17. *Daily News*, 8 February 1916; *SLP*, 11 and 18 February 1916. MEPO2/1698, Reports from Superintendents.

18. For Dominion complaints see *The Times*, 7 and 31 July 1917. For the attack see *The Times*, 23 February 1917; for the Canadian see *SLP*, 25 May 1917, and Oswin Street, 7 September 1917.

19. *The Times*, 16, 27, 29 November, 19 December 1917, 12 February 1918.

20. *The Times*, 24 February, 12 and 19 March 1915; S. Ingleby Oddie, *Inquest*, 1941, pp. 139–40.

21. For Conan Doyle see Andrew Lycett, *Conan Doyle: The Man Who Created Sherlock Holmes*, 2007, p. 369; *The Times*, 6, 7 and 10 February 1917. *Report of the Commissioners of Prisons and the Directors of Convict Prisons, with Appendices (For the Year ended 31st March, 1919)*, Cd. 374, 1919, p. 21. E. Sylvia Pankhurst, *The Home Front: A Mirror to Life in England during the World War*, 1932, pp. 105–6.

22. Robert Hutton, *Of Those Alone*, 1958, pp. 9–11, 32–3. Cecil Chapman, *The Poor Man's Court of Justice: Twenty-Five Years as a Metropolitan Magistrate*, 1925, p. 222. For some south London indecent behaviour charges between men see *SLP*, 27 July 1917, 26 April 1918.

23. Hutton, *Of Those Alone*, p. 38.

24. Mary S. Allen, *The Pioneer Policewoman*, 1925, pp. 9–10. For Boyle and Dawson see *ODNB*.

25. MEPO2/1603, 'Note on Women's Police Organisations', n.d. [c.June 1915]. For the uniform see Allen, *The Pioneer Policewoman*, pp. 24–5, and Mary S. Allen, *Lady in Blue*, 1936, p. 29.

26. Allen, *The Pioneer Policewoman*, pp. 72–3, 273.

27. MEPO2/1710, Memo from Superintendent Sutherland, C Division, Vine Street Police Station on 'Women's West End Night Patrols', 29 November 1916.

28. MEPO2/1603, 'Note on Women Police Organisations', n.d. [c.June 1915].

29. See Edward J. Bristow, *Vice and Vigilance: Purity Movements in Britain since 1700*, Dublin, 1977, Ch. 9; Judith R. Walkowitz, *Nights Out: Life in Cosmopolitan London*, 2012, Ch. 2.

30. Flower (ed.), *The Journals of Arnold Bennett*, Vol. II, pp. 156–7, 7 March 1916; Bennett, *Pretty Lady*, pp. 2–3. Hutton, *Of Those Alone*, pp. 36–7.

31. *The Times*, 19 May and 31 July 1916; Bristow, *Vice and Vigilance*, p. 214.

32. *Report from the Joint Select Committee on the Criminal Law Amendment Bill*, q437ff, Rt. Hon. Ian Macpherson, Under Secretary of State, War Department.

33. Royal Commission on Venereal Diseases, *Final Report*, Cd. 8189, 1916, paras. 116–18.

34. RC Venereal Diseases, *Final Report*, para. 230; see also Bristow, *Vice and Vigilance*, pp. 148–51.

35. For Meyer see *SLP*, 16 February 1917. For Doyle see his letters to *The Times* of 6 and 10 February 1917.

36. *HC Debates*, 1917, Vol. XC, col. 1098ff, 19 February 1917; Vol. XCIII, col. 61ff, 30 April 1917.

37. *HC Debates*, 1917, Vol. XCII, col. 2397, 25 April 1917; Vol. XCIII, cols. 1781–3, 17 May 1917. Association for Moral and Social Hygiene, 'Minute Book of the Police Court Rota Committee 1917–18', 3AMS/A/03/08, 3 December 1917.

38. *The Times*, 3, 7 January, 1 February 1918.

39. *HC Debates*, 1917, Vol. XCVIII, col. 1786, 5 November 1917. *Hackney and Stoke Newington Recorder*, 1 and 22 February, 8 and 29 March 1918.

40. For the controversy over 40D see *HC Debates*, 1918, Vol. 105, cols. 236–7, 16

April 1918; 106, cols. 2397–8, 13 June 1918; 108, col. 202, 17 October, and 1586, 31 October 1918; see also Claire Culleton, A *Working-Class Culture, Women, and Britain, 1914–1921*, New York, 1999, p. 137ff. On the number of VD cases, from all fronts, see Sir W. G. Macpherson, Sir W. P. Herringham, T. R. Elliott and A. Balfour, *History of the Great War Based on Official Documents. Medical Services. Diseases of the War. Vol. II*, 1923, pp. 118ff.

41. Virginia Berridge, *Opium and the People: Opiate Use and Drug Control Policy in Nineteenth and Early Twentieth Century England*, 1999, pp. 246–9.

42. Ibid., pp. 249–57. John Julius Norwich (ed.), *The Duff Cooper Diaries 1915–1951*, 2005, p. 21, 27 November 1915; p. 24, 9 January, and p. 27, 11 March 1916.

43. For Ching Foo Jack and other raids see *The Times*, 3 August 1917; 3 and 21 May, 16 October and 4 November 1918. For the Gibson case see *The Times*, 15 and 24 August 1918; see also Berridge, *Opium and the People*, p. 260, which gives his name as Walter.

44. See *The Times*, 4, 13, 14 and 21 December 1918; 3, 17, 24 January and 5, 8 April 1919; Oddie, *Inquest*, pp. 145–50; Berridge, *Opium and the People*, pp. 260–62. For an interesting fictional representation of this world of 1918 and after see Lady Dorothy Mills, *The Laughter of Fools*, 1920.

45. C. Sheridan Jones, *London in War-Time*, 1917, Ch.1.

46. Ibid., p. 8. For some East End raids see *HKG*, 19 September 1917; *HSNR*, 4 January 1918. For Nereshiner see *The Times*, 19 February 1918; and for other raids 12 February, 2 and 12 April 1918.

47. Flower (ed.), *The Journals of Arnold Bennett*, Vol. II, pp. 237–8, 23 October 1918.

48. Lady Cynthia Asquith, *Diaries 1915–1918*, 1968, p. 411, 17 February 1918; 'pantin' is a jumping jack.

49. Radclyffe Hall, *Adam's Breed*, 1924 (1957 edn), p. 220.

50. *The Times*, 8 August 1916; 5 March 1917. Sir Hubert Llewellyn Smith (ed.), *The New Survey of London Life and Labour. Vol. I, Forty Years of Change*, 1930, p. 296.

10: *Everyone Is So War-Weary!* 1917

1. *Daily Chronicle*, 1 January 1917; *HKG*, 1 January 1917; Playne MSS Collection, Senate House Library, MS1112, Folder 111, Diary 1917, 1 January.

2. Michael MacDonagh, *In London during the Great War: The Diary of a Journalist*, 1935, p. 169, 20 January 1917.

3. For the King see Christopher Addison, *Four and a Half Years: A Personal Diary from June 1914 to January 1919*, 2 vols, 1934, Vol. II, p. 318; for Croydon see H. Keatley Moore and W. C. Berwick Sayers (eds), *Croydon and the Great War: The Official History of the War Work of the Borough and its Citizens from 1914 to 1919. Together with the Croydon Roll of Honour*, 1920, p. 36. For the firm's reluctance to have a TNT plant in Silvertown see Anon., *The First Fifty Years of Brunner, Mond & Co. 1873–1923*, 1923, pp. 55–6.

4. London Hospital, House Committee Minutes, 22 January 1917, Report on Silvertown Explosion.

5. Enid Bagnold, *A Diary Without Dates*, 1918 (Windmill Library edn, 1933), pp. 52–3.

6. *COR*, Vol. XLI, No. 244, April 1917, pp. 154–7.

7. For the claims see *COR*, Vol. XLI, No. 244, April 1917, p. 156. For the rumours see Basil Thomson, *Queer People*, 1922, pp. 196–7; Basil Thomson, *The Scene Changes*, 1939, pp. 322–3. See generally Graham Hill and Howard Bloch, *The Silvertown Explosion. London 1917*, Stroud, 2003.

8. Lady Cynthia Asquith, *Diaries 1915–1918*, 1968, p. 264, 28 January 1917. C. à Court Repington, *The First World War, 1914–1918: Personal Experiences of Lieut.-Col. C. à Court Repington*, 2 vols, 1921, Vol. I, p. 447, 31 January 1917. D. S. Higgins (ed.), *The Private Diaries of Sir H. Rider Haggard*, 1980, pp. 95 and 97, 13 January and 2 February 1917. Gavin Roynon (ed.), *Home Fires Burning: The Great War Diaries of Georgina Lee*, Stroud, 2006, pp. 209 and 212, 8 March and 2 April 1917. Jane Ridley, *Edwin Lutyens: His Life, His Wife, His Work*, 2002, p. 275; 31 Bedford Square is now 29.

9. Asquith, *Diaries 1915–1918*, pp. 268–9; for the laundry basket see Mrs C. S. Peel, *How We Lived Then: 1914–1918: A Sketch of Social and Domestic Life in England during the War*, 1929, p. 57; for the City see James Munson (ed.), *Echoes of the Great War: The Diary of the Reverend Andrew Clark 1914–1919*, Oxford, 1985, p. 180, 7 February 1917.

10. For the queues see *HKG*, 9 February 1917; the *Star*, 7 April 1917. For councils see Bermondsey Metropolitan Borough Council, Council Minutes, 20 February 1917; *HKG*, 6 February 1917, for similar action by Hackney and Stoke Newington. The Coal Controller is cited in Elspet Fraser-Stephen, *Two Centuries in the London Coal Trade: The Story of Charringtons*, 1952, p. 117. For the inquests see *SLP*, 16 February 1917. For coal rationing see Simon Litman, *Prices and Price Control in Great Britain and the United States during the World War*, New York, 1920, p. 150. And generally see Armin Triebel, 'Coal and the Metropolis', in Jay Winter and Jean-Louis Robert (eds), *Capital Cities at War: Paris, London, Berlin 1914–1919*, Cambridge, 1997, pp. 342–73.

11. The colour is recalled in Harold W. Walker, *Mainly Memories, 1906–1930*, 1986, p. 30. For the protest meetings see *SLP*, 23 February 1917. Generally see Sir William Beveridge, *British Food Control*, 1928, pp. 34–40, 98–100.

12. For queues see, for instance, *SLP*, 16 March 1917, and *Observer*, 8 April 1917. Walker, *Mainly Memories, 1906–1930*, p. 30. For the fish and chip shops see *HC Debates*, 1917, Vol. XCII, col. 8, 26 March 1917. Cooke's is in *HKG*, 28 March 1917. Playne MSS, Diary 1917, 13 and 15 March.

13. For voluntary rationing see Beveridge, *Food Control*, pp. 34–5. The posters are in Caroline E. Playne, *Britain Holds On, 1917, 1918*, 1933, p. 65. For voluntary rationing taken seriously see Roynon (ed.), *Home Fires Burning*, pp. 204–8, 3–23 February 1917. Wensley Family Archive (*c.*1890–1950): Correspondence, File 1/6, f143. Higgins (ed.), *The Private Diaries of Sir H. Rider Haggard*, p. 107, 24 May 1917.

14. Playne, *Britain Holds On, 1917, 1918*, p. 68 (bun hogs); Viscount [William] Sandhurst, *From Day to Day: 1916–1921*, 1929, p. 193, 24–7 July 1917 (Rhondda-vous). Higgins (ed.), *The Private Diaries of Sir H. Rider Haggard*, p. 107, 17 May 1917. Roynon (ed.), *Home Fires Burning*, p. 218, 24 May 1917. For prosecutions see, for example, *HKG*, 1 June 1917; *SLP*, 20 April

1917. On these offences, anachronistically labelled a 'black market', see Edward Smithies, *The Black Economy in England since 1914*, Dublin, 1984, pp. 19-37.

15. For the parks see London County Council, *The Council and the War*, 1920, p. 36; *HC Debates*, 1917, Vol. XC, cols. 1655-6, 26 February 1917 (Richmond Park). For Bermondsey and school playing fields see Henry Fuller Morriss, *Bermondsey's 'Bit' in the Greatest* War, 1923, pp. 206-8; for pigs see Bermondsey Metropolitan Borough Council, Public Health Committee Minutes, 15 March 1918. On local advice see, for example, *SLP*, 26 January 1917; for the newsbills see MacDonagh, *In London during the Great War*, p. 179, 10 March 1917. For the first Kitchen see *SLP*, 18 May 1917.

16. For price rises see Litman, *Prices and Price Control in Great Britain and the United States during the World War*, pp. 24-5, 89. Roynon (ed.), *Home Fires Burning*, p. 217, 16 May 1917. For the bus strike see *The Times*, 14, 17 and 18 May 1917.

17. See David Lloyd George, *War Memoirs*, 2 vols, new edn, 1938, Vol. II, pp. 1146-50; James Hinton, *The First Shop Stewards' Movement*, 1973, passim.

18. Commission of Enquiry into Industrial Unrest. No. 5 Division. *Report of the Commissioners for the London and South-Eastern Area*, Cd. 8666, 1917. For wage increases see London County Council, *London Statistics. 1915-20 . . . Vol. XXVI*, 1921, pp. 61-5.

19. On the Albert Hall meeting see Henry Nevinson, *Last Changes, Last Chances*, 1928, pp. 123-4; Brock Millman, *Managing Domestic Dissent in First World War Britain*, 2000, p. 206. Playne MSS, Diary 1917, 18 March. Roynon (ed.), *Home Fires Burning*, p. 219, 9 June 1917.

20. For the fears see Thomson, *The Scene Changes*, p. 332, 5 April 1917. Addison, *Four and a Half Years*, Vol. II, p. 407, 13 July 1917.

21. David Marquand, *Ramsay MacDonald*, 1977, p. 202; *HKG*, 12 January 1917. *HKG*, 23 March 1917.

22. *HKG*, 16 April and 2 May 1917. For Finsbury Park see Ken Weller, *'Don't be a Soldier!' The Radical Anti-War Movement in North London 1914-1918*, 1985, pp. 56-7; Edward Tupper, *Seamen's Torch: The Life Story of Captain Edward Tupper, National Union of Seamen*, 1938, pp. 191-5. For the National Party see Playne, *Britain Holds On, 1917, 1918*, p. 143.

23. For the raids see *HC Debates*, 1917, Vol. XCIX, cols. 860-61, 1169-70, 1628-30, 1978-9 (19, 21, 26 November 1917); Vol. C, cols. 440-42, 853 (5 and 10 December 1917); for the meeting see Vol. XCIX, cols. 2210-11, 29 November 1917; see also Herbert T. Fitch, *Traitors Within: The Adventures of Detective Inspector Herbert T. Fitch*, 1933, pp. 60-63.

24. W. R. Inge, *Diary of a Dean: St Paul's 1911-1934*, 1949, p. 38; for the crowds that day see MacDonagh, *In London during the Great War*, pp. 189-91, and 15 August see p. 210. Reform Club, General Committee Minutes 1908-1919, p. 511, 512, 533 (7 and 21 June, 13 November 1917). *The Times*, 30 July 1917. See also Playne, *Britain Holds On, 1917, 1918*, pp. 146-7.

25. Asquith, *Diaries 1915-1918*, p. 257, 18 January 1917 (Harry Lauder), pp. 322-3, 30 July 1917; John Julius Norwich (ed.), *The Duff Cooper Diaries 1915-1951*, 2005, pp. 60-61, 23 November 1917; Higgins (ed.), *The Private Diaries of Sir H. Rider Haggard*, p. 101, 30 March 1917. Barbara Wootton, *In a World I Never Made: Autobiographical Reflections*, 1967, pp. 49-50.

26. Playne MSS, Diary 1917, 24 April, 15 June; Playne, *Britain Holds On, 1917, 1918*, pp. 76–7.

27. Sandhurst, *From Day to Day: 1916–1921*, pp. 153–4; MacDonagh, *In London during the Great War*, p. 184; Thomson, *The Scene Changes*, p. 331; *Manchester Guardian*, 26 March 1917. The cause appears to have been an anti-invasion exercise interpreted as the real thing.

28. See Joseph Morris, *The German Air Raids on Great Britain 1914–1918*, 1925, pp. 217ff; Neil Hanson, *First Blitz: The Secret German Plan to Raze London to the Ground in 1918*, 2008, Ch. 4; Ian Castle, *London 1917–18: The Bomber Blitz*, Oxford, 2010, pp. 18ff.

29. See Frank Morison, *War on Great Cities: A Study of the Facts*, 1937, pp. 115–16, 215; Hanson, *First Blitz*, pp. 87–105.

30. Bill Goble, *Life-Long Rebel*, 1984, pp. 4–5; see also Morison, *War on Great Cities*, pp. 117–27, 216–17; Hanson, *First Blitz*, pp. 123–49; Castle, *London 1917–18*, pp. 19–23, with a very helpful map; the most complete modern account is in Ian F. W. Beckett, *The Making of the First World War*, 2012, Ch. 9.

31. Playne MSS, Diary 1917, 13 June; *HKG*, 15 June 1917; Hanson, *First Blitz*, pp. 147ff; for the rumours see *Manchester Guardian*, 15 June 1917.

32. Morison, *War on Great Cities*, pp. 118, 127–32, 218–19; Castle, *London 1917–18*, pp. 25–33; Hanson, *First Blitz*, pp. 164–80.

33. *SLP*, 13 July 1917; *HKG*, 9, 11 and 18 July 1917; *Daily Chronicle*, 10 July 1917.

34. Sandhurst, *From Day to Day: 1916–1921*, pp. 176–7, 13–17 June 1917.

35. *HC Debates*, 1917, Vol. XCIV, cols. 28–30, 5 June 1917, and cols. 1283ff, 14 June 1917; Vol. XCV, cols. 512–13, 28 June 1917; for protest meetings see *SLP*, 22 June 1917 (Bermondsey and Rotherhithe). For Haig and French see G. A. R. Riddell, *Lord Riddell's War Diary 1914–1918*, 1933, pp. 254–5, recounting a dinner conversation with Lloyd George on 10 June 1917.

36. *HC Debates*, 1917, Vol. XCV, col. 2102, 12 July 1917. The chagrin is in an editorial in *HKG*, 13 July 1917; until then the paper labelled those calling for warnings as 'Panickies'. For the rankling see Jack While, *Fifty Years of Fire Fighting in London*, 1931, p. 172. MEPO2/1656, Memo. No. 388, 21 July 1917, the 'all clear' arrangements unspecified.

37. Playne MSS, Diary 1917, 5 September; Morison, *War on Great Cities*, pp. 135–9.

38. Ibid., pp. 139ff; Morris, *The German Air Raids on Great Britain 1914–1918*, pp. 232ff; Hanson, *First Blitz*, pp. 213–17; Castle, *London 1917–18*, pp. 44ff.

39. Florence E. Lockwood, *Private Diary*, 1926–29, Part II, pp. 25–6, [24] September 1917. *SLP*, 28 September 1917.

40. Lydia Peile, 'Diary May 1916–Nov. 1917', 94/2/1 (IWM), pp. 219–31, 25 September 1917.

41. For numbers see *SLP*, 7 September 1917; Castle, *London 1917–18*, p. 50, which does not give a citation for the police estimate of 300,000. On the death see David Bownes, Oliver Green and Sam Mullins, *Underground: How the Tube Shaped London*, 2012, p. 100. Lord William Beveridge, *Power and Influence*, 1953, p. 146, citing a letter of 1 October. Norman Flower (ed.), *The Journals of Arnold Bennett*, 3 vols, 1932–3, Vol. II, p. 205; there is an interesting take on class encounters in the tube shelters in 'A Forsyte Encounters the People', in John Galsworthy, *On Forsyte 'Change*, 1930. Playne, *Britain Holds On, 1917, 1918*, pp. 147–8.

42. For the tunnels see MEPO2/1657, Report of Chief Engineer LCC, 11 October 1917, and for sanitary accommodation Bermondsey Public Health Committee Minutes, 27 November and 11 December 1917. For the royal visit see *The Times*, 19 October 1917, and for the Stratford accident see the *Star*, 28 September 1917. London Hospital Minutes, 16 July and 1 October 1917. London County Council, *The Council and the War*, pp. 49–50, the shelterers counted on 23 November 1917.

43. John Bickersteth (ed.), *The Bickersteth Diaries 1914–1918*, 1995, pp. 212–13 (Waterloo); Playne, *Britain Holds On, 1917, 1918*, pp. 147–8 (Richmond Park); Anon. [Albert Lieck], *Narrow Waters: The First Volume of the Life and Thoughts of a Common Man*, 1935, p. 218 (Devon); Higgins (ed.), *The Private Diaries of Sir H. Rider Haggard*, p. 117, 8 October 1917 (the return).

44. Alfred Stokes, *East Ham: From Village to County Borough*, 3rd edn, 1933, p. 179. Playne MSS, Diary 1917, 29 September and 1 October; spelling was never her strong point. Hallie Eustace Miles, *Untold Tales of War-Time London*, 1930, p. 133, 16 September–19 October 1917.

45. Douglas H. Robinson, *The Zeppelin in Combat: A History of the German Naval Airship Division, 1912–1918*, 1962, pp. 262–83. Morison, *War on Great Cities*, pp. 141–50; Castle, *London 1914–17*, pp. 86–9.

46. While, *Fifty Years of Fire Fighting*, p. 178; for the aprons see Stokes, *East Ham*, pp. 181–2, and Castle, *London 1917–18*, p. 55. A. Rawlinson, *In Defence of London, 1915–1918*, 1923, pp. 199–201.

47. *SLP*, 25 May and 1 June 1917; Royal Borough of Kensington, *Annual Report of the Medical Officer of Health for the Year 1917*, p. 7.

48. For the gas-bags see *The Times*, 11 October 1917; Frederick Arthur Robinson, 'MS Diary 1914–1918', 11335 P. 401–402 (IWM), 29 November (cost of conversion) and 15 October 1917 (disgruntlement about the officers); Asquith, *Diaries 1915–1918*, p. 373, 27 November 1917.

49. Higgins (ed.), *The Private Diaries of Sir H. Rider Haggard*, p. 109, 18 June 1917; *HC Debates*, 1917, Vol. XCIX, cols. 1190–91, 21 November 1917.

50. R. D. Blumenfeld, *All in a Lifetime*, 1931, pp. 93–4, 25 September 1917. Wensley Family Archive, File 1/6, f143, Daisy Parsons to Edie Wensley, 29 April 1917. Playne, *Britain Holds On, 1917, 1918*, pp. 44–5.

51. Bermondsey Council Minutes, 6 November and 4 December 1917.

52. Asquith, *Diaries 1915–1918*, p. 314, 22 June 1917. On Chaplin at this time see W. R. Titterton, *London Scenes*, 1920, pp. 141ff. The cinema tragedy is in *The Times*, 30 April 1917.

53. Sydney Moseley, *The Private Diaries of Sydney Moseley*, 1960, pp. 169, 171; Wensley Family Archive, File 1/7, f157, 3 July 1917. *Chu Chin Chow* opened on 31 August 1916 and ran till 1921.

54. Lieut. F. H. Ennor, 'Diary 1917', 86/28/2 (IWM), passim.

55. Stephen McKenna, *While I Remember*, 1921, pp. 218–19; see also John Lucas, *Thomas Beecham: An Obsession with Music*, 2008, pp. 141–5. Asquith, *Diaries 1915–1918*, p. 351.

56. For Victoria Park see *HKG*, 5 December 1917; for Lewisham see *The Times*, 11 December, and the City queues 22 December 1917. See generally Sir William Beveridge, *British Food Control*, 1928, pp. 78, 144–5, 195–201.

57. Playne MSS, Diary 1917, 23 December 1917; Robinson, 'MS Diary 1914–1918', 25 December 1917.

58. *The Times*, 26 December 1917; MacDonagh, *In London during the Great War*, pp. 240–41, Christmas Eve.

11: *The Curse Is Being Removed*

1. Arthur L. Bowley, *Prices and Wages in the United Kingdom, 1914–1920*, Oxford, 1921, Ch. VII and p. 167; there are generally no separate figures for London, but for some London wage rates from 1916 see London County Council, *London Statistics. 1915–20 . . . Vol. XXVI*, 1921, pp. 62–3. Arthur Gleason, *Inside the British Isles*, 1917, p. 23.
2. Alfred Grosch, *St Pancras Pavements: An Autobiography*, 1947, p. 53. Barbara Drake, *Women in the Engineering Trades*, 1917, p. 72, for weighing in the balance. Naomi Loughnan, 'Munition Work', in Gilbert Stone (ed.), *Women War Workers*, 1917, pp. 33, 40.
3. H. J. Bennett, *I was a Walworth Boy*, 1980, p. 43. A. S. Jasper, *A Hoxton Childhood*, 1969 (Readers' Union edn, 1971), pp. 61–6, 71–5. For the unemployment rates see London County Council, *London Statistics. 1915–20 . . . Vol. XXVI*, p. 85.
4. For school dinners see ibid., p. 241. Sir William Beveridge, *British Food Control*, 1928, pp. 327–8. No London-wide statistics on food samples taken by borough councils and found to be adulterated during the war.
5. For Bethnal Green see *HKG*, 1 November 1915. For the LCC see *Report of the Working Classes Cost of Living Committee, 1918*, Cd. 8980, 1918, p. 9. Grosch, *St Pancras Pavements*, p. 53. R. M. Fox, *Smoky Crusade*, 1937, p. 200. John Gray, *Gin and Bitters*, 1938, p. 104.
6. R. D. Blumenfeld, *All in a Lifetime*, 1931, p. 61, 18 April 1916. Mrs Ethel Alec-Tweedie, *Women and Soldiers*, 1918, p. 42, citing an article she published in the *English Review* in April 1916.
7. 'Folklore' is cited in Adrian Gregory, *The Last Great War: British Society and the First World War*, Cambridge, 2008, p. 193. *HKG*, 17 January 1917; *The Times*, 17 September 1917, 6 September 1918. *SLP*, 4 August 1916. For the auction rooms see Paul Morand, *Tender Shoots*, 1921 (1st English translation, 2011), p. 46.
8. Florence Roberts, *The Ups and Downs of Florrie Roberts*, 1980, p. 5.
9. Dorothy Scannell, *Mother Knew Best: An East End Childhood*, 1974, pp. 65–6.
10. Woolwich Metropolitan Borough Council, *Annual Report of the Medical Officer of Health for 1915*, p. 86.
11. COR, Vol. XXXIX, No. 229, January 1916, pp. 1–2. London County Council, *London Statistics. 1915–20 . . . Vol. XXVI*, pp. 76, 78, 153, 217 and 92 (common lodging houses); for elderly people no longer in the workhouse see Wandsworth Board of Guardians, Minutes of the Board, 27 March 1919, Triennial Report of retiring chairman, Canon Hubert Curtis. London County Council, *London Statistics. 1921–23 . . . Vol. XXVIII*, 1924, pp. 66–9 for the historic trends of poor relief.
12. Michael MacDonagh, *In London during the Great War: The Diary of a Journalist*, 1935, p. 196, 28 May; p. 237, 16 December 1917. Sir Chartres Biron, *Without Prejudice: Impressions of Life and Law*, 1936, p. 273. Gleason, *Inside the British Isles*, p. 105.

13. See Jon Lawrence, 'Material Pressures on the Middle Classes', in Jay Winter and Jean-Louis Robert (eds), *Capital Cities at War: Paris, London, Berlin 1914–1919*, Cambridge, 1997, pp. 232–9.

14. For a summary of the tax situation see Ernest L. Bogart, *Direct and Indirect Costs of the Great World War*, New York, 1919, pp. 9–18. Alec-Tweedie, *Women and Soldiers*, p. 43.

15. On the PCWRC see, for instance, *The Times*, 30 October 1914; 27 February, 14 April and 21 June 1915; 31 May 1917. Alec-Tweedie, *Women and Soldiers*, pp. 42–3.

16. Royal Borough of Kensington, *Annual Report of the Medical Officer of Health for the Year 1917*, p. 2. Cases known to the police from *Report of the Commissioner of Police of the Metropolis for the Years 1918 and 1919*, Cd. 543, 1920, Part II, Table I; . . . *for the Year 1917*, Cd. 9204, 1918, p. 11. For inquests see London County Council, *London Statistics. 1915–20 . . . Vol. XXVI*, p. 219.

17. For infant mortality figures for the war years see ibid., pp. 48–9. See also Jay M. Winter, *The Great War and the British People*, 1986, pp. 147–53; and Jay Winter, 'Surviving the War: Life Expectation, Illness and Mortality Rates in Paris, London, and Berlin, 1914–1919', in Winter and Robert (eds), *Capital Cities at War*, pp. 487–523.

18. Lionel Rose, *The Massacre of the Innocents: Infanticide in Britain, 1800–1939*, 1986, pp. 180–81.

19. London County Council, *London Statistics. 1915–20 . . . Vol. XXVI*, pp. 45 (birth rate) and 88 (health visitors). For difficulties in Camberwell see Winter, *The Great War and the British People*, pp. 201–2. For a wartime survey of this new provision see E. W. Hope, *Report on the Physical Welfare of Mothers and Children, England Wales, Vol. I*, 1917, pp. 206ff (and pp. 382–3 for St Marylebone); and for pre-war provision, Janet M. Campbell, *Report on the Physical Welfare of Mothers and Children, England Wales, Vol. 2*, 1917, pp. 82–90.

20. *HKG*, 20 December 1915, 30 March and 5 January 1916.

21. Children's Society Archive, 'Kitchener Memorial Home, Hornsey'. The numbers in care nationally at each year's end were given in the *Annual Report[s] of the Waifs' and Strays' Society*: they were 4,414 in 1913, 4,797 in 1916, 4,866 in 1918 and 4,269 in 1919.

22. CSA case files 19382, 22267, 22036, 22013, 22140 and 22040 (the last two from the same family).

23. CSA case file 22829.

24. Irene Osgood Andrews, *Economic Effects of the War upon Women and Children in Great Britain*, New York, 1918, pp. 164–5. *Annual Report of the Chief Inspector of Factories and Workshops for the Year 1916*, Cd. 8570, 1917, p. 4. For the canteens see David Lloyd George, *War Memoirs*, 2 vols, new edn, 1938, Vol. I, pp. 203–4. For welfare generally see M. B. Hammond, *British Labor Conditions and Legislation during the Great War*, New York, 1919, pp. 216–20; Deborah Thom, *Nice Girls and Rude Girls: Women Workers in World War I*, 1998, Ch. 8; Vicky Long and Hilary Marland, 'From Danger and Motherhood to Health and Beauty: Health Advice for the Factory Girl in Early Twentieth-Century Britain', *Twentieth Century British History*, Vol. 20, No. 4, 2009, pp. 458ff. On the crèches see Rose E. Squire, *Thirty Years in the Public Service: An*

Industrial Retrospect, 1927, pp. 185-7; D'Arcy Cresswell, *Margaret McMillan: A Memoir*, 1948, p. 143.

25. *Annual Report of the Chief Inspector of Factories and Workshops for the Year 1915*, Cd. 8256, 1916, p. 9. Drake, *Women in the Engineering Trades*, p. 75 and fn. Andrews, *Economic Effects of the War upon Women and Children in Great Britain*, pp. 167-8; see also Gail Braybon, *Women Workers in the First World War*, 1981, pp. 115-16.

26. London County Council, *London Statistics. 1915-20 ... Vol. XXVI*, pp. 48-52, 57; London County Council, *London Statistics. 1920-21 ... Vol. XXVII*, 1922, p. 43. Winter, 'Surviving the War', in Winter and Robert (eds), *Capital Cities at War*, pp. 498ff.

27. London County Council, *London Statistics. 1913-14 ... Vol. XXIV*, 1915, pp. 52-7, figures from the 1911 Census. For amenities including baths, see Jerry White, *London in the Twentieth Century: A City and Its People*, 2001, pp. 235-6.

28. Maud Pember Reeves, *Round About a Pound a Week*, 1913, pp. 21-4. For the rents see Helen Bosanquet, 'Housing Conditions in London', *Economic Journal*, Vol. 27, No. 107, September 1917, pp. 330-31. E. Sylvia Pankhurst, *The Suffragette Movement: An Intimate Account of Persons and Ideals*, 1931, pp. 528-9.

29. Dan Rider, *Ten Years' Adventures Among Landlords and Tenants: The Story of the Rent Acts*, 1927, pp. 3-4; David Englander, *Landlord and Tenant in Urban Britain 1838-1918*, Oxford, 1983, pp. 205-6.

30. Rider, *Ten Years' Adventures Among Landlords and Tenants*, pp. 3ff; *EG*, 27 March 1915, p. 396, and 11 September 1915, p. 273.

31. For the nationwide strikes see *EG*, 16 October 1915, pp. 432-3. For Tooting see Rider, *Ten Years' Adventures*, chs. III-V. For London rent strikes generally see *The Times*, 11 October, 16 and 24 November 1915, and Englander, *Landlord and Tenant*, pp. 209-10. For Leyton see *HKG*, 19 November 1915.

32. Rider, *Ten Years' Adventures Among Landlords and Tenants*, Ch. X, has a useful summary; see also Susanna Magri, 'Housing', in Winter and Robert (eds), *Capital Cities at War*, pp. 390-91.

33. See ibid., pp. 374-6; Hugh Quigley and Ismay Goldie, *Housing and Slum Clearance in London*, 1934, pp. 65-8; London County Council, *London Statistics. 1915-20 ... Vol. XXVI*, pp. 134-5.

34. Woolwich Metropolitan Borough Council, *Annual Report of the Medical Officer of Health for 1914*, pp. 115-16. *EG*, 6 February 1915, p. 174.

35. For the Well Hall estate and other government schemes in Woolwich see *History of the Ministry of Munitions*, 12 vols, 1919-22, Vol. V, Part V, pp. 83-7. *The Times*, 22 May 1916. Drake, *Women in the Engineering Trades*, pp. 73-4 and fn.

36. *History of the Ministry of Munitions*, Vol. V, Part V, pp. 23, 26-7, 79-81. For the PLA see *EG*, 11 March 1916, p. 301. For the LCC see London County Council, *Housing: With Particular Reference to Post-War Housing Schemes*, 1928, p. 113.

37. The borough information from 1916 is in Bosanquet, 'Housing Conditions in London', p. 340. The survey in Stanhope Street from November 1915 is in *COR*, Vol. XLI, No. 246, June 1917, p. 240. H. Keatley Moore and W. C. Berwick Sayers (eds), *Croydon and the Great War: The Official History of the War Work*

of the Borough and its Citizens from 1914 to 1919. Together with the Croydon Roll of Honour, 1920, pp. 222-3.

38. Caroline E. Playne, Society at War, 1914–1916, 1931, p. 231; see also Alec-Tweedie, Women and Soldiers, p. 69. EG, 3 April 1915, p. 423. For North Kensington and other districts see Bosanquet, 'Housing Conditions in London', p. 340, and for Bloomsbury see COR, Vol. XLII, No. 247, July 1917, p. 18.

39. For the movement back from the suburbs see COR, Vol. XXXIX, No. 233, May 1916, pp. 218–19; XL, No. 235, July 1916, p. 1; No. 239, November 1916, p. 179. For Stoke Newington see EG, 5 February 1916, p. 157; the advertisement is in HKG, 11 February 1916, for an unfurnished apartment in Rendlesham Road, Clapton.

40. For Harrow and other places see HC Debates, 1918, Vol. 105, cols. 512–13, 17 April 1918; see also cols. 34–6, 520, 1540, 1864–5. The Times, 27 March 1918. The Home Secretary is in HC Debates, 1918, Vol. 104, cols. 1638–9, 11 April 1918.

41. For the difficulties leading to middle-class rent protection see Englander, Landlord and Tenant, pp. 290–94. For the 1915 Act's loopholes see ibid., pp. 242ff, and Rider, Ten Years' Adventures Among Landlords and Tenants, pp. 83ff and 111ff. For the new DORA regulation see HC Debates, 1917, Vol. XCIX, cols. 600–602, 15 November 1917; 1918, Vol. 103, col. 1711, 4 March 1918.

42. For the Gunter estate see The Times, 9 December 1916; EG, 16 June 1917, p. 597. For Hoxton see EG, 15 September 1917, p. 249; HKG, 17 September 1917. For the Cubitt estate see EG, 5 January (p. 1) and 26 January 1918, p. 83.

43. Moore and Sayers (eds), Croydon and the Great War, p. 34.

44. For Tabard Street see The Times, 29 April, 2 and 4 May 1916. For both areas see London County Council, Housing, pp. 111ff, 116ff.

45. For Soho see Bosanquet, 'Housing Conditions in London', p. 339; for Stanhope Street see COR, Vol. XLI, No. 246, June 1917, pp. 239ff. For central London see London County Council, London Statistics. 1915–20 ... Vol. XXVI, p. 135.

46. Ibid., figures for the 'original area' including the County of London and twenty-nine urban areas in outer London.

12: The News Is NOT Good! 1918

1. Caroline E. Playne, Britain Holds On, 1917, 1918, 1933, p. 255. For the sales see The Times, 1 and 2 January 1918.

2. Sir William Beveridge, British Food Control, 1928, p. 201; see also The Times, 3 and 5 January 1918. Gavin Roynon (ed.), Home Fires Burning: The Great War Diaries of Georgina Lee, Stroud, 2006, pp. 241–2, 6 and 22 January 1918. Michael MacDonagh, In London during the Great War: The Diary of a Journalist, 1935, p. 247. Christopher Addison, Four and a Half Years: A Personal Diary from June 1914 to January 1919, 2 vols, 1934, Vol. II, p. 467, 7 January 1918. For the salmon see C. à Court Repington, The First World War, 1914–1918: Personal Experiences of Lieut.-Col. C. à Court Repington, 2 vols, 1921, Vol. II, p. 183, 13 January 1918. Reform Club, General Committee Minutes

1908–1919, 31 January, 7 February 1918; Reform Club Letter Book 1917–18, 31 January, 1 and 4 February 1918, etc.; see also Norman Flower (ed.), *The Journals of Arnold Bennett*, 3 vols, 1932–3, Vol. II, p. 217, 22 January 1918.

3. Beveridge, *British Food Control*, pp. 202, 206–8.

4. For disorder see *The Times*, 18 January 1918. Anne Olivier Bell (ed.), *The Diary of Virginia Woolf. Vol. I, 1915–1919*, 1977, pp. 99–100, 21 January 1918. Viscount [William] Sandhurst, *From Day to Day: 1916–1921*, 1929, p. 228, 4–12 February 1918. Mary Coules, 'First World War Papers, Reuters Papers, Editorial Order 21 January 1918', 97/25/1 (IWM).

5. Robert Graves, *Goodbye to All That*, 1929 (Penguin edn, 1986), p. 223.

6. For the scheme see Beveridge, *British Food Control*, pp. 201–8. Sandhurst, *From Day to Day: 1916–1921*, p. 237, 11–17 March 1918. *SLP*, 1 March 1918.

7. *HSNR*, 8 February 1918; Frank Morison, *War on Great Cities: A Study of the Facts*, 1937, pp. 156–7.

8. The various accounts of the raid and especially the Odhams disaster conflict on points of detail: see W. J. B. Odhams, *The Story of the Bomb . . .*, 1919, pp. 5–10; Morison, *War on Great Cities*, pp. 158–61; Ian Castle, *London 1917–18: The Bomber Blitz*, Oxford, 2010, pp. 66–9. The ink is in Hallie Eustace Miles, *Untold Tales of War-Time London*, 1930, p. 145: some may well have drowned, it seems, through the huge volume of water from the firemen's hoses. S. Ingleby Oddie, *Inquest*, 1941, pp. 141–2; Graves, *Goodbye to All That*, p. 224.

9. Morison, *War on Great Cities*, pp. 162–4, 231–2; Castle, *London 1917–18*, pp. 74–8.

10. Morison, *War on Great Cities*, pp. 165–6, 233; Castle, *London 1917–18*, pp. 78–81; Repington, *The First World War, 1914–1918*, Vol. II, p. 251, 17 March 1918.

11. Morison, *War on Great Cities*, pp. 166–9, 234; Castle, *London 1917–18*, pp. 82–9.

12. For casualties and damage see Morison, *War on Great Cities*, pp. 208–34; Castle, *London 1917–18*, p. 89.

13. *HC Debates*, 1918, Vol. 104, cols. 315–16, 13 March 1918.

14. Sandhurst, *From Day to Day: 1916–1921*, p. 239; MacDonagh, *In London during the Great War*, pp. 251–6, 29 January 1918.

15. Sandhurst, *From Day to Day: 1916–1921*, p. 227, 3 February, and pp. 241–2, 29–31 March 1918, reporting on the situation 'three days ago'. Roynon (ed.), *Home Fires Burning*, p. 247; Frederick Arthur Robinson, 'MS Diary 1914–1918', 11335 P. 401–402 (IWM), 14 March 1918. For the larceny see *HC Debates*, 1918, Vol. 103, cols. 493–4, 18 February 1918.

16. See Trevor Wilson, *The Myriad Faces of War: Britain and the Great War, 1914–1918*, Cambridge, 1986, Chs. 50 and 51.

17. MacDonagh, *In London during the Great War*, p. 281, 27 March 1918.

18. G. A. R. Riddell, *Lord Riddell's War Diary 1914–1918*, 1933, pp. 319–21, 24–5 March 1918. Playne MSS, Folder 126, Diary 1918, 24 March.

19. *Pall Mall Gazette*, 25 March 1918. Playne MSS, Diary 1918, 26 March. London County Council, *The Council and the War*, 1920, p. 7. Romer Wilson, *If All These Young Men*, 1919, pp. 88, 111. Vera Brittain struck an untypically false note when she wrote years later that the crisis 'appeared not to interest London in comparison with the struggle to obtain sugar' (*Testament of Youth. An Autobiographical Study of the Years 1900–1925*, 1933, pp. 429–30).

20. On Hampstead that Easter see *Manchester Guardian*, 2 April 1918. For the horse auction see *SLP*, 26 April 1918. Roynon (ed.), *Home Fires Burning*, p. 257, 23 June 1918; her husband appealed. H. V. Marrot, *The Life and Letters of John Galsworthy*, 1935, p. 443, 22 July 1918.

21. For the success of London Tank Week see Adrian Gregory, *The Last Great War: British Society and the First World War*, Cambridge, 2008, pp. 230–31. The gardens are in Miles, *Untold Tales of War-Time London*, p. 153, 14 August 1918; *HSNR*, 18 October 1918; Todd Longstaffe-Gowan, *The London Square: Gardens in the Midst of Town*, 2012, pp. 207–8; MacDonagh, *In London during the Great War*, pp. 320–21, 16 October 1918.

22. For the meetings see Brock Millman, *Managing Domestic Dissent in First World War Britain*, 2000, pp. 253–6; *HC Debates*, 1918, Vol. 108, cols. 486–7, 11 July 1918. For the destruction see *HC Debates*, 1918, Vol. 101, cols. 1144–5, 21 March 1918. Playne, *Britain Holds On, 1917, 1918*, pp. 302–3.

23. Roynon (ed.), *Home Fires Burning*, p. 254, 28 April 1918.

24. *The Times*, 31 May and 5 June 1918; MacDonagh, *In London during the Great War*, p. 299, 2 June 1918. Basil Thomson, *The Scene Changes*, 1939, pp. 373–4, 4 June 1918. See also Stephen McKenna, *While I Remember*, 1921, pp. 223ff; Judith R. Walkowitz, *Nights Out: Life in Cosmopolitan London*, 2012, pp. 87–9.

25. Playne, *Britain Holds On, 1917, 1918*, pp. 326–7.

26. For the buses and trams see ibid., pp. 344–5; Gail Braybon, *Women Workers in the First World War*, 1981, pp. 80–81. Richard Morris, *The Man Who Ran London during the Great War: The Diaries and Letters of Lieutenant General Sir Francis Lloyd GCVO, KCB, DSO (1853–1926)*, Barnsley, 2009, pp. 127–8; see also Millman, *Managing Domestic Dissent in First World War Britain*, pp. 262–4. Riddell, *Lord Riddell's War Diary 1914–1918*, p. 347, August 1918.

27. *The Times*, 31 August and 2 September 1918.

28. Lady Cynthia Asquith, *Diaries 1915–1918*, 1968, p. 470, 31 August 1918. *SLP*, 6 September 1918.

29. Sandhurst, *From Day to Day: 1916–1921*, pp. 265–6, 31 August to 2 September 1918. See generally the excellent account in Gerald W. Reynolds and Anthony Judge, *The Night the Police Went on Strike*, 1968, Chs. 3–6; and for Henry see his exculpatory biography in *ODNB*.

30. *The Times*, 31 August 1918. *HSNR*, 8 March 1918. *HC Debates*, 1918, Vol. 109, cols. 1531–2, 8 August 1918. Wartime accident statistics are in London County Council, *London Statistics. 1915–20 . . . Vol. XXVI*, 1921, p. 307; the number of fatalities in 2012 was 184 and serious injuries 2,884. MacDonagh, *In London during the Great War*, pp. 318–20.

31. Playne, *Britain Holds On, 1917, 1918*, p. 308; Playne MSS, Diary 1918, 11 May and inserted note under that entry headed 'May 1918 – Psychology'.

32. For the May procession see MacDonagh, *In London during the Great War*, pp. 293–4, 11 May 1918. Joseph G. Broodbank, *History of the Port of London*, 2 vols, 1921, Vol. II, p. 469. Roynon (ed.), *Home Fires Burning*, p. 258, 4 July 1918. Longstaffe-Gowan, *The London Square*, pp. 205–7.

33. Pte. Robert Maddison, 'Diary 1917–1918', PR84/213 (AWM), 28 March 1918 et seq.

34. Henry Nevinson, *Last Changes, Last Chances*, 1928, pp. 130–31. MacDonagh, *In London during the Great War*, pp. 290–91, 20 April, and pp. 303–4, 29 June 1918.

35. Asquith, *Diaries 1915–1918*, p. 421, 12 March 1918; for the jazz band see *The Times*, 9 October 1918, and for the curfew 2 April 1918. McKenna, *While I Remember*, pp. 219–20.

36. Asquith, *Diaries 1915–1918*, pp. 452ff, 23 June et seq.

37. *Aircraft Rag*, Vol. 2, No. 5, November 1918. There is a good picture of the outbreak in H. Keatley Moore and W. C. Berwick Sayers (eds), *Croydon and the Great War: The Official History of the War Work of the Borough and its Citizens from 1914 to 1919. Together with the Croydon Roll of Honour*, 1920, pp. 43–4; see also *SLP*, 25 October, 1 and 8 November 1918. London Hospital, House Committee Minutes, 28 October, 4, 18 and 25 November 1918; see also A. E. Clark-Kennedy, *The London: A Study in the Voluntary Hospital System. Vol. 2, The Second Hundred Years 1840–1948*, 1963, pp. 196–8 – the author qualified as a doctor at the London in January 1918. For statistics see London County Council, *London Statistics. 1915–1920 . . . Vol. XXVI*, p. 52.

38. Repington, *The First World War, 1914–1918*, Vol. II, p. 464. Robinson, 'Diary 1914–1918', 29 September 1918. Playne MSS, Diary 1918, 13 October. Miles, *Untold Tales of War-Time London*, pp. 156–7, recalls this as happening on a Sunday in October, but I have followed Playne, *Britain Holds On, 1917, 1918*, pp. 368–9, as more reliable on dates. MacDonagh, *In London during the Great War*, p. 321, 17 October 1918.

39. For the traffic see *SLP*, 8 November 1918. For the Lord Mayor's Procession and Dinner see E. C. Bentley, *Peace Year in the City 1918–19: An Account of the Outstanding Events in the City of London during Peace Year, in the Mayoralty of the Rt. Hon. Sir Horace Brooks Marshall, KCVO, LL.D, following the Great War of 1914–1918*, 1920, Ch.1.

13: *The Most Wonderful Day in All Our Lives*

1. Winston S. Churchill, *The World Crisis, Vol. III, 1916–1918*, 1927, Folio Society edn, 2007, p. 427. He misremembered 11 a.m. as having been announced by the chimes of Big Ben, but it did not strike the hour until 1 p.m. that day, having been silenced since very early in the war.

2. J. A. Hammerton, *Books and Myself: Memoirs of an Editor*, 1944, pp. 283–4; Edith Summerskill, *A Woman's World*, 1967, p. 24.

3. E. C. Bentley, *Peace Year in the City 1918–19: An Account of the Outstanding Events in the City of London during Peace Year, in the Mayoralty of the Rt. Hon. Sir Horace Brooks Marshall, KCVO, LL.D, following the Great War of 1914–1918*, 1920, pp. 25–6; C. H. Rolph, *London Particulars*, Oxford, 1980, p. 199.

4. Lucy Masterman, *C. F. G. Masterman: A Biography*, 1939, p. 306. Ernest Thurtle, *Time's Winged Chariot: Memories and Comments*, 1945, p. 58. Caroline E. Playne, *Britain Holds On, 1917, 1918*, 1933, p. 393. Hallie Eustace Miles, *Untold Tales of War-Time London*, 1930, pp. 158–60.

5. Michael MacDonagh, *In London during the Great War: The Diary of a Journalist*, 1935, p. 329. Gavin Roynon (ed.), *Home Fires Burning: The Great War Diaries of Georgina Lee*, Stroud, 2006, p. 276. The twinkling is in Playne, *Britain Holds On, 1917, 1918*, p. 393. *SLP*, 15 November 1918.

6. John Julius Norwich (ed.), *The Duff Cooper Diaries 1915–1951*, 2005, p. 85. For the dash to London see, for instance, Gilbert Frankau, *Peter Jackson, Cigar Merchant: A Romance of Modern Life*, 1920, pp. 398–9. Sir Chartres Biron, *Without Prejudice: Impressions of Life and Law*, 1936, p. 284.

7. Arthur C. Armstrong, *Bouverie Street to Bowling Green Lane: Fifty-Five Years of Specialized Publishing*, 1946, pp. 119–20. The question is in Ford Madox Ford, *A Man Could Stand Up –*, 1926, p. 701.

8. Ferdinand Tuohy, *The Crater of Mars*, 1929, pp. 247–8.

9. *The Times*, 13 November 1918.

10. Roynon (ed.), *Home Fires Burning*, p. 277.

11. Mrs Humphry Ward, *Harvest*, 1919, pp. 208–9. Norman and Jeanne MacKenzie (eds), *The Diary of Beatrice Webb. Vol. 3, 1905–1924: 'The Power to Alter Things'*, 1984, p. 315, 4 November 1918.

12. For casualties see Francis W. Hirst, *The Consequences of the War to Great Britain*, 1934, p. 231. Catriona Pennell, *A Kingdom United: Popular Responses to the Outbreak of the First World War in Britain and Ireland*, Oxford, 2012, p. 147, gives regional proportions of men aged nineteen to thirty-eight in London from the 1911 census, and the proportion enlisting before 12 November 1914.

13. For women and demobilisation see Deborah Thom, *Nice Girls and Rude Girls: Women Workers in World War I*, 1998, pp. 187–93. For domestic service see Sir Hubert Llewellyn Smith (ed.), *The New Survey of London Life and Labour. Vol. II, London Industries I*, 1931, Ch. VIII.

14. Sir Hubert Llewellyn Smith (ed.), *The New Survey of London Life and Labour. Vol. I, Forty Years of Change*, 1930, p. 5.

15. Douglas H. Smith, *The Industries of Greater London: Being a Survey of the Recent Industrialisation of the Northern and Western Sectors of Greater London*, 1933, Ch. V. On the aerodromes see *The Times*, 25 April 1919.

16. For the industrial and suburban growth of London in the interwar period, especially in the west, see Jerry White, *London in the Twentieth Century: A City and Its People*, 2001, pp. 26–37, 185–95.

17. Sir Hubert Llewellyn Smith (ed.), *The New Survey of London Life and Labour. Vol. III, Survey of Social Conditions (I) The Eastern Area (Text)*, 1932, Ch. VI.

18. Smith (ed.), *The New Survey of London Life and Labour. Vol. I*, p. 82.

BIBLIOGRAPHY

All books are published in London, unless otherwise stated.

Abbreviations

AWM   Australian War Memorial, Canberra
CSA   Children's Society Archive
IWM   Imperial War Museum, London
LMA   London Metropolitan Archive
TNA   The National Archives

Manuscript Sources

Association for Moral and Social Hygiene, 'Minute Book of the Police Court Rota Committee 1917–18', 3AMS/A/03/08 (Women's Library)

Bermondsey Metropolitan Borough Council, Council Minutes (Southwark Local History Library)

Bermondsey Metropolitan Borough Council, Public Health Committee Minutes (Southwark Local History Library)

Brittain, Frederick, 'World War I Diaries. The Military Hospital Chelsea, Dec. 1914 to Aug. 1915; Aboard the Hospital Ship Egypt, Aug. 1915 to April 1919', 99/51/1 (IWM)

Bunbury, Edith Marjorie, 'Diary of the European War Sept. 1914–Nov. 1915', A/FH/F15/001/002 (LMA)

Church of England Incorporated Society for Providing Homes for Waifs and Strays, case files and other records (CSA)

Coules, Mary, 'First World War Papers. Journal c.June 1914–Nov. 1915', 97/25/1 (IWM)

'Diary of a London Lady (Anonymous)', MISC 29/522 (IWM)

Ennor, Lieut. F. H., 'Diary 1917', 86/28/2 (IWM)

Grant, Philip, 'Brent's Women at war and at peace, 1914–1919', 2010 (Brent Archives)

Gray, G. W. R., *The Rise and Decline of the Park Royal Industrial Estate*, Oxford Polytechnic, Department of Town Planning, MSc Project, 1980 (Brent Archives)

London Ambulance Service records (LMA)

London Hospital, House Committee Minutes (London Hospital Archive)

Maddison, Pte. Robert, 'Diary 1917–1918', PR84/213 (AWM)

MEPO 2, Commissioner of Police Correspondence (TNA)

Meysey-Thompson, H. C., 'Diary 1914–1918', 92/19/1 (IWM)

Moore, Capt. Ralph Ingram, 'Diary 1915–16', PR 88/206 (AWM)

Peile, Lydia, 'Diary May 1916–Nov. 1917', 94/2/1 (IWM)

Pelly, Arthur Roland, 'MS Diary 1915', 91/15/1(IWM)

Playne MSS Collection, MS1112 (Senate House Library)

Reform Club, General Committee Minutes 1908–1919 (Reform Club)

Reform Club Letter Books 1913-1914 to 1918–1919 (Reform Club)

Robinson, David John, 'The Wensley Family at War, Work and Play (1890 to 1950)', unpublished typescript, 2007 (Bishopsgate Institute)

Robinson, Frederick Arthur, 'MS Diary 1914–1918', 11335 P. 401-402 (IWM)

Sainsbury Archive (Museum of London Docklands)

Tower, Winifred L. B., 'Journal, 26 July to October 1914, and Some Diary Notes, October 1914 to February 1916', P476 (IWM)

Wandsworth Board of Guardians, Minutes of the Board (Wandsworth Local History Library)

Wensley Family Archive (c.1890–1950), Correspondence (Bishopsgate Institute)

Newspapers and Magazines

Acton Gazette

The Aircraft Rag. The Magazine of the Employees of the Aircraft Manufacturing Co. Ltd (Brent Archives)

Catholic Herald

Charity Organisation Review (COR)

Daily Chronicle

Daily Mail
Daily News
Estates Gazette (EG)
Hackney and Kingsland Gazette (HKG)
Hackney and Stoke Newington Recorder (HSNR)
Hampstead and Highgate Express
Manchester Guardian
Observer
Pall Mall Gazette
South London Press (SLP)
Star
The Times

Parliamentary Papers

Annual Report of the Chief Inspector of Factories and Workshops for the year 1914, Cd. 8051, 1915
Annual Report of the Chief Inspector of Factories and Workshops for the year 1915, Cd. 8256, 1916
Annual Report of the Chief Inspector of Factories and Workshops for the year 1916, Cd. 8570, 1917
Annual Report of the Chief Inspector of Factories and Workshops for the year 1917, Cd. 9108, 1918
Annual Report of the Chief Inspector of Factories and Workshops for the year 1918, Cd. 340, 1919
Census of England and Wales 1911, *Occupations and Industries Pt. II*, Cd. 7019, 1913
Census of England Wales 1921, *County of London*, 1922
Commission of Enquiry into Industrial Unrest. No. 5 Division. *Report of the Commissioners for the London and South-Eastern Area*, Cd. 8666, 1917
Parliamentary Debates (House of Commons), Fifth Series, 1914–1918 (HC Debates)
Report of the Commissioner of Police of the Metropolis for the Year 1914, Cd. 8188, 1916
Report of the Commissioner of Police of the Metropolis for the Year 1916, Cd. 8827, 1917
Report of the Commissioner of Police of the Metropolis for the Year 1917, Cd. 9204, 1918

Report of the Commissioner of Police of the Metropolis for the Years 1918 and 1919, Cd. 543, 1920

Report of the Commissioners of Prisons and the Directors of Convict Prisons, with Appendices (For the Year ended 31st March, 1919), Cd. 374, 1919

Report from the Joint Select Committee of the House of Lords and the House of Commons on the Criminal Law Amendment Bill and Sexual Offences Bill [H.L.] together with the Proceedings of the Committee, Minutes of Evidence and Appendices, Cd. 145, 1918

Report of the Working Classes Cost of Living Committee, 1918, Cd. 8980, 1918

Royal Commission on Venereal Diseases, Final Report, Cd. 8189, 1916

Primary Sources

Addison, Christopher, Politics from Within, 1911–1918: Including Some Records of a Great National Effort, 2 vols, 1924

Addison, Christopher, Four and a Half Years: A Personal Diary from June 1914 to January 1919, 2 vols, 1934

Alec-Tweedie, Mrs Ethel, Women and Soldiers, 1918

Allen, Mary S., The Pioneer Policewoman, 1925

Allen, Mary S., Lady in Blue, 1936

Andrews, Irene Osgood, Economic Effects of the War upon Women and Children in Great Britain, New York, 1918

Anon., A Record of the Honoured Men of Wimbledon & Merton Who Fell in the Great War 1914–18, with Notes of Local Activities during the Same Period, 1921

Anon., A Soldier's Diary of the Great War, 1929

Anon., The First Fifty Years of Brunner, Mond & Co. 1873–1923, 1923

Anon. [Albert Lieck], Narrow Waters: The First Volume of the Life and Thoughts of a Common Man, 1935

Anon., Sweated Industries, Being a Handbook of the 'Daily News' Exhibition, 1906

Anon., Thomas Hancock Nunn: The Life of a Social Reformer. Written by His Friends for His Friends, 1942

'A People's Autobiography of Hackney', Working Lives. Vol. 1, 1905–45, 1976

Armstrong, Arthur C., Bouverie Street to Bowling Green Lane: Fifty-Five Years of Specialized Publishing, 1946

Asquith, Lady Cynthia, Diaries 1915–1918, 1968

Baedeker, Karl, *London and Its Environs: Handbook for Travellers*, 1911

Bagnold, Enid, *A Diary Without Dates*, 1918 (Windmill Library edn, 1933)

Barbellion, W. N. P., *The Journal of a Disappointed Man*, 1919

Bell, Anne Olivier (ed.), *The Diary of Virginia Woolf. Vol. I, 1915–1919*, 1977

Bellman, Harold, *Cornish Cockney: Reminiscences and Reflections*, 1947

Bennett, Arnold, *The Pretty Lady: A Novel*, 1918

Bennett, H. J., *I was a Walworth Boy*, 1980

Benson, Stella, *This is the End*, 1917

Bentley, E. C., *Peace Year in the City 1918–19: An Account of the Outstanding Events in the City of London during Peace Year, in the Mayoralty of the Rt. Hon. Sir Horace Brooks Marshall, KCVO, LL.D, following the Great War of 1914–1918*, 1920

Beveridge, Sir William, *British Food Control*, 1928

Beveridge, Lord William, *Power and Influence*, 1953

Bickersteth, John (ed.), *The Bickersteth Diaries 1914–1918*, 1995

Biron, Sir Chartres, *Without Prejudice: Impressions of Life and Law*, 1936

Blumenfeld, R. D., *All in a Lifetime*, 1931

Bogart, Ernest L., *Direct and Indirect Costs of the Great World War*, New York, 1919

Booth, Charles, *Life and Labour of the People in London. Series I, Poverty, Vol. I, East, Central and South London*, 1892

Booth, J. B., *Miss 'Billie' Tuchaud: Her Life and Letters*, 1918

Booth, J. B., *The Days We Knew*, 1943

Bosanquet, Helen, 'Housing Conditions in London', *Economic Journal*, Vol. 27, No. 107, September 1917, pp. 330–45

Bowley, Arthur L., *Prices and Wages in the United Kingdom, 1914–1920*, Oxford, 1921

Brittain, Vera, *Testament of Youth: An Autobiographical Study of the Years 1900–1925*, 1933

Brockway, Fenner, *Inside the Left: Thirty Years of Platform, Press, Prison and Parliament*, 1942

Broodbank, Joseph G., *History of the Port of London*, 2 vols, 1921, Vol. II

Brown, Beatrice Curtis, *Southwards from Swiss Cottage*, 1947

Brust, Harold, *In Plain Clothes: Further Memoirs of a Political Police Officer*, 1937

Burke, Thomas, *Out and About: A Note-Book of London in War-Time*, 1919

Burns, C. Delisle, *A Short History of Birkbeck College (University of London)*, 1924

Campbell, Janet M., *Report on the Physical Welfare of Mothers and Children, England Wales*, Vol. II, 1917

Cancellor, H. L., *The Life of a London Beak*, 1930

Carter, Henry, *The Control of the Drink Trade in Britain: A Contribution to National Efficiency During the Great War, 1915–1918*, 2nd edn, 1919

Chapman, Cecil, *The Poor Man's Court of Justice: Twenty-Five Years as a Metropolitan Magistrate*, 1925

Church, Richard, *The Golden Sovereign – A Conclusion to 'Over the Bridge'*, 1957

Churchill, Winston S., *The World Crisis, Vol. I, 1911–1914*, 1923 (Folio Society edn, 2007)

Churchill, Winston S., *The World Crisis, Vol. II, 1915*, 1923 (Folio Society edn, 2007)

Churchill, Winston S., *The World Crisis, Vol. III, 1916–1918*, 1927 (Folio Society edn, 2007)

Colville, Lady Cynthia, *Crowded Life*, 1963

Cooper, Diana, *The Rainbow Comes and Goes*, 1958

Cross, George, *Suffolk Punch: A Business Man's Autobiography*, 1939

Cutlack, F. M. (ed.), *War Letters of General Monash*, Sydney, 2nd edn, 1934

Dearle, N. B., *An Economic Chronicle of the Great War for Great Britain and Ireland*, 1929

Dent, J. M., *The Memoirs of J. M. Dent 1849–1926, with Some Additions by Hugh R. Dent*, 1928

Drake, Barbara, *Women in the Engineering Trades*, 1917

Ezard, Edward, *Battersea Boy*, 1979

Fitch, Herbert T., *Traitors Within: The Adventures of Detective Inspector Herbert T. Fitch*, 1933

Flower, Norman (ed.), *The Journals of Arnold Bennett*, 3 vols, 1932–3

Ford, Ford Madox, *Some Do Not . . .*, 1924 (*Parade's End*, Everyman edn, 1992)

Ford, Ford Madox, *A Man Could Stand Up –*, 1926 (*Parade's End*, Everyman edn, 1992)

Fox, R. M., *Smoky Crusade*, 1937

Frankau, Gilbert, *Peter Jackson, Cigar Merchant: A Romance of Modern Life*, 1920

Fraser, Helen, *Women and War Work*, New York, 1918

Friends' Emergency Committee, *Report for the Half-Year Ending June 30th, 1915*, 1915

Galsworthy, John, *Saint's Progress*, 1919

Galsworthy, John, *On Forsyte 'Change*, 1930

Gardiner, A. G., *John Benn and the Progressive Movement*, 1925

Gibbs, A. Hamilton, *Gun Fodder: The Diary of Four Years of War*, Boston, Mass., 1919

Gibbs, Philip, *The Soul of War*, 1915

Gibbs, Philip, *Realities of War*, 1920

Gleason, Arthur, *Inside the British Isles*, 1917

Goble, Bill, *Life-Long Rebel*, 1984

Golland, Jim (ed.), *When I was a Child: Memories of Childhood in Pinner, Middlesex*, 1984

Graham, John W., *Conscription and Conscience: A History 1916–1919*, 1922

Graves, Robert, *Goodbye to All That*, 1929 (Penguin edn, 1986)

Gray, John, *Gin and Bitters*, 1938

Grey, Edward, Viscount of Falloden, *Twenty-Five Years, 1892–1916*, 2 vols, 1925

Grosch, Alfred, *St Pancras Pavements: An Autobiography*, 1947

Hall, Edith, *Canary Girls and Stockpots*, Luton, 1977

Hall, Radclyffe, *Adam's Breed*, 1924 (1957 edn)

Hambrook, Walter, *Hambrook of the Yard*, 1937

Hamilton, Mary Agnes, *Dead Yesterday*, 1916

Hammerton, J. A., *Books and Myself: Memoirs of an Editor*, 1944

Hammond, M. B., *British Labor Conditions and Legislation during the Great War*, New York, 1919

Hannington, Wal, *Never on Our Knees*, 1967

Harris, H. Wilson, and Bryant, Margaret, *The Churches and London (An Outline Survey of Religious Work in the Metropolitan Area)*, 1914

Hicks, Stephen 'Johnny', *Sparring for Luck*, 1982

Higgins, D. S. (ed.), *The Private Diaries of Sir H. Rider Haggard*, 1980

Hirst, Francis W., *The Consequences of the War to Great Britain*, 1934

History of the Ministry of Munitions, 12 vols, 1919–22

Hobhouse, Stephen, *Forty Years and an Epilogue: An Autobiography (1881–1951)*, 1951

Holland, Sydney, Viscount Knutsford, *In Black and White*, 1926

Hope, E. W., *Report on the Physical Welfare of Mothers and Children, England Wales*, Vol. I, 1917

Humphreys, Mrs Desmond 'Rita', *Recollections of a Literary Life*, 1936

Hunt, Violet, and Hueffer, Ford Madox, *Zeppelin Nights: A London Entertainment*, 1916

Hurley, Alfred James, *Days That are Gone: Milestones I have Passed in South-West London*, 1947

Hutton, Robert, *Of Those Alone*, 1958

Hyde, Robert R., *Industry was My Parish*, 1968

Inge, W. R., *Diary of a Dean: St Paul's 1911–1934*, 1949

Islington Metropolitan Borough Council, *Annual Report on the Health & Sanitary Condition of the Metropolitan Borough of Islington*, 59th Annual Report, 1914

Jasper, A. S., *A Hoxton Childhood*, 1969 (Readers' Union edn, 1971)

Jones, C. Sheridan, *London in War-Time*, 1917

Kirkaldy, Adam W. (ed.), *Industry and Finance (Supplementary Volume), Being the Results of Inquiries arranged by the Section of Economic Science and Statistics of the British Association during the Years 1918 and 1919*, 1920

Kreitman, Esther, *Diamonds*, 1944 (1st English edn, 2010)

Lee, Arnold Charles, *As I Recall: The Memoirs of Arnold Charles Lee*, 2010

Lee, Celia, *Jean, Lady Hamilton 1861–1941: A Soldier's Wife (Wife of General Sir Ian Hamilton). A Biography from Her Diaries*, 2001

Legge, Edward, *King Edward, The Kaiser and War*, 1917

Litman, Simon, *Prices and Price Control in Great Britain and the United States during the World War*, New York, 1920

Lloyd George, David, *War Memoirs*, 2 vols, new edn, 1938

Lockwood, Florence E., *Private Diary*, 1926–9 (Playne MSS, Folder 156)

The London Censorship 1914–1919. By Members of the Staff Past and Present, n.d. [1919]

London County Council, *The Council and the War*, 1920

London County Council, *Housing: With Particular Reference to Post-War Housing Schemes*, 1928

London County Council, *London Statistics. 1911–12 . . .*, Vol. XXII, 1912

London County Council, *London Statistics. 1912–13 . . .*, Vol. XXIII, 1914

London County Council, *London Statistics. 1913–14 . . .*, Vol. XXIV, 1915

London County Council, *London Statistics. 1914–15 . . .*, Vol. XXV, 1916

London County Council, *London Statistics. 1915–20 . . .*, Vol. XXVI, 1921

London County Council, *London Statistics. 1920–21 . . .*, Vol. XXVII, 1922

London County Council, *London Statistics. 1921–23 . . .*, Vol. XXVIII, 1924

London County Council, *Record of Service in the Great War 1914–18 by Members of the Council's Staff*, 1922

Lowndes, Susan (ed.), *Diaries and Letters of Marie Belloc Lowndes 1911–1947*, 1971

Lucy, Sir Henry, *The Diary of a Journalist: Fresh Extracts*, Vol. III, 1923

Macaulay, Rose, *Non-Combatants and Others*, 1916

MacDonagh, Michael, *In London during the Great War: The Diary of a Journalist*, 1935

McKenna, Stephen, *While I Remember*, 1921

MacKenzie, Norman and Jeanne (eds), *The Diary of Beatrice Webb. Vol. 3, 1905–1924: 'The Power to Alter Things'*, 1984

Macpherson, Sir W. G., *Medical Services: General History. Vol. I, Medical Services in the United Kingdom etc.*, 1921

Macpherson, Sir W. G., Herringham, Sir W.P., Elliott, T. R. and Balfour, A., *History of the Great War Based on Official Documents. Medical Services. Diseases of the War*, Vol. II, 1923

Marrot, H. V., *The Life and Letters of John Galsworthy*, 1935

Masterman, Lucy, *C. F. G. Masterman: A Biography*, 1939

Miles, Hallie Eustace, *Untold Tales of War-Time London*, 1930

Mills, Lady Dorothy, *The Laughter of Fools*, 1920

Moore, H. Keatley, and Sayers, W. C. Berwick (eds), *Croydon and the Great War: The Official History of the War Work of the Borough and its Citizens from 1914 to 1919. Together with the Croydon Roll of Honour*, 1920

Morand, Paul, *Tender Shoots*, 1921 (1st English translation, 2011)

Morison, Frank, *War on Great Cities: A Study of the Facts*, 1937

Morris, Joseph, *The German Air Raids on Great Britain 1914–1918*, 1925

Morrison, Lord [Herbert] of Lambeth, *Herbert Morrison: An Autobiography*, 1960

Morriss, Henry Fuller, *Bermondsey's 'Bit' in the Greatest War*, 1923

Moseley, Sydney, *The Private Diaries of Sydney Moseley*, 1960

Mudie-Smith, Richard (ed.), *The Religious Life of London*, 1904

Munson, James (ed.), *Echoes of the Great War: The Diary of the Reverend Andrew Clark 1914–1919*, Oxford, 1985

Murry, John Middleton, *Between Two Worlds: An Autobiography*, 1935

Neighbour, Rose (as told to Muriel Burgess), *All of Me: The True Story of a London Rose*, 1979

Neil, Arthur Fowler, *Forty Years of Man-Hunting*, 1932

Nevinson, Henry, *Last Changes, Last Chances*, 1928

Newnham-Davis, Col. Nathaniel, *The Gourmet's Guide to London*, 1914

Norwich, John Julius (ed.), *The Duff Cooper Diaries 1915–1951*, 2005

Oddie, S. Ingleby, *Inquest*, 1941

Odhams, W. J. B., *The Story of the Bomb: A Brief Account of the Disaster Due to the Dropping of an Incendiary Bomb from a German Aeroplane upon the Premises of Messrs. Odhams, Ltd., on January 29th, 1918, Now Available for the Information of the Shareholders*, 1919

Pankhurst, E. Sylvia, *The Suffragette Movement: An Intimate Account of Persons and Ideals*, 1931

Pankhurst, E. Sylvia, *The Home Front: A Mirror to Life in England during the World War*, 1932

Paterson, Alexander, *Across the Bridges: or, Life by the South London Riverside*, 1911

Peel, Mrs C. S., *How We Lived Then: 1914–1918: A Sketch of Social and Domestic Life in England during the War*, 1929

Pethick-Lawrence, F. W., *Fate Has Been Kind*, 1942

Pigache, D. Nichols, *Café Royal Days*, 1934

Playne, Caroline E., *Society at War, 1914–1916*, 1931

Playne, Caroline E., *Britain Holds On, 1917, 1918*, 1933

Postgate, Raymond, *The Builders' History*, 1923

Pottle, Mark (ed.), *Champion Redoubtable: The Diaries and Letters of Violet Bonham Carter 1914–45*, 1998

Pulling, Alexander (ed.), *Defence of the Realm Acts and Regulations Passed and Made to July 31st, 1915*, 1915

Quigley, Hugh, and Goldie, Ismay, *Housing and Slum Clearance in London*, 1934

Rawlinson, A., *In Defence of London, 1915–1918*, 1923

Reay, W. T., *The Specials – How they Served London: The Story of the Metropolitan Special Constabulary*, 1920

Reeves, Maud Pember, *Round About a Pound a Week*, 1913

Registrar-General of Births, Deaths, and Marriages in England, *Annual Summary of Marriages, Births, and Deaths in England and Wales and in London . . . 1912*, 1913

Repington, C. à Court, *The First World War, 1914–1918: Personal Experiences of Lieut.-Col. C. à Court Repington*, 2 vols, 1921

Riddell, G. A. R., *Lord Riddell's War Diary 1914–1918*, 1933

Rider, Dan, *Ten Years' Adventures Among Landlords and Tenants: The Story of the Rent Acts*, 1927

Roberts, Florence, *The Ups and Downs of Florrie Roberts*, 1980

Rocker, Fermin, *The East End Years: A Stepney Childhood*, 1998

Rocker, Rudolf, *The London Years*, 1956

Rolph, C. H., *London Particulars*, Oxford, 1980

Royal Borough of Kensington, *Annual Report of the Medical Officer of Health for the Year 1917*, 1918

Royce, James, *I Stand Nude*, 1937

Roynon, Gavin (ed.), *Home Fires Burning: The Great War Diaries of Georgina Lee*, Stroud, 2006

Ryland, F. J., *Specks on the Dusty Road*, Birmingham, 1937

Sandhurst, Viscount [William], *From Day to Day: 1914–1915*, 1928

Sandhurst, Viscount [William], *From Day to Day: 1916–1921*, 1929

Scannell, Dorothy, *Mother Knew Best: An East End Childhood*, 1974

Shadwell, Arthur, *Drink in 1914–1922: A Lesson in Control*, 1923

Shaw, George Bernard, *Heartbreak House*, 1919

Slate, Ruth, *Dear Girl: The Diaries and Letters of Two Working Women (1897–1917)*, edited by Tierl Thompson, 1987

Smith, Douglas H., *The Industries of Greater London, Being a Survey of the Recent Industrialisation of the Northern and Western Sectors of Greater London*, 1933

Smith, Sir Hubert Llewellyn (ed.), *The New Survey of London Life and Labour. Vol. I, Forty Years of Change*, 1930

Smith, Sir Hubert Llewellyn (ed.), *The New Survey of London Life and Labour. Vol. II, London Industries I*, 1931

Smith, Sir Hubert Llewellyn (ed.), *The New Survey of London Life and Labour. Vol. III, Survey of Social Conditions (I) The Eastern Area (Text)*, 1932

Smith, Sir Hubert Llewellyn (ed.), *The New Survey of London Life and Labour. Vol. VI, Social Survey II, Western Area*, 1934

Southgate, Walter, *That's the Way It was: A Working-class Autobiography 1890–1950*, 1982

Spensley, J. Calvert, 'Urban Housing Problems', *Journal of the Royal Statistical Society*, Vol. LXXXI, No. 2, March 1918, pp. 161–228

Squire, Rose E., *Thirty Years in the Public Service: An Industrial Retrospect*, 1927

Steed, Henry Wickham, *Through Thirty Years, 1892–1922: A Personal Narrative*, 2 vols, 1924

Stokes, Alfred, *East Ham: From Village to County Borough*, 3rd edn, 1933

Stone, Gilbert (ed.), *Women War Workers*, 1917

Strachey, Ray, *Women's Suffrage and Women's Service: The History of the London and National Society for Women's Service*, 1927

Street, G. S., *At Home in the War*, 1918

Summerskill, Edith, *A Woman's World*, 1967

Thomson, Basil, *Queer People*, 1922

Thomson, Basil, *The Scene Changes*, 1939

Thorne, Guy, *The Great Acceptance: The Life Story of F. N. Charrington*, 1912

Thurtle, Ernest, *Time's Winged Chariot: Memories and Comments*, 1945

Titterton, W. R., *London Scenes*, 1920

Tuohy, Ferdinand, *The Crater of Mars*, 1929

Tupper, Edward, *Seamen's Torch: The Life Story of Captain Edward Tupper, National Union of Seamen*, 1938

Walker, Harold W., *Mainly Memories, 1906–1930*, 1986

Ward, Mrs Humphry, *Harvest*, 1919

Warner, Sylvia Townsend, *With the Hunted: Selected Writings*, Norwich, 2012

Watson, Eric R. (ed.), *Trial of George Joseph Smith*, 1922

Watson, W. F., *Machines and Men: An Autobiography of an Itinerant Mechanic*, 1935

Wells, H. G., *Mr Britling Sees It Through*, 1916

While, Jack, *Fifty Years of Fire Fighting in London*, 1931

Williamson, Joseph, *Father Joe: The Autobiography of Joseph Williamson of Poplar and Stepney*, 1963

Willis, Frederick, *London General*, 1953

Wilson, Romer, *If All These Young Men*, 1919

Winnington-Ingram, Arthur Foley, *The Potter and the Clay*, 1917

Winnington-Ingram, Arthur Foley, *Fifty Years' Work in London (1889–1939)*, 1940

Woolwich Metropolitan Borough Council, *Annual Report of the Medical Officer of Health for [1914–1918]*

Wootton, Barbara, *In a World I Never Made: Autobiographical Reflections*, 1967

Wyles, Lilian, *A Woman at Scotland Yard: Reflections on the Struggles and Achievements of Thirty Years in the Metropolitan Police*, 1952

Secondary Sources

Ball, Michael, and Sunderland, David, *An Economic History of London, 1800–1914*, 2001

Banton, Michael, *The Coloured Quarter: Negro Immigrants in an English City*, 1955

Barker, T. C., and Robbins, Michael, *A History of London Transport: Passenger Travel and the Development of the Metropolis. Volume II, The Twentieth Century to 1970*, 1974

Beckett, Ian F. W., *The Making of the First World War*, 2012

Berridge, Virginia, *Opium and the People: Opiate Use and Drug Control Policy in Nineteenth and Early Twentieth Century England*, 1999

Bird, Samantha L., *Stepney: Profile of a London Borough from the Outbreak of the First World War to the Festival of Britain, 1914–1951*, Newcastle upon Tyne, 2011

Bloch, Howard, and Hill, Graham (eds), *Germans in London: No. 1 East Ham and West Ham Documentary Sources 1865–1919*, 2000

Boghardt, Thomas, *Spies of the Kaiser: German Covert Operations in Great Britain during the First World War Era*, Basingstoke, 2004

Boulton, David, *Objection Overruled*, 1967

Bownes, David, Green, Oliver, and Mullins, Sam, *Underground: How the Tube Shaped London*, 2012

Bradstock, Andrew, Gill, Sean, Hogan, Anne, and Morgan, Sue (eds), *Masculinity and Spirituality in Victorian Culture*, Basingstoke, 2000

Braybon, Gail, *Women Workers in the First World War*, 1981

Bristow, Edward J., *Vice and Vigilance: Purity Movements in Britain since 1700*, Dublin, 1977

Brockway, Fenner, *Bermondsey Story: The Life of Alfred Salter*, 1949

Bush, Julia, *Behind the Lines: East London Labour 1914–1919*, 1984

Cameron, H. C., *Mr Guy's Hospital 1726–1948*, 1954

Castle, Ian, *London 1914–17: The Zeppelin Menace*, Oxford, 2008

Castle, Ian, *London 1917–18: The Bomber Blitz*, Oxford, 2010

Cesarani, David, and Kushner, Tony (eds), *The Internment of Aliens in Twentieth Century Britain*, 1993

Clark, Christopher, *The Sleepwalkers: How Europe Went to War in 1914*, 2012

Clark-Kennedy, A. E., *The London: A Study in the Voluntary Hospital System. Vol. 2, The Second Hundred Years 1840–1948*, 1963

Connelly, Mark, *The Great War, Memory and Ritual: Commemoration in the City and East London, 1916–1939*, 2002

Cox, Jeffrey, *The English Churches in a Secular Society: Lambeth 1870–1930*, Oxford, 1982

Cresswell, D'Arcy, *Margaret McMillan: A Memoir*, 1948

Culleton, Claire A., *Working-Class Culture, Women, and Britain, 1914–1921*, New York, 1999

Donoughue, Bernard, and Jones, G. W., *Herbert Morrison: Portrait of a Politician*, 1973

Englander, David, *Landlord and Tenant in Urban Britain 1838–1918*, Oxford, 1983

Fishman, William J., *East End Jewish Radicals 1875–1914*, 1975

Fraser-Stephen, Elspet, *Two Centuries in the London Coal Trade: The Story of Charringtons*, 1952

Fryer, Peter, *Staying Power: The History of Black People in Britain*, 1984

Fussell, Paul, *The Great War and Modern Memory*, 1975 (illustrated edn, 2000)

Gainer, Bernard, *The Alien Invasion: The Origins of the Aliens Act of 1905*, 1972

Grange Museum of Community History and Brent Archive, *Places in Brent: Twyford and Park Royal*, c.2001

Gregory, Adrian, *The Last Great War: British Society and the First World War*, Cambridge, 2008

Grigg, John, *The Young Lloyd George*, 1973

Grigg, John, *Lloyd George: The People's Champion 1902–1911*, 1978

Grigg, John, *Lloyd George: From Peace to War 1912–1916*, 1985

Hanson, Neil, *First Blitz: The Secret German Plan to Raze London to the Ground in 1918*, 2008

Hill, Graham, and Bloch, Howard, *The Silvertown Explosion: London 1917*, Stroud, 2003

Hinton, James, *The First Shop Stewards' Movement*, 1973

Hochschild, Adam, *To End All Wars: How the First World War Divided Britain*, 2011

Houlbrook, Matt, *Queer London: Perils and Pleasures in the Sexual Metropolis, 1918–1957*, Chicago, 2005

Hugill, Antony, *Sugar and All That . . . A History of Tate & Lyle*, 1978

Jackson, Alan A., *London's Termini*, Newton Abbot, 1969

Kynaston, David, *The City of London. Vol. II, Golden Years 1890–1914*, 1995

Kynaston, David, *The City of London. Vol. III, Illusions of Gold 1914–1945*, 1999

Light, Alison, *Mrs Woolf and the Servants*, 2007

Long, Vicky, and Marland, Hilary, 'From Danger and Motherhood to Health and Beauty: Health Advice for the Factory Girl in Early Twentieth-Century Britain', *Twentieth Century British History*, Vol. 20, No. 4, 2009, pp. 454–81

Longstaffe-Gowan, Todd, *The London Square: Gardens in the Midst of Town*, 2012

Lucas, John, *Thomas Beecham: An Obsession with Music*, 2008

Lycett, Andrew, *Conan Doyle: The Man Who Created Sherlock Holmes*, 2007

McLeod, Hugh, *Class and Religion in the Late Victorian City*, 1974

Marcus, Geoffrey, *Before the Lamps Went Out*, 1965

Marlow, Joyce (ed.), *Women and the Great War*, 1999

Marquand, David, *Ramsay MacDonald*, 1977

Marrin, Albert, *The Last Crusade: The Church of England in the First World War*, Durham, North Carolina, 1974

Martin, J. E., *Greater London: An Industrial Geography*, 1966

Marwick, Arthur, *The Deluge: British Society and the First World War*, 2nd edn, 2006

Mayhew, Emily, *Wounded: From Battlefield to Blighty, 1914–1918*, 2013

Michie, R. C. (ed.), *The Development of London as a Financial Centre*, 4 vols, 2000

Millman, Brock, *Managing Domestic Dissent in First World War Britain*, 2000

Morris, Richard, *The Man Who Ran London During the Great War: The Diaries and Letters of Lieutenant General Sir Francis Lloyd GCVO, KCB, DSO (1853–1926)*, Barnsley, 2009

Neiberg, Michael S., *Dance of the Furies: Europe and the Outbreak of World War I*, Cambridge, Mass., 2011

ODNB (Oxford Dictionary of National Biography)

Panayi, Panikos, *The Enemy in Our Midst: Germans in Britain during the First World War*, New York, 1991

Panayi, Panikos (ed.), *Germans in London since 1500*, 1996

Panayi, Panikos (ed.), *Racial Violence in Britain in the Nineteenth and Twentieth Centuries*, 1996

Pennell, Catriona, *A Kingdom United: Popular Responses to the Outbreak of the First World War in Britain and Ireland*, Oxford, 2012

Pimlott, J. A. R., *Toynbee Hall: Fifty Years of Social Progress 1884–1934*, 1935

Postgate, Raymond, *The Life of George Lansbury*, 1951

Pugh, Martin, *Speak for Britain! A New History of the Labour Party*, 2010

Reynolds, Gerald W., and Judge, Anthony, *The Night the Police Went on Strike*, 1968

Reznick, Jeffrey S., *Healing the Nation: Soldiers and the Culture of Caregiving in Britain during the First World War*, Manchester, 2004

Ridley, Jane, *Edwin Lutyens: His Life, His Wife, His Work*, 2002

Robbins, Keith, *The Abolition of War: The 'Peace Movement' in Britain, 1915–1919*, Cardiff, 1976

Robinson, Douglas H., *The Zeppelin in Combat: A History of the German Naval Airship Division, 1912–1918*, 1962

Rose, Lionel, *The Massacre of the Innocents: Infanticide in Britain, 1800–1939*, 1986

Rubinstein, W. D., *Men of Property: The Very Wealthy in Britain since the Industrial Revolution*, 1981

Schmiechen, James A., *Sweated Industries and Sweated Labour: The London Clothing Trades, 1860–1914*, 1984

Scott, J. D., *Siemens Brothers, 1858–1958: An Essay in the History of Industry*, 1958

Silbey, David, *The British Working Class and Enthusiasm for War, 1914–1916*, 2005

Smith, Angela K., *Suffrage Discourse in Britain during the First World War*, Aldershot, 2005

Smithies, Edward, *The Black Economy in England since 1914*, Dublin, 1984

Survey of London, *County Hall (Monograph 17)*, 1991

Survey of London, *Vols XLIII–IV, Poplar, Blackwall and the Isle of Dogs. The Parish of All Saints*, 1994

Survey of London, *Vol. 48, Woolwich*, 2012

Thom, Deborah, *Nice Girls and Rude Girls: Women Workers in World War I*, 1998

Thorold, Peter, *The London Rich: The Creation of a Great City, from 1666 to the Present*, 1999

Tottenham History Workshop, *How Things Were: Growing up in Tottenham, 1890–1920*, 1982

Vessey, Alan, *Napier Powered*, Stroud, 1997

Vicinus, Martha, *Independent Women: Work and Community for Single Women, 1850–1920*, 1985

Walkowitz, Judith R., *Nights Out: Life in Cosmopolitan London*, 2012

Watson, Janet S. K., 'Khaki Girls, VADs, and Tommy's Sisters: Gender and Class in First World War Britain', *International History Review*, Vol. 19, No. 1, February 1997, pp. 32–51

Weller, Ken, *'Don't be a Soldier!' The Radical Anti-War Movement in North London 1914–1918*, 1985

White, Jerry, *Rothschild Buildings: Life in an East-End Tenement Block, 1887–1920*, 1980

White, Jerry, *The Worst Street in North London: Campbell Bunk, Islington, Between the Wars*, 1986

White, Jerry, *London in the Twentieth Century: A City and Its People*, 2001

White, Jerry, *London in the Nineteenth Century: A Human Awful Wonder of God*, 2007

Whyte, Adam Gowans, *Forty Years of Electrical Progress: The Story of G.E.C.*, 1930

Wilkinson, Alan, *The Church of England and the First World War*, 1978

Williams, Bridget, *The Best Butter in the World: A History of Sainsbury's*, 1994

Williams, S. C., *Religious Belief and Popular Culture in Southwark, c.1880–1939*, Oxford, 1999

Wilson, Charles, and Reader, William, *Men and Machines: A History of D. Napier & Son, Engineers, Ltd 1808–1958*, 1958

Wilson, Trevor, *The Myriad Faces of War: Britain and the Great War, 1914–1918*, Cambridge, 1986

Winslow, Barbara, *Sylvia Pankhurst: Sexual Politics and Political Activism*, 1996

Winter, Jay M., *The Great War and the British People*, 1986

Winter, Jay M., and Robert, Jean-Louis (eds), *Capital Cities at War: Paris, London, Berlin 1914–1919*, Cambridge, 1997

Winter, Jay M., and Robert, Jean-Louis (eds), *Capital Cities at War. Paris, London, Berlin 1914–1919. Vol. 2, A Cultural History*, Cambridge, 2007

Woollacott, Angela, *On Her Their Lives Depend: Munitions Workers in the Great War*, Berkeley, California, 1994

INDEX

abortion 233

Acton 39, 75, 93, 105, 106, 107, 121, 128, 234, 274

Addison, Christopher (1869–1951, Liberal politician) 44, 45, 162, 207, 248

Adelphi 171, 208

Admiralty 39, 40, 81, 111, 124, 125, 128, 129–30, 169, 173, 267

Air Ministry 83, 111, 267–8, 274

air raid precautions and defences (*see also* blackout) 39–40, 88–9, 124–31 passim, 145, 169–70, 175, 213–5, 217–9, 244, 249–54, 275–6

air raids 87–8, 124–9, 168–73, 211–19, 244, 249–52

Airco (Aircraft Manufacturing Co.) 106, 107–8, 242, 265

aircraft manufacture 103, 104, 105, 106, 107–8, 236, 242, 274

Aldwych 128, 217

Aldwych Theatre 45, 135

Alec-Tweedie, Ethel (1862–1940, writer) 65–6, 103, 145, 228, 229, 232

Alexandra Palace 72, 74, 79–80, 91

Alhambra Theatre (Leicester Square) xiv, 143–4, 168, 190, 221

Aliens Act 1905 86

Aliens Restriction Acts 70, 144

Allan, Maud (1873–1956, dancer) 258

Allen, Mary (1878–1964, police officer) 187, 189

Alliance of Honour 48, 151

allotments (see food)

Amalgamated Society of Engineers 10, 101

ambulances 42, 137, 166–7, 169, 210, 211, 256

Americans xiv, 14, 41, 60, 89, 90, 102, 143, 155, 196, 197, 209, 258, 262–4

Amiens 35, 255

Angell, Norman (1872–1967, peace campaigner) 20

Anglo-American Exhibition (1914) 13

Anglo-Spanish Exhibition (1914) 13

anti-conscription movement (*see* pacifists and pacifism, No-Conscription Fellowship)

Anti-German Union 84

Anti-Socialist Union 41

Antwerp 74

Apollo Theatre (Shaftesbury Avenue) 45

Archbishop of Canterbury (Thomas Davidson Randall, 1848–1930) 20, 66, 67

Arlington Street 141, 146, 147

Armistice 83, 89, 94, 144, 267–71

Armstrong, A.C. (publisher) 270

Army and Navy Stores (Victoria Street) 27–8, 99

Army Council 53, 150

Ascot 118

Asquith, Herbert (1852–1928, Liberal politician) 10, 14, 16, 44, 56, 59, 101, 121, 127, 169, 175–6, 220, 241–2, 258

Asquith, Katharine (1885–1976, socialite) 145

Asquith, Lady Cynthia (1887–1960, socialite) 118, 121, 122, 123, 125, 138–9, 142–3, 144, 146, 147, 155, 168, 201, 202, 209–10, 220, 221, 222, 261, 264, 265

Astor, Lady Nancy (1879–1964, hostess) 143

Athenaeum (Waterloo Place) 100, 210

August Bank Holiday 14, 17–23, 110, 122, 162

Australian and New Zealand Army Corps (ANZACs, *see also* Australians, New Zealanders) 112, 122–3, 135, 161, 164, 178, 263

Australians xiii, 86, 122–3, 167, 170, 184–5, 208, 262, 270

Austria 15, 16, 56, 81, 83, 84, 90

Austrian Londoners 3, 69–81 passim, 86, 100, 275

Bagnold, Enid (1889–1981, nurse, writer) 146, 147–8, 200–1

Baker Street 104, 195

Balfour, Arthur (1848–1930, Conservative politician) 130

Band of Hope, 49, 52

Bank of England 17–18, 28, 110, 119–20

bank rate 17–18, 28

Barbellion, W.N.P. (Bruce Cummings, 1889–1919, diarist) 43

Barnes 106

Barrie, James Matthew (1860–1937, writer) 44, 45, 261

Battenberg, Prince Louis of (1854–1921, sailor) 72

Battersea 17, 33, 52, 107

Bayswater 69, 71

Beatty, Sir David (1871–1936, sailor) 67

Beckenham 252

Beecham, Sir Thomas (1879–1961, musician) 164, 222

Belgian Londoners (and refugees) 73–5, 81–2, 96, 98, 119, 139, 144, 179, 180, 187

Belgium (and Flanders) xiv, 16, 17, 19, 21, 23, 24, 31, 35, 38, 41, 73, 98, 122, 129, 212, 266

Belgravia 4, 140, 186–7, 196

Belloc, Hilaire (1870–1953, writer) 44, 142

Bennett, Arnold (1867–1931, writer) 35, 38, 40, 44, 78, 94, 112, 116, 179, 190, 196–7, 217

Bennett, H.J. (memoirist) 226

Benson, Stella (1892–1933, writer) 152

Beresford, Lord Charles (1846–1919, sailor, Conservative politician) 208

Berlemont, Victor (publican) 82

Berlin 2, 9, 23, 46

Bermondsey 18, 28, 31–2, 33, 34, 52, 72, 74, 92, 96–7, 98, 110, 130, 137, 138, 154, 159, 160, 167–8, 174, 183, 205, 212, 222, 233, 240, 242

Bethnal Green 7, 83, 88, 96, 117, 124, 132, 171, 212, 214, 226, 227, 233, 236, 239, 246, 250

Beveridge, William (1879–1963, civil servant) 144–5, 174, 217, 247

Bexley 57

Bezalel, Abraham (Jewish rights campaigner) 87

Bickersteth, Ella (clergyman's wife) 134

Billing, Noel Pemberton (1881–1948, airman and politician) 65, 89, 170, 214, 258–9, 260

Bing Boys Are Here, The 163–4, 168

Bing Girls Are There, The 221

Binyon, Laurence (1869–1943, poet) 142

Birkbeck College 152

Birmingham 97

Biron, Chartres (Metropolitan magistrate) 231, 269–70

Bishop of London (*see* Winnington-Ingram, AF)

Bishopsgate Goods Depot 250, 253

Bisley 14

black Londoners 81, 83, 101, 264

Blackfriars Bridge 112, 172, 199–200

Blackfriars Road, 161, 185

Blackheath 215

blackout 39–41, 44–5, 46, 118, 125, 129, 130–1, 162, 170, 176, 201, 211–12, 221, 242

Blackwall Tunnel 217–8
Blatchford, Robert (1851–1943, writer) 30
Bloomsbury 64, 117, 125, 127, 243, 250
Blumenfeld, Ralph David (American-born journalist) 41, 43, 56, 116, 118, 133, 167, 169, 220, 228
Bond Street 135
Booth, Charles (1840–1916, sociologist) 5, 6–7, 44, 242, 273, 275
Booth, J.B. (journalist) 25, 88–9, 139
Borden, Sir Robert (1854–1937, Canadian politician) 191
Bottomley, Horatio (1860–1933, journalist and politician) 59, 76, 170
Bow Street Magistrates' Court 11, 180, 206, 260
Bowerman, Charles (1851?–1947, Labour politician) 59
Boy Scouts 49, 144, 215
Boyle, Nina (1865–1943, police officer) 187–8
Boys' Brigade 129
Brighton 13, 88–9, 201–11
Bristol 123, 254
British Board of Film Censors 65
British Empire Union 90
British Expeditionary Force (BEF) 23, 32, 35, 42, 50, 51, 52, 64
British Museum 11, 66
British Socialist Party 160
British Summer Time 162
Brittain, Frederick (soldier) 122–3
Brittain, Vera (1893–1970, nurse, writer) 135–6, 146, 148, 166–7, 194
Brixton 27, 31, 65, 73, 117, 152, 171, 183
Brixton Prison 159, 206, 260
Brockway, Fenner (1888–1988, peace campaigner and socialist) 159
Brompton 12, 258, 269
Brotherhood Church (Southgate Road) 160, 161, 208
Brown, Beatrice (memoirist) 22, 23–4, 262
Brunner, Mond & Co. (chemicals manufacturers) 200–1
Brust, Harold (police officer) 71

Bruton Street 141–2, 149
Buckingham Gate 111, 202
Buckingham Palace 11, 21, 22, 24, 25, 39, 152, 176, 209, 266, 269, 271
building workers 1, 6, 9–10, 29–30, 227
Bunbury, Edith Marjorie (social worker) 56–7, 122
Burke, Thomas (1886–1945, writer) 81, 82
Burns, John (1858–1943, Labour politician) 32, 36
buses 10, 32, 37–8, 44, 116, 206, 213, 220, 221, 256, 259, 261–2, 265, 269, 271
Butt, Alfred (1878–1962, impresario) 64

Cable Street 83, 243
Café Royal (Regent Street) 5, 25
Camberwell 33, 73, 90, 109, 122, 135–6, 146, 165–6, 219, 229, 234, 239, 243
Camden Town 102, 160, 193, 236, 250
Cameron, Basil (1884–1975, musician) 72
Canadians xiv, 76, 112, 113, 184–5, 191,193, 208, 209, 262
Cancellor, Henry Lannoy (1862–1929, Metropolitan magistrate) 71
Canning Town 76, 83, 90
Carleton, Billie (1896–1918, actress) 195
Carnegie, Andrew (1835–1919, philanthropist) 44
Carson, Sir Edward (1854–1935, Unionist politician) 15
Casement, Sir Roger (1864–1916, Irish patriot) 165
casualties 120–1, 131, 133, 165–7, 209–10, 236–7, 252, 255, 264, 271–2
Cave, Sir George (1856–1928, Conservative politician) 214–5, 244, 261
Cavell, Edith (1865–1915, nurse) 123
Cenotaph 271
Central Control Board (Liquor Traffic) 57–8, 59

Chancery Lane 128, 268
Chandos Street 35, 39, 142
Chant, Laura Ormiston (1848–1923, puritan) 190
Chaplin, Charlie (1889–1977, actor) 221
Chapman, Cecil (1852–1938, Metropolitan magistrate) 186
Charing Cross Hospital 43
Charing Cross Station 23, 43, 105, 134, 134, 145, 154, 166, 167, 256
charity 36–7, 74–5, 119, 133, 137–44, 220, 232, 251
Charity Organisation Society 52, 83, 137, 139, 230
Charrington, Frederick Nicholas (1850–1936, puritan) 61–2, 64–5
Charteris, Yvo (d1915, soldier) 122, 155
Chelsea 22, 25, 122–3, 141, 144, 146, 158, 222, 233, 245, 251
Childers, Erskine (1870–1922, writer) 44
children's homes 37–8, 138, 235–6
Chinese Londoners 82–3, 194–5
Chiswick 105, 161
Christmas 7, 45–6, 135–6, 142, 153, 157, 174, 176, 222–4, 248, 266
Chu Chin Chow 64, 221–2
Church of England Waifs' and Strays' Society 235–6
Church, Richard (1893–1972, civil servant, writer) 34, 158
churches (see religion)
Churchill, Winston (1874–1965, Liberal politician) 15–16, 39, 81, 124, 130, 174, 256, 267
cinema 7, 47–8, 64–5, 164, 168, 176, 211, 221
City of London 17–20, 27, 28, 39, 66, 69, 72, 78, 84, 90, 93–4, 110, 113–4, 116, 127–8, 157, 162, 164, 195, 202, 208, 212–14, 223, 226, 229, 232, 243, 250, 257, 268, 270
City of London Police 8, 25, 161, 260–1
Clapham 12, 27, 174, 183, 199, 243, 251, 254, 262
Clapton 75, 88, 131

Clapton Orient Football Club 61, 132
Claridge's Hotel (Brook Street) 4, 138
class feeling 1–2, 4–5, 7–13, 28, 32, 47–68 passim, 132, 157–8, 171–4, 202–3, 211, 214–5, 217, 223, 227–32, 248, 249, 252–3, 257, 259
Clerkenwell 127, 219
clubs (see also named clubs) 18, 100, 162–3, 175, 204–5
coal 18, 28, 99, 118, 202–3, 247
Colindale 106, 274
conscientious objectors (see pacifists and pacifism)
conscription 84–9 passim, 132–3, 157–62, 164, 175, 256–7
Cooper, Duff (1890–1954, socialite, soldier) 122, 155, 210, 269
Cornwallis Road (Islington) 80, 98
Coules, Mary (diarist) 39, 40, 75, 121, 128
Covent Garden 58, 187, 250
Covent Garden Theatre (Bow Street) 118
Coventry Street 12, 19, 179, 189
Crayford 57, 103, 104, 108, 206, 242
cricket 14, 118
Cricklewood 106
crime 117–20, 130–1, 161–2, 182, 184–5, 193, 201, 214, 216, 232–3, 254, 261, 270
Crooks, Will (1852–1921, Labour politician) 30
Cross, George (hotelier) 69, 104
Croydon 18–19, 33, 76, 106, 128, 174, 200, 243, 245
Crystal Palace 13, 45
Cuffley (Hertfordshire) 171
currency 17–18, 23, 28, 119–20

Dagenham 104, 159
Daily Mail 120, 170
Dalston 95, 126, 153, 214
dancing 13–14, 86, 115, 138, 197, 204, 264, 268–9
Dardanelles (see Gallipoli)
Darling, Charles John (1849–1936, judge) 258–9
Dartford 245

Dawson, Margaret Damer (1873–1920, police officer) 187–8
Defence of the Realm Acts and Regulations (DORA) 50–1, 57–8, 61, 66, 70, 87, 92, 119, 144, 168, 174, 192–4, 206, 208–9, 219, 221, 244–5, 270
demobilisation 272
Dent, Joseph Malaby (1849–1926, publisher) 94, 154
Deptford 59, 73, 75, 105, 127, 128, 220, 221, 234, 237
Derby Scheme 132–3
Despard, Charlotte (1844–1939, socialist, pacifist) 52
Devonport, Lord (Hudson Kearley, 1856–1934, industrialist) 44, 176, 204
dock labourers 6, 34, 97–8
Dollis Hill 106
domestic servants 6, 102–3, 105, 125, 146, 254
Downing Street 15, 20, 21, 25, 33, 90, 127, 261, 269
Doyle, Sir Arthur Conan (1859–1930, writer) 154, 185, 191–2
Dr Johnson's House (Gough Square) 116
Drake, Barbara (1876–1963, sociologist) 237
drink 7, 8, 46–9, 51–3, 55–61, 63, 67, 98, 119, 163, 170, 183–4, 196, 234, 236, 270, 273
drugs 61, 82, 135, 183–4, 194–6, 264
Drury Lane Theatre Royal 45, 222
Dublin 165, 240
Dulwich 74, 174, 240
Dunn, Kaye (clergyman) 31–2
Ealing 90
Earls Court Exhibition 13, 74–5
East End 3, 32, 42, 61, 82, 83–9 passim, 95–6, 102, 105, 107, 110, 124, 126, 158, 171, 194–5, 203–4, 211, 218, 238–9, 243–4, 259, 275
East Ham 206, 212, 218
East India Docks 20, 97, 160
East London Federation of Suffragettes 12, 36
Eastbourne 17, 19

Easter Rising (1916) 165
Edgware Road 1, 11, 12, 189, 250
Edmonton 103, 105, 203, 219, 240
Edward, Prince of Wales 14, 24, 36, 264
Ehrlich, Dr Paul (1854–1915, German chemist)
Elephant and Castle 11, 217, 253–4
Eltham 242
Empire Day 204
Empire Theatre of Varieties (Leicester Square) 63, 64, 190, 195
Enfield 58, 103, 105, 244
Ennor, F.H. (soldier) 222
Erith 57, 103, 104, 107, 109, 206, 242, 245
Euston Road 216, 243, 246
Euston Station 105, 111, 127, 134, 145, 183, 253, 268
Ezard, Edward (memoirist) 17

F.A. Cup Final (1915) 62, 118
Fabian Society 36
Fabian Women's Group 5
Farnborough 103
Feltham 106
Fenchurch Street Station 212–3
Finchley 228
Finsbury 119, 233, 235
Finsbury Park 30, 160, 208, 209, 257
Fisher, Lord John "Jacky" (1841–1920, sailor) 81
Fitzgerald, F. Scott (1896–1940, American writer) 43
Fitzrovia 81, 179–80, 196
flag days 74, 138–9
Fleet Street 14, 25, 88, 94, 117, 139
Folkestone 212
food – (allotments) 174, 205; (hoarding) 18, 28; (prices) 18, 28, 118, 120, 163, 173–4, 203, 206; (rationing) 174, 204, 223, 243, 248–9; (shortages) 108, 141, 173–5, 203–5, 222–4, 247–8
Food Controller 176, 204–5, 223
football 61–2
Football Association 61–2
Ford, Ford Madox (formerly Ford

Hermann Hueffer,1873–1939, writer) 23, 72, 129, 156
Foreign Jews' Protection Committee 85, 86–7
Foreign Office 23, 25, 39
fortune-telling (see religion)
Fox, R.M. (engineer) 21, 159, 227
France xiv, 16–19 passim, 21, 24, 41, 43, 67, 85, 89, 97, 98, 105, 107, 116, 131, 135, 138, 145, 147, 149–52, 165–8, 191, 193, 235–6, 254–5, 262, 266
Fraser, Helen (1881–1979, suffragette, social worker) 52
French Londoners 3, 14, 20–1, 81, 115, 179, 180, 196, 275
French, Sir John (1852–1925, soldier) 52, 169, 214
Friends' Emergency Committee 78
Fulham 25, 38, 105, 106, 117, 243

Gallipoli xiv, 122–3, 130, 131, 134, 148, 154, 164, 174
Galsworthy, John (1867–1933, writer) 40, 91, 137, 140, 171, 257
gambling 47, 61, 82, 196
Garrick Theatre (Charing Cross Road) 163
General Post Office 111, 135, 150, 151–2, 169, 223, 225–6, 227, 251
German Gymnasium (King's Cross) 3, 214
German Londoners 3, 20–1, 33, 67–8, 69–18 passim, 83–4, 86, 89–92, 100, 118, 156, 161, 179, 275; (anti-German violence) 70, 73, 75–8, 81, 120, 126, 145, 213–4; (internment) 71–2, 75–6, 78–80, 84, 90–1, 98, 117, 175, 258; (pro-German feeling) 31–2, 77–8, 91
Germany 16–19 passim, 21, 23, 25, 27, 31, 56, 83, 84, 90, 91, 266
Giant bombers 215–6, 250–2
Gibbs, Hamilton (writer) 32–3
Gibbs, Philip (1877–1962, journalist) 22, 121
Glasgow 240
Gleason, Arthur (journalist) 60, 225, 231

Golders Green 102, 127
Gotha bombers 211–19 passim, 250–2, 254
Grafton Galleries (Bond Street) 140, 264
Graves, George (1873–1949, entertainer) 45, 63
Graves, Robert (1895–1985, writer) 141, 166, 249, 251
Gravesend 38
Gray, John (memoirist) 227–8
Gray's Inn Road 102, 128
Great Western Railway (GWR) 10, 17, 259
Green Park 23, 38
Greenford 103, 106, 274
Greenwich 53, 105, 120, 174, 217, 242
Grein, Jacob Thomas (1862–1935, impresario) 258
Grey, Sir Edward (1862–1933, Liberal politician) 15, 16, 21, 23, 175
Grosch, Alfred (clerk) 225–6, 227
Guildhall (City) 66, 266
Guy's Hospital 42, 127, 146, 147, 265

Hackney 33, 36, 40, 58, 70, 74, 76, 77, 88, 102, 104, 105, 119, 125, 131, 132, 138, 144, 158–60 passim, 165, 193, 196, 234, 235, 244, 257
Haggard, Sir Henry Rider (1856–1925, writer) 40, 52, 115, 153, 168, 201, 204, 205, 210, 220
Haig, Sir Douglas (1861–1948, soldier) 50, 214, 254–5
Hainault 170
Haldane, Lord Richard (1856–1928, Liberal politician) 258
Hall, Edith (memoirist) 107
Hamilton, Lady Jean (1861–1941, diarist) 134, 154
Hamilton, Mary (1872–1952, writer) 22
Hamilton, Sir Ian (1853–1947, soldier) 50, 134, 154
Hammersmith 25, 238, 239, 243, 260
Hammerton, John A. (journalist) 94, 267–8

Hampstead 17, 27, 98, 132, 153, 159, 170, 204
Hampstead Heath 12, 160, 174, 230–1, 256, 263
Hanover Square 12, 54
Hardie, Keir (1856–1915, Labour politician) 20, 30
Harlesden 105
Harmsworth, Cecil (1898–1978, publisher) 44, 117
Harrods 18, 74, 118, 146, 194
Harrow 76, 244
Havilland, Geoffrey de (1882–1965, aeroplane designer)
Hayes 76, 103, 105–6, 107, 109, 274
health (see also influenza) 232–8
Hedderwick, Thomas (1850–1918, Metropolitan magistrate) 62
Hendon 103, 106, 107–8, 242, 274
Hendon Aerodrome 13, 14, 274
Henley 14, 244
Henry, Sir Edward (1850–1931, police officer) 100, 131, 169, 187–8, 214, 253, 259–61
Hewlett, Hilda Beatrice (1864–1943, aviator) 1–2, 11, 12
Hicks, Stephen (boxer, memoirist) 36–7
Highbury 211
Highgate 117, 141
Hillingdon 162
His Majesty's Theatre (Haymarket) 45, 64, 221
Hobhouse, Stephen (1881–1961, pacifist) 159, 161
Hodge, Gordon (sugar merchant) 69
Holborn 9, 45, 59, 73, 81, 127, 180, 212, 238, 243
Holland 69, 71, 91
Holloway 78, 138, 216
Holloway Prison 185, 192, 193
Hornchurch 170
Hornsey 235
Horse Guards 33, 42
Horseferry Road 123, 178
horses 38, 256–7
hospitals (see also named institutions) 41–2, 74, 122–3, 135, 138, 140–2, 146–9, 165–8, 210

Hotel Metropole (Northumberland Avenue) 111
Hounslow 170, 274
House of Commons 21, 32, 41, 49, 56, 62, 65, 72, 78, 84, 86, 91, 112, 129, 131, 157, 169–70, 173–4, 192, 213–4, 253, 262, 263
Houses of Parliament xiv, 21–2, 89, 110, 209, 263
housing 2, 6, 230, 238–246 passim; (rents) 28–9, 238–41, 243, 245
Hoxton 7, 30, 51, 73, 93, 95, 109, 126, 128, 161, 182, 212, 214, 226–7, 235–6, 245
Hudson, Robert (memoirist) 186–7, 190
Hunt, Violet (1862–1942, writer) 129
Hurley, Alfred (journalist) 23
Hyde Park 1, 9–10, 12–13, 21, 38, 65, 67, 90, 174, 185, 189, 257, 263, 264, 269
Hyndman, Henry Mayers (1842–1921, socialist politician) 20, 30

Ilford 133, 252
illegitimacy 54–5, 232–3, 234
Imlay, Oliver (d1917, Canadian soldier, murder victim) 185
Imperial Conferences 191
Increase of Rent and Mortgage Interest (War Restrictions) Act 1915 240–1, 244–5
Independent Labour Party 30, 159
Indian Home Rule League
infant welfare 234–8 passim
infanticide 55, 232–3
influenza 151–2, 222, 237, 264–6
Inge, William (1860–1954, clergyman) 11, 65, 155, 209
invasion scares 165, 211
Ireland 14–15, 29, 76, 86, 151, 155, 165, 256
Irish Londoners 52, 165
Isle of Dogs 127
Isle of Man 91
Islington 58, 78, 80, 96, 138, 160, 211, 234, 235, 245, 252
Italian Londoners 3, 81, 196, 214, 275
Italy 81

'It's a Long Way to Tipperary' 7, 45, 269–70

Janotha, Maria (German musician and spy) 71
Jasper, A.S. (memoirist) 226–7
Jewish Londoners 3, 63, 79, 81, 84–9, 110, 126, 196, 238, 250, 258; (anti-Semitism) 63, 84–9 passim, 218, 244
Jewry Street 212–3
John Bull 59, 76, 170
John Evelyn sailing barge 126–7
Jones, C. Sheridan (pseudonym of Ada Elizabeth Chesterton, 1869–1962, journalist) 196
Joynson-Hicks, William (1865–1932, Conservative politician) 78, 169, 170

'Keep the Home Fires Burning' 252
Kenney, Annie (1879–1953, suffragette) 102
Kennington 7, 33, 152, 183
Kensington 4, 12, 16–8 passim, 27, 28, 37, 41, 70, 71, 75, 98, 100, 104, 111, 121, 138, 144, 157, 195, 220, 233, 243, 245, 247
Kentish Town 20, 160, 215, 236
Kew Gardens 119
Kilburn 92, 106, 252
King George V (and Royal Family) 21, 22, 24, 56, 61, 64, 152, 164, 175, 200, 204, 209, 214, 218, 248, 252, 264, 269–70
King George's Military Hospital (Lambeth) 181
King's Cross 3, 214, 250
King's Cross Station 105
Kingston 106
Kipling, Rudyard (1865–1936, writer) 89, 210
Kitchener Memorial Home (Hornsey) 235, 236
Kitchener, Lord Horatio (1850–1916, soldier) 35, 49–50, 51, 56, 120–1, 131, 138, 164, 165
Kreitman, Esther (1891–1954, writer) 96

Lambeth 5, 28, 77, 98, 134, 178, 180–5, 203, 205, 214, 228–9, 243
Lane, John (1854–1925, publisher) 44
Lansbury, George (1859–1940, Labour politician) 30, 208
Lauder, Harry (1870–1950, singer) 89, 209, 222
Lavery, Sir John (1856–1941, artist) 142
Law, Andrew Bonar (1858–1923, Conservative politician) 175
Lea, River 103, 274
League of the Man in the Street 59
Lee, Georgina (1869–1965, diarist) 17, 32, 46, 98, 121, 143, 143–6 passim, 156, 165, 173, 206, 207, 247, 254, 257, 263, 269
Leete, Alfred (1882–1933, artist) 35
Leicester Square 63, 163–4, 189, 190, 196
Leighton, Roland (1895–1915, soldier) 115–6, 135–6, 194
Lenin, V.I. (1870–1924, Russian revolutionary) 208
Letchworth Garden City 159
Lewisham 219, 223, 252
Leytonstone 126, 240
licensing hours 53, 57–8
Limehouse 82, 195
Lincoln's Inn 33–4
Lisson Grove 1, 235
Liverpool 76, 87, 159, 194
Liverpool Street Station 116, 127, 145, 212, 214, 217, 220, 269
Lloyd George, David (1863–1945, Liberal politician) 9, 17, 49, 55–60, 67, 90, 101–3 passim, 109, 162, 169–70, 175–6, 204, 255, 257, 259, 261, 266
Lloyd, Sir Francis 'Frankie' (1853–1926, soldier) 50, 211
Lloyd's Insurance 17, 116
Lodge, Sir Oliver (1851–1940, scientist and spiritualist) 154–5
Lody, Carl Hans (1877–1914, German spy) 71
London (Army) District 42, 50
London Ambulance Column 42
London Ambulance Service 117, 127

London and South Western Railway 180

London Bridge Station 43, 145

London Council for the Promotion of Public Morality (see Public Morality Council)

London County Council (LCC) 9, 17, 42, 62–5 passim, 84, 99, 104, 117, 119, 120, 152, 162, 167, 190–1, 205, 212, 218, 221, 227, 228, 242, 256, 261–2, 265

London Fields 155, 214

London Fire Brigade 127, 130, 219

London General Omnibus Co. (LGOC) 37–8, 99–100

London Hospital 42, 46, 72, 74, 82–3, 92, 101, 119, 122, 124, 142, 146, 148, 166, 200, 218, 265

London Labour Party 119, 159, 273

London Museum 66

London Regiment 34, 121, 159

London Rifle Brigade 19

London Season 4–5, 14, 44, 118

London Small Arms Co. 103

London Society for Women's Suffrage 74

London Tank Week 257

London Trades Council 59

Long Acre 195, 250–1, 253

Loos, Battle of 121, 122

Lord Chamberlain (see Sandhurst, Viscount William)

Lord Mayor's Show 35, 96, 112, 130, 164, 266

Lord's Cricket Ground 14, 20, 209, 251

Loughnan, Naomi (munitionette) 107, 226

Lowndes, Marie Belloc (1868–1947, writer) 94, 124

luck 134, 154

Luckes, Eva (1854–1919, nurse) 146

Lucy, Sir Henry (1843–1924, journalist) 123–4, 163

Ludendorff Offensive (March 1918) 254–6

Lusitania 76, 87, 159, 194

Lutyens, Lady Emily (1864–1954, housewife and mystic) 202

Lutyens, Sir Edwin (1869–1944, architect) 94, 271

Lyons Bakers and Corner Houses 12, 42, 204

Macaulay, Rose (1881–1958, writer) 75, 128

MacDonagh, Michael (journalist) 27, 28, 43, 45, 61–2, 65, 97, 100, 110, 112, 116, 132, 162, 164, 172, 174–6 passim, 199–200, 224, 230–1, 248, 253–4, 258, 262, 266, 269

MacDonald, Ramsay (1866–1937, Labour politician) 30, 48, 133, 192, 208

MacDougall, Elithe (social worker) 178

Macready, Sir Nevil (1862–1946, soldier, police officer) 261

Maddison, Robert (Australian soldier) 263

Maida Vale 12, 99, 252, 253

Mall, The 21, 24, 128, 266

Manners, Lady Diana (1892–1986, socialite, nurse) 143, 146–7, 194

Mansfield, Katherine (1888–1923, writer) 22, 23, 116

Mansion House (city) 35, 268

Marble Arch 38, 189

Marchant, James (clergyman) 64

Mare, Walter de la (1873-1956, poet) 142

Margate 17

Marylebone 1, 141, 146, 180, 234–6 passim

Marylebone Station 105

Mason, Lady Evelyn (socialite, philanthropist) 141–2, 149

Massie, Chris (labourer, memoirist) 7

Masterman, Charles Frederick Gurney (1874–1927, Liberal politician, writer) 124

Masterman, Lucy (1884–1977, writer) 134–5, 268

Mathy, Heinrich (d1916, German aviator) 127, 128, 171, 172

May Day 1–2, 9–11, 20, 257

Mayfair 4, 9, 12, 71, 122, 140, 141, 195

McKenna, Reginald (1863–1943, Liberal politician) 29, 44, 71, 124

McKenna, Stephen (1888–1967, civil servant, writer) 4, 22–3, 50, 222, 264

McMillan, Margaret (1860–1931, educationist) 237

Merton 72

Mesopotamia xiv, 138

Metropolitan Police 1, 8, 12–13, 39–40, 53, 65, 71–2, 76–7, 81–2, 100, 112, 125, 130–1, 139, 144, 152, 161, 178–80, 185–9 passim, 233, 248, 259–61

Metropolitan Police Special Constabulary 76, 144–5

Metropolitan Water Board 12

Meyer, Frederick Brotherton (1847–1929, nonconformist clergyman) 183–4, 191

Meysey-Thompson, H.C. (soldier) 33–4, 38

Mile End 37, 61, 170

Miles, Hallie Eustace (food writer) xiv, 35, 37, 74–5, 125, 127, 130, 134, 142, 168–9, 218–9, 266, 269

Military Service (Conventions with Allied States) Act 1917 86

Military Service Acts 86, 87, 157-62

Mill Hill 92, 159

Millbank Military Hospital 42

Mincing Lane 69, 114

Ministry of Food 111

Ministry of Health 111

Ministry of Information 111

Ministry of Munitions 59, 101, 103, 111–12, 162, 201, 236–7, 256, 267, 268, 274

Monash, Sir John (1865–1931, Australian soldier) 167, 170

Mond, Sir Alfred (1868–1930, industrialist) 44, 141

Mons 35, 42–3

Moore, Ralph Ingram (Australian soldier) 122–3, 164

Morel, Edmund Dene (1873–1924, peace campaigner) 209

Morrison, Herbert (1888–1965, Labour politician) 119, 159

Moseley, Sydney (journalist) 222

motor cars 1–2, 18, 24, 33, 37, 38, 42, 93, 105, 116, 162, 220, 262, 269

mourning and loss 43, 121–4, 135–6, 149–554, 209–11

munitions manufacture (see also Ministry of Munitions) xiii, 10, 53–8, passim, 60, 67, 92, 101–9, 120, 129, 144, 175, 188, 191–2, 206, 226–8, 236–7, 240–2, 246, 264

Murry, John Middleton (1889–1957, writer) 22, 23, 116

music halls 7, 8, 35, 61–4, 126, 161, 176, 183, 189–91, 204, 209, 250, 270

Napier Motor Works 93, 106, 109

National (Prince of Wales) Relief Fund 36, 137

National Council on Public Morals 48, 64

National Gallery 11, 66, 163, 164

National Kitchens 205

National League of the Blind 1

National Liberal Club 40, 163, 264

National Mission of Repentance and Hope 66–7

National Party 208

National Portrait Gallery 123

National Union of Clerks 159

National Union of Police and Prison Officers 120, 259–61

National Union of Women Workers 187–8

National Vigilance Association 187

Natural History Museum 66

Naturalization Revocation Committee 90

Neighbour, Rose (memoirist) 107, 109

Neil, Arthur (police officer) 117–8

Neutrality League 20, 30

Neuve Chapelle, Battle of 120, 122, 146, 154

Nevinson, Henry Woodd (1856–1941, journalist) 263–4

New Survey of London Life and Labour 197, 272–3, 275

New Year's Eve 48, 115–6, 135, 149, 153, 199, 247

New York 13, 14, 93
New Zealanders xiii–iv, 262
Newbolt, Henry (1862–1938, poet)
    142
Newington 117, 183
News of the World 17
newspaper sellers 19, 27, 77, 119, 165,
    266
nightclubs 44–5, 61, 63, 115, 163,
    196, 264
Nine Elms 17, 52
No-Conscription Fellowship 160–1,
    208
North London Herald League 30, 160,
    208–9
Northolt 106, 274
Northumberland Avenue 111, 163,
    267
Norwood 174
Notting Dale 185, 220
Notting Hill Gate 155, 195, 217
Nunn, Thomas Hancock (1859–1937,
    social worker) 17, 22, 153–4, 156

Odhams Printing Press 250–1, 253
Old Bailey 117, 193, 258–9
Old Kent Road 70, 73
Old Vic Theatre (Waterloo Road)
    181
Olympia 14, 71–2, 74, 79
Oval Cricket Ground 14
Oxford and Cambridge Club 176
Oxford Street 3, 81, 116, 179
Oxford University 115, 146

pacifists and pacifism 20–2, 24, 27,
    30–1, 133, 156, 158–61, 165,
    207–9, 257–8
Paddington 139, 234, 238, 243, 261
Paddington Station 10, 13, 17, 23–4,
    32, 105, 117, 123, 145, 166, 259
Pall Mall 34, 40, 44, 58, 176
Palmers Green 112, 114, 149, 150,
    151–2, 204, 220
Pals' Battalions 131–2
Pankhurst, Christabel (1880–1958,
    suffragette, patriot) 29, 48, 101
Pankhurst, Emmeline (1858–1928,
    suffragette, patriot) 29, 54, 101

Pankhurst, Sylvia (1882–1960,
    socialist) 12, 29, 36, 53–4, 126,
    160, 185–6, 238–9
Paris 2, 4, 14, 39, 129, 254, 262
Park Lane 141, 146
Park Royal 103, 105–6, 274
Parliament Square 24, 269
Passchendaele 209–10
Paterson, Alexander (1884–1947,
    social worker) 8
Peile, Lydia (diarist) 216–7
Pelly, Roland (soldier) 141–2, 148–9
Pennyfields 82, 195
Pentonville Prison 165
Perivale 103, 274
Peter Pan 45
Pethick-Lawrence, Frederick (1871–
    1961, Labour politician) 22, 24
petrol 162, 220, 269
Pharmacy Acts 194
pianos 96, 228, 247
Piccadilly 40, 141, 142, 219, 249
Piccadilly Circus 12, 19, 115–6, 135,
    187, 189, 196, 270
pigs 205
Pimlico 46, 178, 216
Pinner 99
Playne, Caroline (1857–1948, social
    psychologist, pacifist) 27, 75, 154,
    155, 165, 166, 176, 204, 207, 210,
    213, 215, 217, 218, 223, 243,
    255–6, 258, 262, 266, 268–9
Poor Law (including workhouses) 53,
    74, 83, 98, 100, 110, 173,183, 230,
    236, 272
Poplar 7, 20, 77–8, 82, 97, 127, 171,
    195, 212, 213, 238, 240, 242, 250
population 2
Port of London 6, 11, 38, 70–1, 82,
    83, 92, 97–8, 104, 124, 194, 208,
    225, 242, 262, 274
Portsmouth 181
Post Office Railway 117
Potters Bar 172
poverty (*see also* Poor Law) 5–7, 27,
    34, 36, 93, 224–38 passim, 272–3,
    275
prices 18, 28, 58, 118, 120, 163,
    173–4, 203, 206, 225–6, 231, 239

prisons (see also individual institutions) 98
Professional Classes War Relief
Council 232
profiteering 156, 206, 207, 223, 231,
249, 259
prosperity 94–114 passim
prostitutes and prostitution 19, 48, 61,
176, 177–94 passim
Public Meals Order 204–5
Public Morality Council 63
Punch 123
Purley 18

Queen Alexandra (1844–1925) 123
Queen Anne's Gate 39, 94
Queen's Hall (Langham Place) 164,
208
Queen's Park Rangers Football Club
105
queues 203–4, 217, 221, 222–4,
247–9, 261–2

railway stations (see also named
stations) 42–3, 133–5, 166–8, 178,
187–8, 194, 202, 210
Rainham 104
Rawlinson, Sir Alfred (1867–1934,
soldier, sailor) 219
Rayleigh 114
recruitment (see also conscription)
32–7, 131–3, 156
Red Cross 41, 42, 138, 140, 142, 200
Reeves, Maud Pember (1865–1953,
sociologist) 28, 205, 238
Reform Club (Pall Mall) 34, 39, 40,
44, 58–9, 72, 100, 118–9, 163, 173,
175, 179, 209, 248
Regent Street 5, 82, 116, 271
Regent's Park 13, 140, 160, 174, 216
religion (attitudes to war) 31, 153–4,
160, 257–8; (Church of England)
47–68 passim, 153–5; (puritanism)
7–8, 47–68 passim, 78, 187–9,
258–9; (Quakers) 131, 159, 160;
(Roman Catholic Church) 51–2,
153; (spiritualism and fortune-
telling) 154–5, 209–10
rents (see housing)

Repington, Charles à Court (1858–
1925, soldier and journalist) 159,
201, 266
Reuters News Agency 248
Rhondda, Lord (David Alfred Thomas,
1856–1918, industrialist, Liberal
politician) 205
Richmond (Surrey) 115, 142, 205
Richmond Park 38, 218
Rider, Dan (housing activist) 239–40
riots and rioting 28, 32, 70, 73, 81,
83, 84, 88, 89, 120, 126, 133, 145,
161, 208, 213–4, 248, 261
Ritz Hotel (Piccadilly) 4, 70, 72, 128,
138, 264
road traffic accidents 41, 170, 176,
218, 262
Roberts, Florrie (memoirist) 229
Roberts, Lord Frederick (1832–1914,
soldier) 35, 50, 61
Robertson, Sir William (1860-1933,
soldier) 67, 207
Robey, George (1869–1954, enter-
tainer) 163
Robinson, Frederick (City merchant,
diarist) 22, 28, 35, 46, 116, 162,
164–5, 168, 223, 254, 266
Robinson, W. Leefe (1895–1918,
airman) 171
Rocker, Rudolf (1873–1958, German
anarchist) 33, 79–80, 91
Roehampton 141
Rolph, C.H. (pseudonym of Cecil
Hewitt, 1901–1994, writer) 25, 38,
268
Romanian Londoners 81, 87, 180
Romford 76, 170
Rosebery, Lord (Archibald Philip
Primrose, 1847–1929, Liberal politi-
cian) 56, 59
Rotherhithe 127, 205
Rotherhithe Tunnel 217–8
Royal Academy (Piccadilly) 11, 142
Royal Aircraft Co. (Farnborough) 103
Royal Albert Hall (Kensington) 39, 90,
144, 207, 208
Royal Army Medical Corps 122–3
Royal Flying Corps (RFC) 106, 112,
212

Royal Gunpowder Factory (Waltham Abbey) 103
Royal Military College (Sandhurst) 150–1
Royal Naval Air Service 170, 212
Royal Naval Volunteer Reserve 145
Royal Small Arms factory (Enfield) 58, 103
Royal Society for the Prevention of Cruelty to Animals 137
Royce, James (engineer) 106
Runciman, Sir Walter (1870–1949, Liberal politician) 44, 119
Russia 17–19 passim, 84–9 passim, 138
Russian Londoners (see also Jewish Londoners) 3, 81, 84–9 passim, 156, 180, 214
Russian Revolution 86, 207–9

Sainsbury, John James (1844–1928, grocer) 18, 137
Sainsbury's grocery chain 18, 29, 72, 99, 137, 272
St Bartholomew's Hospital 74, 128, 130, 146, 165, 214
St James's Park 39, 94, 111, 112
St James's Square 263
St Martin in the Fields 33, 153
St Marylebone (see Marylebone)
St Pancras 3, 180, 235, 253
St Pancras Station 105, 251
St Paul's Cathedral xiv, 11, 12, 20, 35, 47, 65, 68, 115, 123, 209, 263, 270
St Petersburg (aka Petrograd) 2, 16, 208
Salter, Dr Alfred (1873–1945, physician and Labour politician) 31
Salvation Army 98
Samuel, Herbert (1870–1963, Liberal politician) 86
Sandhurst, Viscount (William Mansfield, 1855–1921, soldier, Lord Chamberlain) 35, 63–4, 102, 128–9, 132, 163–5 passim, 176, 211, 248, 249, 253, 254, 261
Sankey, Sir John (judge, 1866–1948) 90
Savory and Moore's (chemists) 135, 194

Savoy Hotel (Strand) 163, 195
Scannell, Dolly (memoirist) 229
schools and schooling 49, 104, 123, 152, 162, 205, 212, 218, 227, 265
Science Museum 66
Scotland Yard 71, 79, 117, 130, 149, 215, 259
Scott, Sir Percy (1853–1924, sailor) 129–30
Seamen's Union 82
Second World War xiii, 83, 216, 275–6
Serbia 16–17
Shaftesbury Avenue 45, 164, 187
Shaftesbury Theatre 45, 164
Shaw, George Bernard (1856–1950, writer) 164
Shepherd's Bush 13, 117, 145
Sheppard, Dick (1880–1937, clergyman) 153
Shoreditch 30, 95, 117, 126, 132, 159, 171, 202, 212, 213, 216, 218, 233, 239, 243, 250
Shoreham 17
Siemens Brothers 44, 72, 104
Silvertown 104, 108
Silvertown Explosion (1917) 199–201
Simon, Sir John (1873–1954, Liberal politician) 131
Smith, George Joseph (1872–1915, murderer) 117–8
Smith–Dorrien, Sir Horace (1858–1930, soldier, puritan) 50, 64, 65
Smithfield Market 58, 247
Snowden, Philip (1864–1937, Labour politician) 49
Soho 3, 19, 20–1, 69, 81–2, 94, 161, 179, 195, 196, 246
Soldiers' and Sailors' Families Association (SSFA) 36, 53
Somme, Battle of the (film) 168
Somme, Battle of the 103, 150, 152, 165–8, 170, 175, 236, 254
Sopwith Aviation Co. 106
South Bank 9, 42, 127, 250
South Metropolitan Gas Co. 100
Southall 107, 244, 274
Southampton 42, 181
Southend 17, 79, 125
Southgate, Walter (socialist clerk) 159

Southwark 10, 20, 33, 70, 104, 105, 153, 161, 184, 212, 214, 223, 234, 242, 245–6, 260, 269

spies 70–1

Spilsbury, Bernard (1877–1947, pathologist) 193

spiritualism (see religion)

Squire, Rose (1861–1938, civil servant) 112

Stamford Hill 212, 228

Stamford Street 181, 183

Stanhope Street 243, 246

Stepney 34, 83, 85, 119, 126, 151, 155, 229, 233

Stock Exchange 17, 78, 84, 120–1

Stoke Newington 73, 90, 96, 99, 119, 126, 143, 211, 213, 233, 243, 244, 261

Stoll, Oswald (1866–1942, impresario) 163, 164

Strand 40, 43, 111, 128, 167, 195, 267, 268

Stratford 58, 80, 159, 212, 218, 259

Streatham 171

street shrines 152–3, 210

Street, G.S. (journalist) 155

strikes 8–11, 17, 59, 120, 205–7, 259–61

submarine warfare 97, 208

suffragettes and Votes for Women 2, 11–13, 29, 66, 74, 263–4

suicide 73, 76

Summerskill, Edith (1901–1980, doctor) 268

Swiss Cottage 22, 262

Swiss Londoners 69, 81, 180

Tabard Street area 245–6

tailoring 6, 95–6, 104, 110, 143–4, 244

Tate Gallery 11

taxation 231–2, 245

taxis 27, 32–3, 38, 44, 100–1, 168, 202, 220, 269

Territorial Army 7, 14, 19, 21, 33, 38, 121, 131

Thames, River 38, 106, 108, 115, 118, 125, 144–5, 212, 214, 268, 274

theatres (see also named theatres) 7, 25, 44–5, 100, 128, 131, 135, 138, 142–3, 163–4, 196–7, 221–2, 264, 270

Thomas, Jimmy (1874–1949, Labour politician) 30

Thomson, Basil (1861–1939, police officer) 71, 259

Thorne, Will (1857–1946, Labour politician)

Thorpe-le-Soken 116

Thurtle, Ernest (1884–1954, Labour politician) 27, 34, 268

Tilbury 38, 71

Tillett, Ben (1860–1943, Labour politician) 20, 30

TNT 108–9, 199–201

Tooley Street 72, 92

Tooting 23, 174, 240, 248

Tottenham 104, 119, 248, 252

Tottenham Court Road 3, 81, 180

Tower Bridge 130, 260

Tower Hill 214, 260

Tower of London 71

Tower, Winifred (diarist) 37, 39, 146

toxic jaundice 108–9

Toynbee Hall (Whitechapel) 72

trade unions (see also named unions) 9–11, 29–30, 203

Trades Union Congress 82, 208

Trafalgar Square 20–1, 24, 33, 35, 89–90, 111, 128, 142, 161, 257, 267, 270

trams 10, 38, 39–40, 120, 199, 215, 216, 220–1, 256, 259, 261–2, 265

Treasury 33, 72

Tree, Sir Herbert Beerbohm (1852–1917, actor, impresario) 45

Trocadero Restaurant (Piccadilly Circus) 187, 270

Tube 25, 43, 88, 99, 117, 128, 176, 187, 206, 213, 217–8, 253–4, 263

Tuohy, Ferdinand (journalist) 14, 19, 69, 270

Tupper, Edward (seamen's leader) 82, 208

Union Jack Club (Waterloo Road) 181

Union of Democratic Control 30, 133, 160, 208, 209

University Boat Race 118

Unwin, Thomas Fisher (1848–1953, publisher) 44
Upper North Street (Poplar) 212, 218

Vauxhall 250
venereal disease 50, 191–4
Vickers armament manufacturers 103, 107, 109
Victoria (Westminster) 20, 99, 138, 258
Victoria and Albert Museum 66
Victoria Embankment 169, 215, 219, 250, 267
Victoria Park 11, 103, 160, 208
Victoria Station 20, 23, 43, 105, 134–5, 145, 167, 173, 178, 183, 186–7, 210, 254, 268
Vienna 2
Voluntary Aid detachments 145–8

wages 6, 28, 102, 106, 109, 120, 206–7, 225–6, 228, 237
Walker, Harold (memoirist) 203
Waltham Abbey 103, 169
Walthamstow 115, 203, 208
Walworth 31, 152, 226
Wandsworth Prison 159, 185
Wandsworth 98, 118, 123, 159, 173, 240
Wanstead 38
War Babies 54–5
War Babies' and Mothers' League 54
War Bonds 196, 257
War Charities Act 1916 139
War Office 36, 39, 42, 55, 95, 111–13, 122, 124, 129, 132, 149, 150, 152, 158, 160, 165, 166, 210
War Rents League 240
Ward, Mary (1851–1920, writer and philanthropist) 271
Warner, Sylvia Townsend (1893–1978, writer) 107
Waterloo Bridge 37, 185-6, 250
Waterloo Road xiv, 181–5 passim, 188, 196
Waterloo Station 33, 42, 43, 105, 117, 145, 164, 166, 167, 180–5 passim, 194, 209, 218, 222

Watson, W.F. (engineer) 104
weather 13, 45–6, 97, 115, 119, 132, 157, 176, 201–2, 220, 223, 247, 256, 262
Webb, Beatrice (1858–1943, social reformer) 21, 22, 32, 36, 46, 48, 271
Webb, Sidney (1859–1947, social reformer) 21
Wedgwood, Josiah (1872–1943, soldier, Liberal politician) 91
Well Hall Garden Suburb (Eltham) 242
Wells, Herbert George (1866–1946, writer) 37, 40, 44
Wembley 106, 274
Wensley, Edie (office worker) 112–14, 149–52, 164, 204, 222
Wensley, Frederick Martin (d1916, soldier) 149–50
Wensley, Frederick Porter (1865–1949, police officer) 112, 149–52
Wensley, Harold (d1918, soldier) 150–2
West End 3, 11, 12, 19, 25, 44–5, 69, 76, 81, 82, 83, 88, 108, 115, 116, 121, 135, 140–3, 159, 163–4, 168, 173, 176, 178–9, 186–7, 194–6, 209, 243, 247, 260, 263, 264, 270
West Ham 10, 30, 59, 76, 124, 126, 141, 173
Westminster 119, 180, 186, 192, 233
Westminster Abbey 11–12, 20, 66, 67, 164, 263, 271
Westminster Bridge Road 183, 205
Westminster Cathedral 12
Weybridge 254
White City 13, 106, 107, 185
white feather stunt 35–6, 132, 156
Whitechapel 3, 7, 42, 72, 96, 126, 146, 196, 200, 212, 250
Whitehall 20, 21, 24, 25, 32, 33, 84, 110–11, 118, 128, 135, 145, 218, 255, 268
Whitehall Gardens 111
Whitehall Place 40, 111, 163
Willesden 105, 106
Williamson, Joseph (1895–1988, clergyman) 77–8

Willis, Frederick (hat maker, memoirist) 18–19
Wilson, Havelock (1858–1929, trade union leader) 208
Wilson, Romer (1891–1930, writer) 256
Wimbledon 33, 143, 174, 189, 205
Winnington-Ingram, Arthur Foley (1858–1946, Bishop of London) 47, 48, 54, 60, 63, 66–8, 153–5, 190
Women's Army Corps 114
Women's Imperial Health Association 54
Women's Police Service 54, 187–9
Women's Social and Political Union 29, 48, 54
Women's War Pageant (1915) 101–2
women's work (see also munitions manufacture, tailoring) 38, 99–114 passim, 138, 140–8, 163, 224–7, 236–7, 242, 264, 272, 274
Woodford 220
Woolf, Virginia (1882–1941, writer) 102–3, 115, 248
Woolwich 10, 30, 32, 53–5, 60, 67, 102–5 passim, 120, 124, 127, 128, 130, 146, 148, 169, 171, 200–1, 206, 217, 219, 229–30, 233, 234, 240–2, 244, 248, 251
Woolwich Arsenal 10, 102–4 passim, 128, 130, 206, 207, 237, 241–2

Woolwich Crusade 67
Woolwich Dockyard 98, 241
Wootton, Barbara (1897–1988, sociologist) 210
Workers' Suffrage (later Socialist) League 160
workhouses (see Poor Law)
Working Men's Club and Institute Union 59
Wormwood Scrubs Prison 159
wounded xiv, 41–3, 74, 119, 12–3, 135, 137, 140–2, 147–9, 165–8, 210–11, 221, 271–2

Yeats, William Butler (1865–1939, poet) 142
'Yellow Press' 89, 133
York Road (Lambeth) 181–3 passim
Young Men's Christian Association 108, 138, 145, 183, 184
Young Women's Christian Association 54
Ypres 38, 120

Zeiss, Carl (optical manufacturers) 92
Zeppelin Nights
Zeppelins 39–40, 41, 46, 80–1, 124–31, 133, 135, 145, 169–73, 200, 211, 219
Zoo, London 13

www.vintage-books.co.uk